A GENEALOGY OF LITERARY MULTICULTURALISM

A GENEALOGY
OF LITERARY
MULTICULTURALISM

C HRISTOPHER D OUGLAS

CORNELL UNIVERSITY PRESS
Ithaca and London

First published 2009 by Cornell University Press

Printed in the United States of America

Library of Congress Cataloging-in-Publication Data
Douglas, Christopher, 1968–
   A genealogy of literary multiculturalism / Christopher
Douglas.
        p. cm.
   Includes bibliographical references and index.
   ISBN 978–0–8014–4769–3 (cloth : alk. paper)
   1. American literature—Minority authors—History
and criticism.   2. American literature—20th century—
History and criticism.   3. Multiculturalism in literature.
4. Minorities in literature.   5. Literature and
anthropology—United States—History—20th century.
6. Multiculturalism—United States—History—
20th century.   7. Anthropology—United States—
History—20th century.   I. Title.

   PS153.M56D68 2009
   810.9'3552—dc22   2008039460

Cloth printing   10 9 8 7 6 5 4 3 2 1

❧ CONTENTS

❧ ACKNOWLEDGMENTS

I began this book at Furman University, in Greenville, South Carolina, and finished it at the University of Victoria in British Columbia. I would like to thank colleagues at both institutions for their invaluable suggestions and encouragement, especially William Aarnes, Stanley Crowe, Vincent Hausmann, Nicholas Radel, William Rogers, Brian Siegel, and Robin Visel at Furman, and Gary Kuchar, Robert Miles, Stephen Ross, Cheryl Suzack, and Richard Van Oort at Victoria. I am also grateful to Linda Hutcheon, Daphne Lamothe, Walter Benn Michaels, Samina Najmi, David Palumbo-Liu, Glenn Willmott, and Zhou Xiaojing for critical readings and support. I thank Wafa Buhaisi, Karen Guth, Megan Prewitt, and Meg Stroup, who worked as undergraduate research assistants at Furman University in support of an early version of this project, and especially my graduate research assistant at the University of Victoria, Madeline Walker, for her assistance and editorial work in its late stage. I would like to thank my students at Furman and Victoria for thinking with me through these texts and issues.

For permission to reproduce my article "Reading Ethnography: The Cold War Social Science of Jade Snow Wong's *Fifth Chinese Daughter* and *Brown v. Board of Education,*" originally appearing in *Form and Transformation in Asian American Literature,* I thank the University of Washington Press.

For permission to reproduce my article "What *The Bluest Eye* Knows about Them: Culture, Race, Identity," I thank *American Literature,* where it first appeared.

I thank the University of Notre Dame Library for reproducing the image from *McGee's Illustrated Weekly* that appears on page 232.

This project was begun with support from the Social Sciences and Humanities Research Council of Canada, and it was completed with the help of a National Endowment for the Humanities Fellowship. I am grateful to both agencies for their assistance.

I wish to thank, finally, Lynnette, my constant source of intellectual insight and moral support, and Nathalie and Kaela for their patience and good humor. This book is for them, but for Nathalie especially, who is (almost) as old as this project.

A GENEALOGY OF LITERARY MULTICULTURALISM

Introduction
Multiculturalism's Cultural Revolution

A spectacular articulation of our current paradigm of multiculturalism comes at the end of Barbara Kingsolver's 1998 novel *The Poisonwood Bible*. Its occasion is a visit, by the three surviving and reunited Price sisters, to the royal palace at Abomey, the ancient seat of the kingdom of Dahomey, now a UNESCO world heritage site and a famous tourist attraction. One of its kings constructed his section of the palace with slaves' blood rather than water in the mud walls; he was also buried with forty-one of his wives—that is, he was buried dead but they alive. For one sister, the reactionary Rachel, this and the use of "the skulls of their favorite enemies" (480) as building material are just more indications of African brutality and savagery, and as she points out to Leah, such brutality preexisted European invasion. But Leah (the most sympathetic sister, who has gone native) and, we are to suppose, Kingsolver, are reluctant to criticize such practices, and their reluctance is based on cultural relativism: that "we couldn't possibly understand what their social milieu was, before the Portuguese came" (489). "You just can't assume that what's right or wrong for us is the same as what was right or wrong for them," she continues, in a nice summary of this constitutive principle of multiculturalism (490).

In this and other instances, *The Poisonwood Bible* is one sign of multiculturalism's triumph at the end of the twentieth century. But this example also reveals the paradigm's roots in the anthropological formulation of the culture concept at the beginning of the twentieth century. In fact, the white King-solver drew both this relativist lesson and its example of the palace of skulls directly from an African American anthropologist writing sixty years before. That anthropologist heard this palace described by Cudjo Lewis, one of the last Africans to be brought to slavery in America in 1859, when he recalled his capture by the kingdom of Dahomey and his forced march to its capital. As the palace is glossed,

> The skulls of the slaughtered were not wasted either. The King had his famous Palace of Skulls. The Palace grounds had a massive gate of skull-heads. The wall surrounding the grounds were built of skulls. You see, the Kings of Dahomey were truly great and mighty and a lot of skulls were bound to come out of their ambitions. While it looked awesome and splendid to him and his warriors, the sight must have been most grewsome and crude to western eyes. Imagine a Palace of Hindu or Zulu skulls in London! Or Javanese skulls in The Hague!

What you think of the palace will depend on where you stand culturally: it will be either "awesome and splendid" or "grewsome and crude." Cultures generate values, according to this point of cultural relativism, and neither culture should pretend to objectively or universally judge another's prac-tices. The anthropologist who recorded Cudjo Lewis's tale was Zora Neale Hurston,[1] and her lesson of cultural relativism was that established by her mentor, Franz Boas, as a founding plank in cultural anthropology, and, this book will show, literary multiculturalism in the United States. It is a mark of literary multiculturalism's success and anthropology's theoretical underpin-ning of its project, that Barbara Kingsolver a half century later has learned its lesson—perhaps, I shall suggest, too rigidly.

A Genealogy of Literary Multiculturalism is about the development and tri-umph of literary multiculturalism as it was formed through a circuit of arti-culation between the social sciences and minority literary writers in the middle of the twentieth century. The primary contribution that social science offered these mid-century writers was a comprehensive concept of culture to replace the destroyed notion of race. It was Franz Boas, the famous Columbia Uni-versity anthropologist, who effected both. He conducted a decades-long assault on the scientific basis of racial thought, putting in its place a concept of group differences as not immutable, genetically inherited, natural, and hierarchical, but rather as malleable, learned, conventionally arbitrary, and relative. That move allowed the writers examined in this book to redescribe their difference from white America as cultural, not racial. Boas developed a model of culture as something that endured over long periods of time; that had to be understood and evaluated holistically as encompassing language, religious beliefs, social practices, family organization, folklore, and so on; that was conservative insofar as it was resistant to rapid change; and that needed to be understood in its own relative terms and not against a putative universal Western civilization, which was in any case only another series of related cultures. He argued above all that whatever residual group characteristics were racial—and scholars still debate the extent to which a remnant of racial thinking remained with Boas until his death in 1942—they were no match for the far greater effects of environment and learning. I document the way in which many writers, often after formal or informal training in the social sciences, used their fictional and autobiographical works to displace the traditional assumption of racial difference through a rhetorical deployment of culture—thereby adopting the essential Boasian paradigm shift. If this renovated "idea of culture, radically transformed in meaning" became the central problem whose "working out in detail of the implications" was the task of "much of the social science of the twentieth century" (Stocking, "Franz Boas" 232), that paradigm shift and the working out of its implications is no less true of twentieth-century multicultural literature as well.

Culture and the theorization of difference that it provided came in two different models in the middle of the century, and each entailed different literary politics and aesthetics. The Boasian, or anthropological, model tended to emphasize cultural autonomy, long-term endurance, a pluralist ethos, and only slow transformation. Though Boas to some extent imagined the assimilation of minority cultures into the dominant national society, the political program of assimilation was at odds with some of these qualities of culture as he developed them through his life's work. It was left to another social science tradition, led by the sociologist Robert Ezra Park at the University of Chicago, to provide the different model of culture as something that changed fairly quickly, often in the space of one to three generations, especially in urban spaces and under pressure from the dominant white American society. Chicago sociology shared the major premises of Boas's ideas of racial equality and of cultural difference—in fact, it was intellectually indebted to Boas—but Park emphasized the rapidity with which people's cultural practices and values can change under certain conditions. He studied European immigrants becoming Americans in urban Chicago, and then explicitly extended this model to *racialized* minorities who could likewise be *culturally* assimilated.

In *A Genealogy of Literary Multiculturalism*'s three-phase development hypothesis, each phase is understood as a contest among rival minority group conceptions whose keywords include culture, race, nation, and identity. These dynamic forces corresponded to the emergence or recession of specific social science models about minority groups and their fates. The first phase features culturalist minority writing in the 1920s and 1930s that coincides with the empowerment of Boasian anthropology, its fundamental distinction between culture and race, and its challenge to 1920s nativism. As I show in chapter one, the literary work of Zora Neale Hurston and D'Arcy McNickle exemplified the new Boasian model of minority culture, especially its anthropological characteristics of historical particularism, cultural relativism, dynamic holism, and the disengagement of culture from race. The beginning of this phase is marked by anthropology's successful contest with nativism and its rejection of biological racial theory. Its end is signaled by the growth of a sociological model of minority culture that, while still opposed to race, had a substantially different understanding of the properties of culture.

The second phase, from 1940 to 1965, is exemplified by the sociologically enabled writers Richard Wright, Jade Snow Wong, and John Okada. The University of Chicago's Department of Sociology, led by Robert Park, developed a rival model of minority culture in the United States in terms of modern migration, stages of acculturation in the urban melting pot, and cultural assimilation in one to three generations. As I show in chapters two to four, these integrationist writers adopted Park's extension of cultural assimilation to racial minorities using the sociological concepts of the generation gap, the marginal man, and environmental determinism. Elements characteristic of the previous phase remained forceful in the second one, two examples being the nativist racial logic underlying the internment of Japanese Americans and Melville Herskovits's unsuccessful anthropological argument with Gunnar Myrdal about the existence of African cultural retentions. But the writers of this phase rejected these ideas, with Okada and Wong underlining their assimilability through the generation gap and Wright imagining Bigger Thomas (and himself) in terms of cultural discontinuity. They exemplified the growing dominance of Parkian sociology during World War II and the Cold War liberal consensus, signaled by the NAACP's successful arguing of *Brown v. Board of Education* and the Civil Rights movements that followed. That consensus is likewise exemplified by the State Department's simultaneous support for Jade Snow Wong's book (in the form of sponsoring its translation and her tour in Asia) and *Brown* (in the form of friend-of-the-court briefs on behalf of the NAACP). To the extent that the literature of phases one and two was descriptive and realist, it was intended to combat racial mystification and to give substance and place to this newly defined but contested concept of culture.

The third phase was anticipated by Américo Paredes, whose late 1950s ethnography of Border Mexican Americans used the older Boasian model of culture to formulate minority cultural endurance and continuity, as I show in chapter five. That turn to anthropology and to specific anthropologists like Hurston, Paredes, and James Mooney was constitutive of the new cultural nationalisms following 1965, especially the literary nationalism of N. Scott Momaday, Toni Morrison, Frank Chin, Ishmael Reed, and Gloria Anzaldúa. As I demonstrate in chapters six to nine, their embrace (but qualification) of Boasian anthropology and their simultaneous rejection of Parkian sociology behind the ideal of assimilation were the basis for the cultural and literary nationalist movements that laid the pluralist grounds for our current conception of literary multiculturalism. But the specific innovation of these inaugural multiculturalist writers was to reattach culture to race (thus undoing one of Boas's accomplishments) and to return to an account of existence against which Boas had earlier posed the labor of cultural description. Writers in phases one and two did not use the word and generally did not have a concept of "identity," but as multiculturalism developed, these writers were retroactively understood (wrongly, I believe) to have been talking about identity all along. This phase's break with what had come before was the inaugural multiculturalist writers' rejection of the implications and politics of sociology's model of culture. Its beginning was marked by the sorting of different conceptual keywords (nation, race, culture, identity) for an alternative model of the group. To the extent that this nascent multiculturalism stylistically described cultural practices, description itself failed to get at the essence of the group, which is why the literature of this phase was frequently post-realist.

A Genealogy of Literary Multiculturalism thus proposes a unified field theory of American multicultural literature. As we know, multiculturalism frequently makes its historical reference to eighteenth-, nineteenth-, and early twentieth-century racial oppressions experienced by African Americans, Asian Americans, Native Americans, and Mexican Americans. But the meaning of contemporary literary multiculturalism—its politics and canonical interventions—was determined not so much by those different histories as by the much more recent simultaneous rejection in the 1960s and 1970s of a liberal assimilationist consensus. Rather than treat these traditions as separate entities (as much contemporary criticism does), this book sees the traditions as part of a unified field. Undergirding the common revolt across the different *racial* minority traditions was a not-yet-recognized debate about *culture* between anthropology and sociology. Anthropology and sociology redescribed these populations as culturally different instead of biologically different even as they arrived at divergent answers to questions of accommodation, integration, and assimilation.

This genealogy of multicultural literature is Foucauldian rather than genetic, understanding literature's circuit with social science not as mere influence, but as lines of force, adaptations and transformations, ruptures and continuities, and considerable feedback within the circuit itself. Writers took what they needed from the disciplines of anthropology and sociology, using their concepts to articulate broader aesthetic and political principles about what minority cultures in America meant, and what their futures would be. They sometimes adapted or productively misread that social science; and occasionally their writing, in turn, influenced an anthropology already attentive to stories and a sociology already committed to treating life writing as ethnic data.

This book builds on recent critical attention to the relation between social science and literature. Scholars such as Lee D. Baker, George Hutchinson, Marc Manganaro, Carla Cappetti, Susan Hegeman, Susan Mizruchi, Roderick Ferguson, Henry Yu, and Scott Michaelson have made possible my argument, though each would not agree with all of its conclusions. They have revealed the deep affinities and mutual influences between the social sciences and American literature at the end of the nineteenth and the beginning of the twentieth centuries; many of them, too, have explored the ways in which law and social science have colluded to produce and then call into question the theories and functions of race and culture. My work builds on theirs in a few important ways. First, it continues the story, as it were, past their time frame of early and early-mid twentieth-century literature and social science: as I show here, many minority writers besides Zora Neale Hurston and Richard Wright (for whom this formation has been recognized), including the inaugural multiculturalist writers of the late 1960s and early 1970s, continued to be influenced by or to contest the foundations developed by anthropology and sociology in the first four decades of the century. Second, its comparative, inter-tradition historical account brings into sharper focus how the pluralism at the heart of our current multiculturalism was formed through the rejection of assimilationist literary traditions and politics. And third, my project is informed by Walter Benn Michaels's critical unraveling of the terms "race," "culture," and "identity," taking into account his warning that culture became not social science description but a nativist ambition in American modernism, and that such culturalist ambitions perform the back-door re-entrance of the very racial concepts they were meant to displace.

This genealogical scheme reveals similarities and parallels among the four minority literary traditions even as it prevents a homogenization of the four different traditions and groups into a single, undifferentiated minority object in the dominant society. *A Genealogy of Literary Multiculturalism* develops old distinctions among the traditions in new directions, and its identification of cross-tradition patterns allow for a more profound historical thesis about multicultural literature than has heretofore been possible. We have known, for instance, that there has never been an assimilationist, integrationist tradition in Native American letters (reflected in the dearth of Native writing published in the second phase, the 1940s and 1950s) and that Asian American literature's most important beginnings (aside from the "Eurasian" Eaton sisters) lay in this same phase and evinced its cultural politics. But this literary distinction now appears, I argue, to be part of a larger historical pattern that includes *both* the specific disciplinary formations of anthropology's encounter with the Indian and sociology's encounter with the Asian American on the Pacific, *and* a longer-running and inverse logic about Indians' and Asians' spiritual relation to the American land. The more profound historical thesis allowed by this comparativist approach to multicultural literature is that these traditions have a common grounding in changing conceptions of race and culture; insofar as they are part of a feedback loop with social science, these texts reveal the underlying—and generally sequential—consensuses that eventually developed into the paradigm of literary multiculturalism. It means both that mid-century liberal-consensus Asian American writers drew on different aspects of sociology from those used by their African American contemporary Richard Wright, and that post-consensus Asian American literary nationalists had no explicit anthropological precedent on which to draw, unlike writers in the American Indian, African American, and Chicano traditions, even though they arrived at some of the same answers.

Assessing these traditions as a unified field clarifies how writers understood the logic of racial symbolism in America to be interlocking, and frequently triangulated their answers to such questions through reference to other groups. When Hurston protested the *Brown v. Board of Education* desegregation decision in 1955, for instance, she contrasted the NAACP with the observation that there was "no whine in the Indian," thus invoking anthropology's founding conceit of the Indian who would rather die than give up his culture. Frank Chin's cultural nationalist play *Chickencoop Chinamen* likewise achieves its rumination on Asian American masculinity only by triangulating that identity through reference to Tonto and the Lone Ranger, black vernacular and masculinity, and white femininity. It is no accident that a similar nationalism developed in Ishmael Reed's *Mumbo Jumbo* had members of these four groups—whose descents were African, Asian, Native, and Mexican—join forces as the "*Mu'tafikah*" in order to liberate ethnic art from the "centers for art detention" organized by the Western white colonial powers. These writers understood that the racial symbolism of the nation existed not as sets of separated binaries in singular relations to a constructed whiteness, but as a web of associations and mutual definitions. My method, accordingly, is to crossthread a writer of one group with a writer of another group, even if the writers in question do not always receive equal space. It is by such crossthreadings of Hurston with McNickle, Wong with Ellison, Okada with Momaday, Morrison with Chin, Reed with Anzaldúa, and so on, that the parallels and differences demonstrate the meaningful patterns that constitute the genealogy of literary multiculturalism.

🐾 Race and Culture

Boas and many of these writers were overturning the "particular worldview" of race that had developed over the last three or four centuries (Smedley 7). Audrey Smedley argues that the idea of race reached its strongest articulation by the beginning of the nineteenth century in the United States, and is characterized by five primary traits. First, according to Smedley, is the idea that human groups are "discrete biological entities" (28) that are, second, hierarchically ranked in terms of intelligence, civilization, technological advancement, and so on. Third is the idea that outward physical features—one's phenotype—are a manifestation or correlation of unseen "inner realities" (28), such that physical differences among groups were outward signs of inner essential differences among groups. Fourth is the idea that both the group-based physical differences and the group-based inner differences that they stood for were inherited (through whatever mechanism). The fifth and final idea is that such differences were created by either God or nature, and so were "unalterable," untranscendable (28).

Boas's revolution was to destroy all five traits of this idea of race, at least in terms of most scientific accounts of race. Social scientists argue that race is "socially constructed" and not biologically real precisely because there is a gap between what scientists understand as the biology of group differences and the massive social hallucination of the biology of group differences. Because American society remains compelled by the fantasy of biological race, it is stuck with the reality of social race (Omi and Winant 60). Boas's assault on race used the tools of an older physical anthropology, and it was a largely successful struggle waged by him and his students, including Zora Neale Hurston. What they put in its place was a renovated concept of culture as an explanation for group differences, and the idea of the environment.

While heredity still played an important role, Boas's realignment of the field was to show that the relevant biological inheritance from our parents is our genes, not our race.[2]

But as this book makes clear, the first generation of multicultural writers turned to anthropology's notion of cultural pluralism, but they grounded that pluralism in the very logic of racial difference that anthropology had earlier repudiated. *A Genealogy of Literary Multiculturalism* uncovers the history of that paradox, revealing that multicultural literature today depends not so much on cultural pluralism as on racial prescriptivism. Its polemical dimension is to suggest that we expect racial minorities above all to subscribe to ancestral traditions, and if they do not, to try to discover them through tropes of memory, identity, or blood. The near unanimity on the grammar of identity in the United States today should serve as a warning to us: while multiculturalism might imagine itself in opposition to the Christian right, for example, they share the primacy of the subject position and the language of identity.[3] *Mumbo Jumbo,* for example, makes this point clearly when it imagines racial identities and religious identities not just as parallel ontologies, but as essentially the very same thing. The culture wars are identitarianism's family feud, and they are bad wars for this reason. Just as sustained discussion about ethics is short-circuited by the idea of religious identity—in which ethical behavior is understood to emerge from religious identity—so, too, does America's self-conception in terms of a national identity short-circuit the needed discussion about what it should do in the world and domestically. Statements of identity—cultural, religious, or national—trump discussion of practice; essence continually precludes us from talking about existence in meaningful ways.

How we read multicultural literature for identity or for its supposed cultural data is unfortunately at the heart of our current literary paradigm. *A Genealogy of Literary Multiculturalism* distinguishes the good accomplishments of multiculturalism from the way in which it is too frequently the object of bad thinking and bad faith. The achievements of multiculturalism have been pluralism, tolerance, antiracism, and the dethroning of Western cultures as universal ones. But to the extent that multiculturalism has turned pluralism into the celebration of difference as such, it disables pressing questions of what we should do and how we should live. To the extent that multiculturalism is committed to identity and not description—to essentialism and not existentialism—it is a strategy that distracts us from the real. To the extent that multiculturalism wholly abandons the terrain of evaluation and universalism, it disastrously concedes public questions of ethics, arguments, and evidence. And to the extent that multiculturalism grounds appropriate culture in race (or in any other identity), it reinstalls the disturbing (and faulty) thinking that social being is inherited. In these ways, this book calls for a reformation within the paradigm of multiculturalism.

The kind of disentangling of the payoffs of multiculturalism from what I take to be the ultimately unprogressive modes of its discourse can be seen in a number of recent critical projects. David Palumbo-Liu sees "critical multiculturalism" as eschewing the labor of merely "celebrating the plurality of cultures by passing through them appreciatively" (*Ethnic* 5). Like Palumbo-Liu, concerned about the way minority texts can serve as "proxies" for minority students in the classroom (11–13), Hazel Carby points to the way in which the diversification of syllabi, by adding minority authors to established lists, sometimes takes the place of any political action that might increase access for racialized minority students who are statistically overrepresented among the nation's poor ("The Multicultural Wars" 12). For Carby, the focus on "identity politics" fundamentally distracts us from "material conditions" ("Can the Tactics" 222), a point echoed by Nancy Fraser's suggestion that the "politics of recognition" increasingly displaced, in postwar progressive political discourse, the "politics of redistribution" ("Introduction"), and by Walter Benn Michaels in *The Shape of the Signifier*. Michaels, in *Our America* and *Shape,* has advanced the argument that our cultural pluralism continues to be grounded in a racial identity, an argument echoed by Richard Ford's contention that in some multiculturalist accounts of "cultural rights," "social groups defined by race are treated as analogous to geographically insular cultural minorities and certain indigenous or aboriginal tribes" (7). Ford and Michaels agree that much multicultural logic of identity is racially prescriptive rather than culturally descriptive, precisely insofar as multiculturalism collapses back into notions of racial essence. Paul Gilroy argues similarly against the continued progressive use of the concept of race, and likewise contends, with Ford and Michaels, that we should not give up the possibilities of universals, the procedures of evaluation, and the ideals of cosmopolitanism. We surely want to be able to critically interrogate, to return to an earlier example, Dahomey's palace of skulls. While Boas suggested that killing sometimes needed to be seen in terms of cultural relativism,[4] Cudjo Lewis himself probably wondered, legitimately, whether his head was going to end up as just another brick in the wall, and he might have objected on the simple universalist grounds that one should not do to others' bodies what they would not like done to their own. While their arguments are not the same, what unites these six thinkers is a critique of day-to-day, routine multiculturalism: multiculturalism as it happens on the ground, in public political and social discourse, in classroom teaching, in academic research journals, and in the literature that helped establish our current paradigm.

A Genealogy of Literary Multiculturalism thus delineates the twentieth-century history of American literary multiculturalism from the first phase's initial invigoration of Boas's redescription of biological difference as anthropological cultural difference and pluralism, through the second phase's mid-century, liberal, sociologically modeled consensus on integration and cultural assimilation, to the third phase's return with a difference to a pluralist cultural nationalism that laid the foundation for our current paradigm of literary multiculturalism. In doing so, it answers the question that Hurston's biographer and series editor both asked—why does Hurston's star fade between the 1942 publication of her autobiography and her rediscovery by Alice Walker in the 1970s? It also takes up the question Marjorie Perloff directed to Walter Benn Michaels's *Our America*—"But why did this form of nativism occur in the 1920s and recur in the 1990s? What about the six decades in between?" (100). What interrupted both anthropology's culture and nativism's racism was the rival concept of sociology's culture that contested them both in the first and second phases. Walker's 1970s witnessed a cultural nationalism that was enabled by a return to anthropology's non-nativist culture, a nationalism still being worked through as multiculturalism in Perloff's 1990s. The crucial difference was that newly racialized culture became an ambition, and an identity.

✎ Franz Boas's Cultural Revolution

"I am being trained for Anthropometry and Dr. Herskovitch [*sic*] is calling me at irregular intervals to do measuring," Zora Neale Hurston informed a Barnard College trustee in the spring of 1926. "He works me all day in two or three hour spurts," she continued. "But I have a Job for the Summer and that makes me happy. Dr. Boas says if I make good, there are more jobs in store for me" (Kaplan 82–83). There were indeed more jobs in anthropology for Hurston, ones directed by both Franz Boas and Melville Herskovits. The one she was doing in March 1926 was work that these two white anthropologists could likely not have performed: Hurston was stationed on a Harlem street corner, measuring with calipers the heads of Harlemites as they passed by. It was fieldwork, says one biographer, "that many contemporaries felt only Zora Hurston, with her relaxed insouciance, could have gotten away with" (Hemenway 63).

What Hurston helped enshrine through this work was nothing less than a paradigm shift in twentieth-century social science, and, indeed, in Western intellectual history: that of conceiving of group identity as cultural rather than racial, as environmentally conditioned rather than biologically determined. Boas, whom Hurston called "Papa Franz," and at other times "the king of kings," had been arguing against racial explanations for more than three decades, and had repeatedly posited environment and culture in the place of heredity. It was a mark of his commitment both to methodology and to the remade discipline of cultural anthropology that had him using the techniques of physical anthropology to overturn the racial worldview that those techniques had been associated with. He knew that physical anthropology had to be beaten—and could be beaten—on its own ground. He found a student and ally in Zora Neale Hurston, as he did in Herskovits and many others in the generation of cultural anthropologists he trained at Columbia.

While the data Hurston was collecting was a long series of biometrics, the measurements she was taking might have enabled the calculation of a head's circumference, which "was the most accurate means of judging cranial size in living human beings" (Hyatt 105). Cranial capacity, and hence brain size, and other head measurements like the cephalic index (the "ratio of the greatest breadth of the head expressed in per cents of the length of the head"[5]) had dominated discussions of racial science for several generations. Perhaps the best known practitioner was the Philadelphia physician and scientist Samuel George Morton, who began collecting human skulls—mostly Indian—in the 1820s. He collected over a thousand during the course of his lifetime—"Friends (and enemies) referred to his great charnel house as 'the American Golgotha'" (Gould 83)—and measured the capacity of each by filling the skulls with mustard seeds, and later, lead shot.

Morton published his research, beginning with *Crania Americana,* in 1839. Primarily a comparison between "Caucasian" and "American" (meaning Native) crania volume, *Crania Americana* showed that the mean capacity of whites, at 87 cubic inches, was greater than the mean of Indians, at 82 cubic inches, and substantially larger than smaller sample groups of "Mongolian" (83), "Malay" (81), and "Ethiopian" (meaning African, at 78). Its sequel *Crania Aegyptiaca* (1844) published the measurements of seventy-two skulls from Egyptian tombs. "Morton felt that he could identify both races and subgroups among races from features of the skull" (Gould 93) and found, predictably, that the "Pelasgic" (Greek) skulls had higher capacities (averaging 88 cubic inches) than the "Negro" ones (averaging 73). His final combined tally of his collection of 623 skulls in 1849 reinforced white supremacist views, even as it differentiated different "families" within the "races" (Gould 87). As Stephen Jay Gould puts it, Morton's data

matched every good Yankee's prejudice—whites on top, Indians in the middle, and blacks on the bottom; and, among whites, Teutons and

Anglo-Saxons on top, Jews in the middle, and Hindus on the bottom. Moreover, the pattern had been stable throughout recorded history, for whites had the same advantage over blacks in ancient Egypt. Status and access to power in Morton's America faithfully reflected biological merit. How could sentimentalists and egalitarians stand against the dictates of nature? (85–86)

The major and enduring error, of course, was the initial premise linking brain size and intelligence, which Boas criticized in 1938 by noting that brain size was linked to body stature, and that not all "eminent men's" brains were large (*Mind* 104–5).

Morton was an advocate of polygenesis, the idea that the races were actually different species with independent origins, which appealed to both the slaveholding South and the racially hierarchical North. But it also posed a crucial problem for slaveholding ideology in the middle of the nineteenth century, since it seemed to undercut the biblical account of creation, in which humans were created by God once, not several times as several species. It took some inventive theology to reconcile polygenesis with Genesis, and many pro-slavery theologians and naturalists were unwilling to undertake it. Besides, as Gould notes, "The defenders of slavery did not need polygeny. Religion still stood above science as a primary source for the rationalization of social order" (103–4).

Such is what makes schoolteacher, in Toni Morrison's *Beloved,* all the more impressive. Given that *Crania Americana* was published in 1839 and *Crania Aegyptiaca* in 1844, schoolteacher's head measuring at Sweet Home in the early 1850s places him on the cutting edge of the racial science of his time. It is the head measuring and such, Toni Morrison indicates, that helps drive Sixo mad; likewise, it is hearing schoolteacher direct his nephews to line up her "human" characteristics on one side of the page and her "animal" ones on the other that helps give Sethe the final determination to escape with her children. To be sure, schoolteacher does seem to frame his ownership and punishment of people in religious terms—that God has given him and his nephews care of the slaves—but this is mild compared to the emphasis on the measuring string, the teeth counting, and the questions that all form part of schoolteacher's racial science project.

I place Hurston within the head-measuring lineage of Morton and schoolteacher to illustrate the distance between their project and hers and Boas's. What the anthropologists were arguing against—by using the tools of—was a dominant paradigm of racial science, developed in the last half of the nineteenth century, committed to conceptualizing race as hereditary and biological. Though polygenesis waned, the tradition of physical anthropology that developed during this time continued to regard racial differences as real, inherited, and immutable. The discipline of physical anthropology became the primary articulator of scientific racism in the last half of the nineteenth century; this work was popularly disseminated with important legal consequences. As Lee D. Baker puts it,

> anthropological discourse on race was (literally, in some cases) brought to life in magazines, museum exhibits, and world's fairs. These media were riddled with the writings of anthropologists, journalists, and so-called experts who appropriated early anthropological notions of race to buttress their propaganda. The American public voraciously consumed anthropology as popular culture. Similarly, world's fairs, magazines, and museum exhibits validated anthropology as a professional discipline in the academy because it provided a scientific justification for Jim Crow segregation and imperial domination. (22)

By the 1890s, as Boas's career began, race was the entrenched national consensus about group differences, a fantasy with widespread popular and official support.

Boas's challenge to the prevailing racial paradigm had several important components. First, he used anthropometry to argue against the overwhelming emphasis on heredity, the basis of racial thinking. In its place Boas emphasized a second component, the environment in which humans, like other organisms, develop; to put it simply, Boas greatly altered the weighting from nature to nurture. Third, Boas was methodologically suspicious of the seeking of laws in anthropology (Hyatt 137; Stocking, "Franz Boas" 210); he was constantly attentive to the ways in which exceptions broke patterns, a fact that would have a lasting impact on the ontological problem of what constituted a "race"—or even a "culture." Fourth, and most important for this book, Boas renovated the notion of culture as that which lay at the base of the group: culture, unlike the notion of race it generally went on to replace, had to be learned, and could be changed.

Born in Germany in 1858 to a liberal Jewish household, Boas was ostensibly raised orthodox, though he later claimed that this was merely his parents' "sop for his grandparents" (qtd. in Hyatt 4). He was trained in physics, completing in 1881 his dissertation "Contributions to the Understanding of the Color of Water" on the polarization and absorption of light in water.[6] Boas bore facial scars—he joked that he got them from a polar bear while researching on Baffin Island—from dueling in his university days in Germany, which one biographer believes might have resulted from a confrontation with anti-Semitism (Hyatt 5).[7]

He began his anthropology career with a trip to study Baffin Island Inuit in 1883, and he later moved to the United States and did further work in the Canadian Arctic and in the Northwest, around Vancouver Island. He was an assistant editor of *Science* by 1887, and by the early 1890s had "invented his own techniques" in the field of anthropometry (Hyatt 26). His findings went against the grain. As his later influential essay "Instability of Human Types" described, immigrants' body forms underwent significant changes in the new environment of America: "All these differences seem to increase with the time elapsed between the emigration of the parents and the birth of the child, and are much more marked in the second generation of American-born individuals" (216), he wrote. "Instead of attributing divergent development to heredity, he looked to the influence of environmental factors. It appeared that healthier environments produced healthier children" (Hyatt 27). This dietary and psychological truism—both *The Bluest Eye* and the social science it critiques are built around the idea that "healthier environments produce healthier children"—is so only because Boas fundamentally altered the understanding of environment in the decades that followed. One of his earliest formulations of this argument was his famous speech "Human Faculty as Determined by Race," delivered at the 1894 American Association for the Advancement of Science meeting. It was, Hyatt says, "his first public attack on race prejudice." The speech expressed "Boas's emphasis on culture as a determinant of behavior. Rather than attributing differing mental abilities to differences in race, Boas concluded that environment and the historical process were responsible for such characteristics" (33).

Boas's investigations revealed a fundamental and "decided plasticity of human types" ("Instability" 217). Qualities that were thought to be inherited, biological, and immutable were actually qualities that were fundamentally altered depending on environmental conditions. Boas went on to reason—in a crucial blow to racial thinking—that "if the bodily form undergoes far-reaching changes under a new environment, concomitant changes of the mind may be expected" ("Instability" 217).[8] Boas and his students used biometric techniques and conventions to undo their founding premises that bodily form (including cranial capacity) and other less tangible qualities were almost entirely inherited, and that cranial capacity directly determined intelligence. Boas was not arguing for the so-called blank slate idea, but rather was making a distinction within the concept of heredity. As Melville Herskovits puts it,

His stress on the plasticity of the organism in adapting itself to those structured systems of learned behavior termed cultures arose from the need to underscore the fact that culture is learned so well that responses to it are automatic, not inborn; that specific modes of cultural behavior are not the result of innate abilities, instinctively expressed. Racial heredity, Boas repeated over and over, is meaningless. The significant biological factor, for him, was the actual descent line, not the racial category. (*Franz Boas* 25–26)

For Boas, the pertinent group in terms of inheritance was the family, not race (*Mind* 63). Families might include personality characteristics, because of both heredity and cultural continuity, but a large genetic population like a race could not (*Mind* 129).

Boas's 1894 speech summarizes what would become the central paradigm for his work in the next four and a half decades. His teaching position at Columbia University, obtained in 1896 and held until his death in 1942, was the base from which he established and professionalized cultural anthropology across the nation. By the time he retired, Boas had trained some of the twentieth century's best known and most influential anthropologists, including Melville Herskovits, Margaret Mead, Edward Sapir, Ruth Benedict, Alfred Kroeber, Otto Klineberg, Ashley Montagu, and Zora Neale Hurston. His students went on to help institutionalize anthropology departments nationwide, and by World War II they were staffing and directing "most of the major departments of anthropology in the United States" (Herskovits, *Franz Boas* 65). When Boas came to the discipline in the 1880s, it was dominated by the tradition of physical anthropology and by institutions headed by amateur anthropologists with little or no formal training. He helped drive a professionalizing trend that was both a generational shift and a struggle over institutional power. By 1920 Boas was powerful enough to withstand attacks on him in response to his editorial protesting the American use of scientists as spies during World War I. As Stocking writes, "the Boasian viewpoint on issues of race and culture, which in 1919 was still distinctly a minority current, by 1934 was on the verge of becoming social scientific orthodoxy" ("Anthropology" 43).

Boas's range was wide. He did fieldwork with different Native groups in the Northwest, including early linguistic work, particularly on Vancouver Island, and was one of the organizers of the 1897–1903 Jesup expedition in the Northwest, Alaska, and Siberia, on the questions of human migration and cultural transmission across the Bering Strait. He investigated immigration, arguing in particular against the rising nativist sentiment by showing how the children of immigrants seemed to conform anthropometrically to a white American norm rather than any Old World type. About such changing body types, Boas wrote that "not even those characteristics of a race which have proved to be most permanent in their old home remain the same under new surroundings" (qtd. in Hyatt 109).

Boas's research for the Dillingham Immigration Commission was the sole exception to the forty volumes' general conclusion that too much immigration from Southern and Eastern Europe would produce weak Americans (Hyatt 111). "Boas had attempted," Hyatt writes, "to obtain objective, scientific information for a commission that not only had a predetermined attitude toward immigration, but had been warned by Theodore Roosevelt not to rely on 'too many professors' who might prove that immigration was not a threat to the country" (111). (Roosevelt's comment is one indication that the nativist racism of the first phase sometimes articulated itself against the anthropological notion of culture that arose to contest it; another example of nativist racism constructing itself through a repudiation of anthropological culture comes, as we shall see in chapter seven, from the early horror fiction of H. P. Lovecraft.) Boas's struggle against nativism and anti-immigration led him to write scathing reviews of two of the primary nativist texts of the period: Madison Grant's *The Passing of the Great Race* (1916) and Lothrop Stoddard's *The Rising Tide of Color* (1920). He was livid at the "nordic nonsense" of the 1924 Immigration Restriction Act (qtd. in Hyatt 136).

Boas also worked on behalf of African Americans, arguing that "the low status of blacks in the United States" was due in large part to "the persistence of Euro-American prejudice" and contemporary social structures (Williams, *Rethinking Race* 1). In 1904 he highlighted contemporary West African achievements and "the glories of the African past" (Williams 30), both of which undercut current American stereotypes about African Americans. Invited to Atlanta University by W. E. B. Du Bois in 1906, Boas delivered an address on African history and achievements that left Du Bois, in his words, "astonished":

> Franz Boas came to Atlanta University where I was teaching history in 1906 and said to a graduating class: "You need not be ashamed of your African past"; and then he recounted the history of the black kingdoms south of the Sahara for a thousand years. I was too astonished to speak. All of this I had never heard and I came then and afterwards to realize how silence and neglect of science can let truth utterly disappear or even be consciously distorted. (Du Bois, qtd. in Williams 32)

Although Hyatt claims Boas "followed the lead of W. E. B. Du Bois" in teaching African achievements (97), Williams shows more substantively that Boas had arrived at this idea on his own, and was influencing Du Bois in this regard. Williams argues that part of Boas's legacy was an Afrocentric chauvinism: "Boas not only sharpened the African American intelligentsia's revulsion against Euro-American racism but also, unwittingly, nurtured their belief in distinct, hierarchical attributes in reference to the African past. This tendency resulted in the emergence of various chauvinistic Afrocentric theories of history that have persisted to this day" (1–2). Though this line of influence was somewhat complicated—Boas initially thought African cultures were mostly destroyed in the Middle Passage, and changed his mind only partially and slowly—I argue in later chapters that Boas's vision of cultural continuity and endurance was transmitted through Hurston to the cultural nationalists of the late 1960s and early 1970s.[9]

Boas's argument that early twentieth-century African Americans could take solace in the cultural achievements of early African cultures was not based on a notion of racial kinship or cultural continuity. Rather, Boas's point was an antiracist one within the late nineteenth- and early twentieth-century intellectual milieu in which a group's cultural achievements were understood to be entirely dependent on its supposed racial abilities. That *racially* black people had achieved high *cultural* attainment at other times and in other places was proof that there were no biological impediments to contemporary African American cultural achievements and participation. It was, in other words, an indictment of the contemporaneous American racist environment that kept black people socially and culturally inferior—an indictment enabled by the careful conceptual separation of culture from race.

The distinction between large variations *within* groups and trivial differences *between* them was how Boas imagined racial difference (*Mind* 196). His biographers continue to debate the extent to which he remained a believer of some sort in racial difference over the course of his career; to put it another way, they continue to debate the extent to which Boas, the great destroyer of the racial idea, was racist. Marshall Hyatt suggests that Boas was "not a full-fledged egalitarian," believing in the second decade of the twentieth century in some degree of Negro inferiority. "Although he frequently stated that individual variations within each race were more important than interracial comparisons, he did not suggest that the races were fully equal," Hyatt remarks (88). But Boas seems to have believed with decreasing emphasis that there was some content to the category of race, and even that content was entirely trivial when compared to the environmental and cultural effects on the individual, the much larger overlap in whatever characteristic between racial groups, or the more substantial variation within the group. I agree with Vernon Williams Jr. that Boas was, like Robert Park, a "transitional figure," for whom the racial idea lingered, never to be entirely abandoned (96). That said, Williams significantly and erroneously overestimates Boas's commitment to the idea of race, especially by the end of his life, and misunderstands Boas's tactic of doing physical anthropology in order to refute its major conclusions (see Herskovits, *Franz Boas* 29, and Gould 140).

For Boas, the tendency to over-generalize on the basis of little or faulty data was connected to amateur anthropology's lack of rigorous scientific training. His drive for scientific accuracy was just as important as his liberal views, writes Hyatt: "He could not tolerate generalizations or scientific opinions drawn on faulty data. The pseudoscientific support given to theories of black inferiority ran against his emphasis on meticulous research" (85). The tendency toward premature reduction was connected to another unquestioned but unsubstantiated premise, that of the "evolutionist" argument ranking racial ability according to civilizational achievements. For the scientific world and the public at the end of the nineteenth century, it was no accident that the most advanced civilization was European and the least advanced was (variously) Indian, African, or aboriginal. White civilization was at the top, went the thinking, because the white "race" was inherently—constitutionally, biologically—the most advanced.

While such logic did not necessarily follow from Charles Darwin's work— it was, in fact, a misunderstanding and misapplication of it—this view became associated with the idea of evolution, and much anthropology at the end of the nineteenth century was devoted to expositing racial hierarchies based on a civilization's progress. Boas's argument against this "evolutionary" thinking in anthropology arose as early as 1887, when, as an assistant editor of *Science,* he quarreled with Otis Mason on the Smithsonian's method of classification and display. Subscribing to the generally accepted idea that human societies evolved along a single path determined by racial development, Mason wanted to group similar tools from different cultures in the same display. Boas argued instead that artifacts should be grouped and displayed according to cultural groups, a suggestion that would undo the universal idea of a civilization's linear progression. In so contending against the Smithsonian's system, "Boas directly attacked the underpinning of the evolutionist argument, both by elevating the importance of historical particularism and by arguing for a holistic paradigm in displaying tribal artifacts" (Hyatt 21). His approaches to cultures—historical particularism and holism—were foundational elements around which the new cultural anthropology would be built.

Finally, the new paradigm of cultural anthropology did not just include a renovated concept of culture. It also formalized fieldwork methods for collecting cultural elements. Other anthropologists—Herskovits gives the example of James Mooney, whose anthropology would deeply influence

N. Scott Momaday—were doing fieldwork before Boas, but they were not professionals (Mooney was an army officer) and the discipline had not been formalized and professionalized (Herskovits, *Franz Boas* 65). Boas reconceptualized ethnographic research as a process of collection whereby the researcher lived within the culture as a participant observer. Typically, the fieldworker attempted to learn the language partly by collecting stories from the culture's oral tradition. In addition to treating the culture holistically by taking notes on its many elements (religion, kinship structures, social organization, economy, foodways, etc.), one collected the folktales told by members in their actual settings. The importance of gathering "material" was recent in anthropology, Boas noted in his 1938 *Mind of Primitive Man* (175), a shift for which he became in good part responsible. Folklore provided insight into different cultures' "mode[s] of thought" (222) and constituted data for studying linguistic structures. As Stocking notes, "For Boas, it was above all in their folklore that the 'genius of a people' was manifest. Folklore provided the 'best material for judging their character,' because it embodied their values—what they 'considered good and what bad, what commendable and what objectionable, what beautiful and what otherwise'" ("Franz Boas" 223–24). Boas did such ethnographic collection himself, particularly among the Native groups in the Northwest, but he also sponsored other fieldworkers, including Ella Deloria among the Sioux (Herskovits, *Franz Boaz* 63), and Zora Neale Hurston among central Florida's rural African Americans, two minority anthropologists who would later become literary writers.

✥ Chapter 1

Zora Neale Hurston, D'Arcy McNickle, and the Culture of Anthropology

> I was glad when somebody told me, "You may go and collect Negro folklore."
>
> —Zora Neale Hurston, *Mules and Men,* 1935 (1)

✥ Zora Neale Hurston's Anthropology

Zora Neale Hurston was part of the paradigm shift from racial anthropology to cultural anthropology. In the spring of 1926, her caliper exercises in Harlem were part of the work of refuting racial thinking, for which Herskovits credits Hurston in his 1928 report *The American Negro,* and his 1930 study *The Anthropometry of the American Negro.*[1] But Hurston did several important anthropology "jobs" in the years that followed. These included collecting African American folklore in rural central Florida, studying hoodoo in New Orleans and voodoo in Haiti, talking with the last ex-slave to survive the Middle Passage and collecting music from Jamaica. Hurston had arrived in New York in 1925 to take part in the Harlem Renaissance,[2] but began to attend Barnard College that fall, leaving "two years later as a serious social scientist, the result of her study of anthropology under Franz Boas" (Hemenway 21). In fact, the literary output that made her famous emerged only after this anthropological training at Barnard and in the field. Hurston was an enthusiast for anthropology and for "Papa Franz," and became "a kind of proselytizer for anthropological knowledge," convincing Renaissance colleague Bruce Nugent to sit in on Boas's classes for three years (Hemenway 81). What emerged from her ongoing ethnographic labor was the 1930s constellation of two novels, *Jonah's Gourd Vine* (1934) and *Their Eyes Were*

Watching God (1937), and two ethnographies, *Mules and Men* (1935) and *Tell My Horse* (1938), as well as the 1942 autobiography *Dust Tracks on a Road.* In them, Hurston shaped a vision of African American Southern rural folk culture articulated through the Boasian notion of culture that she had been studying and working with for a decade and a half.

By way of comparison, I crossthread my analysis of Hurston's work with that of D'Arcy McNickle, a Salish writer and contemporary of Hurston's whose 1936 novel *The Surrounded* shared with Hurston's 1930s work a number of culturalist traits. Whereas Hurston trained as an anthropologist before turning to literature, McNickle became an anthropologist after first being a novelist. Nonetheless, what we know of the composition of McNickle's novel reveals that he, too, turned to ethnographic sources for the details and perhaps partly for the model of culture that animates his fiction. For both Hurston and McNickle, vernacular story-telling was central to their first-phase vision of minority cultures in the United States. Both writers likewise understood African American and Salish cultures to be premised on a sense of separation from the white dominant society, and even a certain kind of sovereignty of community; the politics that emerged from both writers was an anti-assimilationist one that saw them contest the 1950s sociologically enabled assimilationist consensus signaled by *Brown v. Board of Education* and the federal Indian policies of Relocation and Termination. Hurston and McNickle are the best representatives of anthropology's general influence on African American and Native American writers of the first phase.

George Hutchinson and Lee Baker have recently argued that Boasian anthropology was a crucial context for, and influence on, the Harlem Renaissance writers emerging to prominence in the 1920s and continuing their work in the 1930s. "Boasian concepts" about culture and race, says Hutchinson, "became bedrock assumptions among 'New Negro' authors of virtually every persuasion" (62). John Dewey's pragmatics was a "constellation in the intellectual field to which virtually everyone responded" (38), as was Boas's cultural anthropology and a growing discourse of cultural pluralism as cultural nationalism. Hutchinson cites in particular Boas's *Journal of American Folklore*'s sustained attention to African American folk culture as being "of critical importance for the Harlem Renaissance and that continued with historic results through the 1930s by way of the Federal Writers' Project" (68). Lee Baker likewise suggests that the 14 issues of the journal devoted to Negro folklore between 1917 and 1937 were a critical Boasian project "appropriated by the promoters of the New Negro Movement," an appropriation completed with Alain Locke's *The New Negro,* which contained fifty references to the *JAFL* (Baker 158).

It was not just Boas's devastating critique of racial ideas that was important to Renaissance theorists and writers like Wallace Thurman, George Schuyler, and Jessie Fauset—whose brother Arthur Huff Fauset was a working folklorist, like Hurston, with both contributing to *The New Negro*—but also the culture concept that came to replace race (Hutchinson 70). Hutchinson sees Boas's anthropology along with Dewey's pragmatism as the theoretical underpinning of the project of cultural pluralism within a cultural nationalism that the Renaissance generally shared with many white critics and writers. "Franz Boas and his students at Columbia University (on West 119th Street and Amsterdam Avenue, just up the steps of Morningside Park from Harlem) were reshaping the anthropological discourse on race literally in the middle of the Harlem Renaissance," writes Lee Baker, and they were no less important in developing the rival notion of culture in its stead (166–67).

Of all the Renaissance-associated writers and critics, it was Zora Neale Hurston who responded most deeply to Boasian anthropology. Hurston does not get much space in Hutchinson's *Harlem Renaissance in Black and White,* but her place is especially important in terms of the genealogy of literary multiculturalism. When a later generation of African American multiculturalists—including Toni Morrison, Alice Walker, Gayl Jones, Ishmael Reed, Alex Haley, and Ernest Gaines—turned to Hurston over and above other Renaissance figures, instead of their most recent antecedents Wright, Ellison, and Baldwin, to substantiate the shape and content of African American culture, they were turning, with far-reaching and not yet understood effects, to the figure most deeply influenced by Boasian cultural anthropology and its concepts. It is important to draw a firmer distinction than Hutchinson does between Boasian anthropology and the different set of emphases in the sociology associated with the University of Chicago's Robert Park. Hutchinson sees the atmosphere of cultural pluralism emerging partly from Park's sociology (Park was a student of Dewey), with the resulting pragmatics-cum-pluralism represented by figures like Charles Johnson, the sociologist trained by Park who was the editor of the Renaissance-sponsoring *Opportunity.* But in fact, three generations of minority writers, intellectuals, and activists understood there to be fundamental differences between the culture concepts of Boasian anthropology and Parkian sociology, an understanding that has crucially shaped the twentieth century's genealogy of literary multiculturalism.[3]

Hurston's training in the Boasian concept of culture brings up one of the key problems of this book—the question of influence and articulation in the feedback loop between social science and literature in the middle of the century. To what degree were the contours of African American culture part of Hurston's thinking before she took classes and did fieldwork under Boas's and Herskovits's supervision? What were the influences of social science ideas on her work? Did they change her vision, or sharpen and help articulate ideas already present? One biographer contends that with anthropological training, Hurston's culture became a "scientific concept" which she could then "confront" both "as subject and as object," suggesting that "the academic discipline provided a conceptualization for her folk experience" (Hemenway 21–22, 62). Houston Baker argues the reverse, that Hurston had to "slip the yoke" imposed by disciplinary anthropology.[4] There is no easy answer to this question of influence or articulation. Many of the qualities that went on to define Hurston's reading of African American culture—its essential health, its creative and not just reactive energy, its sophisticated artistry, its inner complexity—pre-dated her study of anthropological ideas. Other qualities of the culture concept—the full ramifications of historical particularism—probably emerged mostly through her anthropological training. In between is the wide range of qualities and content already present to Hurston, such as the artistic value of black music and folktales, that would be re-interpreted and articulated partly through Boas's work, such as the cultural relativism that said black music and tales were not to be evaluated by Western artistic criteria. As I hope to make clear, there were some aspects of Boas's thought—primarily, the implication of the gradual assimilation of minority cultures into a larger environment—that Hurston rejected, and in this sense she was, like the other writers I examine here, a critical evaluator and consumer of social science ideas. In fact, on some issues, like the idea of the retention of African cultural traits across the Middle Passage, Hurston seems to have embraced this idea before her training in anthropology (Hemenway 74), and then substantiated it with her fieldwork in the next decade.[5]

I want to suggest that there was not so much a "vocational schizophrenia" or ambivalence between her role as an ethnographer and her role as an artist, as there was a mutually reinforcing culturism that deeply infuses both her ethnographic work and her literary work (Hemenway 63, but see also 117 and passim). Hemenway reads Hurston as a budding Renaissance artist who lived in New York between 1925 and 1927, but who trained as a scientist and whose new discipline helped her understand her folklore and culture-specific upbringing. According to Hemenway, a subsequent phase began with her first novel, *Jonah's Gourd Vine* (which was composed after, but published before, the ethnographic work *Mules and Men*), where "her writing exhibits a studied antiscientific approach" (213), forecasting a steady movement toward fiction (215). I think we can better understand the anthropological and fictional work between 1927 (when she went to Florida) and 1942 (when *Dust Tracks* was published), however, as a continuous development of the culture concept in all of Hurston's work, an elaboration of a dominant paradigm of cultural autonomy and difference that is Boasian in several crucial and identifiable respects, but which represents nonetheless a distinct adaptation of Boas's ideas rather than a straight adoption of them.

Her collection work in Florida in 1927 and 1928 was composed as *Mules and Men* between March 1930 and September 1932. Its project is anthropological on a general level, as Marc Manganaro has shown through the affinities of Hurston's work with the famous British anthropologist and disciplinary rival of Boas, Bronislaw Malinowski. *Mules and Men,* like Malinowski's *Argonauts of the Pacific,* "argues for cultural unity through the display of often apparently random and rambling narratives" and then substantiates that "coherence" through reference to the "mythical-magical," contends Manganaro (*Culture* 198). Manganaro shows how *Mules'* fragmented structure contrasted with the "well-wrought" quality of the other great ethnography of 1934, Ruth Benedict's *Patterns of Culture,* thus anticipating postmodern ethnography's views of "culture as porous, as fluid, as mobile, and as less than tidy and wholly synecdochic" (198). But we have yet to realize how thoroughly Boasian Hurston's anthropological project actually was, and with what results for the literary multiculturalism that later turned to her.

Beyond the square one of racial equality, which Hurston accepted and which, as we have seen, she helped corroborate, her work substantiates four further qualities of Boas's emerging paradigm of culture. My admittedly schematic method is to place Boas's theory beside illustrative examples in *Mules and Men,* thus serving the dual purpose of explaining Boas's paradigm of culture and showing how Hurston adapted it for her anthropological and literary work of the 1930s.

Culture as a Dynamic Whole

Mules and Men is carefully framed by Boas's presence. Hurston asked Boas to write the preface, and he makes much of Hurston's double status as an insider informant to, and outside ethnographer of, black Southern rural folk culture. Hurston's introduction famously opens with the calling of the King of Kings himself: "I was glad when somebody told me, 'You may go and collect Negro folklore'" (1). *Mules* begins with the narrator-ethnographer casually driving up to the store porch in Eatonville with a "Hello, boys," where the men are playing cards (7). She openly announces her folklore collecting project, and while this provokes some incredulity, the porch talkers begin supplying Hurston with tales. *Mules and Men* integrates its story collection into a full portrayal of African American verbal and social life. This is not just a kind of deep context for the stories themselves, "the intimate setting in the social life of the Negro" which, Boas says in the preface, "has been given very inadequately" in other collections of African American folklore (xiii). It is a treatment of the stories as an integrated part of Eatonville life and central Florida work-camp culture.

Mules' attention to the culture's verbal life is extraordinarily wide-ranging. Hurston records animal fables, just-so stories, tales with standard characters like John the slave who always manages to ultimately trick "ole Massa" or the Devil, spooky stories about Raw Head, hoodoo doctors, and the squinch owl, and a set of Brer stories (165–73). Interspersed are songs, jokes, and repartee. We hear not only the stories, but the frames for the stories: the challenges to tell, their critical reception, and the counter-tales. We hear "it's so hot that…" contests along with competing tales of the biggest mosquito (98–100), and instruction on the hidden meaning in phrases (125). There is specifyin' and signifyin' (124). There are instructions on how to eat a fish properly, and how to get warm (136), and the older generation's stock despair over the young (137). An entire sermon is included (139–42), as is a church prayer (25–26), and instructions on vernacular: words like "abstifically" (perhaps meaning absolutely and specifically) and "suscautious" (suspicious and cautious) are productively meaningful adaptations of standard English in African American Southern rural culture (35, 111, 228). When Hurston is instructed to "spread my jenk" (65), the ethnographer expertly explains the black idiom (she is to have a good time).

Mules does not offer a formalist account measuring the collected tales against tales from other cultures. Rather, Hurston understands the stories as an integrated part of a larger verbal culture; in turn, those stories and the verbal life of which they are a part are understood to be aspects of the larger social life of the community in Eatonville and the mill camps. What the avoided comparativist scheme would look like is glimpsed only briefly in *Mules and Men,* mostly by way of her footnotes, which stand as a commentary apparatus for the ethnography. The stock character John, for instance, "is like Daniel in Jewish folklore, the wish-fulfillment hero of the race. The one who, nevertheless, or in spite of laughter, usually defeats Ole Massa, God and the Devil" (247). One can see the potential hazards of drawing such cross-cultural comparisons: while measuring John next to Daniel might raise the status of the African American hero, it might also suggest (according to the "evolutionary" model of cultural development that Boas was refuting) that Southern black culture has achieved the level of Hebrew culture—of about 2,400 years ago. Likewise, "among the animals the rabbit is the trickster hero," Hurston notes, except in Florida where Brer Gopher sometimes takes his place (249). Here, too, Hurston avoids what might have been a vast cross-cultural comparison among trickster heroes in Native America, or around the world. Instead, *Mules* follows the Boasian proposition about culture: collected objects (here stories and other verbal bits) are the various and interlocking pieces of a complex whole.

As we have seen, as early as 1887 Boas argued for "classification by tribe, rather than by object. This would illustrate the object's origin, history and development, and would also show its relationship to the culture as a whole" (Hyatt 18–19). Boas eventually won this argument about classification, and it became a founding principle of the cultural anthropology in which Hurston was working. As Hyatt writes,

> In essence, Boas was concerned with more than artifacts and their cross-cultural development. He envisioned his museum display as models for 'detailed study of customs in their bearings to the total culture of the tribe practicing them.' Rather than relying on a comparative methodology that ignored both individual experience and the function of objects within a civilization, this holistic structure pinpointed 'the historical causes that led to the formation of the customs in question and to the psychological processes' responsible for their creation. (42)

Comprehending culture as a dynamic whole, Hurston's collection of folklore uses novelistic devices to narrate the ethnographer's hearing of the tales within a wider social experience. The first part of *Mules and Men* thus incorporates the stories into its portrayal of the larger social life of the community, with emphasis on the social (people's relations to one another, especially heterosexual relationships) and not the economic or political (which is what would have interested Richard Wright).

The stories in *Mules* are mostly understood as authored by the culture, not the individual. They constitute, to use Boas's words, the "autobiography of the tribe" (*Tsimshian* 393). The "lies" are usually known by the audience—and so one supposed lie is received by the comment, "Tain't no such a story nowhere. She jus' made dat one up herself" (30). What the individual does is perform the story, conferring certain accents, making small changes, performing tone, emphasizing some meanings at the expense of others. This kind of repetition and revision at work in the verbal life of Eatonville is a model for African American culture in general and for African American literature specifically. Certain stories count as African American and not, to use Hurston's example, Hebrew, because they are told, changed, adapted, repeated, and revised within a community over extended generations, like the folk songs that Hurston says are built by "incremental repetition" that "accumulates" (269). This kind of repetition and signal revision, to use Henry Louis Gates Jr.'s terminology, is a contender for a definition of African American culture or literature that is not racial and essentialist, but rather cultural and constructed. Hurston's portrayal of the performative aspects of the stories is part of the deep description of African American verbal and social life, which accords with Boas's principle of treating cultures as whole dynamics, the parts of which (stories) must be understood as integrated into other facets of the culture.

✹ Culture as Historically Particular

For Boas, it was important to treat cultures as wholes, and not composed piecemeal of interchangeable parts—a bowl or a trickster to be compared to bowls and tricksters among the Yoruba or Ainu or Kiowa or central Florida saw-mill camps. Treating cultures as complex wholes demanded that one emphasize the specific historical development of traits within the cultures that developed or adapted them. Part of the reason Boas conceptualized cultures as complex but not organic wholes was his important principle of historical particularism, by which one understood cultures and their developments as responding to specific circumstances and not universal principles. For Boas, one payoff of historical particularism was that tracing historical developments—convergence, divergence, adaptation, adoption, and so on—helped reveal the real differences behind the superficial similarities (*Mind* 189). This was one reason to reject accounts of culture that were prematurely universal, like Malinowski's or Freud's. "Historical circumstances, not mental ability, determined a culture's progress," summarizes Hyatt (86). The different levels of civilization were not reflections of innate racial ability, as the racial paradigm Boas was displacing thought. Rather, "historical factors were the crucial determinant of civilizations' advance. This theory not only emphasized equality among races but also pointed to the value of historical particularism in the study of man" (Hyatt 114). Boas avoided seeking cultural laws because cultures develop idiosyncratically according to contingent and specific conditions. To delineate universal structures or levels of accomplishment was counter-productive and reminiscent of the amateur "evolutionists" who liked to rank a culture's civilization, from primitive hunter-gatherers through complex industrial monotheistic democracies. When Boas later changed his strict opposition to cultural "laws," especially upon reviewing evidence for "culture complexes" that seemed to suggest that certain cultural traits happened together in groups (which implied at least a pattern), historical particularism nonetheless remained a cornerstone of cultural anthropology.

Historical particularism is another reason, in *Mules and Men,* for not comparing its tricksters with supposedly universal types. The cultural load that John carries is unique to the African American oral tradition begun in the specific historical circumstances of slavery in the United States. "De first colored man what was brought to dis country was name John," begins one such tale (79). John "didn't know nothin' mo' than you told him and he never forgot nothin' you told him either" (79), a tabula rasa whose power partly emerges from the very naïveté and innocence he is said to possess. It is by being simpler than Massa that John successfully fools Massa. In his postured innocence, he is similar to other tricksters. But the John stories in *Mules and Men* emerge from a particular social history of slavery and Jim Crow segregation. When John saves Massa's children from drowning and is set free out of gratitude, for example, he is instructed to remember he is still a "nigger," and that while Massa and his children "love" John, Missy only "likes" him:

> Fur as John could hear 'im down de road he wuz hollerin', "John, Oh John! De children loves you. And I love you. De Missy *like* you."
> John would holler back, "Yassuh."
> "But 'member youse a nigger, tho!"
> Ole Massa kept callin' 'im and his voice was pitiful. But John kept right on steppin' to Canada. He answered Ole Massa every time he called 'im, but he consumed on wid his bag. (90)

This story of slavery critiques the central sexual dynamic behind segregation, the idea that black men remain a sexual threat to the purity of white women, and so must be kept controlled and disempowered in a caste system, an idea most strongly represented in the 1915 film *Birth of a Nation* and critiqued in books like Charles Chesnutt's *Marrow of Tradition* (1901). The purported emotional dynamic of slavery—again represented in *Birth of a Nation*—wherein masters had essentially benevolent and paternalist relations to their slaves, in fact "loved" them and whose "love" was returned by the faithful slaves to their owners, is also ironically undercut, both by John who keeps walking to Canada under the barrage of declared love, and by the repeated Jim Crow note of "nigger," which reveals instead the racial hierarchy, routine violence, and political disempowerment of African Americans. Affection is not enough, says John's back as he walks away.

Mules, like *Jonah's Gourd Vine* and *Their Eyes Were Watching God,* is remarkable for the almost total absence of white people (at least Hurston thought it might be).[6] In these three books, Hurston is more or less uninterested in white people and white characters; her communities are shown to be almost totally autonomous. The white South is like the weather—a condition that impacts her characters, but not something that they can do anything about, and is best ignored whenever possible. And yet in this John story and others, the slavery setting often conceals commentary on the contemporaneous Jim Crow context in which the Eatonville stories are told; they encode, in other words, the historically particular lessons of racial relations in the South, and subversions and challenges to those lessons. Here the hypocrisy and false-hoods of the system are named, and resistance to them developed. John and his cousins Brer Rabbit and Brer Gopher might have a lot in common with tricksters from other cultures, but if we want to understand what their stories mean, we have to attend to Eatonville culture, or African American Southern rural culture more broadly, in terms of its own historical development.

🖉 Culture as Relative

To see cultures as historically particular and complex wholes was intertwined with a third well-known characteristic: cultural relativism. Because differ-ent cultural groups could not be ranked on a universal scale, but were rather merely the accumulated record of historically specific conditions and devel-opments, the comparison of some cultures as better or more advanced than others was erroneous. A culture's components reflected its past or present needs, not the innate ability of its practitioners.[7] One sees this most clearly in Boas's contribution to the field of "comparative linguistics" (Herskovits, *Franz Boas* 80). Boas contended that languages should be studied through their own structures, not against putatively universal structures derived from European languages. Like other factors in a culture, languages could not be ranked, but rather were living records of historical diffusion and develop-ment; in this respect he argued for linguistic relativism that refused to see different language structures as signs for superior cultures (Hyatt 117). And like languages, cultures had to be assessed in their own terms. Boas assumed a common psychological basis for the human development and experience of cultures, but this unity was not what the "evolutionists" maintained. Refer-ring to the idea of the "psychic unity" of humanity, Herskovits writes, "The evolutionists conceived of it as the expression of human capacity to develop culture in accordance with a set sequence of stages, without reference to time or place. This took specific terms—from sexual promiscuity to monogamy, from food-gathering to agriculture, from animism to monotheism, from pictorial to non-representational art" (54). Boas saw "primitive cultures" as different and not as technologically complex, but at the same time, they were not childlike, and not precursors to Western culture (98). Herskovits asserts that cultural relativism was Boas's "most important contribution" to the emerging cultural anthropology: "It grew out of his tolerance for other ways of life than his own, a recognition of their values, and an understanding of the human misery, degradation and demoralization that can result when one people imposes its way on another" (100). Anticipating one of the payoffs of the multiculturalism that would emerge through his agency, Boas thought that one might get free from one's own cultural prejudice by studying other cultures (101).

Cultural relativism, a cornerstone of Boas's legacy, is a premise for *Mules and Men,* one that was the most obviously political. As many critics have noted, Hurston's representation of black vernacular is crucial, and turned out to be one of the most influential aspects of her work when she was rediscovered by African American writers in the late '60s and early '70s. For Boas, collecting oral arts by "writing down texts, dictated by a speaker of the unwritten language being studied" was one way of studying the language of a cultural group (Herskovits 87). Such collections illustrated both the artistry of a people and their language. In *Mules,* Hurston carefully represents the verbal speech of her informants in their non-standard English; her own voice switches register, so that when she is the ethnographer on the scene speaking with Eatonvilleans she speaks similarly, but when she narrates events (not the tales she transcribed) or explains elements in the glossary, she uses standard English. Hurston's Boasian-inspired strategy is to freely travel back and forth between standard and black vernacular English.

Other elements of cultural relativism are implied through the very absence of the dominant culture in *Mules.* Black stories, preaching, singing, food, verbal play, and courtship are understood in their own terms and not measured against a putative norm or superior style. One could read this as strict neutrality on Hurston's part—which is what Boas urged for ethnographers—or as affirmation and celebration. What distinguished her from some of her Renaissance contemporaries was that she understood black folk culture as already sophisticated and artistic. It did not need to be raised to the level of conscious art by a talented tenth,[8] but only to be conveyed to a wider audience, which she achieved in her anthropological collections, and also in her varied work in musical theater in the '30s and '40s, in which she brought African American and Afro-Caribbean music and dance to mostly white audiences. It is not just the art that was as good as Western or American culture. Voodoo, Hurston instructs in both her 1930s ethnographies, is "no more venal, no more impractical than any other" religion (*Horse* 204). Hurston will not judge these cultural practices by moral criteria other than the culture's own. Cultural relativism is likewise confirmed when Hurston sees mere difference outside of moral questions when recounting Cudjo Lewis's description of the palace of skulls (*Dust* 165). Indeed, this aspect of cultural relativism is likely not a point that Boas taught Hurston, but rather one where Boas's cultural anthropology dovetailed with what Hurston already knew.

❧ Culture Disengaged from Race

Mules and Men joins the qualities of holism, particularism, and relativism of culture to a fourth achievement of Boasian cultural anthropology, the conceptual disengagement of culture, civilization, and language from race. Boas spends a substantial portion of *The Mind of Primitive Man* countering various racist theories that linked culture to race. Accordingly, the understanding in *Mules* is that race and culture are not intrinsically linked but are only historically, conventionally, linked. There is nothing in the stories that is essentially or naturally or organically black, only historically black. This might sound like an obvious point, but to Boas's and Hurston's contemporaries it was not. Eatonvilleans did not tell these stories because they were African American; they told these stories because in that geography emerged a rural culture that passed such stories along from one generation to the next, adapting them along the way. Boas's attention to history helped conceptually decouple culture from race, a cornerstone of cultural anthropology's idea of racial equality. These stories—or certain songs, or dances, or the hoodoo practices examined in the second half of *Mules*—are comprehensible only in terms of the particular developments of this culture; and the fact that they are told or sung or danced by black people is entirely contingent on how things unfolded as they did.

The section of *Mules* on hoodoo likewise displays the influence of the Boasian notion of culture. Hoodoo is treated with the same concern for cultural relativism, holistic complexity, and historical particularism as the folktales that precede it. Hoodoo is a set of cultural traditions descended from African slaves in the Caribbean, reflecting cultural continuity and adaptation to New World conditions such as the presence of the Catholic saints, who only superficially and pictorially stand for the African gods like Legba and Erzulie. When Hurston acknowledges that hoodoo is "not the accepted theology of the Nation" (185), she is recognizing hoodoo's historically contingent development, not normatively judging its values and practices against Christianity. Even what we might from a universalist perspective criticize as not so benevolent—that hoodoo can work curses and even death on people, practices that Hurston the ethnographer partakes in during her participant-observer stint with a dozen or more hoodoo doctors (*Mules* 211)—she is careful not to evaluate such cultural practices by moral criteria other than their own.

The hoodoo section of *Mules* establishes one of cultural anthropology's important tenets, that cultures are long-standing and slow to change, especially in response to outside pressures. This would be one of the key differences between Boas's concept of culture and that of Robert Park's. Asserting that hoodoo "keep[s] alive the powers of Africa," Hurston argues that "Hoodoo, or Voodoo, as pronounced by the whites, is burning with a flame in America, with all the intensity of a suppressed religion. It has its thousands of secret adherents. It adapts itself like Christianity to its locale" (183). The possible retention of African cultures by African Americans was a key question that occupied Boas and two of his students, Hurston and Herskovits. Cultural anthropology eventually answered this question affirmatively, making possible decades later the cultural continuity of Henry Louis Gates Jr.'s *Signifying Monkey* and some versions of Afrocentrism (Williams, *Rethinking Race* 1–2). Hurston's late 1920s fieldwork on hoodoo was some of the first ethnography to establish African cultural continuity, and it is not accidental that her version of social science—the anthropology of culture—was the version taken up by cultural nationalists in the late 1960s and early 1970s.

The version of culture presented in *Their Eyes Were Watching God* is likewise thoroughly Boasian and ethnographically detailed. As in *Mules*, an Eatonville porch is the central site of African American verbal life: we hear language games and courtship rituals (62–71), and the novel pays attention to social structures like hierarchical color preference and their psychological meanings (144–45). Understanding the anthropological bent of the novel helps make sense of some of its departures from fictional conventions. In one extraordinary sequence, a mule occupies the town's (and the reader's) attention for a considerable narrative duration (55–62). While the episode marginally develops Janie's growing alienation from her social status–preoccupied husband, its real purpose is to examine the verbal feats that grow up around the mule's existence. It inscribes jokes directed at the mule (and its owner), tall tales about it, and, when it dies, a "draggin'-out" ceremony attended by many of the town's citizenry, complete with a funeral oration imagining mule heaven. When the people leave, the narrator shifts attention to the buzzard community who will consume the mule—but not before their own ceremonial recognition. The "white-headed leader" of the buzzards, the "Parson," examines the corpse and opens the feast with a ritualized call and response:

"What killed this man?"
The chorus answered, "Bare, bare fat."
"What killed this man?"
"Bare, bare fat."

"What killed this man?"

"Bare, bare fat."

"Who'll stand his funeral?"

"We!!!!!"

"Well, all right now."

So he picked out the eyes in the ceremonial way and the feast went
on. (62)

There is no narrative point to this episode, other than to take pleasure in
performing the folklore tradition in which Hurston grew up, studied in the
field in the late '20s, and wrote up as *Mules* early in the 1930s.[9]

Their Eyes Were Watching God is set in an autonomous and complex whole
rural culture. This culture context explains these excursions from Janie's
story into ethnographic details like stories, social explanations, and verbal
play. Critical consensus, moreover, is that the novel must be understood in
terms of Janie's verbal performance of her story for her best friend Pheoby.
But we can go further than this and say, in view of the focus on the verbal
life of African American Southern rural folk culture in *Mules,* that *Their Eyes
Were Watching God* is of a piece with Hurston's anthropological profession.
The oral tradition that Hurston grew up in and later studied in the field is
in fact the substance of the novel, as Henry Louis Gates Jr. has argued (*Signifying*). And, as with *Mules,* there is a double-voiced effect in which black
vernacular intermixes with standard English. As Hemenway contends, it is
important that Janie learns to take part in the porch talk, for the store porch
"is the center of the community, the totem representing black cultural tradition" (239).

Although Ishmael Reed's 1990 prediction that *Tell My Horse* was "bound
to be the postmodernist book of the nineties" (Foreword xv) turned out to be
not quite correct, his enthusiasm for Hurston's largest work on voodoo traditions is significant. Just as Hurston used most but not all of Boasian anthropology to articulate her conception about African American and African
diaspora cultures, so, too, does Reed adapt Hurston and her anthropology to
his own ends. Though I develop this idea more fully in chapter eight, suffice
it to say here that in his foreword to *Tell My Horse,* Reed frames Hurston not
just in terms of cultural nationalism, but also by the suggestion that culture
should be hereditary. Citing psychiatrists who "trace the mental and physical
health problems of many blacks—in particular the lack of self-esteem—to
the symbolic annihilation to which their culture is subjected by the white-
pride school curricula and media" (xiii), Reed suggests that being severed
from "their ancient religion" is another cause. He thereby imagines that one

could still have a religion that one did not actually practice, and conversely, we might assume, that the religion one practiced might not be hers at all. As I will suggest, this idea of prescriptive and hereditary social identity—what someone's ancestors' religion was, should be hers—is a racial idea reminiscent of the Spanish fear of the *conversos* (Smedley 65–70). Its essential strategy is to subvert the conceptual decoupling of culture from race that was one of Boas's main achievements. This is what makes it possible, as we shall see, for one of Reed's characters in *Mumbo Jumbo* to practice a religion that is not actually his, with terrible consequences.

The reason *Horse* is open to such an interpretation is the particular emphasis on African retentions that Hurston again and again suggests is part of the historically particular development of religion in Haiti and the Caribbean. Hurston's fieldwork among voodoo practitioners substantiates the idea that African cultural traditions were not erased in the Middle Passage, but were transformed by slaves and their descendants. This longevity of culture had always been part of Boas's model, distinguishing it from that developed by Robert Park. In Jamaica, Hurston found many cultural retentions, some substantial and some speculative. Anansi, the West African trickster, "is personified in Haiti by Ti Malice and in the United States by Brer Rabbit," says Hurston (*Horse* 25). The tale of the Three-legged-Horse prompts speculation: "I have the strong belief that the Three-legged-Horse is a sex symbol and that the celebration of it is a fragment of some West African puberty ceremony for boys" (26). "The most universal ceremony in Jamaica is an African survival called 'The Nine Night,'" she says elsewhere, suggesting that "In reality it is old African ancestor worship in fragmentary form. The West African tradition of appeasing the spirit of the dead lest they do the living a mischief" (39). Like Herskovits's work, Hurston's in the Caribbean suggested that it was possible to look for hidden cultural qualities or associations that might not be immediately apparent. That is one reason, besides modeling a much slower process of assimilation, that anthropology would be more valuable than sociology to the cultural nationalists emerging in the late 1960s. Retention of old traits or associations makes possible the work of carefully examining one's practices and values to discover hidden remnants of Kiowa, West African, or Aztec cultures.

What is at times only vaguely suggested in *Mules'* section on hoodoo— that the hoodoo practices "keep alive the powers of Africa" (*Mules* 183)— becomes in *Tell My Horse* a fairly detailed account of retentions, or "survivals," in voodoo.[10] "And right here, let it be said that the Haitian gods, mysteres, or loa are not the Catholic calendar of saints done over in black as has been stated by casual observers," Hurston begins (114). That many of the loa are identified with Catholic saints is only a pictorial shorthand and a later adaptation; the essential characters of Damballah (the chief loa), Legba (the guardian of the crossroads), Loco Attison (work and knowledge), and Erzulie (the goddess of love) are African. Hurston explains that the loa appear in two forms, that of the Rada (benevolent, but sometimes slow to act) emerging from Dahomey, and the Petro (malevolent, but quick to perform services), emerging from Congo or Guinea. Priests likewise divide into the *houngan* who appeal to the Rada and the *bocor* who appeal to the Petro, although there are priests who lead the double lives of both.

African retention is the rule when it comes to the voodoo system, with one exception being Guedé (the messenger of the gods), who is "entirely Haitian" with no African or European antecedent; not coincidentally, he is also the loa who most clearly refers to the ongoing class conflict characterizing contemporary Haitian society (219). Typically, West African pagan beliefs and structures take on superficial Christian associations: thus, Hurston says, "It must have been a joyful thing to the Africans newly arrived in Saint Dominique to find their worship of the dead confirmed in the European All Saints Day, but the services to Baron Samedi or Cimeterre are more than just an expansion of Halloween. The Christian Church has merely given the cult an annual feast day. The rest of it has come out of Africa with adaptations on Haitian soil" (226). Cultural adaptation was complicated, Boas knew: in art and mythology, for instance, outward forms might be transmitted, while "symbolical interpretations" and "mythological use" and meaning might change during such diffusion (*Mind* 244–45). That was why anthropologists used the historical method—because current customs might be associated non-organically with things they were not originally associated with (*Mind* 248).

Throughout *Horse* Hurston takes on the ethnographer's mantle, adopting many of the poses important for the participant-observer fieldworker. She appeals for further study, explaining like an orthodox Boasian that not even a comprehensive survey of the innumerable loa exists (131), and that the use of poisons, while suggestive of African retentions (like the leopard whisker method used in the Gold Coast), is not sufficiently understood by contemporaneous anthropology (238–42). Hurston willingly suspends disbelief when she embarks on a chilling account of the use of zombies by the Petro aspect. Initially she frames her tale of seeing a zombie, "the broken remnant, relic, or refuse" of a woman, through the lesson of cultural relativism: there is a middle ground in Haiti between the living and the dead, a reality different from life "in the shadow of the Empire State Building" (179). She is horrified by, but manages to photograph (for the first time ever), the zombie

Felicia Felix-Mentor. She and a doctor later arrive at a rational explanation for the zombie's mental state by suggesting that perhaps "it is not a case of awakening the dead, but a matter of the semblance of death induced by some drug known to a few. Some secret probably brought from Africa and handed down from generation to generation" (196). While this scientific answer differs from her initial cultural relativist position—that in effect the laws of reality apply differently in Manhattan and Haiti—Hurston largely sees voodoo in relativist terms (204). What emerges from *Horse* is a vision of Afro-Haitian cultural practices through the prism of cultural relativism, historical particularism's dual focus on the processes of adaptation and the retention of African content, and cultural holism, in which voodoo practices and beliefs are seen in terms of the class differences they sometimes articulate, or the gender relations, foodways, song, and dance that characterize early twentieth-century Haitian society.

Just as Hurston's basic assumption in *Tell My Horse* is the equality of races, so too does she accept Boas's conceptual decoupling of culture from race. Voodoo practices and beliefs characterize (mostly lower-class) Afro-Haitian society not because the West African religion is mysteriously connected to a racial quality in black people in the Caribbean, but because actual historical events generated the religious practices of a particular group of people in a particular geography, a situation calling for analysis of structure, content, adaptation, and retention. Voodoo is contingently, not intrinsically, Afro-Caribbean. And importantly, because voodoo is understood in cultural terms, anyone might adopt it. The upper-class Haitians tend to deny voodoo's relevance and reality; Hurston is critical of this denial not because these cultural practices should (according to race) be theirs, but because their avoidance smacks of the same middle-class African American denial of folklife ("My race but not my taste") that Hurston repeatedly found in the United States—it is a matter of social class prejudice rather than cultural assimilation. Likewise, the cultural practices of voodoo can be, as culture, embraced by anyone. The Boasian decoupling of culture from race is thus most spectacularly demonstrated by a white *houngan* Dr Reser, who "walked out of his Nordic body and changed. Whatever the stuff of which the soul of Haiti is made, he was that. You could see the snake god of Dahomey hovering about him. Africa was in his tones" (257). Africa can be in his "tones"—not his "blood"—because this white American, ex-U.S. Navy pharmacist learned a particular set of Haitian cultural practices. This specific figure is ignored, significantly, by Reed in his foreword to the book, for of course the man is practicing not what Reed would call his "ancient religion," but has instead learned a religion that (according to Reed) cannot really be his.

🌿 Culture as Anthropological Description

> Whereas Wright attempted to explode the discursive
> category of the Negro as being formed, historically,
> in the culture of minstrelsy, and as being the product
> of a society structured in dominance through con-
> cepts of race, Hurston wanted to preserve the concept
> of Negroness, to negotiate and rewrite its cultural
> meanings, and, finally, to reclaim an aesthetically
> purified version of blackness. The consequences for
> the creation of subaltern subject positions in each of
> their work are dramatically different. The antago-
> nism between them reveals Wright to be a modernist
> and leaves Hurston embedded within the politics of
> Negro identity.
>
> —Hazel Carby, "The Politics of Fiction," 1994 (34)

The most problematic text for my argument is Hurston's first novel, *Jonah's Gourd Vine,* written in the summer of 1933 and published in 1934. Deeply rooted not just in Hurston's own life but in the cultural collection she had been doing, the book is "less a narrative than a series of linguistic moments representing the folklife of the black South," including oral figures, poetry of the folk, and a transcribed sermon inserted as John's final message to his congregation (Hemenway 192). But it also at times seems to collapse culture and race, the categories Boas has worked to conceptually distinguish.

Jonah's presents an opportunity to delineate more completely the dynamic contest among models of culture central to the genealogy of literary multi-culturalism. Understanding the genealogy in terms of these phases com-prised of contesting claims about culture clears up a number of recent and ongoing critical confusions. I want to build on but complicate the analyses of the rallying point of "culture" in the 1920s by George Hutchinson and Walter Benn Michaels, suggesting that each slightly misinterprets it in oppos-ing ways. The "cultural nationalisms" Hutchinson examines in the first three decades of the twentieth century were not always cultural but just as often regional, racial, or statist; to get a genuine cultural nationalism required a rigorous concept of culture, one that came only through the intervention of Boasian anthropology. Conversely, the anthropology of cultural description practiced by writers like Zora Neale Hurston provided exactly the disci-plinary rigor that resisted the slide into culture as race, identity, or ambition identified by Michaels. Understanding the first phase in terms of nativism's and anthropology's contesting models of culture (with an emerging socio-logical one complicating the picture further, as I show in chapter two) allows us to see how individual writers like Hurston and D'Arcy McNickle could occasionally partake of both, even though they were overwhelmingly and self-consciously committed to the anthropological model. Situating Hurston at the center of the first phase is a way of refining Hutchinson's and Michaels's arguments, but it also recognizes her rightful place, as the African American author above any other to whom third-phase multiculturalist writers like Toni Morrison, Alice Walker, and Ishmael Reed looked back, not just for the content but also for the shape of African American culture.

Jonah's inscribes potentially racial notions of cultural inheritance in three passages, and the first, a description of a dance by black farm workers on Alf Pearson's farm, is the most extraordinary:

> So they danced. They called for the instrument that they had brought to America in their skins—the drum—and they played upon it. With their hands they played upon the little dance drums of Africa. The drums of kid-skin. With their feet they stomped it, and the voice of Kata-Kumba, the great drum, lifted itself within them and they heard it. The great drum that is made by priests and sits in majesty in the juju house. The drum with the man skin that is dressed with human blood, that is beaten with a human shin-bone and speaks to gods as a man and to men as a God. Then they beat upon the drum and danced. It was said, "He will serve us better if we bring him from Africa naked and thingless." So the bukra reasoned. They tore away his clothes that Cuffy might bring nothing away, but Cuffy seized his drum and hid it in his skin under the skull bones. The shin-bones he bore openly, for he thought, "Who shall rob me of shin-bones when they see no drum?" So he laughed with cunning and said, "I, who am borne away to become an orphan, carry my parents with me. For *Rhythm* is she not my mother and Drama is her man?" So he groaned aloud in the ships and hid his drum and laughed. (29)

In this astonishing description, Hurston rehearses and rejects the idea, being popularized by the sociologist Franklin Frazier in the 1930s, that captured Africans had their cultures stripped from them during the Middle Passage.

The passage is framed by one anonymous speaker who declares "Us don't want no fiddles, neither no guitars, neither no banjoes" (29) because "us ain't no white folks!" (28). "Less clap!" the man insists, and so the "skin" of the people is poetically transformed by Hurston into the "drums" retention from Africa. While clapping's rhythm is a universal human trait, the passage connects the "drums" of hands clapping to the "drums of kid-skin" but also the "great drum" made with "man skin." Its lack of ethnic particularity— "Africa" is here treated as a homogenous cultural zone—makes it part of an occasional Renaissance troping of Africa as a mystical but abstract homeland (see Hutchinson 185).

The passage is ambiguous on the question of whether the bearing of the drum is a cultural or a racial trait, a distinction central to Boas's project. Its use of body parts—skin and bones—suggests an attention to the body that resonates with the possibility of racial difference, despite their status as generic human organs. But the fact that the metaphorical drum is hidden away "in his skin under the skull bones" suggests finally that the inheritance is a cultural one after all. What is "under the skull bones" is the brain, thus making the drum a property of the mind and making the ethnically indistinct practices of drumming into learned behavior. This racial moment in Hurston's work seemingly resolves into the transmission of African cultural traditions of clapping and dancing. Boas had written to Hurston in a May 3, 1927, letter while she was on her initial collecting trip in Florida:

> We ought to remember that in transmission from Africa to America most of the contents of the culture have been adopted from the surrounding peoples while the mannerisms have, to a great extent, been retained. For instance, when you compare Negro singing and the singing of white people, it is not so much the musical notation that is different but rather the manner of rendition.[11]

However dubious this distinction between cultural form and content or between notation and rendition, what is clear is that Boas and Hurston were thinking through the transmission of learned traits across the Atlantic.

In two other instances *Jonah's* also ambiguously suggests a racial inheritance. When John gets up to pray in church, for instance, "He rolled his African drum up to the altar, and called his Congo Gods by Christian names" (76). Presuming that John does not know the Congo Gods by their own names, the question we have to ask is, in what sense can they be his Gods if he does not know their names, and perhaps does not even know of their existence? Here, too, the answer might be racial or cultural, or even merely ancestral; but any explanation that held to the mystical hanging-on of African gods under new names as racial would have to admit an equally plausible cultural answer, which is how Hurston understood African religious retentions in Haitian voodoo.

At John's funeral, finally, the drums return:

> And the hearers wailed with a feeling of terrible loss. They beat upon the O-go-doe, the ancient drum. O-go-doe, O-go-doe, O-go-doe! Their hearts turned to fire and their shin-bones leaped unknowing to

the drum. Not Kata-Kumba, the drum of triumph, that speaks of great ancestors and glorious wars. Not the little drum of kid-skin, for that is to dance with joy and to call to mind birth and creation, but O-go-doe, the voice of Death—that promises nothing, that speaks with tears only, and of the past. (168)

Here there is even less clue as to whether the "ancient drum" is a metaphor for cultural or racial continuity. Since the parishioners do not know that their mourning recapitulates the beating of O-go-doe, and no more know the name of O-go-doe than John knows the names of the Congo Gods, it appears to be a submerged, unconscious group practice. It might be either a racial essence sensed but unnamed, or a cultural sensibility passed on through tradition, one equally unnamable except through the Christian terms that they have adopted.

This is the most un-Boasian treatment of African American practices in Hurston's major work, and it was powerfully (and productively) invoked by Black Arts movement critic Larry Neal in 1971, in a reworking of Hurston's anthropological commitments that underpinned African American literary multiculturalism, as I show in chapter six. The drums recall an earlier Renaissance essay of 1928, "How It Feels to Be Colored Me," written after her training with Boas but before her thinking and writing matured in the 1930s. In one famous passage, she compares her reaction to jazz with a white companion's:

It constricts the thorax and splits the heart with its tempo and narcotic harmonies. This orchestra grows rambunctious, rears on its hind legs and attacks the tonal veil with primitive fury, rending it, clawing it until it breaks through to the jungle beyond. I follow those heathen—follow them exultingly. I dance wildly inside myself; I yell within, I whoop; I shake my assegai above my head, I hurl it true to the mark *yeeeeoouww!* I am in the jungle and living in the jungle way. My face is painted red and yellow, and my body is painted blue. My pulse is throbbing like a war drum. I want to slaughter something—give pain, give death to what, I do not know. But the piece ends. The men of the orchestra wipe their lips and rest their fingers. I creep back slowly to the veneer we call civilization with the last tone and find the white friend sitting motionless in his seat, smoking calmly.

"Good music they have here," he remarks, drumming the table with his fingertips. (828)

Hurston invokes the primitivist trope of the jungle to contrast her (innate?) response to the music with the staid (and innate?) response of her square white friend. The bodily response raises the specter of an inherited funk (as Toni Morrison would later put it). But the "*yeeeeooww!,*" like the Asian "aiiieeeee!," embraced ironically a couple of generations later by some Asian American critics, is surely a little over the top, as Hemenway suggests (76).

But if this passage destabilizes the fundamental Boasian conceptual distinction between culture and race, the essay resolves with an entirely Boasian articulation of it. Hurston compares herself to "a brown bag of miscellany" beside "other bags, white, red and yellow" (829). One might dump all the inner qualities into a pile and randomly reassign them to new bags "without altering the content of any greatly." In other words, you cannot judge the contents of the bag by its color. Raising the specter of racial difference only to resolve it through the assertion of culture became a crucial gesture in the social science–articulated minority literature of the first and second phases in the mid twentieth century. Hurston raises the possibility of racial difference—the drum in the skin, the jungle beneath the "veneer we call civilization"—only in order to replace it with a cultural distinction—and so the drum is a trait learned by the mind, "under the skull bones," and her jazzy yeeeeooww! might just as well appear in "other bags, white, red and yellow."

But it is not an accident, according to Walter Benn Michaels in *Our America: Nativism, Modernism, and Pluralism*, that the moment that is the most outrightly racial in Hurston's 1930s work is also the moment most committed to identity, and to a notion of culture as an ambition instead of anthropological description. *Our America* argues that, instead of replacing the incoherent concept of biological race with a coherent concept of ethnic culture, nativist modernism established our strategy for answering the question of which culture we should have by determining first what our race was: "Culture, put forward as a way of preserving the primacy of identity while avoiding the embarrassments of blood, would turn out to be much more effective than incest, impotence, and homosexuality as a way of reconceptualizing and thereby preserving the essential contours of racial identity" (13). The nativist 1920s and the texts of American nativist modernism constituted "something like the research-and-development division of identitarianism" ("Response" 125)—the moment when our commitment to a notion of culture as an ambition and not just a description was first fully worked out. Cultural identity conceals an underlying racial identity, *Our America* contends, a ruse developed in this historical moment of nativist modernism.

In the chapter titled "The Psychology of Imitation," for instance, Michaels addresses Hurston along with other New Negro artists and theorizers like Langston Hughes and Alain Locke. As he shows, Hurston's essay

"Characteristics of Negro Expression" (written around 1930 but published in 1934) shares with other nativist commitments of the time period both the ambition to be oneself and the grounding of that identitarianism in a racial logic. Middle-class African Americans betray their race by imitating whites, Hurston seems to be saying, while "truly cultured" and educated African Americans imitate working-class black folk culture, thereby making the attempt to be who they (in some sense) already are into a project, and making folk culture into a "racial heritage" (90, 93). In understanding culture not as a description of what people actually were doing but rather as a prescriptive ambition for matching one's practices and values to one's already-existing racial identity, Hurston partakes of the nativist logic of the period; and indeed there are other examples of this gesture elsewhere in her work. In her 1928 essay "How It Feels to Be Colored Me," for example, her assertion "My country, right or wrong" (829) likewise declares a preference for one's own on the grounds that it is one's own.

Nevertheless, the 1920s was marked by a countervailing tradition that ran against this logic of cultural-identity-as-racial-ambition characteristic of nativist modernism, a counter-tradition of Boasian anthropology committed to culture as description. As a student of Boas and an anthropologist and literary modernist, Hurston generally (but not always) exemplified this counter-tradition's rival and differently renovated notion of what "culture" was, and in fact this different version of culture generally dominates Hurston's 1930s work, as I have shown. Her ethnographies and novels most often demonstrate thoroughly Boasian propositions about culture: first, that culture is descriptive (of what groups of people actually do or believe) and not prescriptive (a culture is not what a group is trying to become); second, that culture is distinct from, and not grounded in, race; and third, that culture is not determined by, and does not confer, an identity. Hurston worked to collect and transcribe—but not evaluate—African American stories and religious practices. She liked African American tales partly because she thought they were as good as other cultures' stories, and there is not really the sense that she, via a nativist logic, prefers African American tales because they are racially hers. This is why, though she grew up on these stories, she could then go on to "luxuriate" in the "syllables and rhythms" of *Paradise Lost* even before being told "that Milton was one of the greatest poets of the world" (*Dust* 98). Hurston's disdain for adaptations of African American spirituals according to European musical traditions was not a nativist preference for her own, but rather the cultural pluralist declaration that the folk music did not need a European high-culture supplement in order to count as art.

So even as Coolidge was calling for "more culture" and for Americans "to be supremely American" (qtd. in *Our America* 35, 3), and even as the logic of nativism generally called for the preference for one's own, thus imagining culture as prescriptive and opening it up to identitarian ambition, Hurston's work exemplified a counter-tradition of anthropological cultural description that was at times fiercely at odds with this nativist notion of culture. Most Hurston scholars conclude that it is impossible to reconcile her sometimes contradictory statements or to neatly pigeonhole her cultural politics. As we have seen, her work occasionally exemplifies the nativist identity and racial thinking that comprises one of the three competing group ontologies of the first phase. But the vast if incomplete consensus of her oeuvre places her unmistakably within the Boasian paradigm of culture.

Boas opposed nativism not just politically but also methodologically on this question of identity. What Michaels uncovers as the function of identity was contested by Boas's notion of culture. Boas did not believe that cultural practices and values emerged from or coincided with identities of people, or that any practices and values were natural to a group of people in a way that would allow race to be the source of one's proper culture. In conceptually disengaging culture from race, Boas rendered culture as contingent: not arbitrary, since historical particularism explained why some cultural traits dominated certain groups in specific geographical domains, but not naturally or organically tied to a descent population. Michaels is right that "accounts of cultural identity that do any work require a racial component," and that "insofar as our culture remains nothing more than what we do and believe, it is impotently descriptive" (*Our America* 128). But the Boasian-Hurstonian anthropological paradigm of culture was descriptive in exactly this sense: impotent as far as identity was concerned, but powerful and ultimately successful in challenging the racial worldview that had held sway for decades.[12]

In general, both Boas and Hurston exemplified the possibility of a cultural pluralism that refuses both identity and evaluation. Michaels contends that "Pluralism is, in a sense, built into nativism since the essence of nativism is its preference for the native exclusively on the grounds of its being native." As he elaborates,

> it is precisely this pluralism that transforms the substitution of culture for race into the preservation of race. For pluralism's programmatic hostility to universalism—its hostility to the idea that cultural practices be justified by appeals to what seems universally good or true—requires that such practices be justified instead by appeals to what seems locally good or true, which is to say, it invokes the identity of the group as the

grounds for the justification of the group's practices. Thus, although the move from racial identity to cultural identity appears to replace essentialist criteria of identity (who we are) with performative criteria (what we do), the commitment to pluralism requires in fact that the question of who we are continue to be understood as prior to questions about what we do. Since, in pluralism, what we do can be justified only by reference to who we are, we must, in pluralism, begin by affirming who we are; it is only once we know who we are that we will be able to tell what we should do; it is only when we know which race we are that we can tell which culture is ours. (14–15)

This argument that nativism contains a pluralist logic is compelling, but my contention is that the contemporaneous anthropological model of culture that arose to contest nativist racism was pluralist without being necessarily nativist. To put this more bluntly, one cannot have nativism without pluralism, but one can have pluralism without nativism. Boasian anthropology and its various fieldwork projects generated accounts of cultures that were simultaneously descriptive (not based on "prior" questions of "who we are") and non-evaluative.

Michaels's *Our America* thus offers a historical and theoretical correction to Hutchinson's *Harlem Renaissance in Black and White*—and the reverse is no less true. One of Hutchinson's main contentions is that an increasingly dominant intellectual mode of cultural pluralism became the context for Renaissance and other writings of the 1920s. But *Our America* shows how such pluralisms could frequently be racial and national—and committed to identity—instead of descriptively cultural. Conversely, Hutchinson's stress on Boasian cultural anthropology shows how the 1920s deployment of cultural pluralism by African American and white authors and intellectuals was not always covertly racial or framed by ambition, prescription, and identity. It is my argument that a sharpened sense of Boasian anthropology's culture concept and the way it was used by Hurston to articulate her vision of African American Southern rural folk culture is the way to retain the primary insights of these two very important arguments. If Michaels insists (wrongly, I believe) that all pluralisms were necessarily nativist and hence covertly racial in their logic, Hutchinson does not see the way in which pluralist declarations, even ones which invoked culture, could sometimes nevertheless ground themselves in race. Indeed, it is a sign of the contested terrain that many intellectuals were not always clear on the difference between the two—as with Alain Locke's not very precise phrase "cultural racialism" (qtd. in Hutchinson 91; see also Posnock 199–200).

In his chapter on cultural pluralism and cultural nationalism, for instance, Hutchinson traces the "cultural pluralism" of *The New Negro* and intellectuals like Du Bois, Locke, and Horace Kallen, to the pragmatist writings of William James and Josiah Royce and not directly to Boas's anthropology (78–79). As he says parenthetically, "By the end of the 1920s, partly because of Boas' influence, 'culture' would replace blood and spirit as the effective category of group identity for both Kallen and Du Bois" (78). But if culture eventually becomes the vehicle for pluralism only after the intervention of Boas, in what sense does a specifically *cultural* pluralism exist before Boas as merely the influence of pragmatism?[13] If Kallen, a key example for *Our America* of a pluralist who nevertheless retained a nativist logic, "at least in his initial formulations, did not clearly distinguish between biological and cultural aspects of race or nationality" (Hutchinson 86), that fact undercuts Kallen's status as a developer of *cultural* pluralism. And conversely, if "cultural anthropology was a crucial factor in making Dewey understand that a philosophy of experience must take 'cultural' factors into account" (89), this likewise suggests that whatever is pluralist and experiential about pragmatism is not yet fully cultural until it is articulated through the emerging culture concept developed by Boas and other anthropologists.

My point here is that the best account of cultural pluralism comes from the discipline that actually has a coherent notion of culture—and not from those like Kallen who, as Ross Posnock has shown, was unable to conceptually disengage culture from inheritance and race (192). It was this anthropology that influenced Hurston, McNickle, and Américo Paredes, and with them the multicultural pluralism that emerges against assimilation in the third phase of this genealogy. While Posnock asserts that it was Kallen's cultural pluralism that bequeathed identity politics to multiculturalism decades later (23, 192, 197), I am arguing that third-phase multicultural writers were not reading Kallen or other nativists so much as they were reading Hurston (or writers who had read her) and other anthropologists. How multicultural pluralism became attached to the affective work of identity that anthropology had earlier combated is one story of rupture and influence this genealogy uncovers. Michaels, Hutchinson and Posnock do not fully credits how Boasian anthropology developed a culture concept rigorously different from the nativism, nationalism, racialism, and provincialism of the period. Zora Neale Hurston is given marginal space in their studies, but she was, I contend, crucial to the genealogy of literary multiculturalism in the twentieth century.

Even Hurston's autobiography, *Dust Tracks,* is as focused on the culture as it is on herself. It is full of attention to local folk culture, especially at Joe Clarke's porch (45–52), including what must have become one of Hurston's favorite stories, how black people became black (they misheard God's instruction to "Git back" as "Git black," and then they "kept the thing agoing"), which she retells once in *Mules* (29–30) and twice in *Dust Tracks* (50–51, 244–45). She adopts the cultural relativist position that we cannot judge Dahomey's palace of skulls described by Cudjo Lewis, and the Boasian critique of the racial idea, declaring "I learned that skins were no measure of what was inside people" (192). But while Hurston is the most important predecessor of our current literary multiculturalism in her embrace of Boas's turn from race to culture and in culture's qualities of relativism, holism, and particularism, her work generally eschews the notion of identity. My argument here runs counter to Hazel Carby's reading of Hurston's anthropology, in which, according to Carby, "The folk as community remain the 'other,' and exist principally as an aesthetic device, a means for creating an essential concept of blackness" ("Politics" 40). Citing George Marcus and Michael Fischer's critique that 1920s and 1930s ethnographic texts shared with explorer accounts the romantic discovery of unknown people, Carby sees a certain nostalgia and colonialism at work in Hurston's anthropological attitude in *Mules, Horse,* and *Eyes.* Situating Hurston criticism of the 1990s in terms of racial and economic relations that were not getting talked about, she wonders if *"Their Eyes Were Watching God* [has] become the most frequently taught black novel because it acts as a mode of assurance that, really, the black folk are happy and healthy?" (41). For Carby, the fascination with Hurston depended on her anthropological romanticiziation of a rural folk community anchored in the past and in the Caribbean; like many in her 1990s audience, Hurston "displaces" urban "crisis" conditions (chronicled by Richard Wright) with an idealized rural nostalgia.

But Carby sees Hurston as only a consumer, not a critic, of anthropological ideas. Carby, for instance, reads the initial salvage frame of *Mules* unironically (33), whereas Marc Manganaro has more compellingly shown that when Hurston's informant appears to question the narrator's interest in recording stories, she is using him to interrogate the entire ethnographic premise of disappearing cultures (*Culture* 177). In a March 29, 1927, letter to Franz Boas early in her first collecting trip to Florida, Hurston did appear to understand her initial difficulty in terms of the salvage narrative. She writes,

It is fortunate that it is being collected now, for a great many people say, "I used to know some of that old stuff, but I done forgot it all." You see, the negro is not living his lore to the extent of the Indian. He is not on a reservation, being kept pure. His negroness is being rubbed off by close contact with white culture. (Kaplan 97)

Hurston later discovered that the informants were only claiming to have forgotten those old tales, rejecting her queries because of her (initial) non-native pose; in other words, the question of forgetting one's culture was a premise that, Hurston learned the hard way on her unsuccessful 1927 collecting trip, had to be up for grabs rather than assumed.

Like her early informants, Hurston learned to deploy what James Clifford has called the allegory of salvage in modern anthropology—that cultures needed to be recorded in writing before they disappeared. Her writing to the president of Fisk University in 1934 that she had undertaken her Florida ethnography because she was "weighed down by the thought that practically nothing had been done in Negro folklore when the greatest cultural wealth on the continent was disappearing without the world ever realizing that it had ever been" (Kaplan 315) suggested the urgency of her ethnographic mission (and her virtue and heroism). Hurston actually believed that African American rural folk culture was a lived culture still in the process of continual creation—a sign of its health, not decline. I have also argued here that Hurston rejected the assimilationist implications of Boas's paradigm (which is here logically joined to the salvage ethic), rendering her a more complicated consumer of anthropological ideas than Carby gives her credit for. Furthermore, Hurston's status as participant-observer collapses spectacularly when her entrance into the romantic-sexual economy of the labor camps causes a jealous brawl from which she has to flee: these kinds of instances make clear that Hurston is interrogating, not just adopting, the anthropological conventions with which she worked.

A more problematic charge, which I quote in the epigraph to this section, is the essentializing one that Carby levels at Hurston's ethnography: that, in creating a nostalgic and romantic folk rendered from her childhood—and therefore from a time firmly in the past—Hurston's work is committed to identity. As I have shown extensively in this chapter, however, Hurston's ethnographic and novelistic labors in the 1930s and later are generated by a project of cultural description and collection that militates against identitarian and essentialist drives. In fact, for all the differences between Hurston and Wright (differences I address in chapter two), one of the things they shared was a disinterest in identity, the emergence of which as a distinct ontology of the group is a story told in chapters four and seven. Carby fails to show that there is a concept of blackness or Negroness in Hurston at all, and I contend this is not because Hurston is more virtuous than Carby makes her out to be, but because the anthropology she critically consumed had her paying attention to facts. Hurston was drawn to African American stories because she grew up with them and because they are tales of good "sentence" and substantial "solaas," as Chaucer put it (*CT* 1.798); they instruct and they give aesthetic pleasure.[14] But the stories do not make the people who they are.

The lack of "identity logic" in Hurston's work, as Posnock puts it (217), also emerges in her treatment of what the past means. She writes, "Since I wash myself of race pride and repudiate race solidarity, by the same token I turn my back upon the past. I see no reason to keep my eyes fixed on the dark years of slavery and the Reconstruction. I am three generations removed from it, and therefore have no experience of the thing" (253–54). In one sense, Hurston's repudiation of the past, especially that of slavery, contrasts with Toni Morrison, whose *Beloved* has the project of memorializing slavery. But Hurston's commitment to culture *is* a commitment to the past of a certain kind. The tales and verbal practices that she collects and values are historical; such is what an oral tradition is. The past as culture emerges as a set of lived practices and values that can be collected and described, but it does not emerge as a source of "experience" or identity—and in this sense, Hurston's representation of the past, while overstated, has the virtue of emphasizing that culture is transmitted (if only in non-pedagogical ways), not remembered.

Seraph on the Suwanee, whose principal characters are white, likewise signals Hurston's commitment to the Boasian culture concept, and how at odds it was with any notion of identity. Hurston wrote a white book, apparently reversing what *The Harlem Renaissance in Black and White* makes clear was a frequent attention to African American themes by white authors (202–3)—both of which would be frowned upon (and thus rarely attempted) in later decades. Hemenway contends that the novel is the result of Hurston taking seriously white critics' demands that black authors write on "universal" themes (308), but an alternative interpretation is that Hurston believed she could write a novel about a different culture precisely because she understood culture the way an anthropologist would: as something that might be examined and understood, to some significant degree, by an outsider. It is because Hurston believed that culture, and not identity, made people different that she could write *Seraph*. Such is an understanding of culture different from that of Maya Angelou who—in seeming response to Hemenway's criticism of *Dust Tracks*—condemned the presumption of white people writing about African American experience in her introduction to Hurston's autobiography (vii, ix). For Boas and Hurston, cultures were different but not utterly inexplicable or incomprehensible. With hard work, observation, and awareness of one's own cultured position, one might actually understand other human beings and their cultural practices and values.

If Hurston's ethnographic expertise allowed her to imagine that she could accurately write a novel about what white people are like, what are we to make of the use of black vernacular to tell the story and by the characters themselves? "Her aim was to hit a straight lick with a crooked stick" (114), the narrator says of Arvay, who later uses the phrase herself to her daughter: "Call yourself hitting a straight lick with a crooked stick, I take it" (150). This is a line that would be used by Ellison, but it was also used by one of Hurston's characters in *Jonah's Gourd Vine:* "Some folks kin hit uh straight lick wid uh crooked stick," says Brother Harris to Hattie (124). Similarly, *Seraph* glosses Arvay's love by saying, "She had been in Hell's kitchen and licked out all the pots" (153), which would be a line Hurston also used both about herself in *Dust Tracks* (227) and in *Seraph's* mirror novel, *Jonah's Gourd Vine,* in which Lucy says she has "been in sorrow's kitchen and Ah done licked out all de pots" (112).

Jonah's and *Seraph* are complementary texts in many ways, both about marriage and giving oneself wholly to your partner. Both John and Jim call their wives "Li'l Bit" and "Little Bit" (*Jonah's* 82, 95; *Seraph* 57) (just as Big Sweet called Hurston "Little-Bit" when she was under her protection [*Mules* 151]). John asks that Lucy "hug mah neck tight" (*Jonah's* 95), and Jim likewise asks that Arvay "Hug my neck for me. Hug me tight" (*Seraph* 47). Jim at one point uses the African American vernacular phrase "quiet as it's kept" (*Seraph* 172), later used by Toni Morrison to open *The Bluest Eye.* There are thus quite a few idiomatic expressions shared by these two Southern families, one white and one black. Is this African American vernacular improbably ascribed to white people, and so a mark of Hurston's inability to correctly imagine white culture? A better and more culturally accurate explanation is that by the 1940s Hurston saw Southern vernacular in general as evidence of diffusion between white and black rural speech. She suggests the latter in a 1948 letter, writing that she initially thought that poor white Dixie County folk were "copying us," but later came to realize that the shared vernacular styles of rural black and white Floridians suggested a deeper language diffusion between the two groups, initiated when non–English-speaking slaves "learned from the whites" (Kaplan 577–78). In other words, listening to what people were actually saying led Hurston to more strongly comprehend a regional diffusion of cultural practices.

Hurston also compellingly captures white Southern fundamentalist Christianity in the early twentieth century. Arvay dislikes her husband's Portuguese helpers because they are not really white, comparing their daughter's threat to her son to the scantily clad heathens of other lands who lure Christians (212); this kind of rumination mixing sin, sex, and race seems ethnographically correct to the white Christian South of the early twentieth century. But obsession with sin and sex was an element of a shared fundamentalist Southern culture (as seen in *Jonah's* themes). Certainly *Seraph* is a somewhat romanticized version of white paternalism in the segregated South, with the African American family attached to the Meserve family actually calling themselves Meserves. The white son learns to "pick a box" from the family's main black employee and friend—to do black music—and this is approved by his father Jim, who is revealed to be wiser than Arvay. The white bands in New York and New Orleans are "taking over darky music" in the 1920s, the novel reveals; but anyhow this music is "not considered just darky music and dancing nowadays. It's American, and belongs to everybody," the book notes, with Hurston's apparent approval of this example of cultural diffusion and adaptation (176). *Seraph* confirms that Southern "white" and "black" cultural traditions have long been interpenetrating one another, a cultural integration of which Hurston approves. It is based on a model of culture as learned behavior that might be described, not culture as the expression of an identity.

Hurston's alliance with Boas suggests a compelling answer to the question posed by the series editor of Hurston's reissued work, Henry Louis Gates Jr., and one of her biographers, Robert Hemenway: namely, "How could the recipient of two Guggenheims and the author of four novels, a dozen short stories, two musicals, two books on black mythology, dozens of essays, and a prizewinning autobiography virtually 'disappear' from her readership for three full decades" between *Dust Tracks* and her revival by Alice Walker in 1975? (Gates, Afterword 290–91; see also Hemenway 4). In brief, the Boasian model of African American culture that Hurston helped establish in the first phase became slowly eclipsed by a Parkian model of African American culture that grew to contest anthropology's culture in the first phase, becoming itself dominant in the second phase. This was a model of culture that Wright embraced, and that became influential in the integrationist and Civil Rights politics of the 1940s and 1950s. In other words, it was not accidental that Hurston herself became sidelined and her work eclipsed as the rival model of culture, with all its political implications and uses, became ascendant. Then, in turn, it was not accidental when, by the late 1960s, the cultural nationalists seeking to articulate principles of cultural pluralism and resistance to assimilation did so in part by returning to the Boasian model of African American culture that Hurston helped establish.

🍏 Cultural Anthropology and Native American Literature

> It is clear that the Indian, with his inability to preserve his own culture or to assimilate ours, is bound to disappear as a race, if indeed he has not already found his way into the pious hands of the museum archaeologists. His passing is one of the great tragedies of the American continent.
>
> —Marius Barbeau, *Indian Days in the Canadian Rockies,* 1923 (7–8)

There is a sense in Hurston's work that the cultural autonomy of Eatonville is based on sovereignty and separation. The first chapter of her autobiography, *Dust Tracks,* is devoted to the 1886 founding of Eatonville and "the experiment of self-government for Negroes" (6). Eatonville and the nearby white town of Maitland "have lived side by side for fifty-five years without a single instance of enmity" (6); it is economically dependent on Maitland, but is not culturally and socially dependent. The deal struck between them anticipated by nine years Booker T. Washington's vision of economic integration and social separation, and seemed to slightly anticipate by one year the Dawes General Allotment Act (1887) that broke up communally held Native lands and thereby made them economically integrated and available for exploitation.

This semi-autonomous town's sovereignty is crucial to understanding the inner integrity of Eatonville culture, and why it is to be preserved, not lost through assimilation. Both Hurston's childhood experience of growing up in an independent African American culture and her training in the Boasian culture concept put the conservation into her conservative politics. The vibrancy and endurance of African American culture depended on a certain kind of separation; this culture was nurtured by segregation, whatever other evils it inflicted. The simultaneous cultural separation and economic interpenetration of Eatonville is not unlike the situation of the Flathead reservation in D'Arcy McNickle's *The Surrounded.*

Hurston is the most prominent example of what George Hutchinson has argued was the general intellectual context of Boasian anthropology for the Harlem Renaissance; as we shall see in chapters six and eight, it was precisely in this capacity as a literary articulator of the anthropological notion of culture that African American cultural nationalist authors turned to Hurston beginning in the mid 1960s as they sought to depart from the sociological cultural views of the writer who had eclipsed Hurston in the 1940s, Richard Wright. A somewhat similar dynamic was at the center of the interrelation between anthropology and literary production for Native writers during this same period. Social science enquiry and documentary were part of what Alfred Kazin identifies as the dominance of descriptive nonfiction during the 1930s, and were responses to the twin crises of the Depression and the "progressive disintegration of the European order" into fascism (Kazin 363). As Michael Staub describes the generic mood of the period,

> Documentary and ethnography [...] became the Depression era's char-acteristic genres for representing a widespread societal preoccupation with the plight of the disempowered. The 1930s were a time when not only writers sponsored by the Works Progress Administration, but also scores of other ethnographers, documentarians, and journalists sought to preserve oral memories they perceived as rapidly vanishing. (Staub 425)

One of Staub's primary examples of 1930s ethnography is John Neihardt's *Black Elk Speaks,* which was transcribed, composed, and published in 1931. Staub sees Neihardt's narrative strategy as one which thematizes the ines-capable distortions of *writing* the "recollection and representation of Indian speech" (Staub 452)—thus anticipating some of the meta-ethnographic issues raised by postmodern ethnography, which is likewise how Hurston's *Mules and Men* has been read.

One of the other key intersections between anthropology and Native literature in the first half of the twentieth century was Ella Deloria, a Dakota Sioux with whom Boas worked on a grammar of the Dakota language in New York (Herskovits, *Franz Boas* 63). Deloria's work was supervised by Boas at virtually the same time as Hurston's in the spring of 1927, and she later crafted anthropologically inflected literature. Like Hurston working with Herskovits's anthropometry, Deloria was asked to help establish the irrelevance of racial traits and to assert environment and learned culture in their place (Hoefel 189–90). In a further parallel, Deloria acted as an insider ethnographer, collecting stories from the Dakota, which she published as her 1932 collection *Dakota Texts,* just as Hurston's late 1920s collecting activi-ties in Florida were reworked into the 1935 *Mules and Men.* Deloria wrote her novel *Waterlily* in the 1940s, but it was published posthumously only in 1988. It was not only white anthropologists like James Mooney that a gen-eration of Native writers turned to for content, but also to previous Native anthropologists like Deloria or to anthropologically mediated Native texts like *Black Elk Speaks.*

D'Arcy McNickle exemplifies some of the intersections and co-dependency of anthropology and Native literature, demonstrating Boas's larger influence on Native writing in the 1920s and 1930s, widely discussed in recent years. McNickle's novel *The Surrounded* (1936) is a story of cultural difference and change. It is dramatically structured by the return to the Flathead Indian Reservation in Montana of Archilde Leon, a mixed-blood Salish who has been in Portland playing the fiddle for a living. The novel doubles the question of whether the estranged Archilde will be reconciled with Salish culture and life on the reservation by the question of whether his mother Catharine will return to her childhood (and tribal) religion, giving up the Catholicism that she like many others had converted to years before. Central to the novel are questions about culture—what cultures contain, how they are different, whether one can be better or alternatively more appropriate for an individual or a group, and how cultures disappear or are transformed through contact with other cultures.

Like *Jonah's Gourd Vine* and *Their Eyes Were Watching God, The Surrounded* is made possible by the author's research into rural minority oral traditions. "In this story of the Salish people," McNickle writes in a prefatory note,

> are elements which will be recognized as belonging to the story of tribes from Hudson Bay southward. The particular facts may be found in the journals of Ross Cox, David Thompson, Alexander Henry the younger, John Work, Major John Owen; in the journals and other writings of Pierre J. De Smet, S. J., and Lawrence B. Palladino, S. J., and in later writers. Marius Barbeau has collected some fine stories of the Mountain Indians ("Indian Days in the Canadian Rockies"), and to him I am indebted for Big Raven's story of the wistful search for "The Thing That Was to Make Life Easy." The "Story of Flint" was told by Chief Charlot, the last of the Flatheads to leave the ancestral homeland when the Government gave the order to move on. It was collected by Mrs. Helen Fitzgerald Sanders in her "Trails Through Western Woods," an excellent book. (n.p.)

As with *Their Eyes Were Watching God, The Surrounded* reprints stories in the course of describing communal tale-telling. "The story was an old one and nothing was lost," the narrator prefaces the first story of "The Story of Flint" (64), perhaps somewhat ironically since the version we have was retained precisely through salvage ethnography. The story brings the community together, binding the generations:

> When the story was told everybody laughed. It was a very old story, the kind grandmothers told to grandchildren, and it always made people laugh. Archilde had not intended to listen, yet he had heard every

word. The story had amused him in spite of himself. It left a spark of
gay remembrance in his mind. (66)

The oral tradition plays a key role in momentarily drawing Archilde back
into the communal fold: as when Janie is drawn into the group (becoming
submerged in it) during the tales of the mule in *Eyes,* so, too, does Archilde's
stubborn resistance to Salish culture yield slightly upon hearing the tale.

A second story, "The Thing That Was to Make Life Easy," was collected,
McNickle says in the note, in *Indian Days in the Rockies* by Marius Barbeau,
a French Canadian anthropologist who collected Native and French Canadian stories and who had worked with Franz Boas when Barbeau became
assistant editor of the *Journal of American Folklore* in 1915 and president of the
American Folklore Society in 1918. This story likewise draws Archilde back
to the community: "Archilde heard that story also. He wondered at it. And
the more he reflected on it the more wonderful it grew. A story like that, he
realized, was full of meaning" (69).

A third story is told by the blind chief Modeste, who says that he will "tell
it for this boy who has just come home after traveling out to the world. You
have just heard him say that those old days are dead and won't come again.
And it's true. But let me tell this story so he will see better just what it was
like back in those times" (69–70). So framed for Archilde, the story tells of
the history of the Salish, their strength and traditional rivalry with the Black-
feet, a warfare bitterly transformed by the latter's acquisition of guns. The
devastated Salish turned to Catholicism, thinking that the Fathers "would
bring back the power we had lost—but today we have less" (74). Archilde is
softened by the oral history: "For the first time he had really seen it happen,"
and his new visceral comprehension of his tribe's history "destroyed his stiff-
ness toward the old people" (74). Though a different emotional register from
the first, the story also helps reconcile Archilde to the Flathead Salish.

This story also fills out the novel's parallel drama, that of Archilde's mother's
(and hence the older generation's) Catholicism and their earlier rejection of
Salish religious beliefs and practices. It is through the novel's treatment of the
Salish's conversion to Catholicism that its anthropological ethos of cultural
pluralism and cultural relativism become most clear. Catholicism is shown
to be superficial to Catharine, and to Archilde. The missionary project—to
change a tribe's cultural practices within a generation—is seen itself to be
problematic. The hollowness of the Church's promises emerges from the
points of view of Catharine (131) and Archilde (105, 179), and even from
their estranged husband and father Max, who wonders "were they saved or
were they destroyed?" by the culture the Church brings (139). Conversion

brings Catharine not just a new set of religious practices and beliefs, but also a parallel cultural education (by the Sisters) in turn-of-the-century domestic womanhood (170). "The Sisters had taught her many arts but they had not quite taught her to be interested in using them. Possibly there was a deeper reason for her neglect, but on the surface that was what she felt" (171). Cultural transformation is here represented as essentially superficial, a portrayal, as we shall see, that anticipates the palimpsest cultures in N. Scott Momaday's *House Made of Dawn*.

It is Catharine's murder of the game warden—who had shot her other son—that triggers her cultural reconversion. "Something had happened to her" since that moment, the narrator says: "She had lost something. She was a pagan again. She who had been called Faithful Catharine and who had feared hell for her sons and for herself—her belief and her fear alike had died in her" (173). The novel understands that the Church cannot help Catharine address the murder she has committed—its cultural practices are not sufficient, or perhaps not appropriate for what she has done. Instead, in a key event in the novel that parallels Archilde's growing romantic attachment to Modeste's granddaughter, Catharine returns to the tribe's pre-Christian way of registering and mediating guilt—the whip (206). In fact, many in the community have been turning their back on the new teachings and returning to older ways before their individual conversions: "those old people turned back on the path they had come and for a while their hearts were lightened. The old lady, with the red stripes of the whip on her back, slept without dreaming" (211). Likewise, the novel critiques the Church's and government's attempts to eliminate specific Native cultural practices like religious ceremonies and traditional dances (174, 204); in these and other ways, the novel supports the cultural longevity that anthropology's culture had made central.

The novel thus places itself firmly in the anthropological tradition of cultural pluralism and cultural relativism. It is pluralist insofar as it argues for the continuation of traditional ways, and condemns coercive conversions of cultural practices and beliefs. But it is relativist insofar as it seems in part, with its positive portrayal of some of the priests, to suggest that their faith is right for them, just not for the Salish. Father Grepilloux in particular, though he helped effect the tribe's conversion, sympathizes with their loss of "a way of life" (59), is quietly wise in his understandings, and helps both Max and Archilde. The stance that *The Surrounded* adopts, in other words, is the early twentieth-century social scientific approach to religion— in anthropology especially—of treating religion as a cultural formation. This cultural relativism suspends the truth claims of religions, addressing their psychological and cultural terms, but not their metaphysical claims.

Such is McNickle's approach to Catholic and Salish religious beliefs, just as it is Hurston's approach to Catholic and voodoo ones—the ethnographer-novelists will not judge them; though the social sciences are a product of modernity, they somewhat paradoxically suspend religions' truth claims.

My point here is that, while McNickle was not a working ethnographer like Hurston, his incorporation of anthropology-mediated oral tradition into his fiction performs the same work of cultural description, affirmation, and pluralism as it did in her novels. This turn to ethnic culture was recognizable at least to one prospective publisher, Harcourt and Brace, which was one of the big three insurgent presses established in the late 1910s and early 1920s that would go on to publish much literature associated with the Harlem Renaissance (Hutchinson 344). An early draft of *The Surrounded* was rejected by Harcourt, which quoted an anonymous report on the manuscript that it was "Perhaps the beginning of a new Indian literature to rival that of Harlem."[15]

McNickle, in fact, had begun the novel in the late 1920s in New York, not on the Flathead Reservation. In response to one potential publisher's report, McNickle turned to the ethnographic sources in the Columbia University library mentioned in his prefatory note to give cultural substance to the dramatic "skeleton" of his story (Parker 50). In fact, it was during the composition of *The Surrounded,* and especially the last two or so years of its revisions, that McNickle was first introduced in depth to anthropology, through his ethnographic research for his novel, through some work for the Federal Workers Project in 1935 on "Indians and anthropology" (55), and while he was "writing biographical sketches for the *National Cyclopedia of American Biography*" (59) on anthropologists, including Johns Hopkins anthropologist William Gates, with whom McNickle initiated a correspondence about cultural and linguistic relativism (65). While his training in anthropology was not as detailed and formal as Hurston's, McNickle nonetheless came to anthropology through two different paths and was familiar with the central tenets of cultural anthropology, which, by the early 1930s (and in Columbia University's library no less), were dominated by the intellectual influences of Franz Boas and his students. And while *The Surrounded* is not as clearly or as thoroughly orthodox in its concept of anthropological culture as Hurston's 1930s novels and ethnographies are, it shows the signs nonetheless of being articulated through the Boasian culture concept that had become the disciplinary consensus.

But while Hurston did the bulk of her anthropology training (at Columbia and in the field) largely before her literary career, McNickle's career as an anthropologist happened as his literary career was beginning—with its origins in his literary career, since he first turned to anthropology to solve a problem of literary craft. The fact that we can see some aspects of anthropology's culture concept in his work—such as the importance of the oral tradition in terms of a cultural holism, but also his commitment to cultural relativism regarding Catholicism, and an implicit understanding of culture as things that gain meaning through but also change within history—suggests a couple of important ideas about the circuit between literature and social science. The first is that for anyone writing about culture and race in the first phase of the genealogy of literary multiculturalism, Franz Boas's anthropological ideas were unavoidable as part of the intellectual fabric of the milieu. One did not need to be mentored by Boas in order to be affected by his ideas about racial equality and the question of what culture was, especially if (as was true for McNickle) one was writing one's first novel in the late 1920s in New York City. The second point is that one did not need to come to such ideas about culture through the intervention of Boasian anthropology. That McNickle later turned to anthropology says much about the author and intellectual choosing the discipline instead of the discipline determining the ideas of an author and intellectual. McNickle formulated notions of Salish culture in informed dialogue with Boasian anthropology. While his sense of culture is not as sharp as Hurston's was—a fact traceable to Hurston's schooling with Boas—it is nevertheless much closer to the culture concept of anthropology than the other social science discipline becoming influential in the 1920s, University of Chicago sociology.

About the time *The Surrounded* was published, McNickle began working for the Bureau of Indian Affairs under the new leadership of John Collier. Collier administered what became known as the "Indian New Deal" in the second half of the 1930s—a program that reversed the previous assimilationist federal policies with a drive for more "cultural and political autonomy" (Parker 125). Collier's other innovation was to introduce "applied anthropology," "a science of humankind that would establish objective criteria on which to base the policies and programs of Indian affairs," especially the creation of culture-specific tribal constitutions (Parker 72). McNickle became involved in significant changes at the BIA. For a while he was tangentially involved in helping to administer a Japanese American internment camp at Poston, Arizona through an agreement between the BIA and the War Relocation Authority headed by Dillon Myer. It was the arrival as the head of the BIA in 1952 of Myer—whose chief virtue for the Truman administration was his rapid dispersal of Japanese Americans out of concentrated rural areas during and following World War II—that led to McNickle's departure from the BIA and his eventual founding of the Department of Anthropology at the University of Saskatchewan.

That a set of Native American intellectuals and writers have turned to, contested, used, and influenced anthropology even as a rival set of Asian American intellectuals and writers have turned to, contested, used, and influenced sociology, is the pattern that is at the heart of *A Genealogy of Literary Multiculturalism,* and it is a pattern that matters. It is not an accident that after World War II McNickle became an anthropologist, just as Gordon Hirabayashi, the famous litigant of Japanese American internment before the Supreme Court, was becoming a sociologist. It is not merely the facts (though both are true) that American anthropology has historically formed itself through addressing the question of the "Indian" and that American sociology has historically formed itself (in part) through addressing the question of the Asian American that led McNickle to choose anthropology and Hirabayashi to choose sociology. It is, more fundamentally, the different culture concepts that emerged from these rival social science disciplines as they contested together the nativist racial thinking of the first phase. Such differences on the question of culture are at the center of the next chapter.

 Chapter 2

Richard Wright, Robert Park,
and the Literature of Sociology

> A new type of Negro is evolving—a city Negro. [...]
> In ten years, Negroes have been actually transplanted
> from one culture to another.
>
> —Charles S. Johnson, "The New Frontage on
> American Life," *The New Negro,* 1925 (285)

Hurston's famous August 11, 1955, letter to the
Orlando Sentinel is a strange document, at once an anticommunist screed and
a diatribe against the NAACP and its legal accomplishments in overturning segregation (see Kaplan 738–40). At its heart, however, is really Hurston's
opposition to the element of Boas's anthropology that Hurston rejected: the
implication that in contact with a larger, more powerful culture, members of
smaller cultures would gradually desire to adopt the practices and values of the
dominant one. Hurston opposed *Brown v. Board of Education* not solely because
of its implication for black educational institutions (some of which she had
taught at), but on the larger dynamic of what African American culture was,
and what its future would be. She makes this point by invoking American
anthropology's founding conceit of the disappearing Indian, who would rather
die than give up his culture: "The American Indian has never been spoken of
as a minority and chiefly because there is no whine in the Indian. Certainly
he fought, and valiantly for his lands, and rightfully so, but it is inconceivable
of an Indian to seek forcible association with anyone. His well known pride
and self-respect would save him from that. I take the Indian position" (738).
The un-"Indian" strategy is the NAACP's, characterized by "the 'tragedy of
color' school of thought among us, whose fountain-head is the pressure group
concerned in this court ruling" (Kaplan 740): to whine until permitted to give
up African American culture by integrating in the dominant one.

But Richard Wright's paradigmatic African American was already "bereft of a culture," as he put it in his description of Bigger Thomas ("I Bite" 828). In a book that became (in a roundabout way) an actual piece of evidence for the Supreme Court's desegregation decision that Hurston condemned, *Native Son* suggested a picture of African American life as being without any culture worth holding on to. While Hurston's earlier rejection of his book *Uncle Tom's Children* cited the same anticommunist grounds on which she later rejected *Brown,* what was more fundamentally at stake for Hurston about Wright and the NAACP is that they shared a picture of worthwhile African American culture as having, in one sense, already disappeared.

When Richard Wright reviewed *Their Eyes Were Watching God* in *New Masses* in 1937, he criticized what he saw as its racist clichés and its minstrel conventions. Hurston's characters, wrote Wright, "eat and laugh and cry and work and kill; they swing like a pendulum eternally in that safe and narrow orbit in which America likes to see the Negro live: between laughter and tears" ("Between" 25). The next year, Hurston's review of Wright's *Uncle Tom's Children* responded in kind, complaining of its caricatured communist portrayal of black oppression in the South ("Stories"). But Wright's work was influenced not only by communism, but also by reading he had done in the social sciences, particularly by the University of Chicago school of sociology. What was at stake in this literary antagonism between Hurston and Wright was not just a difference in politics and aesthetics—or a clashing of literary egos—but equally and importantly for the genealogy of literary multiculturalism that followed, a disciplinary argument between anthropology and sociology. It was an argument about the shape and future of African American culture in America. It was an argument that Hurston lost; or to put it another way, Hurston lost the battle but won the war—posthumously.

Although the development of anthropology historically preceded sociology by a decade or two, by the 1920s both were dynamic disciplinary forces that were contesting, albeit sometimes unevenly, the racial biology of nativist notions of culture, and both were deeply influencing African American writers and intellectuals of the period. Alain Locke's *New Negro* nicely captures the way the first phase in the genealogy of literary multiculturalism was composed of contesting forces offering differing conceptions of minority cultures. In that collection the Robert Park–trained sociologist Charles Johnson, quoted in the epigraph to this chapter, rendered the Great Migration through tropes of cultural disruption and loss, and while that disjunction might be partially compensated for by a discovery of "heritage," Johnson ultimately folded (as did Park) such cultural pluralism into an eventual cultural merging (297). Melville Herskovits argued there was no cultural continuity across the

Middle Passage, and that African Americans did not have a different culture, but were separated from full participation in white American culture by social barriers—"The same pattern, only a different shade!" he put it (353). (In a few years he repudiated this thesis and, turning 180 degrees, became the most forceful anthropologist for understanding African cultural retentions and survivals.) E. Franklin Frazier cast an approving eye over Durham's Negro middle class, arguing they had "the same" practical business views of the middle class "everywhere" (338). But also present in *The New Negro* was African American anthropologist Arthur Huff Fauset, who argued not only for the existence of a distinct Negro folklore, but that its "animal cycle" in particular had its origins in Africa (240). His contribution, along with Alain Locke's, tried to establish distinctive African American cultural formations and their likely origin in Africa.[1] It also printed Zora Neale Hurston's "Spunk," written before she had begun her Barnard training with Boas, Benedict, and Herskovits. Locke's own exploration of African sculpture and his casting about for language that might capture the continuities and discontinuities—"African spirit," "ancestral heritage" (254), "race psychology" (255), "blood descendants," "direct cultural kinship" (256), "racial idiom" (262), "a racially representative tradition" (266), "culturally awakened Negro artist" (267)—make clear that *The New Negro* instantiated the tripartite struggle among nativist, anthropological, and sociological models of African American culture which characterized this first phase.

This phase between 1920 and 1940 was thus a complex, contested terrain of conflicting concepts of race and culture. My shorthand description of the phase—as beginning with a struggle between nativism and anthropology over the difference between race and culture and ending with a struggle between anthropology and sociology over the model and destiny of minority culture—simplifies the timeline somewhat, but accurately renders the fundamental topography of the phase's contested terrain. Actual anthropologists and sociologists—such as Herskovits and Johnson—had nuanced views that were not always and not entirely identical with the disciplines rendered here in shorthand as anthropology and sociology. But for all their internal complexity, these disciplines modeled culture differently, in ways recognized by key writers and intellectuals in the three phases of the genealogy of literary multiculturalism.

This chapter makes several related arguments in terms of this genealogy. My first argument is that, while some of Wright's biographers, editors, and critics have sought to place him as an antecedent for our current paradigm of literary multiculturalism, it is actually Hurston who was its precursor and enabler. The reason is historical—Hurston's work was more of an influence on early multiculturalist African American writers like Ishmael Reed, Toni Morrison, and Alice Walker—and theoretical, in the sense that (and this is my second argument) third-phase literary multiculturalism could emerge only from the anthropological model of culture used by Hurston, and not the sociological model of culture used by Wright. Through an examination of the sociology of Park and others at the University of Chicago, this chapter argues that Wright's model of culture was profoundly different from the anthropological one that had enabled Hurston, and that the sociological model generally became dominant in the second phase of integrationist and assimilationist literature by racialized minorities between 1940 and 1965. My third argument here is that it is partly through a confusion of the difference between anthropology's and sociology's models of culture that Wright has mistakenly been understood as the progenitor of third-phase literary multiculturalism. Many cultural nationalist and multiculturalist accounts of Wright have failed to see the ways in which Wright's literary politics were actually integrationist, assimilationist, and universalist—the latter two of which are anathema to our current paradigm of literary multiculturalism. If Hurston's conservative politics, her anti-*Brown* position, and her general distrust of radical politics and protest are problems posed to a multicultural tradition that received its inspiration from her and would like to recuperate her, then Wright poses a different (and worse) set of problems. The problem for cultural nationalist attempts to recuperate Wright is his relative disinterest in African American culture as such, or in a cultural pluralism that envisions its endurance.

While some scholars like Carla Cappetti have recognized the ways in which sociology was an enabling and influential discourse for Richard Wright, others like Michel Fabre and Cynthia Tolentino have downplayed or rejected this influence. Fabre's biography characterizes Wright's life as the intellectual journey from Marxism through existentialism to a postcolonial politics; other influences like sociology, naturalism, and literary modernism play decidedly secondary roles. Tolentino goes further by suggesting that sociology was part of the very liberal discourse on race in the 1930s that Wright was challenging in *Native Son* (381). She finds Wright's Marxist revolutionary consciousness to be incompatible with liberal sociology's reformism, suggesting that "This novel shows how liberal attempts to engage with blacks are encoded by the language and tropes of cultural anthropology and sociology most commonly associated with Mary Dalton's school, the University of Chicago" (393). But Tolentino's equating of anthropology and sociology ignores the specifics of sociology and confuses "the liberal segregationist status quo" (388) of the Daltons with the liberal integration that Chicago sociology eventually entailed. As I show here with *Native Son* and as Cappetti has shown with

Black Boy, Wright almost entirely accepted "sociology's traditional authority and function in interpreting the circumstances of black Americans," Tolentino's claim notwithstanding (381).

Conversely, other critics have sought to rescue Wright from his views about African American culture. One such attempted multiculturalist recuperation is Richard Yarborough's 1991 introduction to the HarperPerennial edition of Wright's 1938 *Uncle Tom's Children.* Citing Wright's "Blueprint for Negro Writing," in which Wright claims "Negro culture, and especially in folklore" is the source of black "nationalism," Yarborough recommends it as a guide to reading the stories of *Uncle Tom's Children* (xxi). As he states, "It would be difficult to overestimate the impact of [Langston] Hughes and other black authors on Wright's handling of folk materials, for *Uncle Tom's Children* represents one of the most ambitious and complex fictional uses of black folklore that had appeared to that time" (xxi–xxii). But the pre–*Uncle Tom's Children* publication of Hurston's *Jonah's Gourd Vine, Mules and Men,* and *Their Eyes Were Watching God* constitutes a group of texts whose attention to black folk culture was actually far more "ambitious and complex" than anything in Wright's entire career. The evidence Yarborough provides for this culturalist reading of the stories in *Uncle Tom's Children* is so thin as to suggest that the multicultural paradigm within which he wrote in 1991 demanded pluralist valuations of black culture even where none existed.

Wright's earliest stories display only minimal interest in the elements of black rural Southern culture so central to Hurston. Wright uses black vernacular, but its range and ornamentation is severely limited compared to Hurston's. Yarborough sees the "verbal jousting of the young men in [the first story] 'Big Boy Leaves Home'" in terms of "the rich black cultural freight that they carry" (xxii), but when we hear exchanges like

> "Big Boy?"
> "Huh?"
> "Yuh know one thing?"
> "Whut?"
> "Yuh sho is crazy!"
> "Crazy?"
> "Yeah, yuh crazys a bed-bug!" (17–18),

it is evident that Wright's handling of—as well as interest in and ear for— African American verbal play cannot compare with Hurston's offerings in *Their Eyes* or *Mules.* (On this one point at least it seems Hurston is correct in observing, "Certainly he does not write by ear unless he is tone-deaf" ["Stories" 913].)

A somewhat more significant cultural presence in the stories is African American Christianity in the South, providing the background of "Big Boy Leaves Home" and the ironic title to the second story, "Down by the Riverside," and becoming central in the last two stories, "Fire and Cloud" and "Bright and Morning Star" (in addition, again, to providing titles). But the problem for reading these two stories in terms of "the whole of Negro culture" in order to understand the "character of the Negro people" (to use Yarborough's citation of Wright's "Blueprint") is that both stories turn on the replacement of Christianity by Marxism. In "Bright and Morning Star," the protagonist's two sons have successfully (and correctly, for this story first published in *New Masses*) convinced her to abandon her childhood Christianity of the African American culture in which she grew up (222) and replace it with the "new faith" of class struggle and the interracial alliance of the Communist Party (225). In "Fire and Cloud," the African American preacher protagonist, while earlier born again, is actually born thrice after a savage beating by the local white mob leaders who want to prevent a demonstration: he is "somehow changed" (212) and preaches a new doctrine of "the *people*" (210), which means leading a successful interracial march of poor black and white people to the town where they receive concessions from the mayor. The spiritual that gives the story its title—"*So the sign of the fire by night / N the sign of the cloud by day*" (218)—is reworked and given the new content of class struggle. The story sees Southern African American religious life as a strategy that partly works to enable survival, build community, and diffuse tension, but that must be abandoned in order to solve the underlying conflicts. While Hurston's 1934 short story "The Fire and the Cloud" was a tribute to the African American religious symbol of Moses (and a rehearsal for her 1939 *Moses, Man of the Mountain*), Wright's 1938 "Fire and Cloud" was about emptying that tradition of its false consciousness. Whereas Hurston in *Jonah's* imagines Southern black Christianity as a cultural tradition that conceals an African religious continuity (a theme to which Ishmael Reed returns, as I show in chapter eight), Wright sees Southern black Christianity as the opiate of the masses, but a tradition whose structures and vocabularies can be reworked to the ends of class struggle—which would ultimately be his critique of the church in both *Native Son* and *Black Boy*. Wright's treatment of African American religion cannot count as cultural pluralism because he imagines and desires its disappearance, to be replaced by a universalist Marxism not understood through Boasian cultural relativism.

Just as the solution in the last two stories is the abandoning or subordination of black culture to a universal ethos, so too does the picture of the South as a whole suggest the need to abandon it. Yarborough sees the "motif of the train" in "Big Boy"—four youths keep hearing northbound trains' whistles and the lone survivor, in a slight adaptation, flees a white lynch mob in a northbound truck—resonating with an "Afro-American folklore" that is the "structural glue" connecting this story to the five other pieces in the collection (xxii). But the train motif is centered on the need to escape the oppressive South for the land of freedom and "ekual rights" in the North (19, 28). While this idea certainly is a historical part of Southern black rural culture, it cannot count as celebratory of black culture since its logic is to escape what was the very site of black culture, as Hurston knew, and as a generation of cultural nationalist critics would rediscover, as I show in chapter six.

In fact, the image of the South that emerges from the five stories and one essay of *Uncle Tom's Children* is of a totalitarian state whose race war is held in check only by the constant threat of violence by better-armed and more numerous white authorities and mobs. This is obviously what enraged Hurston when she read the book. The opening essay of the expanded 1940 edition—"The Ethics of Living Jim Crow"—ends with one of Wright's friends exclaiming, "Lawd, man! Ef it wuzn't fer them polices 'n' them ol' lynch-mobs, there wouldn't be nothin' but uproar down here!" (15). This sentiment is echoed in all the stories, and the collection is punctuated by a high body count. From a nationalist perspective, what is useful about *Uncle Tom's Children* is its promise of militant resistance (white men get shot by African American men or women in four of the five stories); but from a nationalist perspective, what is not helpful (in terms of imagining a distinct "nation") is that there is not much culture to speak of. The Jim Crow South is an armed society in a race war, in the face of which there might be militancy, resistance, and survival, but not cultural health. Hazel Rowley suggests that the members of Wright's first writing group in Chicago, before whom he read drafts of most of *Uncle Tom's Children,* "embraced 'Negro nationalism'—writing about black culture, folklore, religion, and sport—but (Wright was adamant about this) they would not restrict themselves to this. Their literary heritage was European, white American, and Negro" (117). While the stories do address African American religion (albeit as false consciousness), Rowley's reading of the influence of Negro culture and nationalism, like Yarborough's reading, is based on reading Wright's later prescriptive "Blueprint" rather than on the details in the stories themselves.

Wright's lack of interest in (and even hostility to) African American Southern rural culture was a result of personal experience articulated through a social science model of culture, just as Hurston's conversely positive portrayal was generated by a different experience and a different model. Sociology's conception of the culture of survival on the margin of the dominant society probably affirmed and gave scientific definition to his own experience of growing up in the oppressive South and then moving north to Chicago. *Uncle Tom's Children* reveals the imprint of sociology, and his later two books, *Native Son* and *Black Boy,* obviously used sociology to articulate his vision of African American culture within the larger context of urban Chicago and mostly-white America.

Wright appears to have come to Chicago sociology through multiple points of contact, though it is not clear exactly when Wright read what he read. *Black Boy* suggests that his first readings in sociology were very early, by 1929 before the stock market crash (327, 338). His biographer Michel Fabre concurs, noting that by 1930 Wright was supplementing his observations and recordings of the South Side of Chicago (where he had moved from the South in 1927) by "referring to the available sociology books in order to characterize different types of black people" (Fabre 86). Other sociology texts may have been recommended to Wright by Mary Wirth, a social worker who interviewed him in 1933 (Rowley 68). Wirth's husband was the University of Chicago sociologist Louis Wirth (a former student-turned-colleague of Robert Park), and the Wirths were to become life-long friends of Wright. Wright joined the local John Reed Club in 1933, and when he was made executive secretary of the club the following year, he began inviting progressive social scientists as guest lecturers, like Wirth, Ernest Burgess of the University of Chicago Sociology department and Melville Herskovits of Northwestern University (Fabre 101). When Wright later visited Wirth at the university, he was given "a reading list of undergraduate books on sociology," one of which was certain to have been Park and Burgess's *Introduction to the Science of Sociology*. Rowley notes, "When they met again a few months later, Wirth was astounded by the thoroughness with which Wright had done the reading" (82). It is unclear whether Park and Wright met before the publication of *Native Son,* but in any case, when Wright left Chicago for New York in May 1937, he was not leaving behind the influence of sociology.

🎵 University of Chicago Sociology

"It occurred to me that if one could discover some means of artificially inducing and stimulating this nervous disease at will, one might possibly solve the American race problem. My sociology teacher had once said that there were but three ways for the Negro to solve his problem in America. [...]

> 'To either get out, get white or get along.' Since he
> wouldn't and couldn't get out and was getting along
> only differently, it seemed to me that the only thing
> for him was to get white."
>
> —George S. Schuyler, *Black No More,* 1931 (11)

It is not incorrect to say that the sociology of the era was developing a technology to help black people "get white." Schuyler's satire, of course, is premised on this *sociological* idea about culture being heard by the hero Dr. Junius Crookman, a *biology* student who literalizes the sociological lesson by developing a machine that transforms phenotype. But one of sociology's crucial innovations was the idea that racialized minorities could become culturally white, if not phenotypically white. The sociology of the era was that developed by the University of Chicago Sociology Department, which became extremely influential, attaining "almost a monopoly status" in American sociology from the 1910s until World War II (Szacki 445). Focused on urban experience, migration, social institutions and neighborhoods, race and questions of cultural assimilation, ghettoes, and delinquency, many of the school's representative ideas were summarized by its most famous practitioner, Robert Ezra Park. Chicago sociology addressed a wide range of issues, and what united them were the idea of the cultural assimilability of racialized minorities, and the possibility of relatively quick changes in cultural practices and values. As this chapter and the next two will make clear, different aspects of the sociological model of culture were used by different writers in different traditions.

"The founding document of Chicago sociology," according to Dorothy Ross, was published in 1912 by William I. Thomas. It was

> a research protocol entitled "Race Psychology: Standpoint and Questionnaire, with Particular Reference to the Immigrant and the Negro." It addressed the central issue that would occupy the ethnic and urban sociology of Thomas and Park, "the backwardness and forwardness of different social groups." The theoretical standpoint Thomas had constructed was crucial to the enterprise, for it placed his subjects in the midst of a changing liberal society and assumed racial equality. (Ross 351)

Although Michael Omi and Howard Winant attribute the social science conceptualization of biological equality to Robert Park's sociology in the 1920s, Dorothy Ross has shown that this change was initiated by Boas in anthropology, and later taken up by Thomas, and through him, eventually Park (Ross 350–59).[2] Furthermore, Ross argues, Thomas borrowed Boas's ethnographic research method: "In developing this research stance, Thomas had taken a great deal from anthropology, not only from Boas' theory of the biological equality of races, but also from the combination of distance and sympathy the strangely human materials of anthropology provided him" (351). Thomas later published, with Florian Znaniecki, *The Polish Peasant in Europe and America* (1918), an important work on immigration and non-pluralist assimilation that set the paradigm for "the new empirical social science" (352).

Thomas met Robert Park at a conference at the Tuskegee Institute in 1912, where Park had been an aide, publicity agent, and ghostwriter to Booker T. Washington for seven years, becoming, as Park put it "for all intents and purposes, for the time, a Negro, myself" (qtd. in Ross 307).[3] Park joined Thomas and the sociology faculty at the University of Chicago the following year, where he contributed to sociology's growing orientation toward realism, empiricism, and hard facts. Park built on the work of Thomas and Boas, embracing their assumption of racial equality and using their empirical research methods, such as gathering data by interviewing urban and ethnic subjects. When his and Ernest W. Burgess's *Introduction to the Science of Sociology* was published in 1921, it became "the dominant text in the field for the next twenty years"; according to Ross, it "disseminated Park's conception of sociology" (359), enabling both theoretically and methodologically Gunnar Myrdal's *An American Dilemma* twenty years later.

Boas was the Charles Darwin of the social sciences: like Darwin, he did not get everything right, and he was not wholly original, but he synthesized into a powerful working model a number of already-existing and new ideas. At the heart of Boas's paradigm shift—the turn from biology to culture—was a powerful set of questions, one of the most important of which worked—and still works—as a kind of universal acid on theories of inherited and immutable difference: namely, what is the evidence for considering a given trait to be the result of biological and heritable difference rather than social, environmental difference? Robert Park, on the other hand, became the chief theorist of migration in American modernity, investigating what happens to individuals and cultural or racial groups when they move to, or within, the United States. Over the course of his career, Park developed several influential concepts, some of which were pursued by his students or colleagues. One of the most important was that of the four stages—competition, conflict, accommodation, and assimilation—through which immigrant communities passed as they became American. Two others were those of the generation gap and the "marginal man," the cosmopolitan subject whose migration makes him "a man on the margin of two cultures," simultaneously a stranger to both ("Human Migration" 354), both of which, as I show in chapters three and four, became central to mid-century Asian American integrationist literature. What these key interests shared was a concept of culture as it was experienced by individuals who were in transition between societies. Parkian sociology shared with Boasian anthropology an interest in the psychological meanings of the cultures they studied, but Park imagined cultural values and traditions as much more fragmented, in flux, patchwork, adaptive, and to be taken up and discarded by migrants and their children. For Park, urban society often contained several competing cultural groups, and he studied how such groups grew, changed, or disappeared.

Thus Robert Park and Chicago sociology took up in earnest the implication of cultural assimilation that Boas had outlined but not pursued. One important difference between Boasian anthropology and Parkian sociology was that the former dealt with rural people and the latter with urban people. But an even more important difference was their competing accounts of the culture concept, with anthropology conceiving of culture itself, characterized by longevity and holism, as an object of study, and sociology investigating people changing their culture, either themselves (in the marginal man) or their descendants (in the more abstract four stages of assimilation).[4]

A key contribution of Park and Burgess's *Introduction to the Science of Sociology* was an anti-nativist theory of progressive assimilation. "The heart of the text," notes Dorothy Ross, "was a group of chapters on competition, conflict, accommodation, and assimilation" (359). Competition was ecological rather than social, the condition of drawing nutrients from the same environment as competitor plants without being conscious of the others' existences (Park and Burgess 504–6). It was an abstract condition that "inevitably initiates conflict, accommodation, or assimilation" (507), all modes in which consciousness of others predominates. Nonetheless, competition is an ecological fact resulting from a kind of geographical accident: Dalton and Bigger Thomas, to anticipate this chapter's discussion of *Native Son*, are in competition merely because of their co-existence in Chicago. If competition was presocial, the second stage of conflict was necessarily communicative and frequently group-based. If competition was a "struggle for position in an economic order" (574), then "the status of the individual, or a group of individuals, in the social order, on the other hand, is determined by rivalry, by war, or by subtler forms of conflict" (574). Bigger's trial and the less formalized lynch-mob pursuit of Bigger that precedes the trial are instances of this kind of group conflict: in both cases, the novel makes clear that racial consciousness is at the heart of the crime and its punishment.

The third stage, that of accommodation, was the "social heritages, traditions, sentiments, culture, [and] technique" that individuals or groups acquired and passed on as tools for dealing with their environment (664). Accommodation included the "cosmopolitan's" ready adjustment to his new "milieu" (666), but also the socially structured subordination of groups like slaves (667) or the enforcement of caste boundaries like those in the South and the North. In *Native Son,* the restrictions on housing (African Americans can rent on the South Side but not generally elsewhere) and vocation (African Americans can drive cars but not pilot planes) would likely have counted as accommodation according to Park and Burgess's theory, as would the more severe social restrictions that the Southern newspaper editor recommends to Chicago readers.

Assimilation was the process that immigrants underwent in "gradually acquiring the culture of the new" country, an idea expressed for Park and Burgess by Israel Zangwill's play *The Melting Pot* (734). If accommodation was adjustment reducing conflict, assimilation represented a "process of interpenetration and fusion" of peoples into "a common cultural life" (735). While assimilation included some mutual change, Park and Burgess most frequently understood this process as losing one's ethnic culture to become American. They distinguished assimilation from amalgamation, the "fusion of races by interbreeding and intermarriage," a process that is "a universal phenomenon among the historical races" (737). Immigration and Americanization framed cultural assimilation: an example in *Native Son* might be the Daltons' Irish American cook, who illustrates the comparative ease with which European immigrants are allowed to participate in national life.

Park and Burgess's four categories are theoretically problematic and have been complicated and developed in sociology in the last eight decades, but they were important in the 1920s and 1930s for thinking through the place of immigrants and ethnic and racial minorities in the nation. The four categories were both synchronic descriptors of social relations and diachronic predictors of how individuals and groups would eventually mesh with larger groups. It was therefore to the last three processes of conflict, accommodation, and assimilation that Park especially looked to theorize the Americanization of immigrant groups. In "Human Migration and the Marginal Man" (1928), he developed this type to explain the immigrant's urban experience of being caught between two cultures, his or her migration occasioning the destruction of the old cultures of "tribe and folk" (353), and the slow embrace of the new.

In "Personality and Cultural Conflict" (1931), Park urged attention to immigrants' "life history documents," like biographies and letters, the use of which he helped pioneer in sociology. Many of them, he wrote, "have been published in recent years, [and] have revealed the manner and extent of the inner moral conflicts to which immigrants and frequently immigrant children are subjected in making the transition from the cultural tradition of the home country to that of the new" (370)—thus suggesting an emerging theory of the generation gap.[5] In "Education and the Cultural Crisis" (1943), Park recognized this generation gap as helping to produce second-generation "marginal men." As with "Human Migration," the fundamental process that interested Park was the break in cultural transmission from parents to children inaugurated by migration to the United States.

This process seemed relatively straightforward for European immigrants, yet Park grappled for years with what would become a central problem in this vision of Americanization: could racialized minorities marked by skin-color difference be assimilated? In one of his first post-Tuskegee publications, "Racial Assimilation in Secondary Groups with Particular Reference to the Negro" (1913), Park opens with the double meaning of assimilation: to adopt the culture of, but also to become incorporated into. Using that era's notion of race—which held that the population of Europe was composed of different racial stocks—he wrote, "There is no reason to assume that this assimilation of alien groups to native standards has modified to any great extent fundamental racial characteristics. It has, however, erased the external signs which formerly distinguished the members of one race from those of another" (205). In speaking of Poles, Lithuanians, and Norwegians (and importantly, not Mediterraneans or Jews, whose racial features were understood to be even more pronounced), Park's point was that the supposed phenotypical differences among these groups are readily "assimilated" into the white "native" norm. For Park, simultaneous cultural assimilation and racial amalgamation liberated the individual: "In obliterating the external signs" (206) of racial difference, Europeans simultaneously became racially white and culturally American.

The problem with this formulation of assimilation, of course, is what it meant for groups whose phenotypical difference exceeded that of Poles or Lithuanians. According to Park, "the chief obstacle to the assimilation of the Negro and the Oriental are not mental but physical traits" (208); or, as he went on to say, "The trouble is not with the Japanese mind but with the Japanese skin. The 'Jap' is not the right color" (208)—he wears a "racial uniform" (208). While this is a progressive, Boasian definition of the problem—against the tide of growing nativism, Park agrees with Boas that whatever racial distinctiveness remains is not an inner one of mental ability preventing full participation in the nation—Park imagines, perhaps realistically in 1913, that cultural assimilation of racialized minorities will happen only to the extent of the disappearance through miscegenation of visible signs of ancestry. The rest of the essay takes its political cue from Booker T. Washington in arguing that the shared social space of slavery—"The kindly relations of master and slave in Virginia" (211)—is different from the virulent racism of the day, which is based on "the Hill Billy and the Red Neck," people "who did not own slaves" (212). This new racism emphasizing segregation and exclusion—Park's essay appeared two years before D. W. Griffith's *The Birth of a Nation*—produces, in reaction, increased race pride and national consciousness among African Americans. It is producing "a nation within a nation," Park quotes Washington as saying (218), in a phrase anticipatory of the black nationalism that emerged following the Civil Rights movement. Park ends the essay on this uncertain note of growing nationalism: the increasing racial segregations and exclusions have forestalled the possible fourth stage of the assimilation of African Americans and Asian Americans.

Historian Dorothy Ross analyzes Park's changing ideas about racial assimilation thus:

> The one area of social life Park had not been able to subdue to his vision of liberal history was race relations. Ecology had its most profound effect on Park's attitude toward race, though it operated in tandem with a transforming personal experience of race relations on the West Coast and in Hawaii. Until the mid-1920s Park remained uncertain about racial assimilation. His books on immigrant assimilation and the immigrant press indicated that the new ethnic immigrants would assimilate to American society. The liberal-ecological process would, in its own good time, wear away their group identities, particularly as immigration from Europe halted. But Negro-white race relations could be different, and after the Chicago race riot of 1919, he sensed a growing "class consciousness" and "race consciousness" in the cities.
>
> What apparently changed his mind was his study of Japanese-American relations, in which he encountered "the younger generation of Orientals." Listening to a young Japanese-American woman, he felt that he was listening to "an American woman in a Japanese disguise." Park went on to a conference in Hawaii, where he was astonished at the mixing of races and described his meetings with the Japanese delegation as "an adventure in friendship." Park's encounter led him for the first time to declare unequivocally the triumph of ecological determinism. "The forces which have brought about the existing interpenetration of peoples are so vast and irresistible that the resulting changes assume the character of a cosmic process.... The race relations cycle ... of contacts, competition, accommodation and eventual assimilation, is apparently progressive and irreversible." (438)

Ross marks Park's changed conception through a reading of his contribution to the "oriental" issue of *Survey Graphic* in May 1926, for which Park wrote both an introductory essay ("Behind Our Masks") and an essay on Pacific migrations and modernity ("Our Racial Frontier on the Pacific"), both of which I discuss in more detail in chapter three. It is in the first essay that Park decides he is unable to discern "the oriental mentality behind the oriental mask" of the young Japanese American woman, and thus claims race as a kind of "disguise" (248).

This was the ultimate logic of Boas's disengagement of culture from race, which allowed Park to reformulate the question of racial assimilation as a question of the barriers raised by social custom. His change from conceiving of race as a "uniform" to a "disguise" or a "mask" is of course to reverse the relation between the racial sign and being. If the uniform is the outward sign of an inner allegiance, the mask and the disguise are the false outer guides to what is inside. Once race becomes recast as a mere mask that falsely disguises American belonging instead of the uniform that signified loyalty elsewhere, then shared culture underneath could become recognized. As I will suggest in chapter four, however, this was a contested position not just in the 1920s but almost twenty years later, when the Supreme Court would not see Park's Japanese American youth as Americans in Japanese "disguise," with future *Brown* Chief Justice Earl Warren telling his fellow governors in 1943, "If the Japs are released [from internment camps], no one will be able to tell a saboteur from any other Jap" (qtd. in Kluger 664).

Park's arguments for the possible cultural assimilation of racialized minorities were profoundly anti-nativist and thoroughly Boasian. Summarizing the Race Relations Survey on the Pacific Coast, he argued that second-generation cultural change was "the most significant" discovery of the Survey; like Boas's work for the Atlantic-oriented Dillingham Commission, Park's work on the Pacific-oriented Survey was the discovery of culture in place of race: that people are characterized by "not so much innate qualities as [learned] conventions" (251). In the essay portion, Park explicitly took a dig at nativist theorizers such as Stoddard and Grant, claiming "civilization is not, as some writers seem to believe, a biological, but a social, product" ("Our Racial" 138). The essay prophetically examines Pacific migration in the modern world, suggesting that new modes of commerce (what we would now call globalized markets and labor pools), new technologies of communication (widespread journalism, radio, and cinema) and transportation were reducing international "social distances." Against such forces, a "mythical entity" like race could be deployed (as in the 1924

Immigration Act excluding Asian immigration), but only in vain since "all the deeper currents of modern life run counter to a policy of racial or national isolation" (141). As he concluded, to reproduce more fully Park's words quoted in Ross,

> The race relations cycle which takes the form, to state it abstractly, of contacts, competition, accommodation and eventual assimilation, is apparently progressive and irreversible. Customs regulations, immigration restrictions and racial barriers may slacken the tempo of the movement; may perhaps halt it altogether for a time; but cannot change its direction; cannot at any rate, reverse it. (150)

Once Park had conceived of assimilation not just as a progressive force but as a natural or even cosmic force, he concentrated on the variabilities of conflicts, accommodations, and assimilations, and on the social barriers that temporarily slowed them.

In "Human Migration and the Marginal Man," he summarized the problem accordingly: "All our so-called racial problems grow out of situations in which assimilation and amalgamation do not take place at all, or take place very slowly. As I have said elsewhere, the chief obstacle to the cultural assimilation of races is not their different mental, but rather their divergent physical traits" (353). America's system of racial caste separation was an instance of accommodation, not assimilation, as he invoked his previous categories (354). At the same time, Park was concluding that, "nation within a nation" notwithstanding, the result of forced segregation was not exactly cultural distinction. The racial laws and etiquette of the South meant that white people and African Americans were still "strangers," he wrote in the introduction to Charles Johnson's 1934 *Shadow of the Plantation*. "One way in which this fact finds expression is in the statement that the Negro has not yet been, and perhaps never can be, assimilated" (76), but Park went on to say that "culturally he be a purely native product" and that the Negro "is not assimilated, though in just what sense this is true it is difficult to say" (77). Park, and Chicago sociology more generally, were thus formulating the question of African American assimilation as a problem of social barriers to be overcome, and not in Hurston's anthropology's terms of a distinct and viable culture existing within the United States. One way to put this distinction is that Park and Chicago sociology were not cultural pluralists: to the extent that there were different African American practices and values, such cultural distinctions were reactions to a racist society that kept the races separated by law and custom.

🎇 Richard Wright and Chicago Sociology

> *In practically all its divergences, American Negro culture is
> not something independent of general American culture. It is
> a distorted development, or a pathological condition, of the
> general American culture.* The instability of the Negro
> family, the inadequacy of educational facilities for
> Negroes, the emotionalism in the Negro church, the
> insufficiency and unwholesomeness of Negro rec-
> reational activity, the plethora of Negro social orga-
> nizations, the narrowness of interests of the average
> Negro, the provincialism of his political speculation,
> the high Negro crime rate, the cultivation of the arts
> to the neglect of other fields, superstition, personality
> difficulties, and other characteristic traits are mainly
> forms of social pathology which, for the most part,
> are created by caste pressures.
>
> This can be said positively: *we assume that it is to
> the advantage of American Negroes as individuals and as
> a group to become assimilated into American culture, to
> acquire the traits held in esteem by the dominant white
> Americans.* This will be the value premise here. We do
> not imply that white American culture is "higher"
> than other cultures in an absolute sense. The notion
> popularized by anthropologists that *all* cultures may
> be good under the different conditions to which
> they are adaptations, and that no derogatory associa-
> tion should *a priori* be attached to primitive cultures,
> is a wholesome antidote to arrogant and erroneous
> ideas closely bound up with white people's false racial
> beliefs and their justification of caste. But it does not
> gainsay our assumption that *here, in America,* Ameri-
> can culture is "highest" in the pragmatic sense that
> adherence to it is practical for any individual or group
> which is not strong enough to change it.
>
> —Gunnar Myrdal, *An American Dilemma,*
> 1944 (928–29)

It was an entirely different conception of minority culture from that of Zora
Neale Hurston and anthropology that Richard Wright embraced when he
articulated his vision of African American citizenship in terms of Chicago
sociology, particularly that of Robert Park. Wright's own account of his discovery of sociology is not understated. In Chicago in 1929, Wright pursued
his self-education by reading Stein, Crane, and Dostoevski, but recalled the
importance of sociology above these "new realms of feeling":

> But the most important discoveries came when I veered from fic-
> tion proper into the field of psychology and sociology. I ran through
> volumes that bore upon the causes of my conduct and the conduct

of my family. I studied tables of figures relating population density to insanity, relating housing to disease, relating school and recreational opportunities to crime, relating various forms of neurotic behavior to environment, relating racial insecurities to the conflicts between whites and blacks. (*Black Boy* 327)

In this extraordinary account, Wright learns about himself and his family through his reading of sociology.

An even more astonishing account of what sociology did for Wright comes in his introduction to Horace Cayton and St. Claire Drake's *Black Metropolis,* where he writes of his

> dumb yearning to write, to tell my story. But I did not know what my story was, and it was not until I stumbled upon science that I discovered some of the meanings of the environment that battered and taunted me. I encountered the work of men who were studying the Negro community, amassing facts about urban Negro life, and I found that sincere art and honest science were not far apart, that each could enrich the other. The huge mountains of fact piled up by the Department of Sociology at the University of Chicago gave me my first concrete vision of the forces that molded the urban Negro's body and soul. [...]
>
> It was from the scientific findings of men like the late Robert E. Park, Robert Redfield, and Louis Wirth that I drew the meanings for my documentary book, *12,000,000 Black Voices;* for my novel, *Native Son;* it was from their scientific facts that I absorbed some of that quota of inspiration necessary for me to write *Uncle Tom's Children* and *Black Boy.* (xvii–xviii)

Here the obvious hyperbole—that he did not know his own story, and that, in fact, he had not even experienced life as an "urban Negro" until he read the sociology of the University of Chicago—signals that we probably should not read this literally, but as an acknowledgment of how deeply sociology helped Wright to articulate his "vision."[6] This statement is not unlike his contention (which would have driven Hurston around the bend) that it was Gertrude Stein's *Three Lives* that "had been the first to fascinate Wright with the beauty of the Negro language" (Fabre 286). In both cases, his own experience seems to have become, if we are to take him at his word, comprehensible to himself only after being circulated through white social scientists and white literary modernists.

Wright read and was influenced by many Chicago sociologists, including Wirth, Park, and Redfield, and likely by the five very important mid-century

African American sociologists trained at the University of Chicago, E. Franklin Frazier, Charles Johnson, Horace Cayton, St. Clair Drake, and Bertram S. Doyle—who were all, with the exception of Drake, supervised and trained by Park. In his introduction to *Black Metropolis,* for instance, Wright cites Wirth's *The Ghetto,* Park and Burgess's *The City,* Stonequist's *The Marginal Man,* Redfield's *Tepotzlan,* Frazier's *The Negro Family in Chicago* and *The Negro Family in the United States,* and Doyle's *The Etiquette of Race Relations in the South* as being particularly important (xix). A seventeen-page "Bibliography on [the] Negro in Chicago," composed for the Illinois Writers Project in 1936, makes clear the range of his readings in sociology. It includes key social science of the period, like Frazier's 1932 *Negro Family in Chicago* (his dissertation supervised by Park), Herskovits's 1928 *American Negro: A Study in Racial Crossings* (which included some of Hurston's anthropometric data), Johnson's 1933 *Economic Status of Negroes* (a report on a conference of that theme), and three important articles by Park himself, including "Racial Assimilation in Secondary Groups" (1913), "Methods of a Race Survey" (1925), and "Mentality of Racial Hybrids" (1931).[7] It was with the first essay, noted above, that Park began construing African American assimilation as momentarily stalled not because of a vigorous black culture but because of racist social barriers. Given Wright's extraordinary claims about the influence of sociology on him, it is reasonable to conclude that he paid careful attention to this material. Wright also knew many of these sociologists personally, developing in later years friendships with Cayton and Myrdal particularly.[8]

In her chapter on Wright, Cappetti shows convincingly how he uses these sociological frames and findings in his autobiography *Black Boy/American Hunger,* noting that it was conceived as "a life history of migration from the South to the North, from rural to urban society, from folk culture to modern civilization" (*Writing* 183). Wright's procedure is often documentary, in the sociological method of reporting on urban characters and their histories (199). The notion of representativeness—as with *Black Boy* generally, but also with the biographical sketches he did of Party members in *Black Boy*—may also have been borrowed from sociology. As Cappetti suggests: "Wright's view of Ross's life-story contains both the sociological idea of the individual as 'typical,' as representative of a group and of its experiences, and the literary idea of narration as a search for order and meaning" ("Sociology" 38). Wright's interest in gangs and delinquency is further evidence of the impact that sociology had on his life (*Writing Chicago* 200–201), but Cappetti's major argument is that the struggles that dramatically structure Wright's autobiography—against his family, his neighborhood institutions like school and church, and then against the Communist Party—mirror sociology's understanding (in, say, texts like *The Polish Peasant*) of the struggle of the individual personality against conformist social forces. "More than simply a record of Wright's experiences, *Black Boy* is a selection of episodes organized, like the sociologists' monographs, around the categories of family, culture, environment, and personality," asserts Cappetti (207).

My task here is complementary to Cappetti's argument. Focusing on Wright's most famous novel rather than his autobiography, I argue that his immersion in Chicago sociology helped him formulate a vision of urban life in terms of the competition, conflict, accommodation, and assimilation cycle. My contention is that it was much more than "tables of figures" and "mountains of fact" that Wright learned from Chicago sociology. This work became for Wright a way of conceptualizing the status of African American culture and what social and political goals it might work toward. These were questions for Wright that, beginning in the mid 1930s and extending into the 1940s, Marxism had incomplete answers for, precisely because, as Wright was to find out, it elided the problem of race that the Chicago school of sociology made central. While the American Communist Party of the 1930s and early 1940s generated many pages of ink devoted to "the Negro problem," it was Wright's experience, centrally dramatized in his *American Hunger* but also in Ralph Ellison's *Invisible Man,* that its commitment was only superficial and tactical.

As we have seen, the square one of the new twentieth-century social science was the paradigm shift inaugurated by Boas's work, of reinterpreting group characteristics as determined by learned culture and local environment rather than by biological race. *Native Son* is simply a study of the central importance of social environment instead of racial heredity in determining individual characteristics. The most crucial episode of that drama—where Wright most compellingly adopts a rhetorical strategy of redescribing difference as environmental and cultural rather than biological—is the extended courtroom scene at the end of the novel. Max's defense of Bigger's crimes rests on how the environment has created the criminal; conversely, the prosecutor appeals to the grossest racial concepts from the nineteenth century in order to suggest that what Bigger has done is, in a sense, natural.

While Max's sociology-inspired defense is offered first, the prosecuting attorney Buckley is given the last word, perhaps signaling Wright's opinion that America was not yet willing to hear sociology's racial truths (and Marxism's class truths), but remained content with its racist traditions. Central to Buckley's case is the Jim Crow logic of the sexual threat posed to white women by black men. But equally central is the racial language he employs. As this demagogue warns the court, "at this very moment some half-human black ape may be climbing through the windows of our homes to rape, murder, and burn our daughters!" (408). Buckley's characterization of Bigger in terms of speciation raises some of the oldest and most racist troping of racial theory: that, as the theory of polygenesis argued, the different races were actually different species. Bigger is rendered "half-human," is likened to an "ape" (413), and also a "dog" (409), "bestial" (408), a "lizard" (409), a "beast" (410, 412), a "cur" (412), and a "rattler" (413). Bigger destroyed Mary's body, says Buckley, joining the racial language to the sexual dynamic animating segregation, because "That treacherous beast must have known that if the marks of his teeth were ever seen on the innocent white flesh of her breasts" he would have been lynched (412).

Buckley is only echoing the conventional discourse of racial biology. Before he is tried, Bigger reads a *Chicago Tribune* account of his crimes, one replete with the concepts of biological race:

> "He looks exactly like an ape!" exclaimed a terrified young white girl who watched the black slayer being loaded onto a stretcher [...].
>
> Though the Negro killer's body does not seem compactly built, he gives the impression of possessing abnormal physical strength. He is about five feet, nine inches tall and his skin is exceedingly black. His lower jaw protrudes obnoxiously, reminding one of a jungle beast.
>
> His arms are long, hanging in a dangling fashion to his knees. [...]
>
> His shoulders are huge, muscular, and he keeps them hunched, as if about to spring upon you at any moment. [...]
>
> All in all, he seems a beast utterly untouched by the softening influences of modern civilization. [...]
>
> He acted like an earlier missing link in the human species. He seemed out of place in a white man's civilization. (279–80)

The article ends by quoting a Southern newspaper's recommendation of lynching, increased segregation, and racial etiquette, and its warning that "a minor portion of white blood in his veins" might have made Bigger more cunning (280–81). While this newspaper account seems over the top in terms of its racist demagoguery—Wright putting too fine a point on it—it is in fact directly modeled on, and sometimes a quotation from, 1938 *Chicago Tribune* accounts of Robert Nixon's murder trial, the courtroom of which Wright had visited (Kinnamon 69 and Fabre 172, 556).

Native Son emphasizes the language of racial biology not because it needs to show that Buckley and his society are racist, but because Wright is centrally interested in dramatizing the conflict between two different accounts of what makes us who we are: biological race versus environment and culture. The purpose of rehearsing the biological language of animalism and speciation is to show that even the discourse of the most immutable and seemingly natural of differences is scientifically wrong. That is why Max's defense is as much an expression of Boas's argument that what have been considered racial traits are actually produced by environment, as it is a Marxist critique of class relations in liberal capitalism. *Native Son* proposes this fundamental substitution: while other African Americans fear that Bigger's crime will mean that white people will think all black people are like this (251), treating Bigger's act in terms of a racial typology (276), Wright agrees with the typology part, but wants the reader to understand environment and upbringing as the new content of the type.[9]

In Max's speech, which Wright supposedly composed "as a repository for his [Marxist] ideological views, as articulated by Bigger's lawyer" (Fabre 173), the Marxist class critique is strangely thin, giving way to the more important sociological understanding. It consists primarily of indicting the hypocrisy with which Dalton the philanthropist gives money for ping pong tables to charities on the South Side, even as he employs Bigger as a chauffeur and owns most of the real estate company that rents substandard housing to Bigger's family at market prices made artificially high because of conventional segregation (386). But despite many critics' interpretation of Max as representing a Marxist perspective (e.g., Tolentino 396, Fabre 173), his speeches are more committed to establishing the social science truths of how deprived environments can produce degeneracy. His language is sociological: "complex forces of society" are revealed by Bigger's crime (382), not racial essence. Max's rhetoric replaces the prosecutor's biological language of racial and species difference with the biological language of ecology, thus directly drawing on Chicago sociology's conception of the city as the organism's environment. There is "a mode of *life* in our midst" that is native to the "soil" prepared by America, he argues (388), and later reverses the product of this metaphor when he imagines that the environment of "the wild forest of our great cities, amid the rank and choking vegetation of slums" produces not "a mode of *life*" but rather a pathological "corpse" (392). In either case, it is not heredity that makes the son "native" (and in this echo of the novel's title comes sociology's vigorous challenge to nativist racism), but rather the "soil" of the urban slum. Picturing urban Chicago in ecological terms renders the organism as something without agency or self-consciousness. Both Bigger and the mob that seeks to destroy him are thus "powerless pawns in a blind play of social forces" of misunderstanding (390), echoing the deterministic side of Parkian sociology. Given these forces and this ecological model of urban sociology, Max suggests that the court should "sit to ponder why there are not more like him!" (394).

The sociological model also allows an indictment of segregation and its psychological effects on African Americans. "Our civilization" has much to offer, says Max, but it keeps black children separated and so prohibits them their enjoyment (394). The allures of white America "are daily taunts. Imagine a man walking amid such a scene, a part of it, and yet knowing that it is *not* for him!" (394). Particularly important to Max in this regard—and prescient of the desegregationist works of the 1950s, Lorraine Hansberry's *Raisin in the Sun* and the Supreme Court's *Brown v. Board of Education*—are the enforcement of racial segregation in real estate and in schools. Real estate restrictions, such as those enforced by Dalton's company, keep African Americans in the "ghetto-areas of cities" (395). One result of such forced separation, as intended, is the regular oppression that helps maintain white power; and white power in turn is maintained precisely as it becomes part of the environment—"part of the natural structure of the universe" (396)—that conditions young African Americans.

Other qualities of sociology that infuse Max's speech clarify Wright's different understanding of "culture" from the anthropological paradigm of Hurston, and from the third-phase cultural nationalists who went on to claim him (not very compellingly) as a predecessor. Most important, Wright's image of a just society is assimilationist: one in which, the artificial barriers of racial segregation having been destroyed, African Americans are fully integrated into America's cities and America's culture. Max asks the court rhetorically, "The more you kill, the more you deny and separate, the more they will seek another form and way of life, however blindly and unconsciously. And out of what can they weave a different life, out of what can they mold a new existence, living organically in the same towns and cities, the same neighborhoods with us?" (397–98). It is segregation that here produces a different "way of life"—that is, a "culture"—but not in the Hurstonian anthropological paradigm of holism, pluralism, health, and equality. The conclusion for Max (and Wright) is Park's argument that there can only be a stunted marginal order around the central civilization. That culture, such as it is, is pathological, as revealed in Max's contention, "This Negro boy's entire attitude toward life is a *crime!*" (400): forcibly and artificially separated from the benefits of the dominant culture, Bigger and those like him are driven to discover some other ecological niche "in the same towns and cities" as whites. Bigger has different cultural practices and values, but they are pathological insofar as Bigger remains unassimilated into dominant American life. When Max says Bigger and others are "excluded from, and unassimilated in our society" (400), his very use of the terminology of assimilation is not accidental, but central to Wright's political vision articulated through Parkian sociology.

If African American culture was not distinct and healthy—as Hurston believed—then there could not be anything for the latter generation's cultural nationalism to be nationalistic toward. On the one hand, Max's language of the "nation within a nation," itself used by Park (who was quoting Booker T. Washington), anticipates the formulation that some Black Arts critics would use a generation later. As Max puts it,

> Multiply Bigger Thomas twelve million times, allowing for environmental and temperamental variations, and for those Negroes who are completely under the influence of the church, and you have the psychology of the Negro people. But once you see them as a whole, once your eyes leave the individual and encompass the mass, a new quality comes into the picture. Taken collectively, they are not simply twelve million people; in reality they constitute a separate nation, stunted, stripped, and held captive *within* this nation, devoid of political, social, economic, and property rights. (397)

The cultural nationalism of the Black Arts movement would, like Max, see "the mass" "collectively," and like Max, it would conceive of that mass as "a separate nation," and again like Max, it would see that nation as forged in the fires of oppression.

But what marks the distance between *Native Son* and the Black Aesthetic c. 1965–1975 is that the solution imagined by Max and Wright—the destruction of the forge itself, and the consequent integration into the dominant culture—is the thing that is to be given up as the failed solution, following the Civil Rights integrationist era between *Brown* and 1965. What made the cultural nationalists to come more like Hurston and less like Wright was their idea that, while a separate culture might have been formed through oppression (in ways that Hurston avoided recognizing but which were central to Wright), it was essentially more healthy and not pathological (which was Hurston's conclusion, and not Wright's), and should be affirmed by African Americans in the United States who already constituted, whether they knew it or not, a "separate nation." The conception of culture that the nationalists arrived at, whatever else they shared with Wright, was actually Hurstonian, partaking of Boasian anthropology rather than Parkian sociology.

Another way to illustrate the difference between Wright's vision and that of the nationalists who came later is the airplane episode. After waking in his family's slum apartment and his victorious battle with the rat, Bigger meets Gus on the way to the poolroom. As they smoke on the sidewalk, a skywriting plane provokes in Bigger a "childlike wonder" (16). They appreciate the writing, and that "Them white boys sure can fly" because "They get a chance to do everything." But Bigger is moved "reflectively, as though talking to himself," to suggest that "I could fly one of them things if I had a chance" (16). The historically specific rather than natural conditions that prevent him from flying the planes are quickly enumerated by Gus: "If you wasn't black and if you had some money and if they'd let you go to that aviation school, you *could* fly a plane" (17). Their response to "all the 'ifs' " is more laughter, but also the continuing analysis of "how the white folks treat us" (17). We are to understand that under more just social conditions Bigger could have focused on aviation school and that with such a possibility, what happens in the next four hundred pages would never take place.

The whole point of Bigger envying flight, in other words, is not that he (or Wright) wants a fleet of black airplanes, or countries of black pilots. Such is actually Ras the Exhorter's nationalist argument in Ralph Ellison's *Invisible Man*. Ellison has Ras, the composite figure made up partly of Marcus Garvey and anticipatory of the black nationalism to come, also look up from a city sidewalk to see a white-piloted airplane in the sky. Whereas Bigger and Gus are moved to consider the oppression that keeps them from flying airplanes, Ras "shook his fist toward the plane and yelled, 'Hell with him, some day we have them too! Hell with him!' " (374). "Him" is the Man, the white-dominated nation, and Ras's nationalist response is to imagine a racial entity that includes a fleet of black planes and black pilots. The integrationist's airplane prompts a critique of the barriers that prevent participation; the nationalist's airplane provokes a promise of a future equivalency in the power of a separate racial "nation" (to use the word of Max, Park, and Washington) or "empire" (a word Garvey used to describe his political goals).

I have stressed here the extent to which Wright's vision and politics were indebted to sociology, just as Hurston's were to anthropology. At the same time, however, Wright's use of social science was just as critical as Hurston's. A strange episode in *Native Son* suggests that Wright's enthusiasm for sociology was more tempered than his declarations in *Black Boy* and *Black Metropolis* indicate. While Bigger is in jail, a slightly crazed "brown-skinned Negro" (342) is placed in the cell with him. The man threatens to "report you to the President" unless the jailors return "my papers" and accuses them of wanting to "destroy all my evidence" (343). Another inmate explains the man's problem:

> "He went off his nut from studying too much at the university. He was writing a book on how colored people live and he says somebody stole all the facts he'd found. He says he's got to the bottom of why colored folks are treated bad and he's going to tell the President and have things changed, see? He's *nuts*! He swears that his university professor had him locked up. The cops picked him up this morning in his underwear; he

was in the lobby of the Post Office building, waiting to speak to the President." (343)

Though the man appears "insane" to Bigger, he screams out what seem like Chicago sociology truths: that "you make us live in such crowded conditions on the South Side that one out of every ten of us is insane!"; that "you dump all the stale foods into the Black Belt and sell them for more than you can get anywhere else!"; that "you tax us, but you won't build hospitals!"; that "the schools are so crowded that they breed perverts!"; that "you hire us last and fire us first!" (344). The man is eventually carted off in a strait-jacket and stretcher, thus invoking the standard literary trope that those who speak truth to power are deemed mad. But the fact that this African American student says that his professor—presumably a white University of Chicago professor of sociology like Park or Wirth—has had him locked up after stealing his labor suggests a possible critique of the way in which African American sociologists (like Du Bois or Cayton or Frazier?) have been estranged or excluded from, or exploited by, the practices of knowledge that sociology produces. Perhaps Wright was aware of instances in which the "huge mountains of fact piled up by the Department of Sociology at the University of Chicago" were unacknowledged borrowings of "all the facts" found by African American sociologists.

A later scene in which Bigger reads newspaper accounts of his crime also suggests Wright's critical attitude toward social science work on race:

> Professional psychologists at University of Chicago pointed out this morning that white women have an unusual fascination for Negro men. "They think," said one of the professors who requested that his name not be mentioned in connection with the case, "that white women are more attractive than the women of their own race. They just can't help themselves." (366)

As with the previous scene of instruction, there is some ambiguity. On the one hand, this could be merely the "duh" factor that sometimes arises in the social sciences: here, the simple truism that prohibition increases desire. But on the other hand, the passage suggests that by the late 1930s Wright had become a critical consumer of social science ideas, which were to be evaluated and not treated as the language of truth arriving from outside society. This seems especially true given the concluding self-satisfied line from the psychologist that black men "just can't help themselves," which dangerously does not care whether the purported special attraction is congenital or learned (and because it does not care, of course the former would be assumed).

Furthermore, Tolentino and Rowley are correct in distinguishing between Chicago sociology's laissez-faire liberalism and Wright's more progressive politics, though neither accounts for the nuances of sociology well enough to make sense of how Wright critically distances himself from the social science discipline that had informed his model of minority culture. Indeed, Parkian sociology was too deterministic for the intertwined progressive integrationist politics of Wright, the NAACP, and Gunnar Myrdal's *American Dilemma*. Park imagined the liberal ethnic assimilation of racialized minorities, even in the face of laws and customs designed to prevent it, as a kind of unalterable natural law; human beings were unable to greatly hasten or slow this process modeled on ecology. There was little room for liberal reform or progressive politics: Park did not necessarily oppose either one, but did not think they could so easily change organic social forces that were already transforming themselves fairly rapidly under modern pressures.

The story of Wright meeting Park nicely captures the conservative strain of Park's liberal sociology. After *Native Son* was published, Wright visited Horace Cayton in Chicago in 1941. Coinciding with his visit was Robert Park's visit to Chicago from Fisk University, where he had been invited by Charles Johnson to join the faculty following his retirement from the University of Chicago. Over Wright's protests, the elderly Park struggled to rise from his seat, saying first, "I rise in your honor, sir," and then posing a challenging question for the newly famous Wright: "How in hell did you happen?" (Rowley 250). One has to laugh with Park, who, in this moment of self-irony, manages to see the way in which the real Wright escapes Park's sociological scheme. Although Park cannot understand (or pretends not to understand) how Wright's environment could have produced someone who seemed so ecologically out of place, the story signifies both Park's (self-conscious) determinism and the problematic fact that Wright, while accepting most of this determinist argument, was himself a partial refutation of it. Park's question—"How in hell did you happen?"—was echoed years later by Ralph Ellison's complaint that "Wright could imagine Bigger, but Bigger could not possibly imagine Richard Wright" ("World" 114). In both cases, Park and Ellison recognized that the deterministic sociological vision animating *Native Son* was problematically, if only partly, refuted by Wright's own career. Park would learn a little more about how in hell Wright happened when he attended Wright's lecture at Fisk in April 1943. His talk was called "What I've Been Thinking," and its stormy reception—Wright later recalled, "It crashed upon me that I was saying things that Negroes were not supposed to say publicly"—led to his decision to write his autobiography *Black Boy* (Rowley 280).

Rowley points to Park's conservatism, his association with Booker T. Washington, and the condemnation of Park's "do-nothing fatalism" by Gunnar Myrdal in *An American Dilemma* (250) as evidence of the difference between Wright and the great Chicago sociologist. These are correct but overstated distinctions because they do not credit the way in which Park's model of culture underpinned not only Wright's first three books, but also *An American Dilemma* and the NAACP's legal strategy in *Brown v. Board of Education* (whose connections I address in detail in chapter three). In fact, the difference between Park's skepticism at reformist programs and the do-something politics of Wright and Myrdal is an argument that took place entirely within the paradigm of culture that Park and Chicago sociology established. The really important difference is not between Park's determinism and Wright, Myrdal, and the NAACP's activism, but between Park's sociological model of culture, shared by Chicago sociology, Wright, Myrdal and the NAACP, and Boas's anthropological model of culture, shared by Columbia anthropology, Hurston, and the cultural nationalists who emerged at the end of the 1960s.

Thus even as Wright was critiquing social science for its occasional reproduction of racist beliefs, its skepticism of political and social reform, and its exploitation and exclusion of people who—by its very own findings and arguments—were entirely capable of producing social science knowledge, he nonetheless articulated his own literary projects through it. Wright's acceptance of sociology's culture concept suggests that those claiming Wright as a predecessor of cultural nationalism, pluralism, and multiculturalism have essentially misrecognized his cultural politics. Such readings not only torque *Uncle Tom's Children* and *Native Son* into a kind of literary nationalism that he objected to, but they also misunderstand his essentially assimilationist stance. In later chapters I show how our current paradigm of literary multiculturalism arose from the cultural pluralisms and black (and red, brown, and yellow) nationalisms of books like Toni Morrison's *Bluest Eye,* Ishmael Reed's *Mumbo Jumbo,* N. Scott Momaday's *House Made of Dawn,* Gloria Anzaldúa's *Borderlands/La Frontera,* and Frank Chin's *Chickencoop Chinamen.* But what has frequently accompanied the entrenching of this multiculturalist paradigm is the attempt to read authors who were not pluralists as though they contained the seeds of the multiculturalism.

Such is true of a wide variety of Wright's critics, from his first literary biographer, Michel Fabre, publishing at the height of black nationalism (1973), through his editor Richard Yarborough writing the introduction to *Uncle Tom's Children* twenty years later, to even a revisionist queering of

Wright's work by Roderick Ferguson in *Aberrations in Black* (2003). Following his account of the composition of *Black Boy,* Fabre remarks:

> Wright's conception of the black man's role in the United States actually foreshadowed that later held by advocates of Black Power in the sixties. Wright himself never opposed integration and in fact did everything in his power to promote it. By integration, however, he did not mean a more or less disguised form of amalgamation, but rather an equality among the several ethnic cultures in American society that would permit them not only to survive but also to enrich the national culture precisely because they had retained their individuality and not been reduced to a common denominator. (260)

Fabre dubiously ascribes to Wright a classically Boasian definition of cultural pluralism—"an equality among the several ethnic cultures"—and a proto-multiculturalist gesture imagining that they all "enrich" the nation. But the evidence for reading Wright as a cultural pluralist is almost non-existent. He did, besides, in his marriage to Ellen Poplowitz, practice "amalgamation" in Park's sense of the word of racial intermarriage, which, Park noted, sometimes attended and frequently hastened cultural assimilation.

Like Yarborough, Roderick Ferguson cherry-picks "Blueprint for Negro Writing" to produce an account of Wright as a cultural nationalist *avant le mot*. Situating what he calls "the black nationalist writings of Richard Wright" (32) beside the discourse of Chicago sociology, Ferguson argues that "Wright formulated his version of cultural nationalism" through a "specifically masculine revolutionary agency" that invoked "heteropatriarchal regulation[s]" derived from Chicago sociology (45). Citing "Blueprint's" claims for African American folklore, Ferguson sees it as the basis of an "African American nationalism" that "could effectively restore African American masculinity" and solve the social disorganization of the kind that, says Ferguson, Chicago sociology repeatedly claimed to locate on the South Side (46). While it is not always clear what nationalism means to Ferguson—at one point it becomes synonymous with Marxism (46)—Ferguson ignores how Chicago sociology understood nationalisms of any kind as only temporary pauses in its vision of ultimate assimilation.

Like Yarborough, Ferguson takes Wright at his own word, even when it is clear that Wright's prescriptive utterances about literature did not match his own creative work. Wright disdains in "Blueprint" previous African American literature characterized by "the voice of the educated Negro pleading with white America for justice" (98)—but of course, *Native Son,* even if its tone is demanding rather than pleading, was nonetheless written primarily for whites with justice in mind. Wright's longest disquisition on African American "culture" comes in this essay as well, where he writes that its two sources are "the Negro church" and "the folklore of the Negro people" (99). The first may initially have been "revolutionary," at least until it "began to serve as an antidote for suffering and denial," but "the archaic morphology of Christian salvation" clearly contends against the revolutionary (and not accommodationist) and universalist potential of Marxism—and so it is not, in Wright's view, a progressive force for African Americans. But in words that bring him as close to Hurston as he ever got—almost as if he'd just read *Jonah's, Mules,* and *Eyes*—Wright continues,

> It was, however, in a folklore molded out of rigorous and inhuman conditions of life that the Negro achieved his most indigenous and complete expression. Blues, spirituals, and folk tales recounted from mouth to mouth; the whispered words of a black mother to her black daughter on the ways of men, to confidential wisdom of a black father to his black son; the swapping of sex experiences on street corners from boy to boy in the deepest vernacular; work songs sung under blazing suns—all these formed the channels through which the racial wisdom flowed. (99)

Wright is not far from Alain Locke's Renaissance formulation when he imagines folklore as the raw material that has yet to achieve artistry "for lack of husbanding by alert intelligence" (100). This folklore was the basis of the "unmistakable" "nationalist character of the Negro people" (100).

The problem with Wright's formulation, of course, is that he did not go on to follow his own advice: *Native Son* is totally uninterested in African American folklore and is outright hostile to African American religious traditions. But as Wright continues, in words that put him at odds with both the cultural nationalists to come and with those who want to read him as a proto-multiculturalist, "The Negro people did not ask for this ["Negro way of life in America"], and deep down, though they express themselves through their institutions and adhere to this special way of life, they do not want it now. This special existence was forced upon them from without by lynch rope, bayonet and mob rule" (100). To the extent that there is a minority culture, in other words, it is a survival strategy produced by exclusion from the dominant society—which is the essential idea, not coincidentally, voiced by Park in the conclusion of his essay "Racial Assimilation."

And if one reads "Blueprint" to its end, Wright sees this nationalism, to the extent that it exists, as something that must be worked through only in order to be ultimately discarded: "Negro writers must accept the nationalist implications of their lives, not in order to encourage them, but in order to change and transcend them" (101). Anticipating Max's sociology-inspired ecological figure, Wright continues "liberal writers of all races can help to break the stony soil of aggrandizement out of which the stunted plants of Negro nationalism grow. And, simultaneously, Negro writers can help to weed out these choking growths of reactionary nationalism and replace them with hardier and sturdier types" (106). Wright's argument in "Blueprint," then, is that Negro nationalism—the "Negro way of life in America" produced by the particular history of racial oppression in the United States—must be abandoned for a Marxist perspective that will ultimately enable African American participation in a fully reformed and critically integrated society. If Bigger was "a Negro nationalist in a vague sense because he was not allowed to live as an American," as Wright wrote in "How Bigger Was Born" (451), the solution is not to make future Biggers more nationalist (nationalist in more than "a vague sense") but to make it possible for each to "live as an American."

The Difference of Culture: Wright's Sociology and Hurston's Anthropology

> [Wright] approached this highly religious country [of the Gold Coast] as an unbending rationalist. To him, ancestor worship and West African juju were ludicrous "mumbo-jumbo" that needed to be eradicated—by force if necessary. He thought the tribal chiefs "preposterous" figures, with their "foolishly gaudy" huge umbrellas and their "outlandish regalia." He wrote in his journal: "Their claims about their ability to appease the dead is a fraud, their many wives are a seductive farce . . . their justice is barbaric, their interpretations of life are contrary to common sense."
>
> —Hazel Rowley, *Richard Wright,* 2001 (429)

My argument, then, is not just, as Robert Hemenway concludes in his discussion of Hurston and Wright, that Hurston was right culturally and that Wright was right politically about their portrayal of black life in the South (333–34). The more significant difference between them is that they understood African American culture in completely different ways. Boasian anthropology, as we have seen, began with the premise of racial equality, conceptually disengaged culture from race, and went on to model culture in terms of dynamic holism, historical particularism, pluralism, and relativism. It was only the implication of gradual assimilation that Hurston did not adopt. Since environment played such a heavy part in conditioning individuals, it would effect the disappearance of cultural traits among the next generations, especially as people moved from the sites of traditional culture, as with the

Great Migration. This problem is mentioned only in passing in *The Mind of Primitive Man,* and is made with respect to immigrant cultural traits (and not African American ones) as a way of providing evidence for Boas's argument that race did not confer cultural traits.

Boas envisioned the study of people undergoing changes in their ways of life because of contact with other peoples, but "it remained for those who came after him to develop the techniques of studying cultural dynamics through research among peoples [...] actually undergoing change in their cultures through contact with other modes of life" (Herskovits, *Franz Boas* 70). More specifically, the problem of acculturation and assimilation became the purview of sociology, particularly that developed at the University of Chicago by Robert Park and others. Park, as we have seen, extended the model of cultural assimilation to racialized minorities, thus pursuing to the end the logic of Boas's disengagement of culture from race through arguing that what applied to European immigration could be extended, under the right conditions, to African Americans and Asian Americans in American cities. It was naming and establishing those right conditions that interested Richard Wright, who explicitly drew on sociology in order to think through the effects of the city on minority communities. Thus the assimilationist implications of Boas's work, which were ignored by Hurston, were developed by Park and embraced by Wright.

To put their differences schematically, we could say that Wright accepted racial equality, was uninterested in the project of treating cultures as composed of complex wholes, agreed with the concentration on historical forces, disagreed with cultural relativism, agreed with the disengagement of culture from race, and agreed with the implied process of assimilation. Indeed, racial equality, the separation of race and culture, and assimilation are social science ideas that unite Boas, Park, and Wright. The real contention between Wright and Hurston was the ideas encompassed by cultural relativism (with Hurston in favor and Wright disagreeing) and implied assimilation (with Wright in favor and Hurston disagreeing). Secondary differences could also be drawn between them in what they thought about cultural holism (for instance, work is an aspect of African American culture important to Hurston because it is part of the social fabric inseparable from tales, social relations, foodways, and so on, whereas labor is important to consider for Wright because by paying attention to such conditions one can identify oppressive social structures that prevent integration) and historical particularism (historical contingencies explain cultural elements and meanings for Hurston, but are sources of economic and social inequalities for Wright).

Hurston's commitment to a different model of African American culture from that of Richard Wright and the integrationists in the NAACP explains her opposition to the forced desegregation decision represented by *Brown v. Board of Education*. It is not that Hurston was in favor of segregation and Jim Crow laws: in December 1945 she declared, "I am for complete repeal of All Jim Crow Laws in the United States once and for all, and right now" (qtd. in Boyd 381).[10] For Hurston, the South was not a site of oppression and the North was not a racial utopia; conversely, black culture was not deprived or pathological insofar as it was not the same as, or missing the supposed beneficial influences of, white culture. The rejection of both these political ideas emerges from her commitment to Boasian anthropology's concept of culture.[11] Her experience of growing up in Eatonville had shown her that African American culture was anything but pathological or deprived, and it could appear so only to the outsider bringing in his own set of supposedly universal but actually culturally specific criteria, thus violating the tenet of cultural relativism.

The project of integration in general, which implied that African American people should become more like white people, was an idea that also contravened Boas's conception of very slow cultural change through gradual adaptation and transformation from within. *Brown*'s politics were not gradual adaptation: *Brown* threatened the wholesale and sudden abandonment by black families of black cultural traditions and black sites of cultural autonomy, like Eatonville and Howard University. For Hurston, who had helped to establish cultural continuities over hundreds of years—America's Brer Rabbit and Haiti's Ti Malice were instantiations of the West African trickster Anansi, just as the deities of Louisiana hoodoo and Haitian voodoo were really the old African gods Damballah, Papa Legba, and Erzulie—to all of a sudden give up these long-standing cultural sedimentations in return for the *Dick and Jane* readers of white American schools (as *The Bluest Eye* would imagine it only sixteen years after *Brown*) was not a positive exchange. The nuance of Hurston's politics was that she was an integrationist but was not in favor of *Brown* partly because it threatened the loss of African American cultural distinctiveness: thus her response to *Brown* was to write her angry letter from her cabin in Eau Gallie. Wright, on the other hand, was an integrationist who did not really care about the loss of black cultural distinctiveness because there was for him nothing much worth saving. African American journalist Ollie Stewart recalled Wright's reaction to *Brown*: " 'He had his glasses off,' he recalls, 'and his eyes were lit up with excitement. He was so happy he accepted a beer, although he usually drank coffee. 'It took a long time,' he practically shouted, 'but . . . no matter what happens, the kids will have the law on their side from now on' " (qtd. in Rowley 440)

According to Robert Hemenway, Hurston's conservatism was composed of a) individualism; b) suspicion of communism; and c) social science philosophy. Hemenway rightly sees the last as the most complicated, though he does not register the profound distinctions within social science philosophy between anthropological and sociological conceptions of culture. Boasian anthropology's culture is more conservative than Parkian sociology's culture, primarily because of their different time frames, with anthropology tracing cultural formation, development, and adaptation over tens or even hundreds of generations, and sociology primarily trying to understand cultural changes within only one to three generations. Boasian culture put the conservation into Hurston's conservatism, just as Parkian sociology put the willingness to abandon African American cultural distinctiveness into Wright's integrationism.

That the difference between Hurston and Wright has not been sufficiently understood as actually a difference between anthropology and sociology stems from insufficient attention to the disciplinary distinction in the first place. According to Hemenway, Hurston

> became a folklorist at a time when white sociologists were obsessed with what they thought was pathology in black behavior, when white psychologists spoke of the deviance in black mental health, and when the discipline of anthropology used a research model that identified black people as suffering from cultural deprivation. Hurston's folklore collections refuted these stereotypes by celebrating the distinctiveness of traditional black culture, and her scholarship is now recognized by revisionist scientists questioning the racial assumptions of modern cultural theory. John Szwed, for example, has shown how Boas's early assertion that race and culture were conceptually distinct eventually led anthropologists into a serious misapprehension. Once race and culture were separated, racial differences could be shown to be statistically insignificant. But while proving that there were no racial differences in mental capacity, anthropologists went on to claim that there were no significant *cultural* differences between the races. Out of a zeal to refute genetic racism, but with an ethnocentric bias, many argued that black Americans [quoting Szwed,] "shared essentially the same culture as white Americans, and where they differed, the differences could be accounted for exclusively as the result of environmental deprivation or cultural 'stripping,' but certainly not as the result of any normal cultural procedures."[12] (Hemenway 330)

There are two problems in this passage, both of which are amplified from their source in Szwed's essay itself. It is true that while Hurston was doing her earliest fieldwork in 1927 and 1928 in Florida, work substantiating African American culture that would eventually lead her to a thesis about African retentions, the sociologist Franklin Frazier appears to have been arguing for the cultural erasure of the Middle Passage. Although Frazier suggested that the black family had "failed to conform" in 1927 (qtd. in L. Baker 178), the account of black culture as pathological developed in the 1930s and 1940s (V. Williams, *Rethinking* 111) to enumerate the social cost of racism and segregation. As Lee Baker suggests, it was the white economist Gunnar Myrdal who turned the screw of Frazier's sociology: "Myrdal employed Frazier's basic arguments that all Negroes could obtain a culture as 'legitimate' as that of Whites, but he articulated the notion that 'the simple folk culture of the Negro' was pathological with more force than Frazier did" (180–81). That expression came most forcefully only in the 1944 *American Dilemma,* as my epigraph above makes clear; indeed, "the key contribution of the sociological approach" to black cultural pathology was "the work done by Gunnar Myrdal" (Szwed 159). Thus Hurston's work and its Boasian anthropological model of culture substantially predated the 1940s sociological motif that African Americans had no distinctive culture and that residual distinctiveness was "pathological."

Second, it is just not true that Hurston wrote at a time when "the discipline of anthropology used a research model that identified black people as suffering from cultural deprivation," as Hemenway asserts (330). Hemenway collapses the anthropological model of culture of the 1920s (which, after all, was premised on cultural relativism) into the 1940s sociological paradigm of the essential pathology of black distinctiveness.[13] This confusion emerges to some degree from Szwed's article itself, where he suggests that Boas's key separation of culture from race and his denial of meaningful racial difference might have led to his dismissal of possible cultural differences between the races. But Szwed's inference about what Boas might have thought is glossed only by a quotation from Ruth Benedict's 1940 *Race: Science and Politics* expressing the idea of the cultural erasure undergone in the Middle Passage (157–58). Szwed argues, based on this one quote, that "these anthropologists"—presumably Boas, Benedict, Herskovits, Ashley Montague, and others—began what seemed at the time like a liberal argument that "Afro-Americans shared essentially the same culture as white Americans, and where they differed" (158), the cause was racist institutions and the cultural erasure of the Middle Passage.

In what follows, Szwed says, "Launched and reinforced by these anthropological conceptions, sociologists took up their own version of the same arguments; they soon went much further," using "statistical surveys" (of the kind cited by Wright) but not any ethnography (159). Szwed names the key sociological players—Park, Frazier, Myrdal, Glazer and Moynihan's *Beyond the Melting Pot,* Kenneth Clark, and so forth—as elaborating what became the "orthodoxy" (160) that "lower-class Afro-Americans have no distinctive culture or subculture of their own and what they do have is a non-supportive or pathological version of 'mainstream' American culture" (161). Szwed correctly notes that Herskovits eventually provided a major counterargument to this developing idea, as did the anthropology of Hurston and three other anthropologists (160, 164). Thus the problem with Szwed's argument is that he notes the central difference between a cultural relativist position (that of Hurston) and the cultural pathology position that later developed, but, aside from the single quotation from Benedict, this distinction clearly falls along disciplinary lines. Contrary to his own evidence, Szwed lumps anthropology and sociology together into (drawing on Albert Murray's phrase) "this social-science fiction monster" (163) of black pathology, even when it is clear that Boas, Herskovits, and Hurston all take a cultural relativist position refusing to measure African American culture in terms of white culture. Even the single Benedict quotation ends with "The Negro race has proud cultural achievements, but for very good reasons they were not spread before our eyes in America" (qtd. in Szwed 158)—a dubious assertion of the pathology of cultural difference from white America. Though Szwed has understood his article to be establishing the destructiveness of "an anthropology of pathos" (171), the evidence he provides can be better understood as a *sociology* of pathos, one that he argues against by, in effect, calling for a return to the Boasian tradition of the fieldworking ethnographer upholding the principle of cultural relativism.

Szwed is otherwise correct in seeing that Herskovits's work substantiating African cultural retentions was a problem for integrationist politics (164), which would prefer a model that understood African Americans as either blank slates or almost culturally white. Likewise, Szwed is right to note (and Hemenway is right to follow his lead) that "there is something of a drift of black ideology in the direction of Herskovits' thesis" (165; see also Hemenway 332). The cultural nationalists of the late 1960s returned to the model of culture developed by Boas and Herskovits and embraced by Hurston, rather than that articulated by Park and Wright.

On the other hand, in Szwed's final conclusion noting the "descriptive and historical materials which anthropologists can provide, especially to those colonized peoples who have for so long been cut off from their own histories and traditions" (172), he unintentionally names his era's solution to the vexing problem introduced by the separation of culture from race and cultural relativism: which culture is one, or should one be, practicing? How can one be "cut off" from her "own" history and traditions? In Szwed's account, colonized people—like African Americans—are cut off from "their" traditions, which are theirs not because they are the traditions that the group practices. The group does not practice its traditions; its culture and the traditions they practice (for they must be doing something) are not "theirs." The problem here is, what kind of notion of tradition does one need for it to be a person's even though the person is not doing it? This logic entails not just cultural pluralism, but that minority people, whether "colonized" at home or abroad, should not necessarily do what they are doing, but should do what their ancestors did. As I will argue in more detail in chapter six, this formulation answers the question of which culture we should have by using race. This momentary slippage to race from culture in Szwed—an anthropologist who must know better—becomes emblematic of the productive indistinction between the terms that marks the post-integration third phase.

If I am insisting on this disciplinary difference between the models of culture developed by anthropology and sociology in this first phase of the genealogy of literary multiculturalism, it is because this difference structured the genealogy of African American literature in phases one, two, and three, but also, as I will show, it similarly structured the genealogy of the Asian American, Native American, and Mexican American literary traditions. Hurston's relative disappearance between the 1942 *Dust Tracks* and her rediscovery in 1975 in Alice Walker's *Ms.* article (as both Henry Louis Gates Jr. and Robert Hemenway put it) roughly coincides with the second phase's eclipse of the anthropological model for African American culture and the ascendance of the sociological model for African American culture. I thus, somewhat arbitrarily but not without reason, date the beginning of what I am calling the second phase of the genealogy of literary multiculturalism from the publication of Wright's *Native Son,* which was profoundly influential as a Book of the Month Club offering, and later as a citation in social science research, and the subject of a film by Orson Welles. *Native Son* marks in my genealogy a turning point, wherein the contested models of culture of the first phase gradually waned (with, for instance, Hurston's *Dust Tracks* effectively marking the end of her largest readership and nativist racism spectacularly grounding the 1942 internment of Japanese Americans) as a liberal consensus developed around the sociological model of culture permitting (and sometimes compelling) the cultural assimilation of racialized minorities. As the tide began to turn in 1965, cultural nationalists reacted against this sociological model (Toni Morrison's *Bluest Eye*) or responded favorably to the anthropological one (Ishmael Reed's *Mumbo Jumbo*), or sometimes both (N. Scott Momaday's *House Made of Dawn*). Cultural nationalist authors in this third phase—who established the multicultural literature paradigm we have today—frequently articulated their literary and political projects through a return to Hurston's anthropology and a rejection of Wright's sociology. They were in fact reacting against the sociologically enabled liberal consensus regarding the cultural assimilability of racialized minorities, which is the subject of chapters three and four.

❧ CHAPTER 3

Jade Snow Wong, Ralph Ellison, and Desegregation

> To be sure, when one undertakes the study of the Negro he discovers a great poverty of traditions and patterns of behavior that exercise any real influence on the formation of the Negro's personality and conduct. If, as Keyserling remarks, the most striking thing about the Chinese is their deep culture, the most conspicuous thing about the Negro is his lack of a culture.
>
> —E. Franklin Frazier, "Traditions and Patterns," 1934 (194)

Thus far I have concentrated on the African American literary tradition, with a brief foray into Native American letters represented by D'Arcy McNickle. My more substantial turn in this chapter and the next to the Asian American literary tradition requires some explanation. It is my argument that a dynamic contest among rival models of culture marked what I am calling the first phase of the genealogy of literary multiculturalism, which generally begins with anthropological culture's challenge to racial conceptions of group difference, and ends with the growing challenge to anthropological culture of sociological culture, whose dominance characterizes the second phase of the genealogy. But not all four of the literary traditions were equally represented in the three phases, or before. Of the four literary traditions treated in this book, the African American tradition has historically been the largest (in terms of the greatest number of texts) as well as the oldest (with, probably, Native American literature and oral arts). I have thus necessarily given priority to the African American tradition, as there are few Asian American, Native American, or Mexican American equivalents (in terms of literary importance and influence) to the African American writers of the 1920s and 1930s. That changed in the decades that followed, as writers in these other traditions transformed the multicultural and American literary canons.

The disciplinary differences between Hurston's and Wright's concepts of culture went on to structure the genealogy of African American literature in the rest of the twentieth century, but, additionally, roughly the same differences also structured the developments of the Asian American, Native American, and Mexican American literary traditions. The contesting accounts of what minority culture is and what will happen to it in the United States characterized the development and literary politics in the African American tradition, but they no less characterized the shape of the other three traditions. This is not to say that anthropology and sociology always played the same roles and formed the same circuits with the three traditions as they had in the African American one. For example, sociology understood the African American and Chinese American communities differently—even oppositely, as is suggested by Franklin Frazier in the epigraph to this chapter. A more aggressive way to put this would be to say that Frazier made the sociological argument for the lack of a distinct African American culture by way of Chinese America, just as his mentor and teacher Robert Park had solved the question of the cultural assimilability of racialized African Americans through reference to the American in Japanese disguise in Hawaii. If, as I argue in this chapter and the next, sociology was the discourse underlying the emerging liberal consensus about the cultural assimilability of racialized minorities during the second phase, Frazier's observation indicates that sociology had to provide a different technology for incorporating Asian Americans than that it had provided for African Americans. Chicago sociology understood black America as suffering from cultural indistinction and pathology, but it understood Asian America in terms of a "generation gap," whereby children were separated from the "deep culture" that Frazier saw characterizing their parents. Crossthreading Jade Snow Wong and *Brown v. Board of Education* reveals their shared sociological sensibility, even as Ralph Ellison's work and politics test the limits (but also reveal the strengths) of my three-phase development hypothesis. It is thus the differences in how sociology and anthropology structured the literary traditions of these four communities as well as the similarities that bear further examination. The sociologically enabled liberal consensus of the second phase—which I date from the publication of *Native Son* in 1940 to the passage of the Voting Rights Act, the passage of the Immigration and Naturalization Services Act, the Delano strike, and the Watts riot (all 1965)—was one that Asian American and African American writers generally favored but was a top-down consensus forcefully administered upon non-consenting Native American and Mexican American communities.

One remarkable year in this emerging consensus is 1953. In the year that the Korean War ended and one year before the Supreme Court struck down *Plessy v. Ferguson,* Jade Snow Wong later recalled that

> the State Department sent me on a four-months' grant to speak to a wide variety of audiences, from celebrated artists in Kyoto to restless Indians in Delhi, from students in ceramic classes in Manila to hardworking Chinese immigrants in Rangoon. I was sent because those Asian audiences who had read translations of *Fifth Chinese Daughter* did not believe a female born to poor Chinese immigrants could gain a toehold among prejudiced Americans. (Introduction viii)

It was no coincidence that Jade Snow Wong was in Asia effectively stumping for *Brown v. Board of Education* because both her autobiography *Fifth Chinese Daughter* and *Brown* were fundamentally and explicitly enabled by the sociological model of minority cultures in the United States. The State Department's submission of friend-of-the-court briefs on behalf of the NAACP's Legal Defense and Educational Fund, even as it was simultaneously sponsoring Wong's ambassadorial foray to Asia, can be considered an official authorization of this sociological vision—just as was the Supreme Court's approving citation of this kind of social science in *Brown's* famous footnote 11. *Fifth Chinese Daughter* and *Brown* are signals of the triumphant 1950s liberal sociological argument that Richard Wright had embraced in the late 1930s and the 1940s. The State Department's simultaneous approval of Wong's autobiography and the NAACP's case is one sign of this emerging liberal consensus; another sign is the fact that *Fifth Chinese Daughter* was a Book of the Month Club choice in 1950 (Wildermuth), just as *Black Boy* had been in 1945 and *Native Son* had been the primary selection in 1940.[1]

In fact, a cluster of forces was represented by this sociological model of racial equality and the cultural assimilability of racialized minorities: the "resettlement" of interned Japanese Americans during and after World War II; *Brown;* the Civil Rights movements it helped inaugurate between 1955 and 1965; the federal Indian policies of Termination and Relocation; the protest literary tradition represented by *Native Son* and *Black Boy;* and the Cold War integrationist ethnic minority literary tradition of such key books as *Fifth Chinese Daughter,* Pardee Lowe's *Father and Glorious Descendant,* John Okada's *No-No Boy,* Monica Sone's *Nisei Daughter,* and even, in a slightly different form, Ralph Ellison's *Invisible Man.* This alliance was constituted by a social science that examined the disappearance of minority cultures, a politics of integration and civil rights, and a literature that attested to the Americanizing power of official, national culture. It would be this consensus that cultural nationalist writers such as Toni Morrison, N. Scott Momaday, Ishmael Reed, Frank Chin, and Gloria Anzaldúa contested, beginning in the third phase about a decade and a half after *Brown*.

This chapter substantiates this alliance and the attendant cultural politics, examining some of its contingent by-products for the Asian American literary tradition. *Fifth Chinese Daughter* and *No-No Boy* are crucially canonical books in the Chinese American and Japanese American literary traditions (as are, to a lesser degree, *Father and Glorious Descendant* and *Nisei Daughter*). The way that sociology and social psychology helped Wong, Okada, Sone, and Lowe articulate what a minority culture was and what happened to such minority cultures in America would become fundamentally important to Asian American literature.

Sociology was studied by an unusual number of early Asian American writers, a fact that continues to structure literary critical arguments about the cultural politics in Asian American literature, as well as readers' expectations, and critics' expectations of those readers' expectations, about how Asian American literature supposedly offers true and representative accounts of Asian American communities. Jade Snow Wong (1922–2006) and Pardee Lowe (1904–?) were formally trained in sociology during their university careers. According to Frank Chin, John Okada (1923–1971) "graduated from the University of Washington heavy into English lit, and, in John's words, 'narrative and dramatic writing, history, sociology'" (Afterword to Okada 259). He later completed an M.A. at Columbia University in 1949, either in sociology (Ling, "*No-No*" 142) or English (Chen 281). Monica Sone (1919–?) finished a B.A. at Hanover College and an M.A. at Case Western Reserve in clinical psychology in 1949. In addition to these four writers, Louis Chu (1915–1970), author of the well-known *Eat a Bowl of Tea* (1961), completed a B.A. in English and sociology at Upsala College, and later an M.A. in sociology at New York University in 1940. Park's tale about "listening to an American woman in a Japanese disguise" ("Behind" 248) is of course the source of the title for *American in Disguise*, the 1971 autobiography by Japanese American sociologist Daniel Okimoto. Thus, while I am framing my argument about the sociological version of culture through reference to Wong and Okada, I intend them to serve as synecdoches in a larger argument about the lasting impact of sociology on the Asian American literary tradition—what it means, in short, for there to have been a turn to sociology and not anthropology for many Chinese American and Japanese American writers in the mid twentieth century.

One of the problematic effects of this sociological influence, in ways that sometimes echoed African American receptions of *Native Son* and *Black Boy,* were the social science expectations of truthful, accurate, and representative insider knowledge of the communities. Later writers have had to contest not just the cultural politics of the social science models of what culture was, but also the implicit claims to social science documentation with which such books have sometimes been received—one spectacular example being the use of *Native Son* as social science evidence for the damaging effects of segregation, a circular use that ended up being approved in *Brown's* footnote 11.

Such expectations, and expectations of expectations, were behind a curious mid-1990s writerly protest from Asian American literature's most popular writer, Amy Tan. "I am not an expert on China," Tan declared in the Fall 1996 issue of the *Threepenny Review:*

> Contrary to what is assumed by some students, reporters, and community organizations wishing to bestow me with honors, I am not an expert on China, Chinese culture, mah jong, the psychology of mothers and daughters, generation gaps, immigration, illegal aliens, assimilation, acculturation, racial tension, Tiananmen Square, the Most Favored Nation trade agreements, human rights, Pacific Rim economics, the purported one million missing baby girls of China, the future of Hong Kong after 1997, or, I am sorry to say, Chinese cooking. (5)

Excerpted for the December 1996 issue of *Harper's,* Tan's article mourned the way her fiction is read in terms of the ethnographic knowledge it supposedly provides about Chinese America, and, by apparent extension, Chinese society. "I am alarmed," she wrote, "when reviewers and educators assume that my very personal, specific, and fictional stories are meant to be representative down to the nth detail not just of Chinese Americans but, sometimes, of all Asian culture" (5). Tan told of receiving a permission request to reprint an excerpt from *The Joy Luck Club* in a multicultural anthology; in the proposed excerpt, related Tan,

> a woman invites her non-Chinese boyfriend to her parents' house for dinner. The boyfriend brings a bottle of wine as a gift and commits a number of social gaffes at the dinner table. Students were supposed to read this excerpt, then answer the following question: "If you are invited to a Chinese family's house for dinner, should you bring a bottle of wine?" (5)

In other examples, a literature professor informed Tan that he taught her books, but criticized passages depicting "China as backward or unattractive" or describing "spitting, filth, poverty, or superstitions," and a male student in line at a book-signing asked her loudly, "Don't you think you have a responsibility to write about Chinese men as positive role models?" (7).

These readerly reactions seem naïve, but Tan's faux surprise at being read as a cultural authority—at being taken as an authoritative chronicler of real American lives of Chinese descent—is also remarkable. Tan, protesting too much, might have read Sau-ling Wong's 1995 indictment of her work in her article on "the Amy Tan Phenomenon." Reading the reviews of Tan's novels by white American reviewers, Sau-ling Wong found that Tan was lauded for the presence of both cultural details and myth in her fiction, which shares with "quasi-ethnographic Orientalist discourse on China and the Chinese" the qualities of "temporal distancing" and "authenticity marking" (184). Wong suggested, contra Tan's denial of ethnic expertise, that she was "in effect inviting trust in her as a knowledgeable cultural insider and a competent guide familiar with the rules of the genre in question: quasi ethnography about the Orient" (188). Though Wong took note of the counter-Orientalist possibilities in Tan's work, she argued forcefully against letting Tan off the hook: "*Joy Luck Club* is not a misunderstood, co-opted ethnic text that has been unfortunately obscured by a culturalist haze and awaits recuperation through class- or gender-based readings" (194).

While Sau ling Wong was certainly right to point out Tan's complicity in structuring the ethnographic reception of her novels, the problem she names is not peculiar to Tan, but one that haunts Chinese American fiction, and Asian American literature more generally. Social science paradigms about culture continue to structure Asian American literature and its public reception, even in the academy that, Sau-ling Wong notes at the end of her article, constructs an Asian American canon different from that of the publishing industry. The reception and the production of Chinese American fiction are still laboring under certain regulations formed at the interstices of citizenship and the social sciences half a century ago. This way of reading Tan's work can be traced to the publication of Jade Snow Wong's *Fifth Chinese Daughter* in 1950. Wong's autobiography responded to, and accepted the terms of, the social science paradigm shift from biological race to ethnic culture, and the model of that culture envisioned the generational disappearance of difference rather than longevity and continuity. This model's increasing influence had a diplomatic dimension, with the U.S. State Department translating *Fifth Chinese Daughter* into several Asian languages and funding Wong's four-month speaking tour through Asia. During the Korean War and the entrenchment of the Cold War domino theory in the region, and during a domestic debate on the status of African American citizenship in the form of the Supreme Court's hearing of *Brown v. Board of Education,* American foreign policy needed to be buttressed in these Asian countries by a propaganda portraying the United States as an international beacon of democracy, liberty, and, importantly, racial harmony. Jade Snow Wong's autobiography helped accomplish this task.

✹ The Cold War Sociology of *Fifth Chinese Daughter* and *Brown v. Board of Education*

> For civilization is not, as some writers seem to believe, a biological, but a social, product.
>
> —Robert Park, "Our Racial Frontier on the Pacific," 1926 (138)

Fifth Chinese Daughter arrived on the literary scene attended by expectations of providing ethnic knowledge about the Chinese in America, following as it did the more established Chinese American prose genres of autobiography and travel writing. In her original "Author's Note" to the first edition, Wong acknowledges its role in providing information to a white readership, declaring her intention to make her book "a careful record of an American Chinese girl's first twenty-four years" (xiii). *Fifth Chinese Daughter* is a tale of growing up in a California Chinatown, and of negotiating between Chinese custom and the ways of the surrounding mainstream American culture. Told chronologically, Wong's book speaks of the conflict between "Jade Snow," as she calls herself, and her father, and depicts along the way details of Chinese foodways and cultural practices.

Importantly, the book interprets this generational conflict as a clash between Chinese and American cultures. In her "Horatio Alger account in Chinese guise," as Patricia Lin Blinde puts it (qtd. in Amy Ling 120), Wong fights for her independence and puts herself through college. By the end of the autobiography, her success and Americanization are measured not only by her employment in a wartime shipyard, but by her prize-winning essay on absenteeism in the armaments industry, incorporated into a report to President Roosevelt, and her public christening of a Liberty Ship for the merchant marine (197); not only by her dual career of writing and ceramics, but by her ownership of the "first postwar automobile in Chinatown" (244). In a new introduction to the University of Washington Press's 1989 re-edition of her work, however, Wong went beyond claiming her text as a "record" of her experience of these things, for *Fifth Chinese Daughter* not only provided Americans with knowledge of the Chinese in America, but provided Asia with knowledge about America. Her book, she recalls, created "more than the hoped-for understanding of Chinese by Americans. Beyond America (even including Chinese), *Fifth Chinese Daughter* could offer insight into life in America" (vii).

Fifth Chinese Daughter thus structures a social science reading of culture in two directions. The first direction partakes of the kind of ethnography already established by Chinese American autobiography and travel writing: it provides a white American audience with knowledge of the Chinese American community, and, by a problematic extension, expands to include a knowledge of other Asian ethnicities in different Asian countries. The logic of this extension is expressed in a passage recalling a visit by a Vietnam-bound soldier:

> I have been rewarded beyond expectations. I recall a handsome young paratrooper in full military dress who appeared at my San Francisco studio on his way to Vietnam. He came to thank me for writing the book, which he had read in a Texas military base, for he would better understand the Asians where he was going. (vii)

Wong betrays no impulse to urge the paratrooper to distinguish among Asian peoples, or between Asians in Asia and Americans of Asian descent. Wong's Cantonese speaking Chinatown will stand for Asia in the most general sense for this young soldier. But the other direction of cultural reading is as interesting as the first. Wong's book, in translated form, will provide Asian peoples with a sociology of America. Translated by the State Department into several Asian languages, including, according to Wong, those of "Japan, Hong Kong, Malaya, Thailand, Burma, East India, and Pakistan" (vii), Wong's narrative of how a "female born to poor Chinese immigrants" (viii) made good in America functioned as a window onto contemporaneous economic, social, and cultural realities in the United States.

When Wong explicitly frames her work in terms of American citizenship (unbelieving Asians read Wong's tale of life among "prejudiced Americans" while she is "a female born to poor Chinese immigrants"), she takes up American law's long historical distinction among citizens based on race. The State Department organized Wong's tour in response to a crisis in this racialized citizenship law. Its juridical dimension had been working its way through the courts between the publication of Wong's 1950 work and her tour in 1953, and in 1954 it took the form of the desegregation decision in *Brown*. In three decisions announced in June 1950, *Sweatt v. Painter, McLaurin v. Oklahoma State Regents,* and *Henderson v. United States,* the Supreme Court began to undermine the legal basis for the separate-but-equal distinction. During this time, the U.S. government intervened on behalf of the NAACP (Kluger 252). This intervention included a submission by Secretary of State Dean Acheson, who wrote in December 1952 that "racial discrimination in the United States remains a source of constant embarrassment to this government in the day-to-day conduct of its foreign relations; and it jeopardizes the effective maintenance of our moral leadership of the free and democratic nations of the world" (qtd. in Dudziak 111–12). The domestic crisis in racialized citizenship had external implications for U.S. foreign policy, declared the head of the State Department only months before the same Department sent Jade Snow Wong on a tour to reinforce American "moral leadership" in Asia.

Indeed, the Truman administration recognized the international implications of segregation for American foreign policy. Asian, African, and Latin American attention to American race discrimination posed a profound obstacle to the portrayal of the United States as an upholder of democratic liberty in opposition to communist tyranny (Dudziak). Of particular concern was Asia, which seemed to be up for grabs in the Cold War, with communism advancing particularly in China, Korea, and later in Vietnam (Klein, "Family Ties"). The State Department responded in part by sponsoring speaking tours by American minorities such as Jade Snow Wong in Asia and Louis Armstrong in Africa (Von Eschen; Dudziak 99–100), even as it withheld the passports of those critical of domestic race relations, like Paul Robeson (Rowley 395–96). Meanwhile, State Department officials such as Acheson also partook in friend-of-the-court briefs in segregation cases. Justice Department briefs also stressed the foreign policy considerations of segregation, quoting Acheson in his capacity as secretary of state at length (Dudziak 105–11). As Mary Dudziak suggests, both the international hostility (save in South Africa) toward American segregation and the Justice Department's briefs for *Brown* were cast in terms of citizenship (82, 110). The State Department recognized the importance of this domestic citizenship debate for foreign policy: on May 17, 1954, within an hour of the reading of the *Brown* decision, the Voice of America broadcast the news to the world in 34 languages (Kluger 711; Dudziak 113).

The State Department understood *Fifth Chinese Daughter* and *Brown v. Board of Education* as texts that could be put to strategic use in the Cold War. And, crucially, they were viewed by the State Department as useful interventions precisely because they registered—and were made possible by—the social science paradigm shift from race to ethnicity, and more specifically, Chicago sociology's extension of ethnic assimilation to racialized minorities. Within the context of a collapsing colonial world, in which subaltern peoples were militating against European rulers abroad (Indochina, North Africa,

South Asia) and domestically (the African American demands for the integration of the armed forces following World War II and against Jim Crow), the State Department understood *Fifth Chinese Daughter* to be suitable for the purpose of reinforcing "moral leadership" in Asia because it was not a radical manifesto on Wong's struggle to become American. What was valuable was its ambivalent, ethnic response to the historically racialized institution of citizenship. Wong's book laid claim to national mythology and citizenship, and her culturalism permitted the fundamental inscription of the minority subject into the national fabric. It redefined citizenship from the domain of racial whiteness into cultural whiteness.

While most commentators necessarily speak about Wong's project of cultural mediation between America and China,[2] none has addressed the way that this mediation is produced by Wong's introduction to the social sciences. Social science discourse not only conceptually enables this text's mediation, it also, by substantially determining its content, allows Jade Snow Wong to see herself, as if for the first time. In her first semester at San Francisco Junior College in 1938, she finds, among Latin and chemistry, that "sociology was the most stimulating," a new discipline that "completely revolutionized her thinking, shattering her Wong-constructed conception of the order of things" (125). Its lesson most generally is that of culture, including the terms "norms," "mores," and "folkways," as well as an exploration of "the historical origins of the family."

But such abstract ideas gain traction only at the moment that they are invoked to explain the difference between her family's practices and those of white American families. What falls "suddenly upon Jade Snow's astounded ears" is her sociology instructor's statement that

> "There was a period in our American history when parents had children for economic reasons, to put them to work as soon as possible, especially to have them help on the farm. But now we no longer regard children in this way. Today we recognize that children are individuals, and that parents can no longer demand their unquestioning obedience. Parents should do their best to understand their children, because young people also have their rights." (125)

"Jade Snow heard no more" of the lecture as she analyzes the cultural difference between her family and those described by the sociologist. The American cultural "norm" is individualism, and Wong is moved to see her family practices as evidence of culture: while her family was "living in San Francisco in the year 1938," they still practiced familial rules produced in "the Chinese world of thirty years ago," rules that threatened to make her "a woman in old

China" instead of "a woman in a new America" (125). The model of culture here is sociological rather than anthropological—culturally normative rather than culturally pluralist—as Wong wonders "was it possible that Daddy and Mama could be wrong?"

It is this "devastating discovery" (Wong 125–26) announced by sociology that leads directly to her own American "declaration of independence" from her family's strict Chinese rules shortly thereafter. She delivers this speech to her family "in a manner that would have done credit to her sociology instructor" (128), thus adopting both the discourse and posture of her new-found social science. This discipline allows her a cognitive structure placing her "Chinese" family beside the "American" culture, aspects of which she aspires to. In fact, it is this sociological disciplining of culture that generates one of the book's most dramatic and explicit confrontations between Chinese and American practices. Quoting her instructor, Wong tells her father, "There was a time in America when parents raised children to make them work, but now the foreigners regard them as individuals with rights of their own. I have worked too, but now I am an individual besides being your fifth daughter" (128). Her father's first response is a cultural one: citing Confucius and his "organized philosophy of manners and conduct," he criticizes the American theory of individualism (128). But after Wong persists, arguing that her "independence" in working her way through college should be matched by social autonomy (129), her father responds with the finality of race: "Your skin is yellow. Your features are forever Chinese. We are content with our proven ways" (130).

Wong's fundamental strategy is to counter such racial reasoning by rhetorically deploying culture, thus placing her in the tradition of Hurston and Wright, who answered the specter of biological difference with learned difference. This strategy is foreshadowed early in her book when she confronts a young classmate who throws his blackboard eraser at her, and taunts her with the racial slur, "Look at the eraser mark on the yellow Chinaman. Chinky, Chinky, no tickee, no washee, no shirtee!" (68). As she calmly walks away from him, her musing replaces racial difference with cultural difference:

> Jade Snow thought that he was tiresome and ignorant. Everybody knew that the Chinese people had a superior culture. Her ancestors had created a great art heritage and had made inventions important to world civilization—the compass, gunpowder, paper, and a host of other essentials. (68)

This is the early sign of *Fifth Chinese Daughter*'s sociology-enabled strategy of reconceptualizing what it means to be "yellow" as a matter of culture and not of race. Her father's trump card—"Your features are forever Chinese"—is finessed by Wong's notion of culture, the thing by which she hopes to find "a middle way" between Chinese and American practices and values (131).

Sociology is thus the vehicle through which the autobiography's central project of mediating cultures takes place. And so, "By the end of her first year of junior college, she had been so impressed by her sociology course that she changed her major to the social studies" (132). Its lessons spill into other classes as well. In a foreshadowing of the ethnographic reading dynamics that would govern the reception of multi-ethnic American literature for decades to come, literature corroborates her sociological discovery of culture when, in an English class devoted to exploring "individual expression," she learns "that her grades were consistently higher when she wrote about Chinatown and the people she had known all her life" (132). From this moment on, a new figure of subjectivity animates *Fifth Chinese Daughter:* Wong begins to describe herself as an observer of the community to which she has hitherto belonged. A "critical spectator" rather than a "participant" at a local wedding (143), Jade Snow takes some of her college classmates on a tour of her father's clothing factory. She comments, using an interesting ocular metaphor, "Although everyone seemed more or less at home, the parents as well as guests, Jade Snow suddenly felt estranged, for while she was translating conversation between instructor and parents, she was observing the scene with two pairs of eyes—Fifth Daughter's and those of a college junior" (165). We need to understand this powerful estrangement as a social science effect akin to her writing in the third person (in a move that allows us to see her culturalist explanation for writing her autobiography in the third person, that it is "Chinese habit" [xiii], as itself performative of cultural difference). This feeling becomes acute when she completes her degree in sociology and economics: "after two years away from them and from Chinatown, she now felt more like a spectator than a participant in her own community" (199).

Zora Neale Hurston had likewise adopted an ocular metaphor to describe the subtle dissociation needed to write social science out of one's lived culture. In her introduction to *Mules and Men* she wrote:

> From the earliest rocking of my cradle, I had known about the capers Brer Rabbit is apt to cut and what the Squinch Owl says from the house top. But it was fitting me like a tight chemise. I couldn't see it for wearing it. It was only when I was off in college, away from my native surroundings, that I could see myself like somebody else and stand off and look at my garment. Then I had to have the spy-glass of Anthropology to look through at that. (*Mules* 1)

Hurston's formal training in anthropology and Wong's formal training in sociology produce powerful estranging effects as they both learn to look at their respective communities through the lens of culture. In finally imagining Eatonville, Florida, and San Francisco's Chinatown as cultures, they discover themselves in ways that echo Richard Wright's extraordinary claim to not having discovered the meaning of his own story until he read Chicago sociology.

Minding the Gap: Jade Snow Wong's Sociology of Separation

> Something extraordinary is taking place in these same children.
>
> —Robert Park, "Behind Our Masks," 1926 (249)

My argument is not that the ocular power of anthropology and sociology becomes false, ethnocentric "white" lenses for Wong, Hurston, and Wright, blurring the "real" Chinatown, Eatonville, or Chicago, or that auto-ethnographic self-comprehension muddies the informant's pure information (see Michaelson 46–48). Rather, it is important to understand how social science ideas offered a powerful mixture of benefits and pitfalls to these canonical writers, ones with important consequences for the development of multicultural literature. The primary benefit was the destruction of biological race and its replacement by a comprehensive theory of the social, as culture and environment. Not just a political benefit eventually enabling significant civil rights advances, this idea was also beneficial because it was truer: conceiving of group differences as cultural and environmental rather than biological is a more accurate picture of the world. But one of the pitfalls—and there are others—was the assumption of cultural authority heightened by the adoption of social science discourse. Tan's ostensible dismay at readers' expectations of her cultural expertise is directly traceable to Wong's and other earlier Chinese American writers' social science willingness to represent and explain the totality of culture.

One of the primary tropes in Wong's sociological autobiography of cultural conflict is the figure of the generation gap. While the generation gap is an obvious idea within any systematized theory of assimilation or acculturation—observing merely that a smaller community's changing values and practices will frequently take the form of a younger generation embracing things their parents may resist—it was a central part of Chicago sociology's project.[3] It is no accident that Wong's sociologically framed declaration of independence rhetorically links the *cultural* difference between American and Chinese families to a *generational* difference between her traditional parents and her own American individualism. This was one of the key lessons learned from the Race Relations Survey on the Pacific Coast, as Park argued in the 1926 *Survey Graphic* article "Behind Our Masks." As he puts it, "What has happened more than once in the history of the Jewish people, is precisely what has happened to the Oriental on the Pacific coast; what is happening, in a very special sense, to the second and third generation of Orientals" (248).

Park understood the four-stage process of cultural assimilation involving competition, conflict, accommodation, and assimilation as a generational dynamic extendable to racialized minorities who, unlike Jews, would not "become invisible" (247) during the process of Americanization because of what he elsewhere calls their "racial uniform." What the Race Relations Survey on the Pacific revealed, according to Park, was that many earlier Japanese came to stay in California to settle but had been prevented by American nativist law (showing that law produced rather than responded to sojourning), which encouraged a different affect: "Many of them would like to return to Japan, but their children prefer to stay here" (249). One of the Survey's primary conclusions was thus evidence of the generation gap among Asian American communities on the Coast: "Meanwhile, something extraordinary is taking place in these same children. They are growing up to be Americans" (249). Park continued, "For the Oriental who is born in America and educated in our western schools is culturally an Occidental, even though he be racially an Oriental, and this is true to an extent that no one who has not investigated the matter disinterestedly and at first hand is ever likely to imagine" (249).[4]

In *Asian/American: Historical Crossings of a Racial Frontier,* David Palumbo-Liu recognizes Park's centrality in defining modernity's "seam" between Asia and America across the Pacific, particularly in his *Survey Graphic* article "Our Racial Frontier on the Pacific" (giving the subtitle to Palumbo-Liu's book) and in Park's theory (later developed by Everett Stonequist) of the "marginal man." Palumbo-Liu sees Park as probing the workings and limits of Americanization during the 1920s and 1930s: "Assimilation, then, was both a psychic *and* a somatic phenomenon, the latter now presenting in concrete form the actuality of Americanization (and, conversely, if certain bodies *won't* change, or do so only recalcitrantly, then it is taken as an index to their resistance or inability to assimilate)" (85). Palumbo-Liu criticizes Park for not examining the "material histories of American racism" (87) as it pertained to Asian Americans and for suffering from translation errors about what it means to "save face" in Chinese culture, thus reinscribing cultural stereotypes about Confucian conformist etiquette and Western individualism as social science truth (88).[5] Despite Park's recognition of how Americanized the younger generation of Asian Americans were, Palumbo-Liu argues that Park never conceived this process as moving beyond the limits of phenotypical difference: "Nevertheless, this all but complete Americanization ultimately fails, since, as Park himself attests, the uneradicable sign of race cannot be ignored, even by people of goodwill" (89). Park's student, Stonequist, likewise imagined this barrier as dissolvable only through intermarriage (89–90).

While this sentiment is not how Park's essay ends—rather he proposes that cross-racial "personal friendships are the great moral solvents" that disintegrate the "social distance" caused by physical differences ("Behind" 254), thus concluding like Wong on a hopeful note—Palumbo-Liu is nevertheless correct that Park and Wong lack a fully worked out theory of the social construction of race, which would later show how racialization is not merely left-over biological ideas but constantly re-energized contemporary processes that take place with each generation. In other words, Park and Wong are hopeful about the progress of modernity, whereas Palumbo-Liu speaks from a post–Civil Rights era vantage point, with its knowledge that ending the legality of segregation and prejudice did not change the material economic status of many minorities, did not recognize the continued vitality of the social construction of race, and did not sufficiently critique the falsely universal cultural claims of the dominant American society. That the "irreversible" ("Racial Frontier" 150) process of assimilation might be stalled for some period at mere "accommodation" because of phenotypical traits was an open-ended question for Park. As we shall see in the next chapter, Park was noticeably silent about the internment of Japanese Americans, a historical fact which undercut his optimistic assessments.

But the Parkian sociology that Palumbo-Liu contends is central to the early twentieth-century theorizing of the Asian/American "seam" was also the specific academic discourse through which Wong, Okada, and other Asian American writers articulated their work, and which has hence deeply informed Asian American literary traditions. This sociology has reverberated in Asian American literature and criticism since the 1920s, and we have yet to understand the importance of Asian American writers' turn to Chicago sociology instead of Boasian anthropology. My argument is not that Park's work on the generation gap among Asian American communities on the West Coast is the origin of Wong's culturalist interpretation of the dramatic struggle for independence that ensues between herself and her parents. Rather, Wong is "astounded" by sociology's ideas because she experiences the shock of recognition: sociology in some sense tells her what she already knows, but does so in a highly articulate and theoretically developed way with the imprimatur of the scientific truth of a general social law. She speaks of her own experience amplified and expressed through the concepts of the social science work she studied. She in turn strengthened, for both the literature and social science that followed, the circuit of articulation between the fields, providing another layer of sediment in the Chinese American literary tradition and helping to form the expectations that Tan, two generations later, has to throw off by denying any expertise on the "generation gap."[6]

This gap allows Wong's Americanization even as she retains some Chinese values and practices, so long as they are not at odds with the American ones she generally prefers. The progress of Americanization is understood to be, as Park imagined, progressive and irreversible, and so when her much younger brother is born, "Jade Snow, old enough to be her brother's mother, began a program of interpreting, enforcing, and supplementing her parents' teaching, to bridge a gap of over half a century between parents and son" (205). Bridging this "gap" takes a cultural form of introducing American stories, but also a social form of introducing him to "people and experiences of the Occidental world" (209). As Palumbo-Liu usefully points out, "Most critical appreciations have done little with the fact that the father, for all his 'traditional' precepts, is actually himself an important transitional figure: Christianized, he believes that women should be freed from certain oppressive rules" (139). In this sense, Wong merely continues the journey of acculturation begun by her father, an act of assimilation that has her give up Chinese cultural values when those values collide with her "process of Americanization" (139). Her Americanization proves her father's dark warning wrong, though Wong is too polite to point this out.

In her 1989 introduction, she notes that, just as she and her husband have Americanized their child-rearing practices, thus rejecting many of their parents' ways, so too "our children have developed differently from my generation" (x). Wong speaks of finding a "middle way" between Chinese and American cultures, but that project amounts to figuring out which Chinese practices and values fit into her Americanizing self. The autobiography in fact ends on the perfectly rendered note of the American dream, as she discovers the twin cultural projects of writing and ceramics:

> Jade Snow was deliriously happy. What a wonderful way to live! Write when she wanted to, and make pottery when she wanted to. She could call her soul her own, strike her own tempo as she carved her own niche. How far she would get would depend on how hard she wanted to work, not on anyone else's whims or prejudices. (236)

Once this vision triumphs in the last chapter, her sense of "the fatalism that was at the core of all Chinese thinking and behavior, the belief that the broad pattern of an individual's life was ordained by fate although within that pattern he was capable of perfecting himself and accumulating a desirable store of good will"—which she has previously stated as needing to be combined in a "middle way" (131)—has completely dissolved into her American success. Thus sociology not only methodologically makes possible her realistic, carefully descriptive portrayal of Chinese America, it also informs the content of that portrayal, as a newly ethnicized community whose children are gradually losing Chinese cultural distinctiveness and embracing American practices and values.

Jade Snow Wong's speech to Asian audiences on her State Department–sponsored 1953 trip similarly deploys this rhetoric of cultural difference and displays the unsettled problems that accompany it. Her speech casts the "old-world Chinese standards" in which she was raised, including the "standard of Chinese womanhood" and the "doctrines of Confucius," against the "American new-world values" which she learns at school and in the culture at large, including the "American principles of freedom and independence," as well as the lessons of "individuality, self-expression, and analytical thought" (*No Chinese Stranger* 94–95). For Wong, these two sets of cultural values represent "conflicts" which must be resolved. But, problematically, this cultural conflict is necessarily imagined in the racial terms that the United States had not abandoned: "This discovery [of conflicts] becomes a turning point in the life of any member of the second generation as he asks, 'Am I of my father's race or am I an American?'" (95). To affirm the latter possibility, of course, meant changing not one's "race," but rather one's culture. Nonetheless, in ultimately reconfiguring her difference as cultural rather than racial, Wong mirrored the NAACP's vision of the usefulness of sociology for establishing arguments for integration and assimilation, as they were concurrently arguing in *Brown*.

One cost of this paradigm shift becomes apparent when Wong records a reaction to her speech in Malaysia. She was questioned by an "uninvited East Indian," who asked, "From your speech, Miss Wong, do you imply that there is no prejudice in the United States?" (82). Wong's answer reveals that her value to the State Department was partly due to her Booker T. Washington–like logic on race prejudice:

There was a sudden silence. It was the first time she had been asked this publicly. She talked about prejudice where she had found it in employment and housing; but she emphasized that in the United States racial prejudice had never stopped her from getting where or what she wanted, and that the dimensions which her ancestral culture had added to her life offset occasional disadvantages.

"Fear of prejudice and the excuse it offers for personal failure are chronically more damaging to a person of a minority race than to expect the reality of encountering and dealing with prejudice." (82)

Her answer comes only months before *Brown;* the East Indian's reply is not offered. The cost of this Boasian turn from *biological* to cultural difference was that it occasionally rendered invisible the construction of race as a *social* reality through which continuing oppression and differences of economic and political power took shape. As Robert Lee says of another Cold War orientalist text, "Chop suey ethnicity erases from memory the history of the Chinese in America as a racialized minority" (175), making impossible any analysis of the racialized structures of power and prejudice that endure. Parkian sociology lacked an account of the social process of racialization, such as was later developed by Michael Omi and Howard Winant.

Fifth Chinese Daughter was received as expert sociological testimony, making clear that Wong's strategic use of the paradigm shift from race to ethnicity was to have a lasting generic legacy. Writing for the *New York Times Book Review,* Joyce Geary understood the text to be "not so much the story of her life as it is a story about San Francisco's Chinatown," thus accepting the text's invitation to be read as cultural typography. *Commonweal's* E. V. R. Wyatt similarly recognized culture, assimilation, and the generation gap to be its themes: "Jade Snow's story is a study of the conflict in the lives of Chinatown's younger generation—a conflict between the weight of Chinese tradition and the freedom of American ways." An anonymous reviewer in the *New Yorker* likewise understood the text to be representative of a newer generation of "Chinese upbringing" achieving a "break with Chinese traditions" (Review 1950).

Fifth Chinese Daughter's publication in 1950 thus helped concretize a dynamic of social science reading, a dynamic which continues to inflect the debates within the Asian American community about Chinese American writing, and the reception of that writing within the larger, predominately white, Anglo-America.

✾ The Sociological Consensus in the Second Phase, 1940–1965

> Drawing on the economist Gunnar Myrdal's *American Dilemma,* the State Department developed a clear strategy that acknowledged that discrimination existed but hastened to add that racism was a fast-disappearing aberration, capable of being overcome by a talented and motivated individual.
>
> —Penny M. Von Eschen, "Who's the Real Ambassador," 2000 (117)

The State Department's simultaneous approval of *Fifth Chinese Daughter* and the NAACP's case for *Brown v. Board of Education* was based on their shared liberal integrationist vision of the ethnic assimilability of America's racialized minorities. If the perceived problem with Asian Americans was that they had too much culture, as Franklin Frazier cited, the perceived problem on the other hand with African Americans was that they had too little culture. Sociology was the solution to both problems, from Wong's and the NAACP's points of view, though Jade Snow Wong drew on slightly different aspects of Parkian sociology than did Richard Wright and the NAACP. By downplaying cultural longevity and survivals and emphasizing instead the notions of modernity, migration, and fairly rapid cultural change within a dynamic that assumed racial equality, Asian Americans through the generation gap could lose some of their Asian culture. Conversely, African Americans through processes of urbanization and integration would be able to assume the dominant culture's mores, working habits, and family structures.

The social science confluences behind *Brown* have not always been easy to trace. *Brown's* footnote 11, "destined to become one of the most debated in the annals of the [Supreme] Court" (Kluger 708), names seven social science works, including Franklin Frazier's *The Negro in the United States* (1949), a report on racial preferences among school children by the social psychologist Kenneth Clark that I discuss in chapter six, and the very chapter from *Personality in the Making: The Fact-Finding Report of the Midcentury White House Conference on Children and Youth* (1950) that cites Wright's *Native Son* as a "fictional case history" of Negro reaction to prejudice and discrimination (143). The footnote ends with the line "And see generally Myrdal, *An American Dilemma* (1944)."[7] One racist opponent of desegregation, Carleton Putnam, suggested that the Court's final note to "see generally Myrdal" was "an effective way of saying 'see generally Boas and his disciples,' for Myrdal's *American Dilemma* was Boas from beginning to end" (qtd. in Hyatt 99). In one sense Putnam was correct, since it was Boas's paradigm shift from biological race to culture that emerged as the scientific and social scientific consensus by the middle of the century. But Putnam's blame missed the point that the sociological model of culture that animated the NAACP's case was profoundly different from Boas's anthropological one.

In what could be (erroneously) seen as a rebuttal to Robert Park and not a dependence on his work, Myrdal's long study ends with a critique of Parkian sociology. As Fred Matthews puts it, *An American Dilemma* "concluded by dismissing Park and his students as having transmitted a 'naturalistic and, therefore, fatalistic philosophy' with the implication that 'man can and should make no effort to change the "natural" outcome of the specific forces observed. This is the old do-nothing (laissez-faire) bias of "realistic" social science'" (184). Whereas *An American Dilemma* concludes, "We are entering an era where fact-finding and scientific theories of causal relations will be seen as instrumental in planning controlled social change" (Myrdal 1023), Matthews contends that the difference between Park and Myrdal was not that Park thought change would be "evolutionary," but that "the *mechanism* would not be that of social engineering—rather, it would be largely through the struggle and transformation of the peoples concerned" (185). Park saw migration and cultural change in modernity as an almost natural law, and in this respect he never departed from the kind of political and social conservatism of his early mentor, Booker T. Washington. At the same time, however, it is important to see that Myrdal and the other social science behind the NAACP's challenge to segregation were wholly within the tradition of Chicago sociology, with Park's work as its theoretical foundation, even if Myrdal and the NAACP torqued that social science so that it might be put into the service of accelerating, or at least enabling, the process of assimilation and cultural change in a way that departed from its orthodox objectivism.

One of the best accounts of the intersection of social science, race, and law is Lee D. Baker's *From Savage to Negro: Anthropology and the Construction of Race, 1896–1954*. Baker likewise sees Parkian sociology instead of Boasian anthropology at the heart of *Brown*. When the NAACP's Legal Defense and Education Fund began considering the grounds for a challenge to segregation laws, the organization turned to the newly reputable social sciences, which were becoming authoritative in the courts. The NAACP's legal team, emerging from Howard University Law School, some of whom had been "trained in sociological jurisprudence," selectively chose evidence from the disciplines of anthropology, sociology, and social psychology (Baker 168). As Baker makes clear, they carefully teased apart various social science threads, accepting Boas's concept of racial equality but, strategically, not his anthropological concept of slow cultural historical change, opting instead for Park's more culturally flexible model of social evolution involving the stages of competition, conflict, accommodation, and assimilation, the very model that underpinned *An American Dilemma* (179).

The anthropological model of culture's emphasis on pluralism, holism, and historical particularism was problematic for the Howard team of Charles Hamilton Houston, Thurgood Marshall, and Robert Carter. Accepting anthropology's racial equality, they "discarded the emphasis on cultural history. This group embraced the sociological view of Negro culture that Robert Park advanced at the University of Chicago" (177). Baker shows that the two models of culture animated different sets of cultural politics: while "the Boas-influenced cultural specificity argument" enabled some New Negro Movement members who "attempted to forge an ethnic identity centered on the construction of a cultural homeland" (177), Parkian sociologists argued instead that Negro culture had progressed, but that non-cosmopolitan, non-middle-class Negroes "deviated from American cultural and behavioral standards" in response to "deleterious environmental conditions, racial discrimination, and the heritage of slavery" (178). Especially problematic was anthropology's construction of minority cultures' historical endurance: "Howard social scientists found the cultural specificity thesis incompatible with assimilation because it implied that the cultural patterns of African Americans were long-standing, slow to change, and ostensibly irreversible" (179).

The NAACP, *Brown,* Park, and Myrdal thus found themselves opposed to the anthropological model of culture, a fact, we have seen, behind Hurston's rejection of *Brown. An American Dilemma* argued that *"American Negro culture"* was a *"distorted development, or a pathological condition, of the general American culture"* and its proposal that *"it is to the advantage of American Negroes as individuals and as a group to become assimilated into American culture"* (928, 929; italics original) profoundly violated the Boasian principles of cultural relativism and pluralism. Myrdal worked with both Herskovits and Frazier, but *An American Dilemma* was much more indebted to the latter's sociology. In fact, Myrdal had requisitioned from Herskovits a "research memorandum—which was published as *The Myth of the Negro Past"* (Baker 277n48), but he rejected that research in *An American Dilemma* and somewhat dismissively wrote of *The Myth of the Negro Past*'s attempt "to glorify African culture generally and to show how it has survived in the American Negro community," an idea that was generally being rejected by African American intellectuals who doubted the argument that "Negroes should retain 'their own' cultural heritage and not lose it for the general American culture" (Myrdal 753–54).[8]

As Lee Baker shows, what was at stake for *An American Dilemma*'s sociology—and hence for *Brown* and the Civil Rights movements that followed—was a struggle with anthropology's rival notion of culture. That translated into *An American Dilemma*'s praise for Herskovits's work on anthropometry (which made the Boasian point of racial equality—thus footnote 11's citation of *An American Dilemma* indirectly credited Hurston's help during her summer labor as Herskovits's student), but avoidance of his work on African cultural survivals in America (which was making the different Boasian point about historical particularism). Herskovits's ideas about retentions were attacked by Frazier and Myrdal, since they "suggested to African

Americans that traditions and values passed on from their despised ancestors were in fact significant ways of life that deserved protection—and the price of losing this valuable heritage, which would be destroyed through complete assimilation, would be too high" (Williams, *Rethinking Race* 100).[9] The sole usefulness of anthropology for the NAACP was work that "demonstrated that there was no scientific proof of hereditary differences in intelligence or temperament and concluded that environmental factors could explain the differences among racial groups" (Baker 200).

Importantly, the sociological model of minority culture articulated by Chicago sociology, worked through by Franklin Frazier, and adapted by Gunnar Myrdal's team, implied a pathological quality in African American culture. Park and Wright's work suggested that any distinctive way of life arising from social and legal barriers based on racial prejudice would be marginal and psychologically reactive rather than healthy. Wright "greatly admired" *An American Dilemma* and became friends with Myrdal (Fabre 586n9, 349). When the NAACP awarded the Spingarn Medal to Wright in 1940 for his "powerful depiction in his books, *Uncle Tom's Children* and *Native Son,* of the effect of proscription, segregation and denial of opportunities to the American Negro" (qtd. in Rowley 238), it was prizing the sociological model of culture in Wright's work.

If the sociological construction of African American minority culture as pathological was the theoretical step that enabled cultural assimilation, a converse sociological construction of Asian Americans as characterized by the generation gap, along with the notion of the model minority, became the theoretical step that enabled their cultural assimilation. Thus Robert G. Lee argues that the model minority became a Cold War possibility in this larger paradigm shift: "The representation of Asian Americans as a *racial* minority whose apparently successful *ethnic* assimilation was a result of stoic patience, political obedience, and self-improvement was a critically important narrative of ethnic liberalism that simultaneously promoted racial equality and sought to contain demands for social transformation" (145). Lee understands this new representation to have been made possible by "an emergent discourse of race in which cultural difference replaced biological difference as the new determinant of social outcomes" (145). These changes were underway in Jade Snow Wong's time: as she was embracing sociology in 1938, Gunnar Myrdal began work for *An American Dilemma*. If overtly racial social science had helped buttress exclusionary citizenship in *Dred Scott* and *Plessy* (Baker 15, 28),[10] mid twentieth-century social science appeared to open up the possibility for citizenship, or so it seemed to Myrdal, and to the NAACP after him.

🐾 Ralph Ellison's Ambivalent Culture: Sociology and the Constitution

> To That Vanished Tribe into Which I Was Born:
> The American Negroes
>
> —Ralph Ellison, epigraph to *Juneteenth,* 1999 (vii)

When Jade Snow Wong's contemporary, Ralph Ellison, reviewed Gunnar Myrdal's *An American Dilemma* in 1944, Ellison placed Myrdal within a social science tradition that haunted Ellison for the rest of his life.[11] He rightly understood Myrdal's work within—and as an overturning of—a social science tradition that had been devoted to proving African American inferiority after Emancipation; Myrdal, Ellison says, "has used his science to discredit all of the vicious non-scientific nonsense that has cluttered our sociological literature" (305). Ellison's review is generally positive; like *An American Dilemma* and historians of sociology (see Matthews), Ellison understood the difference between Myrdal and Park to be one of general indebtedness and specific rejection of the latter's sense of the impossibility of social engineering, what Ellison calls its "timidity" (307).[12] While Park understood prejudice as a natural reaction to the pressures of accommodation, Ellison generally approved of Myrdal's transformation of prejudice into a question of morality and national psychology (311).

But Ellison's ambivalence about sociology centered on a quotation whose phantasmal presence had haunted his career since he first encountered it in a sociology class at Tuskegee between 1933 and 1936, a time contemporaneous with Wright's discovery of sociology and shortly before Wong's. In fact, almost thirty years after the fact, Ellison would frame his decision to be a writer through this traumatic encounter:

> Yes, and the question of the nature of reality which underlies American fiction and thus the human truth which gives fiction viability. In this quest, for such it soon became, I learned that nothing could go unchallenged; especially that feverish industry dedicated to telling Negroes who and what they are, and which can usually be counted upon to deprive both humanity and culture of their complexity. I had undergone, not too many months before taking the path which led to writing, the humiliation of being taught in a class in sociology at a Negro college (from Park and Burgess, the leading textbook in the field) that Negroes represented the "lady of the races." This contention the Negro instructor passed blandly along to us without even bothering to wash his hands, much less his teeth. Well, I had no intention of

being bound by any such humiliating definition of my relationship to American literature. (Introduction, *Shadow and Act* xx)

This quotation became the fulcrum of a discarded, unpublished chapter of *Invisible Man* and was recited by Ellison in his review of *An American Dilemma*.

In the review, relating Park's career to the racist social science that had come before him, Ellison wrote,

> But for all his good works, some of Park's assumptions were little better. The Negro, he felt "has always been interested rather in expression than in action; interested in life itself rather than in its reconstruction or reformation. The Negro is, by natural disposition, neither an intellectual nor an idealist, like the Jew; nor a brooding introspective, like the East Indian; nor a pioneer and a frontiersman, like the Anglo-Saxon. He is primarily an artist, loving life for its own sake. His *métier* is expression rather than action. He is, so to speak, the lady among the races."
>
> Park's descriptive metaphor is so pregnant with mixed motives as to birth a thousand compromises and indecisions. Imagine the effect such teachings have had upon Negro students alone! Thus what started as part of a democratic attitude, ends not only uncomfortably close to the preachings of Sumner, but to those of Dr. Goebbels as well. (*Shadow and Act* 307–8)

The textbook's wider context for this quotation justifies Ellison's connection of the "lady of the races" idea to Goebbels, for the section is indeed an exploration of racial, and racist theory. The section of Park and Burgess's *Introduction to the Science of Sociology,* 2nd edition (1924), called "Temperament, Tradition, and Nationality" was originally a 1918 article by Park ("Education and Its Relation"). It begins with Park's statement that:

> The temperament of the Negro, as I conceive it, consists in a few elementary but distinctive characteristics, determined by physical organizations and transmitted biologically. These characteristics manifest themselves in a genial, sunny, and social disposition, in an interest and attachment to external, physical things rather than to subjective states and objects of introspection, in a disposition for expression rather than enterprise and action. (138–39)

Theories of biological race do not get much clearer than that. Once we understand that both Boas and Park were in the middle of a paradigm shift, it is not surprising that residual biological thinking still existed in their work— especially their earlier work, as with this quotation that so revolted Ellison.

The textbook as a whole was more thoroughly grounded in the Boasian paradigm shift from racial theory to environment and culture, and it continued that transformation through its various editions, just as Park's work did in the 1920s and 1930s, as he moved, for example, through his *Survey Graphic* work on race relations on the Pacific. In this passage, either Park has recast social stereotypes as science, or, alternatively, one could imagine that many African Americans with whom Park came into contact while working for Washington at Tuskegee between 1905 and 1912 might have appeared to this white man in the Jim Crow South as "genial" and "sunny" and disposed to "expression" rather than "introspection"—which is to say, only performative of the racial role of the time.

However he arrived at this picture, what is startling about it is not only that it is a residue of biological thinking, but also that, first, he is deaf to how environment is another—better—explanation for racialized behavior than is nature or biology, and, second, he does not imagine how racial roles themselves are shaped by social expectations. Given these supposed biological constraints, Park went on to argue that African Americans adapted themselves to their environment (like any organism) by taking up "such new customs, habits, and cultural forms as it was able, or permitted to use" (139). For Park, the adaptation of American culture by Negroes was not in the areas of philosophy, science, technical expertise, or other markers of advanced civilization, but in that area that they racially excelled in: namely, expressive arts. (While Ellison's hero would be "a brooding introspective" and something of an "intellectual" and "idealist," he would continue to have problems figuring out how to act rather than merely "express").

Park's "lady among the races" became the center of an unpublished chapter of *Invisible Man,* one following directly on the news that the narrator is to be expelled from Tuskegee. In it, the dazed narrator makes his way to his teacher Woodridge's dormitory to ask him about Emerson, whom the white trustee directed the narrator to read. There, a slightly drunk and thoroughly cynical Woodridge begins to disabuse the naïve narrator of his earnestness, his general credulity in believing the promises of the trustee, of Bledsoe, of Tuskegee, of hard work and merit, and generally, of the South and of America.[13] His credulity extends to sociology:

"You study sociology?"

"I did last year."

"Well your sociology textbook teaches that we comprise what it describes as the 'Lady of the races'. Do you remember that?"

"Of course. It's from Robert E. Park."

"You believe it, don't you?"

"I don't know. It's in the textbook.... I suppose so."

"Then even if the rumours about me were true, it shouldn't cause any
surprise, should it? If you belong to the lady of the races, then everything's ok. All things are possible[—]a man is actually a woman.
[I]sn't it all right to become a 'lady'?" (167)

The rumors about Woodridge are that he is gay, we are to understand, with
Ellison ironically extending Park's original metaphor of the "lady of the
races," and Woodridge has come to despise the literary and cultural authorities he teaches. "They built illusions against life and I accepted them," but
now he denies them because "This [perhaps his gay status and the homosexual reality suppressed by Western cultures] too is a part of reality and any
book that fails to include it is obscene" (168). He begins to destroy his books,
including "Shakespeare and Balzac" by stomping on and biting them (168),
but Ellison has later corrected his manuscript by hand, crossing out Shakespeare and writing in the margin "only naturalism not Shakespeare" and
writing above the line "Zola" (168). The revised passage suggests Ellison's
intentional narrowing to the realist-naturalist tradition that cannot apprehend the real, just as its associated cousin sociology is to be dismissed as a
corpus of "illusion" instead of fact, as with Ellison's enduring horror at Park's
rendition of African Americans as the "lady of the races." Roderick Ferguson
is probably right when he says, regarding this draft chapter, "While Wright
employed sociological theory to presumably clarify the position of African
Americans within the social and economic transformations of the 1930s,
Ellison regarded sociological theory as fundamentally distorting" (56).

In reviewing Ellison's revulsion and Park's phrase, Daniel Y. Kim also suggests that the "central trope of his novel was intended as an ironic reversal of
one of Park's assertions: that racially marked Americans are hindered from
assimilating fully into larger culture primarily because of the high visibility of
their racial difference." Kim cites two later "dismissive references" by Ellison to
the idea of "high visibility" (310n1). Park's "lady among the races" was a defi-
nite remnant of biological thinking in his work, expressed early in his career,
but still around to negatively affect Ellison in the 1930s, and which Wright
and Wong, who presumably also read this line in the 1930s, are silent about.
But Ellison gets Park's chronology wrong in his review of *American Dilemma:*
it is not that he starts with a "democratic attitude" and ends up devoted to
biology, but rather that Park's ideas, like sociology in general, were gradually
abandoning biology for better explanations of group behavior and values, ones
that Wright at least agreed were more "democratic" (308). The other point

to make, then, is that Ellison's revulsion at this section of the *Introduction to the Science of Sociology* is not a synecdoche for a wholesale rejection of Chicago sociology. A more accurate way to put Ellison's relation to Chicago sociology would be to say that his objection was its determinism and the lack of agency it accorded, not its overwhelming rejection of biological thinking in favor of the roles played by environment and culture in forming the individual.[14]

Interestingly, Ellison's only major reservation about *An American Dilemma* is its project of cultural assimilation. Like Hurston, Ellison rejects the idea that African American culture is pathological, though like Wright and Park, Ellison agrees that much of the culture has been reactively formed in the crucible of historical race relations in the United States. "Much of Negro culture might be negative," Ellison wrote, "but there is also much of great value, of richness, which, because it has been secreted by living and has made their lives more meaningful, Negroes will not willingly disregard" (316). But the other side of this coin was Ellison's famous insistence that black culture was already American, and that, conversely, much of American culture was already Negro: that jazz and spirituals, for instance were "still being subjected to a constant process of assimilation," and that both "have been absorbed into the musical language of the culture as a whole" ("Some Questions" 268).

Kenneth W. Warren's recent revaluation of Ellison and his legacy for cultural politics exposes both the limits and strengths of my three-phase framework for the genealogy of literary multiculturalism. Warren incisively points out that Ellison rejected a number of sociological tenets, finding them too deterministic and loathing the racial residue in Park's thought, but also rejecting visions of African American life that had no room for black agency and individuality. But, suggests Warren, "Ellison's position did not call for a scorched-earth policy against sociology" (94). Instead, Ellison thought that sociologists (among others) did not account for "the dispersal of ideas, styles, or tastes in this turbulent American society" (94). "His point," says Warren, "was that despite the best efforts of the segregationists, the goods of the world's culture had been available to the Negro and had played a role in shaping his tastes and sensibilities. Likewise, and equally important, the Negro, despite his segregation, had been a powerful force in creating American culture as well as the culture of the modern world" (94).

Ellison's understanding of cultural influence thus developed in two directions: it was not just that African Americans were exchanging a pathological culture for white American culture (as Wright and Frazier hoped), or that African Americans had a distinct culture that was threatened with being forgotten (as Hurston and anthropology feared), but that African American cultural formations had been fundamentally influential on the larger

American culture, and that Negro culture was thoroughly American. Ellison was in accordance with Park and Burgess's notion that minority cultures "contribute" elements to the larger "American civilization," and that cultural "assimilation" is a two-way process of interpenetration and influence (*Introduction* 734–84), although this was an idea more theoretically conceded than rigorously explored by Chicago sociology. To see the Negro "as the heart of American culture" was not a new idea, Warren notes (64), and Ellison's insistence on this point accorded with a different (and submerged) thread of Chicago sociology from that developed by Frazier and Myrdal. Indeed, regarding Ellison's concern for modernity's effects on African American culture that had always been creatively cross-fertilized with the dominant culture, Warren argues, "Perhaps more influenced by Chicago school sociology than he realized, Ellison here adopts what was a commonplace social analysis of twentieth-century black America in which folk societies under slavery were argued to have exhibited a cohesiveness and shared sense of identity not evident in modern industrializing societies" (72). Ellison's vision of black culture as distinct but always composed of mixed elements ultimately makes him, notes Warren, "not entirely assimilable to black nationalism" (19).

Ellison's complicated account of culture is reflected in the respect accorded African American culture in *Invisible Man,* but also the novel's sense that culture as such cannot be a solution, the place of return. In seeing a minority culture as valuable but nevertheless asserting a larger American narrative, Ellison is in accordance with the sociologically inspired integrationist tradition of Wright, Wong, Okada, and, to use an important Mexican American example, José Antonio Villareal's *Pocho.* As with these other (mostly 1950s) texts, the questions *Invisible Man* raises are ones of individualism within the nation—a question wholly amenable to the Civil Rights politics of the 1950s. "Significantly," Ellison wrote in 1958 in response to a question about whether Negroes should adopt white values "in place of 'Negro values,'" "we are the only black peoples who are not fighting for separation from the 'whites,' but for a fuller participation in the society which we share with 'whites.' And it is of further significance that we pursue our goals precisely in terms of American Constitutionalism" ("Some Questions" 270).

Ellison is here referring, of course, to *Brown v. Board of Education* and to the early Civil Rights movement. Indeed, if *Fifth Chinese Daughter* was seen as suitable propaganda for a State Department advising the Supreme Court to overturn *Plessy* for Cold War foreign policy reasons, *Invisible Man* seemed to provide the very legal strategy whereby the African American lawyers successfully argued it. *Invisible Man* mirrored the political method of the Howard team in arguing *Brown* before the courts. The novel ends with a plea that the originary documents of the nation provide the "principles" through which African Americans might claim full membership in the nation—even though they were the very texts which strategically equivocated on who exactly constituted a "person" in the new nation. Though Wong arrived at a liberal integrationist vision of cultural assimilation and individualism through the midwifery of sociology, Ellison arrived at a very similar picture through "American Constitutionalism."

The conclusion of *Invisible Man* sees the narrator hibernating in his underground space, preparing, as he says, for a more overt action to come. It is here that he reflects on the numerous discarded ideologies that had interpellated him into the American scene: Booker T. Washington's compromise with segregation, the Communist Party's blindness to issues of race, and Ras the Destroyer's black nationalism. In the novel's ambiguous epilogue, the narrator returns to his grandfather's enigmatic instructions to "Live with your head in the lion's mouth. I want you to overcome 'em with yeses, undermine 'em with grins, agree 'em to death and destruction, let 'em swoller you till they vomit or bust wide open" (16). "I could never be sure of what he meant" by this riddle (16), the narrator recalls in chapter one; and when in the epilogue he muses that "I can't figure it out; it escapes me" (575), he seems no further along. But in the final pages, Ellison's invisible man eventually understands that his grandfather's advice was, as he puts it now, "to affirm the principle on which the country was built and not the men" (574).

This final claim mirrors in substance and in style the LDEF's legal strategy before the courts. But its strategy parallels Ellison's narrator's plea even more directly than this. Peggy Cooper Davis, examining the rhetorical strategies of Marshall, Carter, and their opponent, argues that Marshall and Carter realized that historical precedent was not on their side, as segregation had been upheld in the courts of the nation for three-quarters of a century since *Plessy v. Ferguson*. David Garrow, in arguing a similar point, remarks that *Brown* "symbolizes the post-1954 Court's repudiation of historical intent and meaningful evidence of historical intent" (74). Ellison's narrator follows a similar path by insisting on the division between, on the one hand, the principle—say, that all men are created equal and their inalienable rights include life, liberty, and the pursuit of happiness—and, on the other hand, the founders who spoke the principle but purposefully separated citizens from chattel. As Ellison's narrator muses on his grandfather's advice,

> Could he have meant—hell, he *must* have meant the principle, that we were to affirm the principle on which the country was built and not the men, or at least not the men who did the violence. Did he mean

say "yes" because he knew that the principle was greater than the men, greater than the numbers and the vicious power and all the methods used to corrupt its name? (574)

Ellison here realizes, as did Marshall and Carter, that the principle had to be separated first from the historical intent of the men who formulated and corrupted it, and second from the precedents that later helped entrench that corruption.

In a second point, what is key is the very uncertainty that marks the narrator's musing about his grandfather's advice. Peggy Davis reveals that, rhetorically, Marshall and Carter used many "mental state verbs" in their oral arguments, such as "I think," "I believe," and "I submit." These signaled a tactical deference to the Court, but also produced the Constitution as an open document needing interpretation and reinterpretation. In Davis's words, "The legal arguments of Carter and Marshall are in the negotiable, and arguably deferential, terms of thinking and saying. [On the other hand, the defending counsel] seizes authority to announce the meaning of the constitutional text" (37). As she explains, "[His] combination of direct assertions and authority frames has the effect of painting the constitutional question as settled. By contrast, Carter and Marshall craft their uses of authority frames both to give hierarchical eminence to principles upon which they wish to rely, and to express interpretive possibilities" (38). Like Marshall and Carter, the invisible man highlights his own role as an interpreter of texts—in this case, his grandfather's words, and, by extension, the principle of the nation to which his grandfather alludes. It is an invitation to interpret and thus to pragmatically refashion.[15]

Thus, even though Ellison rejected the sociology that had been so important for Wright's and Wong's visions of Americanization, he was nonetheless part of the emerging liberal Cold War consensus on the integration of racialized minorities into national culture. Ellison is between Wright and Hurston in his commitment to African American culture. He saw African American culture much more positively than Wright did, and made much more use of it in his literary work than Wright did (as with the influence of blues, jazz, and folklore in *Invisible Man*). On the other hand, he did not mourn its possible disappearance as much as Hurston did, believing that African American culture had already interpenetrated and assimilated—and been assimilated into—white dominant culture, a belief he demonstrated in terms of music and a point Hurston had made four years earlier in her *Seraph on the Suwanee*.

In terms of this genealogy of multiculturalism, Ellison was, like Wright and Wong, a pre-multiculturalist writer: as his later reception by a generation of black nationalists would demonstrate, he was correctly perceived for the most part as hostile to the third phase of cultural nationalism that developed shortly after the Civil Rights era (see Warren 1–23). He was not so concerned with the possibility of cultural loss, a trope that motivated the anthropology-inflected Hurston, or the trope of cultural rediscovery and renewal that was central to the anthropologically inflected cultural nationalisms that were to come. Ellison was part of the ascendant liberal consensus on the Americanization of racialized minorities, a period ending with the passage of the Voting Rights Act and Ellison's attendance at the White House Arts Festival, both in 1965. That emerging consensus made it possible for him to conclude his novel with the famous nationalizing (but not nationalist) line, "Who knows but that, on the lower frequencies, I speak for you?" (581).

❧ CHAPTER 4

John Okada and the Sociology of Internment

> "Seven children," Papa Noda said proudly, counting with his fingers. "Seven treasures. I am not famous. I work all day and I am poor. But I have seven plants. Seven healthy, growing plants." [...] "I am always a gardener. I like work," he would say proudly. "I'll have seven strong plants in my family, yes. They'll root in the rich California soil and grow big. Maybe some day a fine blossom."
>
> —Toshio Mori, *Yokohama, California,* 1949 (110, 113)

"If we are children of America and not the sons and daughters of our parents, it is because you have failed." Such is the "message of great truth" offered by a young sociologist on a visit, of all places, to an internment camp during World War II in John Okada's *No-No Boy* (125). This Japanese American sociologist, newly returned from graduate work "at a famous Eastern school" (124) lectures the older generation of Japanese Americans on not understanding their children. "How many of you," the sociologist asks, "are able to sit down with your own sons and own daughters and enjoy the companionship of conversation?" (124–25). Americanization is indexed by family, he suggests to the interned citizens and immigrants: "Change, now, if you can, even if it may be too late, and become companions to your children. This is America, where you have lived and worked and suffered for thirty and forty years. This is not Japan. I will tell you what it is like to be an American boy or girl. I will tell you what the relationship between parents and children is in an American family" (125). This cross-generational message generally falls on the deaf ears of the older generation who cannot learn, this late in their lives, what the novel imagines as a correct insight. But one couple—Kenji's parents—leaves the lecture to seek their daughter at a dance in the camp's mess hall, where she practices American culture to "blaring music" (125).

This scene invokes *No-No Boy*'s primary rhetorical strategy of national identity and belonging: the generation gap now figured as the family broken and rearranged. The lecture is virtually identical to the one delivered—by a sociology instructor—to Jade Snow Wong, who, as we have seen, hears with "astounded ears" that "parents should do their best to understand their children, because young people also have their rights" (Wong 125). "You should understand me," Jade Snow tells her father, having comprehended the lesson (128). The 1957 *No-No Boy*'s scene of the young Asian American, educated in sociology, delivering a rebuke to parents for not knowing their Americanized children, is an obvious tribute to a similar scene from *Fifth Chinese Daughter.*

Okada's repetition as homage of the sociological trope of the generation gap is only partly ironic revision, signaled by the distance between the situations: the Chinese American student sits in a classroom at San Francisco Junior College and delivers her own sociology lecture in 1938, whereas the Japanese American parents sit in an internment camp in what must be 1943 or 1944. Wong, in fact, had been noticeably silent about the internment taking place during the war years as she finished at Mills College and began work in the wartime shipping industry. At Mills, for instance, one of her friends had been a Japanese American student called Teruko, "members of whose family were affiliated with the royalty of Japan" (Wong 157); Wong would have known her presumably between the fall of 1940 and the spring of 1942 when she graduated. *Fifth Chinese Daughter* does not mention what happens to her, and is likewise totally silent about the internment. Like Wong—but more profoundly—Boas, who died in December 1942, and Park, who died in 1944, were also publicly silent about it. And while the wartime *American Dilemma* framed America's continued discrimination against African Americans as an international war issue that sometimes made it difficult to persuade other countries of the Allied cause, Myrdal's book was likewise silent about the similarly race-based discrimination at work with the internment of Japanese Americans. *No-No Boy* thus takes up the enduring problem of phenotypical distinction and the ongoing social construction of race as they were instantiated in the events of the internment. Upon the internment foundered the liberal ideas of mid-century social science—Boas's racial equality and the separation of culture from race, and Park's assertion of the cultural assimilability of racial minorities through the generation gap.

Okada's parody of Wong's scene of instruction indicates the racial wrench that was thrown into the works of the sociology-influenced dream of *Brown,* the Civil Rights movement, and assimilative citizenship: that racialized minorities were not going to be easily culturally assimilated because of enduring phenotypical distinctions that continued to be racialized. I want to frame *No-No Boy* in the dynamics of what I am calling the second phase of the genealogy of literary multiculturalism: that as Okada began writing the novel in 1950 (Chen 281), the NAACP was in the early stages of the cases that would lead to *Brown v. Board of Education,* following a legal strategy prophesied at the end of Ralph Ellison's just-published *Invisible Man,* and Jade Snow Wong published her autobiography and then stumped throughout Asia on behalf of the State Department, promoting the United States as a nation of enduring racial equality and harmony. In this Cold War setting, and in the midst of an energetic national anticommunism, the United States began to target other communalist groups in the country: namely, the Indian tribes, whose sovereignty came under attack with the passing of the Termination bill in 1953, directing that treaty relationships between the federal government and the individual tribes be terminated, and individual Indians be assimilated into the modern, urban world. While Okada was composing the novel, *Brown* was announced, and then followed up with the Supreme Court's 1955 direction that schools begin to integrate "with all deliberate speed"; some months later at the end of 1955, the year Okada apparently finished writing his novel (Chen 281), Rosa Parks refused to cede her bus seat in the same row as a white passenger, thereby, according to popular history, inaugurating the Civil Rights movement.

The context for the composition of *No-No Boy* was the emerging national liberal consensus about the cultural assimilation of racialized minorities. In this chapter, I argue that Okada, like his Japanese American contemporary Monica Sone, adopted Park's theory of the generation gap—with even more energy than Chinese American writers such as Wong. Okada likewise instantiated a second sociological figure, that of the marginal man, making its use central to Asian American literature in the second phase. When *No-No Boy* was published in 1957, it constituted a warning to sociology's model: unlike the Irish, Italians, or Jews, some Americans would be distinguished from others by enduring phenotypical distinctions racialized by society, with the result, as *Hirabayashi v. United States* and *Korematsu v. United States* showed, that race would be an enduring category of citizenship and national belonging in the United States for the foreseeable future. Okada, in other words, wrote in an America still exhilarated—or, for some, dismayed—by post-*Brown* hopes, but he did so looking back to the racial logic of the internment, a lesson that made the new paradigm severely problematic. Okada's solution was not to abandon its dream—in fact, the novel understood the dream of assimilation to be already underway—but to imaginatively supplement it with Cold War national affect, an act that recalled Ralph Ellison's novel earlier in the decade.

No-No Boy tropes the collapse of Parkian sociology, with the "American in Japanese disguise" now revealed in internment logic as a Japanese in Japanese "uniform," in terms of the family destroyed, reconfigured, and unbearably mutated. The novel's preface introduces its central opposition between biology and national belonging:

> The Japanese who were born Americans and remained Japanese because biology does not know the meaning of patriotism no longer worried about whether they were Japanese-Americans or American-Japanese. They were Japanese, just as were their Japanese mothers and Japanese fathers and Japanese brothers and sisters. The radio had said as much. (viii–ix)

In the internment's logic, familial descent and kinship relations are understood to trump birthright citizenship and national belonging. The novel works out one such son's renegotiation with America through the gradual destruction and unnatural mutation of his family and its internal relations. This image of the family destroyed was suggested by the internment itself, in which Japanese American families were sometimes separated into different camps, and even occasionally into different nations, and during which draft-age Japanese American men were forced to choose between enlisting or going to prison, even while their siblings and parents remained detained in government-run "concentration camps." *No-No Boy* imagines such strains of separation entropically: relations snap, the family structure disintegrates, and the positions of the members change.

The protagonist, Ichiro, is one "no-no boy" who chose prison over war service.[1] Returning home from prison after the war, he discovers that his mother believes Japan has won the war and news to the contrary is American propaganda. Against his mother's delusion of Japanese ships arriving any day to take them "home," his father drinks heavily. His mother's first act when he comes home is to reaffirm the biological, familial connection that the preface has suggested. "I am proud to call you my son," she says to Ichiro, which the narrator glosses as:

> It was her way of saying that she had made him what he was and that the thing in him which made him say no to the judge and go to prison for two years was the growth of a seed planted by the mother tree and that she was the mother who had put this thing in her son and that everything that had been done and said was exactly as it should have been and that that was what made him her son because no other would have made her feel the pride that was in her breast. (11)

To argue against this genetic logic—the logic of race as a biologically meaningful category—the situation of internment and its aftermath demands the destruction of the family and its bonds. Upon Ichiro's return, his mother seeks to underscore his genetic descent from her to the Japanese American community, some of whom had sons who accepted the draft. *No-No Boy's* imaginative destruction of Ichiro's family begins here, as the narrator notes that although "the family group is a stubborn one and does not easily disintegrate," Ichiro or the narrator already regards his mother as "the woman who was only a rock of hate and fanatic stubbornness and was, therefore, neither woman nor mother" (21). This is the first insistence of what becomes a central rhetorical gesture in *No-No Boy:* the repudiation of familial relation. As her "sickness of the soul" deepens, she is described as "a woman, a mother who is also a stranger" (104). Ichiro's father is "neither husband nor father" (116). Ichiro and his brother Taro are now "strangers" (17) as well. "The reason," the novel explains, "why Taro was not a son and not a brother was because he was young and American and alien to his parents" (19). When Taro, having turned eighteen, leaves to join the army, he is a "son who was not a son but a stranger" (68). After Taro betrays Ichiro to his friends, who want to beat up a no-no boy, Ichiro imagines the fraternal bond as having been destroyed, for Taro is "my brother who is not my brother" (81). In *No-No Boy,* the mother is not a mother, nor the father a father, the sons are not sons, nor are they brothers; even the voluntary bond of husband and wife has ruptured.

No-No Boy thus registers and tropes the strains placed on Japanese American families interned during World War II. These were not just the practical strains of separation and internal strife about whether to accept the draft. These were also theoretical strains based in the problems of biology, race, and citizenship. With this rhetoric of familiacide, the novel repudiates the biological ties of family that the logic of internment depended on. This repudiation takes place not only on the intergenerational level, but also on the intragenerational level, where the consanguinity of Ichiro and Taro must be metaphorically destroyed so that Taro can avoid repeating his brother's mistake of saying no to America, which would otherwise happen because, their mother believes, of their blood descent. Ichiro's "mistake," as the novel constantly renders it, of saying no to America, is likewise figured as a flaw generated by his bloodline. His mother's Japanese essence, and now her madness, may also be his own. The problem is not that there is a generation gap between the Isei and the Nisei, as the young sociologist imagines, but that there is not enough of a generation gap between them. In Ichiro's case, the intergenerational ties must be severed in order to make space for national belonging.

No-No Boy's interest in the power of racial identity centers on Ichiro's mother, and the novel's gutsy move is to craft her according to the logic of internment itself. Deeply loyal to the Japanese emperor, she embodies the alarmist government and military fears about the Japanese American community. Both the government—implicitly upheld by the Supreme Court—and Ichiro's mother understood this loyalty to be a racial trait, not cultural consent. Ichiro's mother sees those Japanese Americans who enlist in the U.S. Army as traitorous to Japan and to the race. Race cannot be displaced by cultural consent, but it does need to be completed by culture.[2] This is what it means for Ichiro's mother to imagine herself as the "tree" and Ichiro the "seed"; in similarly biological language, she imagines the Boasian separation of cultural practice from biological race as bodily death. "I will be dead when you begin to cease to be Japanese," she tells Ichiro (42). She sees the signs of American cultural practices among the younger generation as betrayal, and destroys a record player, perceiving in American music the danger of assimilation.[3]

> All she had wanted from America for her sons was an education, learning and knowledge which would make them better men in Japan. To believe that she expected that such a thing was possible for her sons without their acquiring other American tastes and habits and feelings was hardly possible and, yet, that is how it was. [...] it was like denying the existence of America. (205)

Such racial notions were the logic behind internment in the early 1940s. While *Korematsu v. United States* disingenuously denied "racial prejudice" as the basis for the policy, the dissenting justices recognized it for what it was: in the words of Justice Jackson, it was a decision based on a "different racial stock," since German and Italian aliens (let alone American citizens of German or Italian descent) were not interned. Though neither *Hirabayashi* (1943) nor *Korematsu* (1944) challenged internment as such, they made clear that the Supreme Court would have upheld the racial logic of the internment if it were challenged.[4] American law had long depended on notions of biological racial difference, and *Hirabayashi* and *Korematsu* were consistent with the general legal acceptance of race. Accordingly, we have to see a sea change affecting the Court (which had many of the same members) between the 1944 *Korematsu* and the 1954 *Brown v. Board of Education*, a sea change enabled by the legal establishment's increasing acceptance of social science work on race and culture in the first half of the twentieth century.[5]

This constitutional problem is at the heart of *No-No Boy*. The Court's intervention during the internment was to uphold the theoretical probability of individual identity, but to argue that from the white majority perspective, it was impossible to tell how individuals were different from the group. The entire group, accordingly, needed to be detained. In *Hirabayashi*, for instance, the Court noted the continued cohesion of the group on the West Coast, and said that the Japanese Americans "have prevented their assimilation as an integral part of the white population"—an assumption that Robert Park's Race Relations Survey had called erroneous, pointing instead to nativist and exclusionist law as slowing Asian American assimilation. Though the Court found that "Distinctions between citizens solely because of their ancestry are by their very nature odious to a free people," it found that in the case of an emergency, this ostensibly "odious" process (which was actually quite ordinary, in view of segregation, systematic disenfranchisement, and racial immigration policy) could be countenanced.

As was later pointed out, however, there were ways to ascertain the loyalty of these 112,000 detainees, but they went largely unused. Peter Irons makes clear that potentially provocative material about the racial beliefs of those conducting the evacuation—particularly those of General John L. DeWitt, head of the Western Defense Command and of the camps—was carefully and illegally concealed from publication and from the Supreme Court (*Delayed* 5–6). (Evidence of this suppression would lead to a writ of *coram nobis* in 1983, voiding Korematsu's original conviction.) DeWitt's February 1942 memorandum recommending mass evacuation, for example, argued:

> In the war in which we are now engaged racial affinities are not severed by migration. The Japanese race is an enemy race and while many second and third generation Japanese born on United States soil, possessed of United States citizenship, have become "Americanized," the racial strains are undiluted. To conclude otherwise is to expect that children born of white parents on Japanese soil sever all racial affinity and become loyal Japanese subjects, ready to fight and, if necessary, to die for Japan in a war against the nation of their parents. [...] It, therefore, follows that along the vital Pacific Coast over 112,000 potential enemies, of Japanese extraction, are at large today. (qtd. in Irons, *Delayed* 108–9)

That DeWitt rests his case on an old-fashioned notion of biological race—of the kind that Boas had been critiquing steadily for four decades—is clear; what is surprising is that *No-No Boy* instantiates DeWitt's exact logic in the person of Ichiro's mother, for whom "racial affinities are not severed by migration" or by generations. DeWitt also denies, as though in direct reference, Robert Park's finding in the *Survey Graphic* issue that "extraordinary" assimilation was taking place among the children of Asian immigrants.

John Okada directly confronts the notion of biological race that animated the internment. His strategy is identical to that of Zora Neale Hurston,

Richard Wright, Jade Snow Wong, and, we shall see in the next chapter, Américo Paredes: to stage the conflict between race and culture in order to replace the former with the latter. The particular model of his social science–articulated culture concept is sociological, like Wright's and Wong's, and not anthropological, like Hurston's and Paredes's, thus reflecting his integrationist and assimilationist politics. The specific sociological task at hand for Okada is to separate the Japanese American from Japanese cultural continuity in the United States. In this way, his sociological strategy is unlike Wright's—whose work generally embraced Franklin Frazier's argument that black culture was deprived insofar as it departed from the dominant culture—and more like Wong's, who embraced sociology's generation gap as the idea by which her own Americanization might be highlighted. While both *Fifth Chinese Daughter* and *No-No Boy* use the generation gap to separate the protagonists from their parents' cultures, Okada turns its screw, producing a text that, unlike Wong's, has no interest in preserving minimal ethnic foods, customs, or holidays.

It is only the generation gap between the cultural ways of the parents and those of the children that can destroy the biological transmission at the heart of the racial logic of both Ichiro's mother's metaphor of the tree and the seed and General DeWitt's assertion that "the racial strains are undiluted" in second- and third-generation Japanese Americans. The generation gap performs the same function in *No-No Boy* as it did in *Fifth Chinese Daughter,* except that in Okada, Japanese culture must be abandoned with a totality and speed unnecessary to the gradual divestment of Chinese culture found in Wong. Indeed, the urgency of destroying the racial logic behind internment—the logic of which, remember, not even the great liberal thinkers Boas, Park, and Myrdal could bring themselves to publicly condemn or even recognize—leads Okada to so radically embrace sociology's cultural transformation in the generation gap and the concept of Americanization that he adopts a rhetoric of familiacide by which all family ties are destroyed.

Near the end of the novel, for instance, following his mother's suicide once she begins to realize the truth of the war's outcome, Ichiro is disgusted at her Buddhist funeral's empty ceremony: the priest, for instance, recites "the unintelligible mumbo-jumbo revered by all the old ones present but understood by none" (191). "It had been quite a show and this was the final scene," muses Ichiro, "If it all added up to something, he had missed it. He wanted very much for all of it to come to an end" (192). Ichiro, in fact, leaves before the funeral proceedings are over. Not only has the family been destroyed—and his mother in fact removed from the drama—but Japanese culture itself has been rendered "meaningless" as the funeral eulogies Ichiro cannot bear to hear (194). There is some irony in the fact that Okada, like

Wright, became an author heralded by cultural nationalists in the 1970s, given the dispatch with which both authors willingly abandoned minority cultural continuity in the United States.

❧ Marginal Men and "Resettlement"

I want to extend this discussion of how crucial sociological ideas were for mid-century integrationist Asian American writers by looking at another sociological idea that helped them deploy the culture concept in place of race and theorize the process of changing one's culture. This idea was Robert Park's "marginal man," and it is a concept through which mid-century minority writers like Okada, Wong, and Wright expressed their sense of being on the margins between cultures, incompletely assimilated into the dominant culture, a bicultural affliction creating a heightened awareness of culture itself.

In 1928, following his work on the Pacific Race Relations Survey, Park theorized the marginal man as a peculiar product of migration and modernity, first typified as the European Jew emerging from the ghetto. He was

> a cultural hybrid, a man living and sharing intimately in the cultural life and traditions of two distinct peoples; never quite willing to break, even if he were permitted to do so, with his past and his traditions, and not quite accepted, because of racial prejudice, in the new society in which he now sought to find a place. He was a man on the margin of two cultures and two societies, which never completely interpenetrated and fused. The emancipated Jew was, and is, historically and typically the marginal man, the first cosmopolite and citizen of the world. He is, par excellence, the "stranger," whom Simmel, himself a Jew, has described with such profound insight and understanding in his *Sociologie.* ("Human Migration" 354)

Park suggested that recent autobiographies of Jewish immigrants in America showed evidence of the marginal man's "divided self" (355).[6] This formulation of "divided self," of course, strongly echoes W. E. B. Du Bois's concept, in his 1905 *Souls of Black Folk,* of the "double consciousness" experienced by African Americans. David Palumbo-Liu suggests that one difference between the two concepts is that the marginal man is in cultural conflict, but double consciousness registers the effects of power for "nationals without [full] citizenship" (*Asian* 299). Du Bois "removed the onus from individual psychic dysfunctionality and placed it on institutional racism," Palumbo-Liu notes, whereas notions of the marginal man's "divided self" or, later, an Asian

American "dual personality," "tended to repathologize the individual racial and ethnic subject and make the psychic instability of the subject a product of his or her own inability to make cultural choices" (300).[7]

Park's 1928 article on the marginal man became the seed for his student Everett V. Stonequist's doctoral dissertation, published in 1937 as *The Marginal Man*. Richard Wright read *The Marginal Man* in 1945 after he had written his autobiography, *Black Boy*, but he readily recognized himself in Stonequist's work, writing in his journal "I AM the marginal man!" (Fabre 585n9). Here once again is the social science shock of recognition, as when Wong hears her sociology instructor's lesson: sociology does not so much convey a new thought as articulate in a theorized and methodical fashion one's own experience. Richard Wright's next major work, *The Outsider* (1953), extensively used the marginal man concept, making it anticipatory of Okada's *No-No Boy* four years later.

Wright's book is so steeped in the language of the marginal man concept that it can serve as a gloss on the theory, helping us understand its later significance for *No-No Boy*. *The Outsider*'s protagonist is Damon Cross, a man who becomes free from society's untruths and empty mores when he is mistakenly identified as killed in a subway wreck. This social freedom brings responsibility and dread—the book is more steeped in existentialism than it is in sociology—to an already alienated outsider who can now leave behind his pointless job, his separated but powerful ex-wife, and his mindless friends. Cross kills a friend who threatens his new anonymity, and the novel, like other existentially influenced works of the 1950s such as Patricia Highsmith's *The Talented Mr. Ripley* and *Deep Water*, adopts thriller conventions of murder, evasion, and identity detection to structure the existential drama about social freedom. Cross's antagonist is a New York D.A. named Ely Houston, who is intellectually suitable because they are both marginal men, potential outsiders to and observers of the social world on account of what the novel imagines as their analogous visibility, of Cross being black and Houston being "a hunched-back man" (497). "My personal situation in life has given me a vantage point from which I've gained some insight into the problems of other excluded people," Houston tells Cross when they first meet, before Cross is a murder suspect. Cross realizes that Houston, "in identifying himself with Negroes, had been referring to his deformity. Houston was declaring himself to be an outsider like Cross" (499). The novel approves of this parallel, its point that being black and being deformed give one potential access to double consciousness.

Though trained in law, Houston has obviously been reading a lot of Chicago sociology. "Negroes were transported to this country and sold into slavery, then stripped of their tribal culture and held in bondage; and then allowed, so teasingly and over so long a period of time, to be sucked into our way of life," Houston states, in a fairly accurate summary of sociology's and Myrdal's trope of cultural loss in the Middle Passage (499). But Houston continues, seemingly cognizant of the social and legal changes afoot, "We are not now keeping the Negro on such a short chain and they are slowly entering our culture" (499). It is in such a transition from segregation to full cultural membership that Wright has Houston draw on Park and Stonequist's marginal man to theorize what the process will be like:

> Negroes, as they enter our culture, are going to inherit the problems we have, but with a difference. They are outsiders and they are going to know that they have these problems. They are going to be self-conscious; they are going to be gifted with a double vision, for, being Negroes, they are going to be both *inside* and *outside* of our culture at the same time. [...] Negroes will develop unique and specially defined psychological types. They will become psychological men, like the Jews.... They will not only be Americans or Negroes; they will be centers of *knowing,* so to speak. (499–500)

This is straight "marginal man" theory, right down to the invocation of the Jew and the suggestion of the "type."

Wright's adaptation of Park and Stonequist's marginal man, a figure situated in the middle of, and yet prevented from fully achieving, cultural assimilation, is to make his cosmopolitan position of outsider/insider a privileged existential one. Another way to put this is to say that Park understood the marginal man to be a detour or side-effect during the process of assimilation. "All our so-called racial problems," Park wrote before introducing the concept of the marginal man, "grow out of situations in which assimilation and amalgamation do not take place at all, or take place very slowly" ("Human Migration" 353). By 1953, the Parisian Wright, though still an integrationist and assimilationist, did not want to give up the privileged existential position, diagnosed by Park as "the marginal man," of being an observer and critic of culture itself. Cross is both inside and outside the culture, as are, in their own way, Houston, and Wright himself. In the genealogy of multiculturalism, *The Outsider* thus shares the same place as the novel published the previous year that it resembles: Ralph Ellison's *Invisible Man*. Both novels privilege the growing self-consciousness of the protagonists, their existential separateness from and critique of the social, and their universal rather than cultural groundings, although the horizon ultimately remains national for Ellison in a way that it does not for Wright.

The agony and privilege of the margin is likewise the conclusion of another 1950s novel articulated through the sociological vision of the marginal man: John Okada's *No-No Boy*. Without *The Outsider*'s existential ethos, *No-No Boy* offers a more strictly Parkian reading of the "divided self" that is created when complete assimilation is denied "because of racial prejudice." As with *The Outsider*, *No-No Boy* has two marginal men at its center. Just as the legal antagonists Cross and Houston are revealed to share the status of marginal men, so too does the no-no boy Ichiro share this status with his friend Kenji, even though Kenji is his supposed opposite, having served in the war (and lost part of a leg doing so). They become friends because, even though they have arrived at their self-consciousness from opposite paths, they recognize in each other their marginality: they are critical observers of the social world to which, though wholly culturally American, they are not permitted to totally assimilate because of their "racial uniform," as Park put it ("Human Migration" 353). The novel describes the friendship between Ichiro and Kenji as a meeting of national and existential opposites:

> one already dead but still alive and contemplating fifty or sixty years more of dead aliveness, and the other, living and dying slowly. They were two extremes, the Japanese who was more American than most Americans because he had crept to the brink of death for America, and the other who was neither Japanese nor American because he had failed to recognize the gift of his birthright when recognition meant everything. (73)

While Park's first 1928 formulation of the marginal man saw it as an immigrant trait, he gradually extended the theory in the 1930s to the children of immigrants (such as Ichiro and Kenji), thus joining the figure of the marginal man to the trope of the generation gap. In 1931, again citing what would become "life writing" in literary studies, Park argued, "The life history documents of immigrant peoples, many of which have been published in recent years, have revealed the manner and extent of the inner moral conflicts to which immigrants and frequently immigrant children are subjected in making the transition from the cultural tradition of the home country to that of the new" ("Personality" 370). In 1943, a year before his death, Park suggested that between first- and second-generation immigrants there might be "a more or less complete break in the cultural succession" ("Education and the Cultural Crisis" 317). And in one instance, Park then went on to see the second-generation American as especially typifying the marginal man:

> Some of the consequences referred to are so obvious and so marked that they have produced in the second generation a recognizable personality

type sometimes described as "the marginal man," i.e., the man who lives on the margin of two cultures—that of the country of his parents and that of the country of his adoption, in neither of which he is quite at home. We know, in a general way, for reasons that are not at present wholly intelligible, that this so-called "marginal man" is likely to be smart, i.e., a superior, though sometimes a superficial, intellectual type. (318)

But what sets Ichiro apart from other no-no boys like his superficial friend Freddie and what sets Kenji apart from other gung-ho Japanese American soldiers like the equally superficial Bull are their deliberations on the war, on the double-bind posed to interned Japanese American men to serve in the war or be imprisoned, and on ethnicity, race, and nation.[8]

Ichiro, for instance, wonders about his mother and Kenji:

> Was it she who was wrong and crazy not to have found in herself the capacity to accept a country which repeatedly refused to accept her or her sons unquestioningly, or was it the others who were being deluded, the ones, like Kenji, who believed and fought and even gave their lives to protect this country where they could still not rate as first-class citizens because of the unseen walls? (104)

No-No Boy, here and elsewhere, underlines the racialization processes in the United States that continually remake race as socially real. Ichiro recalls attending a church with another internee during internment, and though they are welcomed, he is sickened when he discovers that a lone black man is viciously ostracized by the Christian congregation (229–32).

This scene echoes Kenji's earlier disgust at the Club Oriental, when he discovers that the Chinese American landlord will not allow black men into his bar. Kenji leaves in dismay, but the event prompts this meditation:

> Was there no answer to the bigotry and meanness and smallness and ugliness of people? One hears the voice of the Negro or Japanese or Chinese or Jew, a clear and bell-like intonation of the common struggle for recognition as a complete human being and there is a sense of unity and purpose which inspires one to hope and optimism. One encounters obstacles, but the wedge of the persecuted is not without patience and intelligence and humility, and the opposition weakens and wavers and disperses. And the one who is the Negro or Japanese or Chinese or Jew is further fortified and gladdened with the knowledge that the democracy is a democracy in fact for all of them. (134)

But as this democratic vision begins to flourish, Kenji imagines scenes that forestall the promise: 1) a European immigrant refusing to sit beside a black man on a bus, 2) a Chinese American girl "flaunting" her white prom date before other Asian Americans, 3) a Japanese American, feeling good about not being Chinese, being refused service in an Italian restaurant, and 4) a black man passing for white who "becomes hated" by other African Americans (135–36). Though "Kenji thought about these things and tried to organize them in his mind so that the pattern could be seen and studied and the answers deduced therefrom. And there was no answer because there was no pattern" (136), it is unclear why he cannot see the obvious: the need for the despised to despise is of course a "pattern."

These marginal man musings make Kenji one of the most expressive and sympathetic philosophers of ethnic and racial difference in the novel. But the novel not only critiques racism, but also ethnic identity as such. The other marginal man, Ichiro, for instance, when approached by a Japanese American waiter who is eager to express affiliation, responds by mourning ethnic enclaves, and thinks it would be ideal if a consensual nation could somehow replace familial descent as the basis for human loyalty:

> He had heard how a Chinese from China by the name of Eng could go to Jacksonville, Florida, or any other place, and look up another Chinese family by the same name of Eng and be taken in *like one of the family* with no questions asked. There was nothing wrong with it. On the contrary, it was a fine thing in some ways. Still, how much finer it would be if Smith would do the same for Eng and Sato would do the same for Wotynski and Laverghetti would do likewise for whoever happened by. Eng for Eng, Jap for Jap, Pole for Pole, and like for like meant classes and distinctions and hatred and prejudice and wars and misery. (157; emphasis added)

In place of the biologically extended family, Ichiro imagines here the superior "brotherhood of man" (see Marc Shell, *Children of the Earth*). Kenji, however, remains the primary theorizer of the problem and the solution. He recalls the Japanese American community returning to Seattle after the internment and thinks that the few who scattered to New York or Arkansas "had learned that living in big bunches and talking Jap and feeling Jap and doing Jap was just inviting trouble" (163).

As with Ichiro's meditation above, Kenji's vision is not of cultural pluralism, but of cultural assimilation. "Pretty soon," Kenji says,

> it'll be just like it was before the war. A bunch of Japs with a fence around them, not the kind you can see, but it'll hurt them just as much. They bitched and hollered when the government put them in camps and put real fences around them, but now they're doing the same damn

thing to themselves. They screamed because the government said they were Japs and, when they finally got out, they couldn't wait to rush together and prove that they were. (164)

In good Parkian fashion, Ichiro responds with an ethnic comparison: "They're not alone, Ken. The Jews, the Italians, the Poles, the Armenians, they've all got their communities" (164). Kenji agrees, but seems to condemn the idea of ethnic communities as such, which he blames on the older generation. And as with Park, who extended the ideal of cultural assimilation to racialized minorities even as he wondered whether this process would finally be complete only once race had disappeared, Okada's understanding of racialization suggests that cultural assimilation might have to be accompanied by a procedure that might diminish the "visibility" of the minorities: namely, miscegenation. Kenji recommends to Ichiro that he eventually "Go someplace where there isn't another Jap within a thousand miles. Marry a white girl or a Negro or an Italian or even a Chinese. Anything but a Japanese. After a few generations of that, you've got the thing beat" (164). This theory of racial amalgamation, which seems to be what it would take to finally bring the biological into line with the patriotic, is not really denied by either Ichiro or Kenji, but it is imagined as perhaps only "a fine dream," and not a practical model for action (164). When Ichiro reports Kenji's words to Emi, she says, "He only meant that things ought to be that way" (170). Like Park, *No-No Boy* imagines amalgamation as the possibly necessary step to the full cultural assimilation of racialized minorities.

What is so striking about Kenji's musings on the need to dissolve ethnic communities—and what has not yet been recognized in criticism on *No-No Boy*—is the extent to which they concord with the government policy of dispersing and resettling Japanese Americans away from the West Coast and into mostly white communities during and after the internment. This policy is most associated with the head of the War Relocation Authority, Dillon S. Myer. As early as 1943, Myer's solution to the "racial problem" of Japanese American communities on the West Coast was a policy of planned dispersion (Drinnon 29, 50). This policy became the official plan of the Roosevelt administration (59), and eventually resulted in fifty thousand Japanese Americans being dispersed (at least initially) away from the Coast (60). Richard Drinnon suggests that the "evacuation" of Japanese Americans echoed the policy of Indian removal between 1813 and 1855 (39), and shows how dispersion and assimilation became official Roosevelt administration policy, as overseen by Myer. But what has only recently and incompletely been uncovered is the fact that a more immediate model than Indian removal for Japanese

American resettlement lay in the University of Chicago sociology's theories of migration, urban change, and the four progressive stages of assimilation.

In his excellent account of Asian Americans and sociology, Henry Yu concludes, "In a curious way, resettlement, by taking small, isolated groups of Japanese from the West Coast and spreading them across the American landscape, fit perfectly into the assimilation cycle's definition of how to expose Orientals to American society" (188). A recent urban planning dissertation by Ayanna Sumiko Yonemura suggests that the fit between sociology and resettlement was more substantive than merely "curious," providing its intellectual context and sometimes direct influence. As she puts it, "although these phrases don't actually appear in WRA documents, sociological terms such as 'narrative of generations' and 'assimilation cycle' reverberate strongly throughout WRA resettlement policy. Employing these concepts, the sociologists provided a way to organize the data they collected in the camps, and WRA administrators used the social science data to implement resettlement policy" (87). Yonemura argues that both the geographical emphasis on migration and the policy of resettling individuals rather than small groups "can be traced to the Chicago sociological theorists" (90).

Three connections between Chicago sociology and internment are suggestive of how this line of influence came about. Yu and Yonemura note the presence of both anthropologists and sociologists as researchers at the internment camps, particularly with the Japanese Evacuation and Resettlement Study (JERS) led by Berkeley sociologist Dorothy Swaine Thomas, wife of William Thomas, the man who had drawn Robert Park from Tuskegee to Chicago (Yu 121–23).[9] A second connection came in early 1943 when Dillon Myer attended a race relations seminar at the University of Chicago, which was likewise attended by both Robert Park and his son-in-law Robert Redfield. Yonemura believes that "either Myer or one of his staff members gave a presentation at the seminar" (93n27). Redfield latter wrote Myer that Park had afterwards opined that it was "the best seminar in the minorities and race relations field that the University had ever held," an evaluation he seemed to link to the participation of War Relocation Authority staff. Redfield concluded, "I drove away from the meeting with Dr. Park, and he said after a little that he was greatly impressed by the realistic and penetrating analysis which the Authority officers had given to their problem. He said that it gave him a new pride in his country."[10] No record appears to exist as to what the WRA's presentation entailed, but, given that the first leave policy geared toward college-educated, Christian Nisei was formulated in July 1942 and implemented in March 1943 (Yonemura 88, 136; Drinnon 50), it is safe to assume that part of what made Park proud might have been his own, now officially embraced, theoretical labor in enabling an assimilative answer to the "problem" of internment.

Beyond Yu and Yonemura's research, I would like to offer a third connection between sociology and the WRA policy of resettlement, one that might account for how resettlement grew out of early leave policies for Midwestern and Eastern college-bound Nisei, policies seemingly formulated almost immediately after "evacuation" had been carried out. Robert W. O'Brien became the director of the National Japanese-American Student Relocation Council in 1942, an organization formed for the purpose of advocating that Nisei college students be allowed leave the camps in order to finish their college educations at non-West Coast institutions. This involvement appears to have grown out of his position as "an assistant dean of arts and sciences at the University of Washington" (Girdner and Loftis 336), a capacity through which he was trying, by March 1942, to arrange future study arrangements for some imminently evacuating Nisei students.[11] But O'Brien was also, apparently simultaneously, a sociology student and probably already the doctoral candidate of Washington professor Jesse Steiner. In his testimony to the Tolan Committee hearings on February 28 and March 2, 1942, O'Brien stated that "my training in the last 12 years has been in the area of sociology concerned with minorities and their assimilation and usefulness to the total American pattern."[12]

Steiner, in turn, had been a student of Park's at the University of Chicago, and had written a 1917 dissertation titled "The Japanese Invasion: A Study in the Psychology of Inter-Racial Contacts." O'Brien's 1945 dissertation, "The Changing Role of the College Nisei during the Crisis Period: 1931–1943," was thoroughly grounded in Chicago sociology, citing both his supervisor's work and also Park's seminal essays "Behind Our Masks" and "Human Migration and the Marginal Man," and Stonequist's larger *The Marginal Man*. In a 1944 section of his dissertation published as his article "Selective Dispersion as a Factor in the Solution of the Nisei Problem," O'Brien explicitly argued that Nisei college student dispersion during internment was a blueprint for resettling Japanese Americans across the country during and after the war for the purpose of "early and rapid assimilation" (147).

O'Brien's access to WRA information and camps, necessary for his dissertation's data, suggests a working relationship at least. I would like to hypothesize further that the work of this sociology doctoral candidate and assistant dean to help Nisei finish college in the Midwest and his explicit sociological theorization of how this might provide a pattern for postwar resettlement suggest the most important influential link we have yet between Chicago sociology and the WRA's policy of resettling Japanese Americans away from the Coast during and after the war. It is through O'Brien, as well as Myer's own contact with Chicago sociologists and the existence of the Japanese Evacuation and Resettlement Study, that sociology's culture provided the theoretical grounding for the government policy of Japanese American resettlement.

Sociology thus provided a double-edged sword regarding Japanese American internment. On the one hand, Steiner and O'Brien offered a vigorous defense of Japanese American loyalty, integration, and assimilation at the Tolan hearings on whether to evacuate Japanese Americans from the Coast. Although Steiner conceded that "enemy aliens" might need to be evacuated from "areas adjacent to defense plants and military and naval establishments," and equivocated on second-generation Japanese Americans educated partly in Japan, he, like O'Brien, defended the loyalty of the Nisei and suggested that the FBI might investigate (with the JACL's help) specific individuals suspected of disloyalty. Steiner several times invoked the existence of German and Italian aliens and second-generation American citizens as a point of comparison, arguing that as long "as I hear of no emphasis upon the removal of German aliens and Italian aliens from the Atlantic coast, I do not see why we should try to remove them [Japanese aliens] from the Pacific coast" (Tolan). O'Brien likewise emphasized Nisei loyalty and integration, arguing against their evacuation, and agreed with Steiner that evacuation should be considered solely for "enemy aliens from only selected defense areas and selected coast counties."

The liberal reading of Japanese American loyalty and assimilation was predicated on the central sociological findings of racial equality, the cultural assimilability of racialized minorities, and the Asian American generation gap. Such was the progressive edge of liberal sociology's sword, and, paradoxically, such was likewise its conservative and oppressive side. The policy of resettlement was not pluralist but coercive: while O'Brien stopped short of recommending a policy of forcing Japanese Americans to resettle away from the Coast after the war, the planning that he envisioned and Myer conducted was suffused with psychological manipulation of incarcerated people, the assumptions of cultural supremacy and normativity, and an illiberal social engineering that authoritatively told people what was best for them (see Drinnon). Sociology's culture underwrote a theoretical resistance to race-based internment policies, but it also underwrote the "liberal consensus" of the second phase, even if that consensus was sometimes forced onto a population without its consent.

What makes *No-No Boy* so extraordinary, however, is how closely its cultural politics mirror this sociological imaginary, even if Ichiro, Kenji, and Emi agree that the "fine dream" of dispersal (and amalgamation) must be voluntary rather than coerced policy.[13] Okada demurs at forced dispersion but he does not demur at its goal of cultural assimilation. While Ichiro and Kenji share the sociological position of marginal men and its heightened social consciousness, the novel draws a strong distinction not so much between their Americanizations—because they are both culturally American in their actual practices and values, and not at all Japanese—but between the Americanizations of their respective families. If the Chinese American, sociologically trained Pardee Lowe was able to make his father "truly an American" by marrying a white woman (297), Kenji's decision to be drafted and his loss of a leg in the war provide the mechanism whereby his family can finally claim what seems like unambiguous, healthy national belonging.

It is Kenji's father, after all, who takes the young Japanese American sociologist's message to heart, and has gotten to know his children, as an American parent should. Kenji has gangrene, and as the novel unfolds, doctors try to arrest its growth by amputating more inches from the few that his leg has left. We are to understand that Kenji's patriotic sacrifice in the army and the healthy American relationships in his family are inextricably linked. Though he has given his leg in the service of "Uncle Sam" (59), as he puts it, in language that joins the familial and the national, this adoption has not come at the expense of his biological family, but has rather enabled that family to become fully American in a way that Ichiro's family is not. For Kenji's father "had long forgotten when it was that he had discarded the notion of a return to Japan but remembered only that [it] was the time when this country which he had no intention of loving had suddenly begun to become a part of him because it was a part of his children" (120). Though Kenji's dad rents property (117), his children and their spouses purchase it, and the family itself is highly idealized in its American practices of watching the baseball game, sitting down to large family dinners of chicken and lemon meringue pies (no Japanese food here), talking about cars, and drinking whiskey.

Kenji's father has become American because, like his children and grandchildren, he does American things. Even though his father wonders if he should have prevented Kenji from serving in the war, Kenji questions what the result would have been:

> maybe you would have kept me from going into the war and I would have stayed out and had both my legs. But, you know, every time I think about it that way, I also have to think that, had such been the case, you and I would probably not be sitting down and having a drink together and talking or not talking as we wished. If my leg hurts, so what? We're buddies, aren't we? That counts. (123)

It is at this point that the father recalls the lecture from the young Japanese American sociologist about enjoying "the companionship of conversation," which, the novel clearly wants us to understand, has been a message internalized to the extent that Kenji and his father are now "buddies." The healthy resolution of the generation gap, in other words, comes by following the young Japanese American sociologist's advice: immigrant parents should get to know, and thereby become like, their Americanized children. This family contrasts highly with Ichiro's dysfunctional one, in which relations of mother to son, brother to brother, and husband to wife have been entirely destroyed by the war, and so must be described in terms of an ongoing familiacide.

Okada likewise uses Kenji's sacrifice-enabled Americanization to address another conundrum of race, culture, and assimilation, one resonating deeply with the logic and language of the internment. As we have seen, General DeWitt believed that people of Japanese descent might be born in the United States, but that something genetic prevented them from forming loyalty ties to their nation of birthright citizenship. This image of the Asian sojourner in America has a long history, and is part of what makes the "Asian" racially meaningful. Japanese Americans might be born on this "soil," as DeWitt puts it, but they are unable to have a true relation with the land. John Okada summons just such soil as a way to confront the internment's logic and its dependence on the enduring notion of the Asian as a sojourner in America. Kenji's choice of joining the army, for instance, has "made it so that you can put your one good foot in the dirt of America and know that the wet coolness of it is yours beyond a single doubt" (64). In one sense, he can put his one foot into the "dirt" and know it is his precisely because he cannot so place his other foot. Similarly, contrasted to Ichiro's sojourning mother is the Kumasaka family, whose son died on the European front: "But now, the Kumasakas, it seemed, had bought this house, and [Ichiro] was impressed. It could only mean that the Kumasakas had exchanged hope for reality and, late as it was, were finally sinking roots into the land from which they had previously sought not nourishment but only gold" (26). This sense of "sinking roots into the land" emerges, we are to understand, partly because of the Kumasakas' dead son, in the same way that Kenji can put his foot into the "dirt" because he has sacrificed his other leg.

Okada thus counters the long-standing "sojourner" stereotype of the Asian American in the American imaginary, the supposed multi-generational search for "not nourishment but only gold," by insisting on a spiritual relationship to the land attained most forcefully by those Japanese American families whose sons served in the war. It is likewise no accident that another crucial mid twentieth-century work of Japanese American literature, Toshio

Mori's *Yokohama, California,* also takes up the language and logic of Japanese American children especially developing "roots" in this "soil," as we see in the epigraph to this chapter. Ichiro imagines his mother's spirit returning to Japan after her death; unlike her, he and his father will now spend the family savings to fix up the store, fully settling in the United States. Kenji's family has had a head start in putting down roots, expedited in no small way by the father's engagement with a sociology that called for Japanese American parents to understand, and in some ways emulate, their American children "with change in their pockets and a thirst for cokes and beer and pinball machines or fast cars and de luxe hamburgers and cards and dice and trim legs" (34–35). It is likewise no accident that Emi, who is part of Ichiro's nationalizing therapy as I will show, owns "forty acres" of farmland (83). She is grounded in the land in the way that a city dweller could not be. But perhaps more important, this allusion to the African American hopes of "forty acres and a mule" following the Civil War suggests a somewhat fraught parallel between slavery and internment, in which systematic racial injustice *this time* appears to be on its way to being mended—in other words, Emi really does have forty acres, and consequently the patriotism and sense of belonging Ichiro needs.

🍂 John Okada's Cold War Patriotism

> The difference between democratic constitutional theory and democratic social practice in the treatment of minorities can be a large one. [...] Isolated communities of the concentration-camp type will not promote cultural assimilation and integration into American life, nor will they be in line with constitutional principle and the announced American war aims, which stress the values of human freedom and racial equality.
>
> —Everett V. Stonequist, "The Restricted Citizen," 1942 (149, 155)

No-No Boy's complexity and literary interest arise partly because it pays attention to the processes of racialization, distinguishing it along with *Invisible Man* from other 1950s texts like *Fifth Chinese Daughter* or Monica Sone's *Nisei Daughter.* Space does not permit me to develop a reading of Sone's Japanese American autobiography, but it is, with the works by Wong and Okada, representative of the possibilities of liberal assimilative social science–articulated Asian American literature of the second phase. Its central opposition is between the racial ties of what Sone repeatedly calls "blood" and that which comes to replace it, cultural conflict between Japanese and American cultures, which is eventually resolved through the generation gap between the older immigrant community and their American children. As with Okada, internment provides a kind of test for the new social science vision, and Sone herself was one of the early benefactors of the early release program described by O'Brien ("Selective Dispersion"), allowing her to leave Minidoka for Midwest higher education. Trained in clinical psychology, she casts the marginal man as a kind of "split personality" (238), with the internment especially producing her, in an interesting bodily metaphor, as "two-headed" (19, 158). But her overall alliance with sociology—including its central recasting of biological difference as disappearing cultural distinctions—is indicated in part by a 1979 introduction by University of Chicago–trained sociologist Frank Miyamoto.

More prone to cultural description (like Wong), Sone emphasizes (like Okada) the generation gap as an aid to non-pluralist assimilation, but is less honest (like Wong) about the continuing processes of racialization and American racism than Okada. By 1957, the hopes of *Brown* were in full swing, and the Civil Rights movement and its promise of integration had begun in earnest. *No-No Boy*'s wary reminder to the second phase's optimism about cultural integration and assimilation is that minority groups marked as visually different were not just another category of ethnic that might go through the stages of competition, conflict, accommodation, and assimilation, gradually losing through the generations their group-based distinction from majority society. This is what it means for Kenji to wistfully speak of racial amalgamation as what it would really take to make race disappear—to make *Plessy* or *Korematsu* or *Hirabayashi* impossible. Despite this warning, *No-No Boy* stays true to sociology's answer of the ethnic assimilation of racialized minorities through the technology of the generation gap and the experience of the marginal man.

That answer comes partly through the contrast between Ichiro's mother, who stands for the power of biological attachment, for race itself, and Emi, who becomes a surrogate mother/lover who might help birth Ichiro as an ethnic American after all, and, in a new twist, as a patriotic one at that. Not surprisingly, the novel's juxtaposition of the sociologically correct American family, and the sociologically dysfunctional, nationally uncertain family, is figured through attention to gender. As we have seen, the novel describes Ichiro's family as one in ruins, with the biological relations of son, brother, mother, father being undone by the conflicts attending internment. But the novel also describes a corresponding—or perhaps causal—decay in the gender identities of the family as well. Ichiro's mother, for instance, is described as "neither woman nor mother" (21). The family's gender roles seem to have been reversed, with his father cooking and his mother sitting at the table waiting to speak with him (40). Indeed, Ichiro increasingly senses that his mother and father, or his ex-mother and ex-father, have somehow switched the usual pattern: "Pa, he's just around," Ichiro thinks. "Pa's okay, what there is of him, but he missed out someplace. He should have been a woman. He should have been Ma and Ma should have been Pa. Things would have worked out differently then" (112). Ichiro rejects his manly mother who ultimately can birth only biological attachment to Japan and things Japanese. His existential search for America takes him into the arms of Emi, a Japanese American friend of Kenji's who provides Ichiro with the sexual and national therapy that helps him move away from the biological toward the patriotic. In obvious opposition to his mother's "flat-chested" and "shapeless" body (10), Emi is "slender, with heavy breasts, had rich, black hair which fell on her shoulders and covered her neck, and her long legs were strong and shapely like a white woman's" (83). But even though, or perhaps because, Emi's body is decidedly womanly, her therapeutic mediation for Ichiro returns to biology in order to resymbolize this movement.

Ichiro is first introduced to Emi by their mutual friend Kenji, who, returned from the war with his war-wound, has had his own existential problems to work out with Emi's help. Emi's husband—who, it happens, strikingly resembles Ichiro—likewise served in the war, but has stayed in Europe beyond the call of duty, and not sent for her. So cast off, but because "there's always more [love] because you're a woman," as Emi puts it (168), Emi wants to help Ichiro. Ichiro gets over his initial conventional shock that Kenji has brought him to Emi's house to make love to her, and all three are reconciled to the idea of sex as a kind of mutual therapy, for, as Kenji says, "she needs someone. Just like you need someone" (89). This national therapy takes the form of talk, sex, and more talk, in stages that suggest the inability to evade the biological ties that prevent patriotic, national belonging. As they lie in Emi's bed, they discuss their parents' shared belief that Japan won the war and Ichiro's belief that, because of his mother and his bad decisions, he has "ruined my life and I want to know what it is that made me do it" (91). Emi answers by stating the citizenship problem that had arrested the sociological possibility of racial assimilation: "It's because we're American and because we're Japanese and sometimes the two don't mix. It's all right to be German and American or Italian and American or Russian and American but, as things turned out, it wasn't all right to be Japanese and American. You had to be one or the other" (91). This explicit reference to the different treatment of aliens and citizens of different descents during World War II draws the heavy distinction between ethnic minorities and racial minorities.

This statement of citizenship effects does not help Ichiro resolve his own mistake in choosing not to serve in the war, and so, as he begins to sob in bed beside Emi, the novel tells us that "Emi reached out her free hand and drew his face against her naked breast. Lost and bewildered like a child frightened, he sobbed quietly" (92). What is striking is not that the posing of the question of citizenship and belonging seems to have a sexualized answer, but that it seems to vividly imagine Emi as becoming a substitute for Ichiro's mother right as that therapy takes place. This maternal gesture of drawing the sobbing child toward one's breast is somehow seen as an answer to the citizenship problem posed above—one in which the biological has opposed the patriotic, or, to use Werner Sollers's terms, descent has gotten in the way of consent. In a way, the novel would have us understand that Emi is the mother that Ichiro should have had—her body, after all, is shapely "like a white woman's" in the way that his mother's boyish form is not, as though instantiating Boas's original antiracial point that the environment produces different bodily effects on the children of immigrants. Emi is the mother Ichiro should have had, for she has a body which would make him American, not Japanese. Just as Kenji has gained a new "Uncle" through his service in the war, thereby becoming American, Ichiro's parentage must also be reimagined as almost an adoption.

In the nationalizing talk therapy the next morning, Emi begins articulating the answer of right feelings to the problem of enduring racialized citizenship that is developed by Kenji, Ichiro, and others, an answer not ironized by Okada. On the one hand, *No-No Boy* works by capturing the facts of internment and national belonging as a set of problems, a complexity that needs to be rendered, rather than, as with *Fifth Chinese Daughter,* an answer to be more or less easily arrived at. *No-No Boy* thus construes Ichiro's "mistake" as saying no not just to the two questions on the loyalty questionnaire, but to America itself. "Redemption" is still possible, to quote the novel's spiritualized metaphor, because "he was still a citizen" (51). He imagines time as healing the wounds of internment, for it will

> destroy the old Japanese who, living in America and being denied a place as citizens, nevertheless had become inextricably a part of the country which by its vastness and goodness and fairness and plenitude drew them into its fold, or else they would not have understood why it was that their sons, who looked as Japanese as they themselves, were not Japanese at all but Americans of the country America. (51–52)

Cultural belonging might erase the memory of racialized difference, Ichiro imagines, in a passage that describes culture as practices rather than as identity: "I will buy a home and love my family and I will walk down the street holding my son's hand and people will stop and talk with us about the weather and the ball games and the elections" (52). At this early point in the novel, he dismisses the possibility as a dream, but it is resuscitated by Emi during their talk. Emi thinks he has made a mistake that needs confession, and she expresses the post-*Brown* hopes of assimilative belonging: "This is a big country with a big heart. There's room here for all kinds of people" (95). Emi also thinks that the nation made a mistake with internment, and sees that national mistake as equal to Ichiro's refusals: "They made a mistake when they doubted you. They made a mistake when they made you do what you did and they admit it by letting you run around loose. Try, if you can, to be equally big and forgive them and be grateful to them and prove to them that you can be an American worthy of the frailties of the country as well as its strengths" (96).

But then, in an extraordinary speech that is neither ironic nor counter-manded by anything else in the novel, Emi recommends patriotism as the answer to Ichiro's citizenship problem:

> It's hard to talk like this without sounding pompous and empty, but I can remember how full I used to get with pride and patriotism when we sang 'The Star-Spangled Banner' and pledged allegiance to the flag at school assemblies, and that's the feeling you've got to have. [...] Next time you're alone, pretend you're back in school. Make believe you're singing 'The Star-Spangled Banner' and see the color guard march out on the stage and say the pledge of allegiance with all the other boys and girls. You'll get that feeling flooding into your chest and making you want to shout with glory. It might even make you feel like crying. That's how you've got to feel, so big that the bigness seems to want to bust out, and then you'll understand why it is that your mistake was no bigger than the mistake your country made. (96)

The problem with this patriotism, however, is that it is exactly the kind of national essentialism that Okada critiques in the Japanese. America here is to be measured not on actual practices and values (which would have to, as strict observation, include the facts of internment and Jim Crow along with the Declaration of Independence and discourses of liberty), but on an idealized, essential, transcendent, and unchanging image of an America that never was.

Importantly, Ichiro responds by being slightly encouraged in the face of this national essentialism, in a way that he was not when faced with his mother's cultural essentialism. "What's so good about being Japanese?" he rightly asks his mother after her insistence on its importance (103). She cannot answer this, of course; because she is committed to identity, Japanese is good because it is Japanese. But when faced with the same kind of logic by Emi—though now displaced onto a situation of consent rather than descent—Ichiro does not demand to know "What's so good about being American?" This is the question we might expect him to ask when faced with the facts of a number of things including internment, Ichiro's most immediate context. Not asking this question, even following the allusion to America's own "mistake" of internment, indicates a turn to essentialized national identity. America might have made a "mistake," but only insofar as it departed from its true values, values which are not to be gleaned from a study of practices, but which are asserted a priori as fact, irrespective of practice. In this sense, it is no surprise that the passage is couched in terms of the religious experience of confession, forgiveness, holy song, the rising "shout [of] glory," and the oceanic feeling of oneness with the world—or at least the nation. What makes *No-No Boy* a patriotic Cold War American novel is its approval of the notion that national identity is experienced religiously. *No-No Boy* asserts that both America and Ichiro made complementary, equal mistakes that can be mutually forgiven through an embrace of patriotism, an answer that goes uncriticized throughout the rest of the novel, even though patriotism's emotional structure is identical to the ethnic tribalisms that the novel repeatedly condemns elsewhere.

It is instructive at this point to crossthread my reading of Okada's Cold War patriotism as a form of national identity with a substantially similar expression of Cold War patriotism as national identity that emerges at the end of Ralph Ellison's *Invisible Man*. Both these 1950s novels begin to delineate one of the fundamental questions of *A Genealogy of Literary Multiculturalism*: Where, and for what reasons, does the concept and keyword "identity" emerge? If one of the stories of twentieth-century multicultural literature is its turn to thinking about the locus of difference as culture instead of race, what, in turn, does identity do that neither race nor culture could accomplish? Writers in the first and second phases did not use the word, or have a concept of, "identity": what united Hurston, McNickle, Wright, and Wong is their use of the concept of culture, even though their models for it were substantially different. One exception appears to be Ellison's 1952 use of it in *Invisible Man*. Ellison's narrator, boomeranged from his college, speaks of "the obsession with my identity," which is glossed by the questions, "Who was I, how had I come to be?" (259). But by the end of the novel, as he faces Ras the Destroyer in the Harlem riot, that question about the individual becomes folded into a larger problem of national ontology:

I looked at Ras on his horse and at their handful of guns and recognized the absurdity of the whole night and of the simple yet confoundingly complex arrangement of hope and desire, fear and hate, that had brought me here still running, and knowing now who I was and where I was and knowing too that I had no longer to run for or from the Jacks and the Emersons and the Bledsoes and Nortons, but only from their confusion, impatience, and refusal to recognize the beautiful absurdity of their American identity and mine. (559)

By the end of the novel, he thus appears confident in understanding "who I was," and that knowledge appears to entail "the beautiful absurdity of their American identity and mine."

Jonathan Arac sees Ellison's 1952 use of "identity" as "one beginning for a discursive cluster involving *identity*" (198), one I wish to place beside Okada's use only five years later, also in the Cold War period. Contextualizing the problem, Arac says:

> In our current usage, the term seems wholly ambivalent along the axis of necessity and freedom: The term is used to name both what you can't help being and also what you choose to become. No doubt this saturation of the spectrum is one cause for the term's appeal. In its history as a term, *identity* has undergone transformation and reversal. Its fundamental sense is *sameness,* but it is nowadays understood within a discourse of difference. (204)

Arac traces Ellison's probable use of the keyword to Kenneth Burke, who criticized the "bourgeois" opposition between "individual" identity and "environment" (203), and to the psychologist Erik Erikson, for whom identity is most importantly the "ability to experience one's self as something that has continuity and sameness" (qtd. in Arac 209). *Invisible Man* "discredits the terms *history* and *progress* and proposes in their stead the term *identity*" (211), and Ellison's use of the word turns him toward a liberal individualism, explains Arac: "This turn to the lessons of one's own life is sloganized in the book by the term *identity,* from which I began" (214–15). Arac elaborates that "first, the discourse of identity and the discourse of history interact in the book's master trope of *invisibility.* Invisibility is the figure for the difference between identity as self-possession ('I am who I am') and as dispossession ('how they see me'), and in this text *dispossession* specifically means being (un)seen as preterite" (215). In Ellison's adoption of the jeremiad, glossed by Arac through Sacvan Bercovitch's work, Arac argues that the novel finally "asserts the glorious model of 'America' against the dreadful shortcomings of what I will call 'actually existing Americanism'" (215). "This," Arac concludes, "is Ellison the patriot, who supported the Vietnam War" (215).

Arac's essay makes clear the way the invocation of identity in Ellison is attached to a kind of Americanism, and even patriotism. On the one hand, Ellison preserves an idealism, recognizing that American actuality is different from its stated ideals, and so invokes the latter on behalf of liberally reforming the former. And indeed, Ellison's framing of the problem in terms of "absurdity" is totally apt, if we recall Albert Camus's definition in the *Myth of Sisyphus* of absurdity as the structure wherein hope and desire (but not faith) are undertaken in the face of the facts of real existence (16). In this sense, Ellison's pragmatic invocation of "the principle on which the country was built" in order to enact social change is the deployment of hope against the real. As Arac argues, "Ellison was profoundly committed to the idea of America. Like Martin Luther King Jr., he summoned the actually existing United States to transform itself in accord with its own stated principles of human equality, principles and statements that had themselves arisen out of revolutionary and civil warfare. His resistance to identity politics did not prevent him from affirming, and exploring, an American identity" (205).

But what does it mean for Arac to acknowledge that the "stated principles of human equality" that were never instantiated in the republic were nonetheless part of an "American identity," one to be affirmed by Ellison? And what does it mean for Ellison to describe as "the principle on which the country was built" an ideal that was not actually practiced when the country was built? What does it mean, in short, for one to posit as a facet of an "identity" a "value" or principle that was not practiced, as though it were something that was practiced? This seems to me the sleight of hand that patriotism as national identity came to perform in the Cold War 1950s: even in the face of acknowledging that the nation did not actually practice human equality, it nonetheless affirmed it as a principle of the nation, as part of the nation's identity. But are our values things that we actually do, or things that we say that we do? Do we not need, in other words, a theory of hypocrisy to distinguish between an account of being based on the description of what a nation actually does and an account of being based on the description of what a nation says it is doing?

Perhaps the problem lies not in invoking ideals that have not yet been instantiated, but in calling them American. The ideal of human equality is universal, not American, and to make the mistake of naming it American is to make it part of American identity in a way that it never was in a descriptive sense. Arac makes clear that Ellison's notion of identity comes to him, through Burke and Erikson, from psychology. But was it not psychology in the first place which taught us that self-possession and self-continuity were kinds of mirages of experience—that our selves were not coterminous with our selves, and we did not have self-knowledge? If so, it appears (and why Arac does not underline this more clearly I am not sure) that Ellison misappropriates identity from Burke, or appropriates a concept that Burke has already misappropriated from Freud. In both cases, identity in Ellison becomes the (false) self-possession of the individual and of the nation: the nation content to characterize itself not according to what it actually does but according to an idealized and descriptively false version of itself. The issue here is not only having ideals that you fail to live up to, but attaching universal ideals to a nation and understanding the nation as the horizon in which the instantiation must take place, the forming of a bond between a value and a nation that has not existentially existed, or, to use Arac's terms, of treating the optative mood as though it were definitively indicative (197–98).

Arac is right to invoke Bercovitch and his analysis of how the American jeremiad and rituals of dissensus that followed deploy themselves through a comparison of actual practice with stated ideals. And Ellison is insightful in invoking Camusian absurdity as the structure recognizing the fundamental distinction between desire and the real. The problem is Ellison's invocation of identity, a technology whereby a universal ideal is attached to a nation that did not practice the ideal. An idea is not the same as an identity. National identity as patriotism pretends to make it possible to have an ideal that the nation does not practice. Ellison's use of national identity turns us away from existence, a betrayal of his invocation of Camus and his debt to existentialism. It is not accidental that this is the exact moment of patriotism: that he will be proud to be part of a country not because of what it has done but because of what it has pretended to be. And as we have seen, it is this exact account of national identity as patriotism that provided the emotional resolution in John Okada's *No-No Boy*. In both cases, national identity is a form of transcendence: patriotism as national identity brings their characters (and their authors) outside of the real; identity, in fact, is invoked precisely to work against a description of the real.

My argument is that John Okada and Ralph Ellison do not have concepts of Japanese American identity and African American identity, but instead a concept of "American identity," as Ellison terms it at the end of *Invisible Man*. And it is from this field of the nation that a notion of identity is first introduced into the genealogy of American literary multiculturalism. *No-No Boy* marks a fascinating moment in the genealogy of multicultural American literature. Though the novel registers and protests against the racial exclusions of internment, it ultimately upholds the sociological dream of the cultural assimilability of racialized minorities. But, importantly, *No-No Boy* is one of the first texts to supplement this sociological program of assimilation and civil rights with a powerful Cold War notion of national identity, of identity as such.

It is the hypothesis of *A Genealogy of Literary Multiculturalism* that identity as a way of thinking about being emerged not in continuity from an American nativism of three decades before, but from a Cold War political milieu increasingly pressed to define national character. My argument will be that the later multiculturalists, including Morrison, Momaday, Reed, and Anzaldúa, were not reading or responding to the classic 1920s nativists like Stoddard or Grant, or the literary expression of their commitments to identity that runs through American modernism, as Walter Benn Michaels has shown in *Our America*. The introduction of identity itself emerged from a wholly other context: namely, in response to the emerging American Cold War strategy of supplementing its ideological contest against communism with a fantasy of national character fundamentally unrelated to any social science commitment to empiricism and objectivity. Identity became a technology for separating the question of what a nation is from what it actually does. Thus, in his approval of Emi's recommendation of "how you've got to feel," Okada supersedes the question of what the country does with proper feelings about that country. He likewise abandons the novel's own trenchant critique of ethnocentrism, the preference for one's own group. A decade later, Black Arts movement theorists, like the Chicano movement theorizers, looked to the emerging postcolonial nationalisms for models on which to theorize the African American and Mexican American "nations" within America, but such cultural nationalisms were also reacting to the suffocating Cold War power of national identity as patriotism. In these ways, though African American authors were reviving Hurston's anthropological concept of culture and Chicano authors were extending Paredes's anthropological concept of culture, both groups began to attach culture to this Cold War/ postcolonial interest in national identity, to identity as such, in a fashion that neither Hurston nor Paredes sanctioned.

✒ CHAPTER 5

Américo Paredes and the Folklore of the Border

> Ahab's hunt is symbolic of the American thrust
> toward Asia. [...] Much violence has already occurred
> in the American experience, as the name of the ship
> suggests: The Pequots were a tribe of Connecticut
> Indians destroyed by whites in the seventeenth cen-
> tury. The extinction of the Pequots, it becomes clear
> in the discussion on "Loose-Fish," must be viewed
> within the context of European and white American
> expansionism. "What was America in 1492 but a
> Loose-Fish, in which Columbus struck the Spanish
> standard by way of waifing it for his royal master and
> mistress?" observed Ishmael. Writing shortly after the
> American war against Mexico and after California
> had been placed in "the hands of an enterprising
> people," Melville has Ishmael ask: "What at last will
> Mexico be to the United States? All Loose-Fish."
>
> —Ronald Takaki, *Iron Cages,* 1979 (287–88)

In the summer of 1954, Américo Paredes col-
lected 363 ballads and other songs from the Mexican American communities
of the Lower Border area in South Texas. *Brown v. Board of Education* was only
weeks old—it had been announced on May 17th of that year. John Okada
was nearly finished writing *No-No Boy,* and Jade Snow Wong had toured
Asia the year before to talk about *Fifth Chinese Daughter.* Ralph Ellison had
won the National Book Award for *Invisible Man* the year before; N. Scott
Momaday, another Southwesterner, would shortly attend the University of
Virginia Law School, where he would meet a different National Book Award
winner—William Faulkner. Zora Neale Hurston, another famous regional
folklore collector, was struggling to write a manuscript about Herod the
Great and would shortly write a letter to the *Orlando Sentinel* denouncing
Brown v. Board of Education. D'Arcy McNickle had left the Bureau of Indian
Affairs a couple of years earlier, unhappy with its turn to assimilationist
policies. A recent English graduate from Howard University named Chloe
Anthony Wofford, who had just changed her name to Toni, would the next

year complete a master's at Cornell, just as Paredes in the previous year had completed his master's at the University of Texas at Austin. In the year before Paredes's fieldwork, Richard Wright had visited Ghana, where he was dismayed by his cultural estrangement from African ways.

To so summarize this scene of minority letters in the 1950s is to begin describing a fascinating moment of transition. The protest and integrationist tradition is ascendant: books like *Native Son, Invisible Man, Fifth Chinese Daughter,* and *No-No Boy* emphatically declare their Americanness, a declaration made possible in part by the newly ethnicized and deracialized status of their heroes. The American belonging of the son, man, daughter, and boy was premised on a sociological vision that imagined severed cultural traditions and generation gaps, an imagination summarized by Michel Fabre's account of Wright's decidedly non-anthropological trip to Africa:

> In hunting for the possibility of some "precise ancestral reality," he had, for the time being, assumed the existence of a shared identity between Africans and American Negroes, although he had always refused, as did sociologist E. Franklin Frazier, to consider the "African survivals" in Afro-American culture very significant. It was more an hypothesis, which when disproved, led him to exclaim in stupefaction: "I was black, they were black, but my color did not help me," a refrain denoting frustration, if not anxiety. (402)

The tradition that would have been able to see African culture in African American ways—which in fact had substantiated "African survivals"—was past its time, as is suggested by Hurston's failed literary ambitions in, and denunciations of, the integrationist 1950s.

But this was also a transitional moment in that, at the very moment of the triumph of the liberal, sociologically enabled ethnic model of national assimilation at the heart of the second phase of the genealogy of literary multiculturalism, it was not yet clear that in the pipeline, as it were, were people in their early twenties who would grow up to contest its solution. Within the increasingly dominant liberal consensus brewed anxieties about the loss of African American distinctiveness envisioned by *Brown,* for which Toni Morrison would later offer a literary refutation of the social science it entailed. Likewise, the young law student would turn away from the law so central to integrationist texts like *Brown, Native Son, Invisible Man,* and *No-No Boy*—and, we shall see, the border ballad studied by Américo Paredes—and embrace instead the anthropology that provided a model for, and gave content to, Native cultural longevity in the Southwest. But even as Hurston's star waned and Momaday's was yet to rise, there was a middle anthropological tradition represented by Américo Paredes in the 1950s.

Paredes graduated from the University of Texas at Austin with a B.A. in English and philosophy in 1951 and with an M.A. in English (folklore) and Spanish in 1953. In the summer of 1954 he completed the field research that led to his 1956 Ph.D. dissertation on *El Corrido de Gregorio Cortez,* and its cultural contexts and historical sources. Published two years later, *"With His Pistol in His Hand": A Border Ballad and Its Hero* (1958) was to become a classic of the Mexican American literary tradition. Paredes's maturity as a scholar of Mexican American folklore and culture spans the 1950s milestones from the NAACP's early court cases (1951–1953) leading to *Brown* (1954), *Brown II* (1955), Rosa Parks's refusal to leave her seat (1955), and the beginning of the Civil Rights movements. Against this backdrop of a national debate about the place of newly ethnicized minorities in the United States, Paredes researched and published his scholarship substantiating the cultural presence of an ethnic minority along the Rio Grande.

While one can only speculate about what Paredes knew of the contemporaneous activities of authors like Wright and Wong and Okada, he clearly understood the connection between sociology and assimilation that animated their work, *Brown,* and the Civil Rights movements in this second phase. His early novel *George Washington Gómez,* composed between 1936 and 1940, has its Mexican American protagonist embrace sociology when he marries a white sociologist, on his way to Parkian cultural assimilation through racial amalgamation. He imagines his blond-haired and blue-eyed children learning only English, raised away from his own south Texas roots, thus anticipating Kenji's solution of geographical isolation, intermarriage, and cultural integration (282). The end of the novel is devastatingly critical of this sociologically enabled solution of the cultural assimilation of racialized minorities—and, out of sync with the ascendant sociological imagination of the 1940s, it remained unpublished for half a century, until 1990. The novel is about the Mexican American community in Brownsville, Texas (called "Joneseville-on-the-Grande" in the novel), but anthropology had not yet provided for Paredes a model of cultural endurance. In one scene, the young protagonist Guálinto listens to the adults telling ghost stories (86–92). But unlike similar scenes in McNickle's and Hurston's 1930s books, the oral tradition does not do any cultural work—the stories just terrify Guálinto. The stories have local Mexican American settings and characters, but they are not interpreted as cultural artifacts in terms of cultural belonging, as they are for Hurston and McNickle. The more anthropological notion of culture that distinguishes *Pistol* from *George Washington Gómez* awaited Paredes's formal training in the anthropology of folklore in the 1950s.

Paredes's case offers an instructive answer to the chicken-and-egg question of *A Genealogy of Literary Multiculturalism:* the degree to which social science ideas informed literary writers' concepts of culture and attendant cultural politics, or merely helped articulate already-existing thoughts, "[giving] tongue to interesting thoughts of my own soul, which had frequently flashed through my mind, and died away for want of utterance," as Frederick Douglass described his discovery of a book on Catholic emancipation (84). Paredes's novel shows his awareness and condemnation of two social science modes, that of assimilationist sociology, but also that of pre-Boasian amateur ethnography. The latter is represented by Hank Harvey, a self-taught "expert" on Mexicans who knows only a few words of Spanish and whose false expertise consists of regurgitated stereotypes, racist jokes, and a cultural deafness to the historical and social situation of Mexican Americans on the border. He is a snapshot of amateur anthropology before Boas's professionalization of the discipline (the character must have started his work in the 1890s), and his speech at Guálinto's high school graduation is a source of embarrassment and outrage to the Mexican American community (270–74). In other words, even before attending university Paredes had a pretty accurate understanding of the stakes of social science for his community. But only formal training in the anthropology of folklore gave sharp contours to the object of study, with culture emerging as a primary problematic in Paredes's oeuvre. Importantly, it was the anthropologically framed 1958 *Pistol* and not his pre-anthropological *George Washington Gómez* that influenced a generation of Chicano writers and critics.

What makes *"With His Pistol in His Hand"* so interesting is partly the fact that it is a cusp text: like the hero and the culture that are its objects, it is a book on the border, a book that straddles the demarcation central to *A Genealogy of Literary Multiculturalism,* dividing the integrationist, assimilationist, sociology-inspired tradition from a culturalist one that came before it and another multiculturalist one that would come after it. Writing in the second phase, Paredes both echoed the Boas-Hurston emphasis on distinction, particularity, and continuity, and anticipated to some degree the pluralism and relativity of the third phase. In some respects, his book is an excellent candidate for the protest tradition: like *Native Son* it delineates the racial injustice and lawlessness of American law, but unlike *Native Son* and like *Brown* its hero eventually prevails (somewhat) through the pragmatic use of American law based on the recognition, like that in *Invisible Man,* that principle and not precedent is the route to successful appeal. And like Wong working in the San Francisco wartime shipyards, and like Okada's Kenji who dons the uniform, Paredes in his account of Mexican American history recognizes the Americanizing power of the united fight during World War II against common enemies in Europe and Asia—an account experienced personally by Paredes himself (as with Okada, and to a lesser degree, Ellison in the merchant marine [Jackson 297]). On the other hand, Paredes, through the anthropology of folklore, substantiates the continued cultural distinctiveness and vitality of the Mexican American communities along the Rio Grande. That cultural endurance is signaled by the *corridos,* or border ballads, that continue to be sung a decade after the Americanizing war, although Paredes wonders aloud (without the irony that characterized Hurston's musing on the same anthropological question) whether they will be forgotten when "the last old man dies" (*Pistol* 107).

A more representative example of second-phase Mexican American literature is José Antonio Villarreal's 1959 *Pocho,* a Cold War integrationist novel that likewise ends with its protagonist Richard in the U.S. Navy. Published one year after Paredes's *Pistol,* this "veiled autobiography" is considered by Juan Bruce-Novoa to be "the first Chicano novel" (37). *Pocho* shares with other ethnic minority 1950s works like *Invisible Man, Fifth Chinese Daughter, No-No Boy,* and *The Outsider* an accent on individualism and a downplaying of one's ethnic group. It is perhaps for these reasons that Ramón Saldívar remarks, "*Pocho* has always been somewhat of an embarrassment to Chicanos" (*Chicano Narrative* 65), by which he means those Chicano writers and intellectuals emerging with the third phase's cultural nationalisms of the late 1960s. While Villarreal was trained in English literature (like several Chicano writers) and not sociology (like several Asian American writers), there is nonetheless the sense of Richard turning away from his parents' culture toward a national culture, recognizing that assimilation cannot be accomplished in a single generation because it places too much stress on his family. As with *Black Boy,* and in anticipation of Richard Rodriguez's *The Hunger of Memory,* the protagonist's desire to learn takes him away from ethnic culture and toward participation in the majority American one. Wright's, Villarreal's, and Rodriguez's disinterest in, and occasional hostility toward, the value of cultural pluralism puts them at odds with the multicultural paradigm that emerged in the 1970s—something these writers share with Ellison, Wong, Okada, and Sone as well. As becomes clear in his interview with Bruce-Novoa, Villarreal has a vexed relation with the cultural politics of the Chicano movement (38–48), the seeds of which can be seen in *Pocho.*

Américo Paredes, on the other hand, though writing more or less simultaneously with Villarreal, "is now widely recognized as having articulated the terrain of Chicano cultural studies and established the very ground for 'border writing'" (R. Saldívar, "Borderlands" 273). But Paredes, and *Pistol* in particular, have had a significant impact beyond a narrowly construed border-writing tradition. Ramón Saldívar sees in the "great ethnographic work of América Paredes (1958) on turn-of-the-century border ballads" a "model for understanding Chicano literature" as a literary tradition emerging in opposition to American culture ("Narrative" 17). Given this influence, "it is not surprising," José David Saldívar has said, "that Chicano literary historians and cultural critics often mention the momentous impact América Paredes's *"With His Pistol in His Hand"* had on Chicano literature" ("Chicano" 173).[1] The Chicano literary and cultural studies explosion beginning in the late 1960s was thus underwritten by Paredes's Boasian model of culture.

🐦 *El Corrido de Gregorio Cortez* and Border Culture

> (The person who really knows a lot more about the people of Jonesville is don América Paredes.)
>
> —Rolando Hinojosa-Smith, *Estampas del Valle,* 1973 (82)

"With His Pistol in His Hand": A Border Ballad and Its Hero is a detailed examination of *El Corrido de Gregorio Cortez* in its cultural context and historical origins. The *corrido*'s several variants and the prose legends about its hero are based on the story of the real Gregorio Cortez, a peaceful Mexican American who in 1901 shot in self-defense a local sheriff looking for a horse thief in Karnes County, Texas. While neither Cortez nor his brother had stolen the horse, due to confusion arising from translation and the Anglo tradition of excessive force, the sheriff shot Cortez's brother before being shot himself by Cortez. Cortez fled the scene, attempting to get out of the "lynching belt" where he would be at the mercy of the Texas Rangers (the sheriff had once been a Ranger), and to get to the Lower Border area, where law enforcement included some Texas-Mexicans (*Pistol* 78), and where he would be more likely to be arrested and tried. By the time he was betrayed by a "Judas" and captured, "the chase had taken ten days, during which Cortez walked at least one hundred twenty miles and rode more than four hundred on the brown and the sorrel mares. He had been chased by hundreds of men, in parties of up to three hundred. He had killed two sheriffs and fought off many posses" (79). Cortez had successfully evaded lynch law, and a lengthy series of legal battles ensued. He was finally acquitted of the murder of the sheriff who shot

his brother in a verdict that "was a victory not only for Cortez but for all Mexicans in Texas. Especially interested were the Borderers, who for half a century had seen respectable citizens transformed into outlaws by the application of 'Ranger law,' according to which a man was killed if he did not defend himself, or was tried for murder and hanged if he did" (93). He was, however, sentenced to life for the murder of the second sheriff, and served time until he was pardoned by the governor in 1913. After briefly fighting for General Huerta in the Mexican Revolution, he died somewhat mysteriously in 1916.

El Corrido de Gregorio Cortez is the song that developed in the Lower Border area shortly after Cortez's arrest in 1901. It is composed of four-line stanzas, of which an example is

Decía Gregorio Cortez
con su pistola en la mano:
—No corran, rinches cobardes,
con un solo mexicano

which Paredes translates as:

Then said Gregorio Cortez,
With his pistol in his hand,
"Don't run, you cowardly rangers,
From just one Mexican." (156)

Paredes collected nine variants of the song during his field research (variants A through I), plus a printed Mexico City broadside version, and he prints them together with a hypothetical version X, which he cobbled together from the stanzas of A through I, and which he takes to be the probable original version. *"With His Pistol in His Hand"* likewise reprints twenty pages of prose legends that accompany the songs.

What was crucial, according to Paredes, about the *corrido* variants and legends, was their relation to Mexican American culture. "It was as if," Paredes writes, "the Border people had dreamed Gregorio Cortez before producing him, and had sung his life and his deeds before he was born" (125). Paredes shared the Boasian folklore premise that the value of studying oral traditions was that stories and songs encode specific cultural values: paying attention to folklore is a way of doing cultural anthropology. Since the Mexican American border culture generates the *corrido* tradition, studying its variants gives the social scientist access to the circumstances, values, and particularities of the culture itself. Particularly important to Paredes's analysis of Mexican American border culture were the Boasian characteristics of historical particularism and cultural holism.

Like Hurston's, Paredes's anthropological concept of culture insisted on the historical specificity of the Mexican American border culture and its meanings. He gives only passing reference to comparative folklore studies (medieval European balladry, for instance), emphasizing instead the social, economic, legal, and political conditions that shaped the border culture and its *corridos*. At the heart of his account of early and mid twentieth-century Mexican American culture is a history that begins (for Paredes) with the settlement of the Spanish province of Nuevo Santander in 1749, in what is now the Lower Rio Grande Border area. The Native population was "absorbed into the blood and the culture of the Spanish settlers" (9), a process of assimilation by amalgamation more complete than the account by Gloria Anzaldúa would suggest three decades later. The Lower Border society was agricultural and ranch-based, composed of "tightly knit groups whose basic social structure was the family or the clan" (9), patriarchal in nature and under the "democratizing influence of a horse culture" (10). It produced a social order of communal amusement and decision-making, fostering a rich oral tradition whose importance Paredes contrasts to "the reading habit of the Protestant Anglo-Saxon, [which was] fostered on a veneration of the written words in the Bible" (14).

One of the most decisive shaping influences on the developing border culture, not surprisingly, was the border. "It was the [1848] Treaty of Guadalupe that added the final element to Rio Grande society, a border. The river, which had been a focal point, became a dividing line. Men were expected to consider their relatives and closest neighbors, the people just across the river, as foreigners in a foreign land" (15). With this legal and juridical imposition of an artificial demarcation—artificial in the sense that it is drawn through the middle of a cultural community rather than along it—border culture became characterized by the theme of cultural conflict itself. Paredes's Boasian method in understanding the *corrido* that developed on the border was to trace its growth in terms of the specific historical circumstances of the community. His central question was how the culture developed in response to historical conditions, a development registered by transformations in the oral tradition.

Accordingly, Paredes traces the songs of the area according to patterns of settlement and conflict. The Spanish *romance* arrived with the earliest Spanish settlers and has been preserved, reflecting some cultural continuity but not an identification with Spanish culture. The *copla*, the *verso*, songs about fighting Indians, and the *décima* all have their place in this history of the oral arts of the border people (129–31). But Paredes traces the historical emergence of the *corrido* tradition to political and military upheavals beginning around

1836: "civil war, Indian raids, and the English-speaking invasion" (132), all of which were interrelated (with, for instance, the Anglo-Texans, and then Anglo-Americans, supplying "Indians" to attack Mexican settlements even as they considered various imperial plans for Mexican territory). These tensions were not resolved with the end of the U.S.-Mexico war in 1848, since a new border divided the Mexican Rio Grande community.

Economic and racial exploitation of the new Mexican Americans followed the Treaty of Guadalupe, leading to Juan Nepomuceno Cortina's 1859 revolt against the United States. Cortina "was the first Border Mexican to 'fight for his right with his pistol in his hand,'" and though the revolt was put down, he became a Union guerilla against the Confederacy in the Civil War that followed (134–35). Such conflicts, frequently energized by political events south of the border, continued to characterize the border area, culminating in its unofficial participation in the Mexican Revolution beginning in 1910. With such history, border mythology—so important to later Chicano literature and to other Southwest texts like Leslie Silko's *Almanac of the Dead* and Cormac McCarthy's *Blood Meridian* and border trilogy—begins to take on its meanings of cultural conflicts and mixings, artifice, refuge from questionable jurisdiction, militarized citizenship, sedimented colonial settlement, and so on. Cortina, symbolizing the theme of how cultural conflict on the border can become armed resistance, "is the earliest Border *corrido* hero that we know of," writes Paredes (140), the prototype that would be perfected by *El Corrido de Gregorio Cortez*.

In tracing song forms according to patterns of settlement, Paredes accounts for the growth of the *corrido* by assessing the importation and adaptation of other forms to the border area. Mexico also saw a parallel development of the *corrido,* which gradually replaced "the *décima* as the most important ballad form" (142). Ballads from Mexico on the themes of "filial disobedience" and "the girl who is killed at a dance by a jealous suitor" arrived on the border where they were "widely sung," but Paredes argues that such ballads were not themselves created by border ballad-makers, whose interest "seems to have been on matters other than these" (142). The "moody and dark" lyrical ballad was likewise imported but not imitated by border ballad-makers, since it spoke only minimally to the problems and conditions of that particular culture.

Similarly, the border *corrido* borrowed from Greater Mexico balladry some elements of the outlaw *corridos,* but they were not directly imitated because "the hero of the border conflict" is not a "mere outlaw," or a "Robin Hood" (143). The smuggler is only slightly different: "The smuggler occupied in the Borderer's scale of values a much higher place than the robber, a place

very close to that of the Border hero fighting for his right. This is not surprising if one remembers the average Borderer's hostile attitude toward the
Rio Grande as an international boundary" (144). Border conflict *corridos*
share with smuggling ballads the fight against the *rinches*—the Texas Rangers,
expanded now to mean Anglo-American law enforcement—but the border
conflict *corrido* is uninterested in smuggling *corrido* conventions like operation details or imprisonment because such details do not develop the theme
of cultural conflict central to the indigenous border *corrido*. Paredes offers a
theory of artificial selection to account for the origin and evolution of the
border *corrido*. What is imitated—reproduced—are only adaptations from
abroad that answer to the particular cultural meanings already in place.

Paredes understands the Cortez ballad according to a historically particular anthropological model of culture that explains "the gradual emergence
of the *corrido* as the dominant form of Lower Border balladry" (149). The
history of the border area encourages specific artistic dominance: "One can
see the balladry of the Lower Border working toward a single type: toward
one form, the *corrido;* toward one theme, border conflict; toward one concept
of the hero, the man fighting for his right with his pistol in his hand" (149).
Just as the key adaptation in African American culture of the Moses stories
makes sense only through reference to African American history (as we
shall see in chapter eight), so too do the adaptations in Mexican American
culture of Spanish elements make sense only through the specific history of
Mexicans along the Rio Grande. "As the *corrido* emerges, it assimilates the
romance survivals that had come from Spain" (149), Paredes summarizes, and
other forms give way as the "Border conflict dominates as a theme" (149).
He continues,

> Ballads are received from Greater Mexico, from Cuba, even from the
> United States, but their themes, mostly proletarian, are not imitated.
> The local ballads all take on the complexion of conflict. The term
> *rinche* (Texas Ranger) is extended not only to possemen but to border
> patrolmen, immigration officers, prison guards, and even to Persh-
> ing's soldiers when they are in pursuit of the border raider Pancho
> Villa. (150)

El Corrido de Gregorio Cortez is thus an excellent example of Boas's fundamental argument that cultural elements had to be understood historically
rather than only functionally or psychologically.

Just as Paredes's model of culture is fundamentally in accord with the
Boasian principle of historical particularism, so too is it dependent on an
account of cultural holism: that cultural elements are interlocked and must be

understood as part of a larger dynamic entity. Folklore accordingly encodes a community's mores, which can be seen in the prose legends about Cortez. They portray Cortez's brother Román as a kind of trickster who dupes an arrogant Anglo-Texan into a bad horse trade (36–38), thus initiating the charge of horse thievery that sets Cortez's flight in motion. Paredes comments on the legend's reflection of border values:

> Román plays the part of the anti-hero. He is what men should not be: loud, boisterous, disrespectful, an eternal joker. Men should be quiet and hardworking, excellent vaqueros and good farmers. They should be respectful to their elders, peaceful in manner, and ready to defend their right. In other words, they should be like Gregorio Cortez, who is not only a projection of the Border Mexican's reaction to border conflict but a pattern of behavior as well. (118)

As with Hurston's brief comparison between John and Daniel, Paredes notes only in passing the trickster and "Coyote" (118) archetypal dimensions of Román, dwelling instead on what the character means for Mexican American culture considered as a whole set of values, traditions, habits, and beliefs.

Paredes's devotion to this anthropological model of culture explains his lack of interest in comparative folklore. He notes, for instance, "Unlike John Henry and Paul Bunyan, however, Cortez is not a prodigy. His feats are due to industry rather than to superhuman powers" (119), and briefly quotes Frazer's *Golden Bough* (239), but it is culture as such that is the object to be substantiated and understood. Comparative folklore is an easy temptation to be avoided: Cortez is akin to Robin Hood (he struggles on behalf of the people), and like an outlaw or smuggler (he fights the *rinches*), but these connections miss the central theme of cultural conflict. Where Paredes is most approving of cross-cultural comparison, as when he compares border balladry to Scottish balladry, it is because of their shared historical circumstance—being on the losing side results in "the most stirring" ballads (244)—and not because of a supposed transcultural archetype or symbol.

"With His Pistol in His Hand" became centrally important for the Chicano literary tradition that emerged most forcefully as part of multiculturalism at the end of the 1960s and in the 1970s partly because of its account of minority cultural endurance in the face of a dominant society. It is not an accident that Paredes's seminal account of cultural conflict and endurance was anthropological. Rather, it was the very Boasian qualities of Paredes's model of culture that enabled the picture of a culture disregarded and outnumbered but nevertheless fighting back, preserving its "right." Paredes imagines Mexican American culture, or more particularly border culture,

as oppositional, emerging from its beginnings with a sense of almost being swallowed by the larger dominant society. Once the ex-Mexicans became U.S. citizens in 1848, what might have happened, given enough time and the influx of Anglo-Americans, is eventual assimilation—as had happened to the Native population that amalgamated with and assimilated into the society of the early Spanish settlers, according to Paredes's account. But the Rangers "exacerbated the cultural conflict on the Border," according to Paredes, producing an unintended consequence:

> The assimilation of the north-bank Border people into the American commonwealth was necessary to any effective pacification of the Border. Ranger operations did much to impede that end. They created in the Border Mexican a deep and understandable hostility for American authority; they drew Border communities even closer together than they had been, though at that time they were beginning to disintegrate under the impact of new conditions. (32)

Paredes, of course, was no more pro-Ranger or pro-Anglo racism than Hurston was pro-Klan or pro-segregation. But they share a certain ambivalence (to put it most strongly) in their recognition that forced separations sanctioned by law, violence, custom, and racism allowed Mexican American culture to flourish on the border and African American culture to flourish in the South.

Contemporary changes likewise force Paredes to muse on the longevity of the *corrido*. As he notes, Cortez's grandsons fought in World War II, in which Paredes himself served as the editor of a U.S. Army publication. The war effected a change in cultural relations, Paredes writes: "Until the rise of Hitler in Germany and the beginning of World War II, a majority of Border Mexicans continued to think of themselves as a people apart. Unlike other American minorities, they directed their energies not toward being accepted into the majority but toward maintaining their own individual rights as members in an aloof enclave struggling to keep its own identity." But economic changes in Mexico dissipated the border culture area, and "with the advent of World War II greater numbers of north-bank Borderers began to think of themselves seriously as Americans. Like the unreconstructed Southerner—whom he resembled in some respects—the Border Mexican was surprised to find that the peoples of Europe and the Pacific thought of him as just another American" (106). It is instructive that Paredes sees border Mexican Americans as more similar to another conquered people (to use a Southern trope) than to "other American minorities," by which he certainly means African Americans and might mean Asian Americans (given the recent history of internment).[2] Changed historical circumstances result in changing cultural formations, among which is the foreseen disappearance of the *corrido*. In World War II the "Texas-Mexican" still fought *con su pistola en la mano* to defend his right but he found himself fighting alongside the "Anglo-Texan" against a common enemy "whose acts in Europe made the worst Ranger painted by Border folklore look like an amateur" (106–7). Accordingly, Brownsville's war hero doesn't have *corridos* made about him, "for he was not the hero of the Border folk but of the American people" (107). Since the basis of the border *corrido* was conflict with Anglo society, it has no place in narrating the fight against fascism in Europe.

Paredes ends this musing about assimilation with a poignant resignation, a note different from both the tone of the cultural pluralism that characterized Hurston's work and the tone of third-phase multiculturalism to come. What makes *"With His Pistol in His Hand"* an interstitial text committed somewhat to cultural survival in the integrationist 1950s is Paredes's sense that it is perhaps inevitable that Mexican American cultural traditions will pass. After World War II, he writes, "the old folk communities straddling the international line at the Rio Grande were absorbed into their respective countries. The era of border conflict passed, but its heroes survived in the *corridos* and the legends, to linger in the memories of a new generation until the last old man dies" (107). As conditions of racial oppression and Ranger lawlessness pass (or at least lessen), according to this view, the cultural response to which they gave rise will also decline. The only compensation for this loss of legend and song is that "perhaps they will live longer than that" as the universal values of "dignity" and "courage, even in defeat": just as the English now sometimes celebrate the very Scottish heroes who were their ancestors' enemies, so too might the *corrido* heroes become sung by Anglo-Americans (107). Eventual cultural disappearance seems likely to Paredes, as it was not to Hurston, even though this was something to be a little mournful about, as it was not for Wright or Okada.

For Paredes, *El Corrido de Gregorio Cortez* is fundamentally about culture, and that culture's anthropological model entailed not just historical particularism and cultural holism but other ingredients of Boasian culture as well. Paredes insisted on a mode of cultural relativism in assessing culture, as is evident in his comparison between the Cortez ballad's indigenous variants and one rewritten for a Mexico City broadside. Not only does the broadside variant insert a Mexican patriotism absent from the original, it is also marred by a hackneyed *redondilla* stanza crafted by a writer attempting to be literary beyond his ability. In contrast, "The maker of the Border *corrido* makes no effort to be original or literary, and by staying within the ballad traditions of his people he succeeds in composing in a natural and often a forceful style" (183). This is the same kind of insistence on the artistic validity of folklore shared by Boas and Hurston, and here, as with them, it is asserted to counter the supposed universal aesthetic criteria of high European art. Paredes's stature in Chicano studies is also partly due to his stand against the scholarly tradition of hispanophilia in assessing cultural formations in the Spanish-speaking Americas. That entailed both the relativist insistence that Mexican American culture (and other Spanish-speaking cultures) be measured on their own terms, and not evaluated as a degraded tradition imported from Old Spain, and the historical emphasis on comprehending cultural survivals as adaptations to local conditions of conflict ("Folk Base" 14).

The fourth element of cultural anthropology fundamental to Paredes's work is, again, one that he shares with other minority writers in the 1930s and 1940s: the use of Boas's paradigm shift from race to culture. Like Hurston, Wright, Wong, Okada, and others, Paredes not only counters racist ideas, but replaces the idea of race itself with a better account of group difference, one based on culture. "*El Corrido de Gregorio Cortez,* then, is a Border Mexican ballad, 'Mexican' being understood in a cultural sense, without reference to citizenship or blood" (xi), Paredes warns in the introduction. Describing the settling of Nuevo Santander, Paredes writes:

> In succeeding generations the Indians, who began as vaqueros and sheepherders for the colonists, were absorbed into the blood and the culture of the Spanish settlers. Also absorbed into the basically Spanish culture were many non-Spanish Europeans, so that on the Border one finds men who prefer Spanish to English, who sometimes talk scornfully about the "Gringos," and who bear English, Scottish, Irish, or other non-Spanish names. (8–9)

Paredes's displacement of race by culture is most obvious in the first passage just quoted, in which he distinguishes the ballad tradition under study as emerging from a culture and not a race, but it is likewise true of the second, where "blood" is not the figure of deep biological racial difference (of the kind that Boas was refuting), or a metaphor for cultural difference (which is what it sometimes would become in multiculturalism), but a term for distinguishing among stocks of descent populations characterized in part by phenotypical difference.

Paredes's deployment of culture to displace race comes most profoundly at the moment in which he begins, as José David Saldívar has put it, "a critique of southern white supremacist ideology" that underlies the border conflict and the ballads the region thus produces ("Chicano" 171). Calling this racial ideology "Anglo-Texan legend," Paredes cites its content as including the propositions that "the Mexican is cruel by nature," is "cowardly and treacherous," and is "as degenerate a specimen of humanity as may be found anywhere," a degeneracy "due to his mixed blood, though the elements in the mixture were inferior to begin with" (16). As Paredes described this theory of mixed blood, the Mexican "is descended from the Spaniard, a second-rate type of European, and from the equally substandard Indian of Mexico, who must not be confused with the noble savages of North America" (16). The racial construction of Mexicans has been developing since the 1830s in American society, Paredes says, and has recently found articulation in scholarship. Paredes's chief example is Walter Prescott Webb's 1935 book *The Texas Rangers,* which he quotes at some length:

> Without disparagement, it may be said that there is a cruel streak in the Mexican nature, or so the history of Texas would lead one to believe. This cruelty may be a heritage from the Spanish of the Inquisition; it may, and doubtless should, be attributed partly to the Indian blood.... The Mexican warrior... was, on the whole, inferior to the Comanche and wholly unequal to the Texan. The whine of the leaden slugs stirred in him an irresistible impulse to travel with rather than against the music. He won more victories over the Texans by parley than by force of arms. For making promises—and for breaking them—he had no peer. (qtd. in Paredes 17)

Paredes also quotes Webb's earlier 1931 account of the Central American Indian with whom the Spanish interbred, and "whose blood, when compared with that of the Plains Indian, was as ditch water" (qtd. in Paredes 17). While the Spanish "heritage" presumably suggests learned attributes rather than natural ones—thus dubiously turning Inquisition torture practices into an element of "Spanish" culture transmitted for hundreds of years—supposed Mexican cruelty is to be partly attributed, says Webb, to "Indian blood." It is blood that makes "Mexican nature" what it is, according to this biological account of the group. As Paredes ironically remarks about this quotation, "Professor Webb does not mean to be disparaging. One wonders what his opinion might have been when he was in a less scholarly mood and not looking at the Mexican from the objective point of view of the historian" (17).

But for Paredes, what makes Mexican "nature" is not blood but culture. Paredes thus repeats the central strategic displacement of race by culture that characterizes American minority writing in the first and second phases of the genealogy of literary multiculturalism. Like Wong deploying Chinese culture against her father's "your skin is yellow"; like Max arguing for the environmental explanation of Bigger's crime against the prosecutor's racial one; like Hurston turning the drum's survival across the Middle Passage from being an African bodily quality into an African cultural retention: Paredes counters racist discourse by entirely displacing the idea of race itself and putting in its place a (now positive) account of learned group difference. To be sure, central to Paredes's project is replacing the negative content of racist white Anglo stereotypes with positive group characteristics. Paredes sees the *corrido* as having already done this through its reversals of the white supremacist construction of Mexicans. Thus Cortez is not cowardly but courageous in the face of overwhelming odds; he is not "cruel" but peaceful until provoked; his word is to be trusted, unlike that of the Anglo-Texan Rangers. But more important than positing positive content in place of negative stereotypes was the fundamental strategy of displacing altogether the notion of biological race by replacing it with a renovated and social science–substantiated notion of culture.

The Mexican American's newly ethnic status is revealed by one humorous episode told in the prose legend. Texas tradition allowed the governor to pardon prisoners, especially when a plea for pardon was made by a man's wife, mother, or promised bride. Cortez's legend fills this role with President Lincoln's daughter, who falls in love after seeing him behind bars. She promises to request the governor's pardon if he will marry her. The legend has Cortez ponder this vision of assimilation by amalgamation:

> He could see himself already like a German, sitting on the gallery, full of ham and beer, and belching and breaking wind while a half-dozen little blond cockroaches played in the yard. And he was tempted. But then he said to himself, "I can't marry a Gringo girl. We would not make a matching pair." (52–53)

Like the musings of *No-No Boy's* Ichiro and Kenji, and like Fred Korematsu with his Italian American girlfriend, and like the sociological vision at the end of *George Washington Gómez,* what Cortez momentarily imagines is Park's vision of assimilation through amalgamation. In playfully imagining the Anglo-American as a German, the legend recognizes how easily ethnic, how much like a European immigrant, he might become—and indeed already is. He could be "like a German" by adopting the cultural practices of eating ham and drinking beer, of belching and breaking wind. He could adopt them, of course, because culture has no natural relation to race, as Boas showed: beer and ham, belching and breaking wind, are not racially German or white, but are only culturally German or white. And in a brief nativist gesture (which Paredes is notably silent about), the legend has Cortez prefer his own.

Cortez, Paredes later points out, "refers to himself as a Mexican, but the word has no national connotations. Its meaning is cultural; it is a word that describes Cortez and his kind of people, and to him it is almost equivalent to man, just as to most people of Spanish background *cristiano* (Christian) has come to mean 'person'" (183). The *corrido* thus empties "Mexican" of both its national and racial meanings, establishing instead—from Paredes's point of view—"Mexican" as a cultural description. It is in such a way that *"With His Pistol in His Hand"* deploys a theory of culture to counter the theory of race, which was still popular in the United States but, by 1958, no longer a legitimate vision of the world in American social scientific, intellectual, liberal, or legal circles. And because he was so historically close to this not-very-old conceptual shift, Américo Paredes, like Wright and Okada and Wong, never uses biological metaphors (like "blood" or "hybridity") to talk about the newly instantiated paradigm of culture.

⚡ Paredes and Chicano Folklore

> It is obvious that in the tales of a people those incidents of the everyday life that are of importance to them will appear either incidentally or as the basis of a plot. Most of the references to the mode of life of the people will be an accurate reflection of their habits. The development of the plot of the story, furthermore, will, on the whole, exhibit clearly what is considered right and what wrong.
>
> From these points of view it seemed worth while to review connectedly those ideas which are either implied or described in detail. Material of this kind does not represent a systematic description of the ethnology of a people, but it has the merit of bringing out those points which are of interest to the people themselves. They present in a way an autobiography of the tribe.
>
> —Franz Boas, *Tsimshian Mythology,* 1916 (393)

For Franz Boas, folklore was an avenue not only into the languages of different groups, but into their customs, ways of life, values, and folk practices as well. Boas investigated how the dissemination and adaptation of tales worked, and understood that culturally important things appear in stories, either in passing or as basis of plot, and often reveal that culture's sense of right and wrong, as he wrote in the one thousand-page *Tsimshian Mythology.* The study of folklore was thereby the study of culture (Stocking, "Franz Boas" 225). Boas helped found the American Folklore Society and its publication, the *Journal of American Folklore,* which he edited between 1908 and 1924. Américo Paredes published in this journal and also edited it between

1969 and 1973 from his post at the University of Texas at Austin where he had become a professor of English in 1965 and a professor of anthropology in 1966.[3] The journal published Zora Neale Hurston and Marius Barbeau and had many issues on Negro folklore. As Baker and Hutchinson have shown, there were continuities and influences between Boasian anthropology, including the anthropology of folklore, and the Harlem Renaissance theorizers and practitioners. A parallel set of influences occurred a generation and a half later, with Américo Paredes as the central figure. A scholar of folklore and editor of the very folklore journal edited earlier by the father of American cultural anthropology, Paredes was also crucial to the scholarly and artistic substantiating of Mexican American culture, laying a basis for the Chicano literary movement beginning in the 1960s.

What I am claiming, then, is that an anthropological model of culture underwrote Chicano literary multiculturalism in the third phase for both historical and theoretical reasons. The historical line of influence from Boasian anthropology passed directly through Paredes to the generation of Chicano writers coming of age in the 1960s and 1970s. But the theoretical grounding of these Chicano multiculturalist writers was no less important, given anthropology's model of culture and its qualities of historical particularism, holism, relativism, and longevity. For instance, Rolando Hinojosa, author of the important Klail City Death Trip novels, gives a particularly anthropological account of the "living and unifying culture born of conflict with another culture" ("This Writer's" 122) from which his literary work takes shape, one that closely matches the details and emphasis on historical particularity of Paredes. He notes that the importance of place in his writing is also seen in *Pistol,* and admits to using "the folklore and the anthropology of the Valley" in his literary work (123). Tomás Rivera, author of the equally important *...y no se lo trago la tierra/...And the Earth Did Not Part,* argues that "the impetus to document and develop the Mexican-American community became the *raison d'être* of the Chicano Movement and its writers," and that many writers did so by paying attention to the community's oral and folklore traditions ("Mexican-American" 125). Rivera offers as an example a character from one of Hinojosa's novels (in which the narrator actually recommends Paredes, as seen in the epigraph to the previous section), and cites its "folkloric elements and popular expression" (128) that help to construct community. Rivera was "fascinated" by *"With His Pistol in His Hand"* when he discovered it, and explains that his "role as documentor" took its inspiration from seeing what Paredes had done with Gregorio Cortez and his community (Interview 150). Jonathan Handelman likewise sees Paredes as "a forerunner to the writers of border fiction" (23), who displaced the frontier hypothesis with the emerging border paradigm. As Handelman says,

"Paredes's groundbreaking work prepared the way for the great outpouring of fiction and criticism centering on border conflict that we have seen in the past ten to twenty years" (25), enabling such authors as Rudolfo Anaya, Ana Castillo, and Sandra Cisneros. Ramón Saldívar has also written that "Rivera and Hinojosa simply make explicit [in their voiced tributes to Paredes] an influence that is implicitly felt by all of the major developers of Chicano fiction" ("Américo Paredes" 11). In these direct and indirect ways, the kind of cultural nationalism found in canonical Chicano letters can be traced directly through Paredes to a Boasian account of culture.

Paredes became the founding director of the Mexican American Studies Program at the University of Texas at Austin in 1972. This fact suggestively indicates that the emergence of both literary multiculturalism and ethnic studies in American universities was enabled by the anthropological model of culture. As Ramon A. Gutierrez argues in "Ethnic Studies: Its Evolution in American Colleges and Universities," the ethnic studies programs founded in the mid-late 1960s originated when minority students "demanded that the study of race and ethnicity be removed from the disciplinary homes they had long occupied in departments of sociology and anthropology, where race and ethnicity were pathologized, problematized, or exoticized" (158). But as we have seen, the pathologization and problematization of race and ethnicity were more frequently the hallmarks of sociology than Boasian anthropology. In any case, notes Gutierrez, "the political turn in the mid-1960s from a movement for civil rights to nationalism was accompanied by a rejection of assimilation and a demand for cultural autonomy and national self-determination" (158). The same sociological vs. anthropological distinction that underlay the cultural models of civil rights and assimilation vs. cultural nationalism was also the distinction that underlay the development of ethnic studies and literary multiculturalism.[4] While *"With His Pistol in His Hand"* is only a proto-multiculturalist text, Paredes's own career nicely summarizes the emergent possibilities, for literary multiculturalism and ethnic studies, of the anthropological culture concept.

My point is not that Paredes and the Chicano literary writers influenced by him were orthodox Boasians, or that they uncritically accepted the tradition of cultural anthropology as it had been practiced since the 1920s. My argument is rather that the critique of cultural anthropology in which Paredes took part (with many others, like Vine Deloria) was a series of corrections and refinements worked out largely within the Boasian paradigm of cultural anthropology. In other words, the fact that Paredes and (we shall see) Anzaldúa, Momaday, and Reed have so clearly been influenced by anthropological fieldwork and are working within cultural anthropology's paradigm means that we need to investigate critically rather than take at face value the just criticisms of white Anglo ethnographers among Mexican American and Native communities made by Paredes and Deloria.

For example, anthropologist Renato Rosaldo, while recognizing the breadth of influence of Paredes and his "pioneering work from the late fifties," observes that what was merely an uncritical cultural observation for Paredes—that border culture is patriarchal in social and familial structures—must now itself come under critique "after more than fifteen years of recent feminist scholarship" ("Fables" 87), not only morally but descriptively, in terms of imagining the gender conflicts that must have arisen in what Paredes paints as a too coherent system.[5] Nevertheless, according to Rosaldo, Paredes has played a crucial role in developing the very field for such scholarly and critical revaluations and corrections:

> Lest there be any confusion, my purpose in underscoring the mythic quality of Paredes's poetic characterization of early south Texas-Mexican society is not to demean his work. Gregorio Cortez was a crucial figure of resistance for the south Texas-Mexican imagination through the late fifties and into the sixties. At the time Anglo-Texan white supremacy was even more virulent than today, and the Chicano movement had not yet appeared on the horizon. Indeed, if I were to have a patron saint for these intellectual labors (which I am not about to do) it would be Américo Paredes, not, for example, Fredric Jameson. (87)

Rosaldo cites Paredes's "sophisticated conception of culture that attends to history, politics, and relations of inequality," culture "as bound by circumstances, constantly changing, and internally diverse" (87). Rosaldo suggests that Chicano Studies grew out of a critique of prevailing social science work on Mexican Americans, a critique in which Paredes took part: "In Paredes's hands, the critique of anthropology becomes both more devastating and more constructive" ("Chicano" 408) as he uncovers the "subtle (and therefore more pernicious) unconscious perpetuation of stereotypes" and mistranslations (thus repeating a theme from *El Corrido de Gregorio Cortez* and from *George Washington Gómez*) in Anglo anthropologists' treatment of Mexican American communities (409). Paredes corrects portrayals, but also argues that the ethnographers must become aware of how their own empowered interrogative positions complicate the ethnographic project. In one instance, he argues that sometimes informants just tell ethnographers what they think they want to hear, as a way "meant to test the waters" to see if the ethnographer is content with the already existing racist imaginary (410).

These and other critiques of anthropological practice in the years since the work of Boas and his students and successors Mead, Benedict, and Herskovits are valid, and sorting through them would require more space than I have. I need to briefly explain, however, why, despite such critiques and overarching claims like that of Paredes and Deloria that Chicano writers or Native people in general have rejected anthropology, it is nonetheless true that the genealogy of multiculturalism traces directly back to an anthropological concept of culture. The answer is that, while there is proper contestation of the practice and theory of cultural anthropology, the central anthropological paradigm of culture is nevertheless being upheld and refined. To correct errors of representation and translation is not to overturn cultural anthropology, but to pursue its project. In this sense, the critique of Anglo anthropology's arrogance and errors, as outlined by Rosaldo, is not contesting what Boas thought about culture. The other aspects of such critiques are refinements of Boas's paradigm, but not refutations of it. Rosaldo suggests that Paredes was already questioning the role of writing and the authority of the ethnographer, anticipating the concerns of the postmodern anthropology of James Clifford and George Marcus.[6] This too is a refinement of the practice of cultural anthropology, not a refutation of the Boasian revolution.

Paredes's brilliant and compelling essay "On Ethnographic Work among Minority Groups: A Folklorist's Perspective" demands that ethnographers register the limits of language "fluency" and recognize the performance and agency of individual informants, their own implication in (often humorous and multiply parodic) informant speech acts, unconscious bias, and so on. The essay crucially questions traditional ethnographic methods (in ways that anticipate Maxine Hong Kingston's similar complications in *The Woman Warrior,* as I suggest in the conclusion), but not the ethnographic project, or the Boasian model of culture it is built around. Even Rosaldo's and Paredes's emphases on the internal divisions and stratifications within culture, or other anthropologists' Marxist-influenced attention to how economic conditions shape and are in turn shaped by culture, elaborate and build on the Boasian paradigm of culture as historical, relative, holistic, and conceptually distinct from race. In fact, some of the critiques of anthropology named by Rosaldo as examples could be seen as a return to the Boasian principle of non-evaluation (what looks like laziness is probably just a different order of cultural priorities) and attention to his warning against forming generalizations too quickly. To see culture as internally stratified, hierarchical, in tension, and in process is to pursue questions that Boas raised about how culture worked, and in particular what the role of the individual might be within a culture that would dominate, but not determine, individual consciousness. In short, within the discipline in general, but certainly for the purposes of a genealogy of literary multiculturalism that attends to its mutual articulations with the social sciences, the salient distinction is the model of culture proposed by Boas, challenged later by sociology, and then returned to (with a difference) by a generation of multiculturalist authors by the late 1960s.

🍃 Intimations of Identity

> Chicanos did not know we were a people until 1965 when Cesar Chavez and the farmworkers united and *I Am Joaquín* was published and *la Raza Unida* party was formed in Texas. With that recognition, we became a distinct people. Something momentous happened to the Chicano soul—we became aware of our reality and acquired a name and a language (Chicano Spanish) that reflected that reality.
>
> —Gloria Anzaldúa, *Borderlands/La Frontera,* 1987 (85)

A border text, *"With His Pistol in His Hand"* recalls the first phase's cultural pluralism and anticipates the third phase's multiculturalism, even as it is researched and published during the second phase dominated by the sociologically inspired liberal politics of integration and assimilation. Like *Native Son* and *No-No Boy,* Paredes's study is about a racialized outlaw. Wright and Okada understood that one's race is in large part what made their protagonists outlaws in the first place: the expectation of racial criminality partly or entirely produces the supposed crimes of the African American and Japanese American heroes. As with Gregorio Cortez, Bigger and Ichiro are not really required to do anything; all three men are keenly aware of the white racism that forms the environments of their acts.

That said, these three books understand the law as a place where the racialized outlaw might speak back to the institutions of power. Though Bigger (represented by Max) is ultimately sentenced to die, and while the various pleas or counteraccusations launched by other Japanese American internees during the draft also ultimately fail in the preface to *No-No Boy,* the legend about Cortez says that he "talked for a long time to the judges, telling them about their own law. When he finished even the lawyer who was against him at the start was now for him" (50). Gregorio Cortez is thus not unlike Thurgood Marshall and Robert Carter who several years before had also told the judges "about their own law"; as Ellison's invisible man also understands, principles of justice, if not precedent, can be invoked in the argument that the law itself is not performing for justice. The key difference is not between texts in which racialized outlaws invoke the law and lose (like *Native Son* and *No-No Boy* and *Korematsu* and *Hirabayashi*) and texts in which racialized outlaws invoke the law and win (like *Brown* and *Invisible Man* and *"With His Pistol in His Hand"*) but between the racialized outlaws willing to appeal to (and hence construct) American justice on the one hand (which is all these texts) and those, as we shall see with N. Scott Momaday's *House Made of Dawn,* in which the only recourse of the racialized outlaw is silence, since his culture is fundamentally different from that of American society. In this way, Paredes's 1958 book is strikingly similar to the liberal, protest, integrationist books and Supreme Court decisions of the 1940s and 1950s.

On the other hand, Paredes is not committed to the politics of assimilation, but is interested in the question of cultural distinctiveness and longevity. In general, he answers that question less aggressively than either Hurston who came before him or anthropology-influenced multiculturalist authors like Momaday or Reed who followed. There is one fascinating moment, however, in which *"With His Pistol in His Hand"* is a premonition of the multiculturalism to come. Discussing the variants of the *corrido,* Paredes sees the variants as stages in the evolution of the *corrido,* and sees variant G as "one of the best" (198). Variant X, for instance, has the quatrain

> Then said Gregorio Cortez,
> With pistol in his hand,
> "Don't run, you cowardly rangers,
> From just one Mexican." (156)

But G subtly changes its mood to

> Then said Gregorio Cortez,
> With pistol in his hand,
> "Ah, how many mounted rangers
> Against one lone Mexican!" (171–72)

G guts the other variants' boastfulness and, replacing "cowardly rangers" with "mounted rangers," changes the tone to tragedy and defiance. Paredes sees this variant's emotion as one that "the Border Mexican identified with his own," making Cortez at last into "the prototype of the hero of border conflict, not only on a physical but on a cultural plane" (199). On this new "cultural plane" culture itself is at last at stake for the *corrido.* Paredes interprets Cortez's last words in variant G, "Ah, how many mounted rangers / Against one lone Mexican!" (172) as "expressing the Border Mexican's realization that he too is outnumbered and that he must lose his struggle to keep his own way of life" (199).

What is novel about this variation—or at least about Paredes's interpretation of it—is the emergent idea of cultural loss. The other variants, including the one Paredes construes as the original, have insisted on Cortez's "right": that is, his right to self-defense and to not have himself and his family harassed by the Texas Rangers and other elements of Anglo-American lawlessness posing as law. The ballad has been based on a universal moral account, in which Cortez is properly understood to uphold a "right" that is not recognized, reliably and in practice, by the supposed "law" of the land. But Paredes's praise for variant G is based on its expression not of this desire for his "right," but of the sense that Mexican Americans in the border area are losing their "own way of life"—that is, their cultural distinctiveness. Although up until this new interpretation we might have understood *El Corrido de Gregorio Cortez* as a musing on white supremacy and the lack of justice in America—putting it squarely in the protest tradition of Wright's *Native Son,* the book that also devotes a good portion of its words to detailing its hero's escape from the law that is not based on universal justice—variant G offers a proto-multiculturalist position. Its cultural pluralism arrives with the very anthropological concept of cultural loss: as with the disappearing Indian, G signals a passing of Mexican American border culture.

But Cortez has not actually been defending his "way of life." What would it be, based on the *corrido*—his right to fly from the unjust law? But in what sense could this "right" be considered a cultural practice? We know that his "right" is not just a cultural "way of life" but a universal ethos (or, more accurately, whether one has his "right" depends not on one's culture, but on one's gender), given the fact that the legend suggests the original arresting sheriff facing Cortez with a pistol in *his* hand also has a "right." As the legend puts it, with a momentary homoerotic whiff, "Now he and the Major Sheriff met, each one pistol in hand, as men should meet when they fight for what is right. For it is a pretty thing to see, when two men stand up for their right, with their pistols in their hands, front to front and without fear. And so it was, for the Major Sheriff also was a man" (40). It is with Paredes's slight misreading—this swerve from thinking about *Cortez* as being about a right to being about cultural loss—that Paredes at once harkens back to the older anthropological tradition that his folklore study is rooted in, and anticipates the pluralist ethos of the post-1965 cultural nationalisms.

Such is what marks this transitional text's place between the sociologically articulated integrationist literature of the second phase and the anthropologically articulated multiculturalist literature of the third phase. One quality that the Américo Paredes of *"With His Pistol in His Hand"* shares with his fellow folklorist Zora Neale Hurston is that he does not depend on, or have much interest in, the problem of identity. To return to an earlier quotation, the sole invocation of the word in *Pistol* is when Paredes writes:

> Until the rise of Hitler in Germany and the beginning of World War II, a majority of Border Mexicans continued to think of themselves as a people apart. Unlike other American minorities, they directed their energies not toward being accepted into the majority but toward maintaining their own individual rights as members in an aloof enclave struggling to keep its own identity. (106)

Identity appears to be a kind of ambition to be distinct, and seems supplemental to, and more marginal than, the idea of culture that *Pistol* is far more interested in.

This supplementarity seems confirmed in a slightly more expansive use of the concept in his essay "The Problem of Identity in a Changing Culture," published in 1978, twenty years after *"With His Pistol in His Hand,"* during the ascent of multiculturalism. While the title seems to promise a focus on "identity" and how that concept might supplement the folklorist's sense of what a "culture" is, in fact the notion of identity in the essay remains marginal. Grounding his account in the history of the border area, Paredes analyzes the mutual views, stereotypes, and derogatory terms that Anglos and Mexicans use for one another. Identity emerges only at the moment in the essay where he considers the self-reflection that is forced on one group by the immediate presence of another group, how "our awareness of other groups besides our own is intimately related to our consciousness of ourselves as a group" (40). The "need to establish one's identity" is the result when the group has to label the outsiders and so "ask the question of emerging national consciousness: 'Who are we?'" (40). Each group could be said to have had a culture until the moment of contact, but "identity" is here understood as a kind of technology of group differentiation. While the Anglo does not really acknowledge his cultural borrowing from Mexico (like the ranch culture that would later be adapted and transformed into the "cowboy" image) and so does not suffer from an "identity crisis,"

> The Mexican, on the other hand, has always been on the defensive in the border situation, afraid of being swallowed whole. He does not have to be sophisticated or an intellectual to realize the risk to his way of life that culture contact entails. The folklore shows his preoccupation about remaining Mexican even when he is becoming most Americanized. (41)

Identity here, as with the momentary use in *Pistol,* is linked to a couple of emerging ideas. One is "national consciousness" so central to decolonization,

Cold War ideology, and the cultural nationalisms that had emerged in the United States in the preceding decade. The other is the idea—and here we finally get the logic that the title seems to promise—of how you could still remain "who you are" even if you were becoming "Americanized."

In other words, identity allows us to answer the question of "who we are" without necessary reference to what we do or what we think—what our actual culture or cultural mix is. "Identity" is an emerging technique—still fairly marginal for Paredes—for answering this question in a way actively opposed to the answer that a cultural anthropology of description might give.[7] Such a concept of identity has a structure akin to Okada and Ellison's emerging use of national identity as patriotism: it was precisely by not taking into account the descriptively true practices of the nation that one achieved the proper affect for the nation, now conceived as having an "identity." The connection between Okada and Ellison's notion of national identity (deployed in order to think about national ontology unencumbered by actual practices and values) and Paredes's notion of cultural or ethnic identity (deployed in order to think about "remaining Mexican even when [one] is becoming most Americanized") is more than just a shared structural need to overcome description, however. As noted above, Paredes suggests that identity is intricately related to "emerging national consciousness: 'Who are we?' " This formulation suggests the possibility that, when the cultural nationalists and inaugurators of the third phase of literary multiculturalism cast about for a vocabulary of difference in the late 1960s and 1970s, one such available language was that of American national identity, itself having been recently deployed as a supplemental Cold War strategy meant to distract from actual American domestic and international practices and values. The way identity organizes and calls forth proper affect by means of suppressing the question of actual cultural practices will be the subject of more detailed analysis in chapter seven.

I would like to end this chapter with some questions about this emerging notion of identity. What does it mean to begin to think about a population as characterized by an identity instead of as a culture? What does it mean for Paredes to invoke this supplement to culture in the moment when culture is not enough, and what does it mean for Paredes's work on culture to be reinterpreted by some later critics as being primarily concerned with identity rather than culture?[8] In short, what work does identity do that culture does not do? If the genealogy of literary multiculturalism was shaped by an interest in the studies and concepts of cultural anthropology, what was the supplement provided by the notion of identity that has since become absolutely central to current discourses of critical and literary multiculturalism?

✿ CHAPTER 6

Toni Morrison, Frank Chin, and Cultural Nationalisms, 1965–1975

> When Wright placed Bigger Thomas and Mr. Dalton in a northern setting and pointed up the fact that Bigger's condition resulted from Dalton's hypocrisy, he opened a Pandora's box of problems for white liberals and Negro leaders, neither of whom could bring themselves to share his vision. [...] This liberal ideology—both social and literary—of the northern Daltons has [recently] become the primary target of the Afro-American writer and critic.
>
> —Addison Gayle Jr., *The Black Aesthetic,* 1971 (xix)

Américo Paredes's anthropology was a residual formation during the integrationist second phase of racialized minority literature (1940–1965), but it also anticipated the turn to anthropology's culture characteristic of the cultural nationalisms developed in the following decade, nationalisms that went on to lay the foundations for our current paradigm of literary multiculturalism. As I will show in these next four chapters, these cultural nationalisms in the African American, Asian American, Native American, and Chicano traditions were instantiated through a double gesture of refuting assimilationist sociology and returning to the Boasian principles of cultural anthropology that had enabled authors like Zora Neale Hurston, D'Arcy McNickle, and Américo Paredes. These refutations and returns were frequently explicit, as writers and intellectuals in the four traditions overtly contested the integrationist assimilationism that had come before, but they were also sometimes covert, with lines of influence and circuits of articulation that can be traced nonetheless.

This chapter examines the cultural nationalisms developed in the African American and Asian American literary traditions. The first section looks at Toni Morrison's 1970 novel *The Bluest Eye* in conjunction with Addison Gayle's 1971 collection *The Black Aesthetic;* together with Ishmael Reed's *Mumbo Jumbo* (addressed in chapter eight), they form a constellation of African American literary and cultural nationalism articulated through a refutation of *Brown*'s sociology and a return to Hurston's anthropological project. The second section deals with an analogous constellation for Asian American letters: Frank Chin's plays *The Chickencoop Chinaman* (written in 1971 and first produced in 1972) and *The Year of the Dragon* (1974) and the 1974 *Aiiieeeee!: An Anthology of Asian American Writers,* edited by Chin, Jeffery Paul Chan, Lawson Fusao Inada, and Shawn Wong. The next chapter examines N. Scott Momaday's 1968 *House Made of Dawn,* a novel—said to have begun the Native American Renaissance—likewise characterized by this double gesture. Chapters eight and nine extend this genealogy of literary multiculturalism by looking at two literary works that took up and mythically extended the anthropological question of cultural survivals, Ishmael Reed's *Mumbo Jumbo* and Gloria Anzaldúa's considerably later work *Borderlands/La Frontera.*

Toni Morrison's *Bluest Eye* is an inaugural novel of American literary multiculturalism. Absolutely crucial to its multiculturalist ethos is its rejection of sociology's model of culture, in which newly ethnicized racial minorities were, like other ethnic groups, to assimilate into the dominant white society. Also crucial to its emerging multiculturalism was its rejection of the integrationist politics that sociology's culture had fostered: as we shall see, Morrison and Hurston rejected segregation, but understood that integration was not the political panacea that it was sometimes imagined to be in the 1950s liberal consensus. Likewise important for *The Bluest Eye*'s status as an inaugural multicultural text was a nascent alternative model of culture that echoed Hurston's anthropological one. Although Morrison does not specifically articulate multiculturalism through Franz Boas's culture concept, her work shares some of the qualities of that concept, which can in a limited way be traced to Hurston's influence. As a post-protest, post-realist novel, *The Bluest Eye* mirrored the Black Aesthetic demand that books by black authors speak directly to African Americans. In its critique of assimilation and its substantiation of a rich African American cultural tradition (especially in the form of black vernacular), *The Bluest Eye* accorded with *The Black Aesthetic*'s principle that African American cultural, national, and racial distinctiveness was not to be abandoned.

The Asian American cultural nationalism that emerged in the early 1970s was, like other cultural nationalisms, pluralist in its declarations and anti-assimilationist in its politics. If *The Bluest Eye, The Black Aesthetic,* and *Mumbo Jumbo* are crucial articulations of a larger literary and cultural movement known as the Black Arts movement, *The Chickencoop Chinaman, The Year of the Dragon,* and *Aiiieeeee!* were analogously the locus of an emerging Asian American cultural and literary nationalism. Like the black nationalism it explicitly took as its model, Asian American cultural nationalism articulated itself through a rejection of the sociological model of minority culture and its trajectory of assimilation; it likewise rejected the vision of racial amalgamation that for Robert Park seemed to promise to hasten the cultural assimilation of racialized minorities. Black nationalism rejected the pathological interpretation of African American culture central to the sociology of Frazier and Myrdal, and Asian American cultural nationalism analogously rejected the pathological interpretation of Asian American psychology as suffering from a "dual" or "split personality" disorder that Monica Sone and some social psychologists understood as the result of living between two cultures. This literary and cultural nationalism explicitly rejected the integrationism and assimilationism of the sociologically enabled Jade Snow Wong, and it framed its own project through a productive misreading of John Okada's *No-No Boy,* just as (we shall see) Larry Neal analogously argued for Hurston's antecedence as a black nationalist by misreading her crucial distinction between culture and race and other nationalist and multiculturalist critics productively misread Richard Wright as a cultural nationalist.

Because there had never been a substantial anthropological tradition in Asian America (the converse of the fact that there had never been a sociological tradition in Native America), the Asian American cultural nationalists did not directly turn back to Boas or anthropology for a model of culture to combat the sociological one they were rejecting. Nonetheless, in struggling simultaneously against the assimilating "model minority" image of Asian Americans (as folks even more successful in the white world than many white people) and the stereotypical indistinction between Asian Americans and Asians, the Asian American cultural nationalists arrived at a solution stressing the historical particularism of Asian American cultures. That solution would have been utterly recognizable to Boas, Hurston, McNickle, and Paredes as the insistence that cultural practices and values adapted over time to environmental and historical circumstances. One such historically particular facet of Asian American cultures was language, and the Asian American cultural nationalists emphasized the historical development of Asian American vernaculars that borrowed and transformed white English, African American vernacular, and Asian immigrant speech. While it is not possible to trace direct influences from anthropology to these Asian American cultural nationalists, the documented interpenetrations among these Asian American writers and intellectuals and African American and Chicano ones (who were themselves, I am arguing, taking up the substance and models of minority cultures developed by their foundational authors Zora Neale Hurston and Américo Paredes) suggest that the anthropological principles of pluralism, holism, relativism, and particularism were indirectly available to those Asian American nationalists who rejected the assimilationist project of the earlier sociological model.

🍃 What *The Bluest Eye* Knows about Them

> This myth of the creation of the white race, called "Yacub's History," is an inversion of the racial death-wish of American Negroes. Yacub's plan is still being followed by many Negroes today. Quite simply, many Negroes believe, as the principle of assimilation into white America implies, that the race problem in America cannot be settled until all traces of the black race are eliminated.
>
> —Eldridge Cleaver, *Soul on Ice,* 1968 (101)

When *The Bluest Eye* sets up another example of the way in which the novel's object, Pecola, is damaged by the U.S. racial order circa 1941, Toni Morrison performs an extraordinary series of literary moves to create the scene. The panorama of Junior sadistically tormenting Pecola by hurling his mother's cat at her is prepared by tracing the boy's action back to his mother's character, thus continuing the novel's standard procedure of explaining characters through extended forays into family history—as it does with Cholly, Pauline, Soaphead, and ultimately Pecola. But his mother's genealogy, instead of familial, is typological: that of a type of persons who, characterized together, are losing a cultural identity that is rightfully theirs because of their racial ancestry.[1]

"They," Morrison collectively terms this type, "come from Mobile." Or, perhaps, "Aiken. From Newport News. From Marietta. From Meridian"(81). What distinguishes "these particular brown girls" is that they are learning "how to get rid of the funkiness. The dreadful funkiness of passion, the funkiness of nature, the funkiness of the wide range of human emotions" (82, 83). Setting up a fundamental ambivalence, *The Bluest Eye* on the one hand locates funk as a species-wide quality; we all have, or once had, funk. On the other hand, this quality is understood to have been already lost by white people in a process that was either racial or cultural (perhaps this loss is what makes someone white); accordingly, funk is the heritage of the "particular brown girls," who are threatened with its loss. The funk is embodied and racialized through the various phenotypic differences that mark the social construction of race and that threaten to overwhelm the whitening process: "They hold their behind in for fear of a sway too free; when they wear lipstick, they never cover the entire mouth for fear of lips too thick, and they worry, worry, worry about the edges of their hair," which has been straightened with "Dixie Peach" (83, 82). In this struggle, it seems as if culture as learned behavior might combat an inherited, biology-derived identity.

Or at least that is the possibility that *The Bluest Eye* takes up: whether, following desegregation and the Civil Rights movement, African Americans could or should adopt dominant white cultural practices and values. In a generative moment in the genealogy of literary multiculturalism, the novel tells the story of a black girl in 1941 who is all but destroyed by her desire for white beauty and by other African Americans acting in response to the oppression of white racism and cultural normativity. *The Bluest Eye* thus staked a claim in the national debate about minority culture and citizenship that took place during its composition (1962–1970), a debate shaped not only by literature but also by social science and law. A cornerstone of our current paradigm of literary multiculturalism is this novel's rejection of integrationist law and assimilationist social science, although the novel's discomfort with group ontology is not characteristic of the multiculturalism it helped inaugurate.

While that discomfort characterizes *The Bluest Eye* as a whole, it is not on display in Morrison's vigorous and extended typology of the "brown girls," who learn in school "the rest of the lesson begun in those soft houses with porch swings and pots of bleeding heart: how to behave" (83). The body continually seems to threaten this process, and as such it is the focus of behavioral practices (and products) that help to whiten these "brown girls": "They wash themselves with orange-colored Lifebuoy soap, dust themselves with Cashmere Bouquet talc, clean their teeth with salt on a piece of rag, soften their skin with Jergens Lotion" (82). The narrator goes on to describe their future husbands as not knowing about the sexual reticence (detailed for three paragraphs) produced by their carefully ordered worlds: "Nor do they know that she will give him her body sparingly and partially. He must enter her surreptitiously, lifting the hem of her nightgown only to her navel" (84).

Not strangely, perhaps we are to understand, the product of this surreptitious acknowledgment of the body is a boy whose identity as "colored" (as his mother calls them) is continually threatened by the body's intrusion into cultured order. Even though Geraldine has her son's hair cut "as close to his scalp as possible to avoid any suggestion of wool" with a part "etched into his hair by the barber," and even though she puts more Jergens onto his "light-skinned" face "to keep the skin from becoming ashen," her son's body resists the cultural practices that might erase or mitigate racial difference (87). "The line between colored and nigger was not always clear; subtle and telltale signs threatened to erode it, and the watch had to be constant" (87). But the novel establishes Junior's almost innate desire for blackness:

> Junior used to long to play with the black boys. More than anything in the world he wanted to play King of the Mountain and have them push him down the mound of dirt and roll over him. He wanted to feel their hardness pressing on him, smell their wild blackness, and say "Fuck you" with that lovely casualness. He wanted to sit with them on curbstones and compare the sharpness of jackknives, the distance and arcs of spitting. In the toilet he wanted to share with them the laurels of being able to pee far and long. (87)

Junior's desire for blackness is strongly signaled in sensual and sexual terms, terms tactile, auditory, olfactory. The boys will "roll over him," their "hardness" will press on him, they will say fuck together, and they will, wielding their penises, pee together. All of these could be described as cultural practices (which, together or separately, do not appear to have any intrinsic meaning whatsoever)—so that comparing jackknives, playing rough, peeing and spitting together, saying "fuck you" could be understood to be performative of "black" boyhood "culture." But the text draws our attention to the ways in which these things seem to be true to the body, in a way that an equally performative "white" "culture," exemplified by Geraldine's efforts, is understood to be inauthentic, at least to the bodies of Geraldine and her son. That is, in both this typology of the "brown girls" and the narrower description of Geraldine and Junior that follows it, the novel does not model culture as performative. While doing certain things and holding certain values might abstractly constitute a culture, the text devalues that culture in favor of an identitarian, body-based, essentialist "culture" which has its origin and true value in race. That these girls are "brown" is the condition for but also the cause of this slippage between race and culture; being racially mixed permits and necessitates a cultural answer. In other words, and as Walter Benn Michaels argues about Oliver La Farge's *Laughing Boy,* "Biology is an essential but not a sufficient condition of an identity that here requires a relatively autonomous set of practices to complete its constitution" (*Our America* 119).

The ostensible narrative purpose of Morrison's extended typology in *The Bluest Eye* is to introduce Geraldine, who accounts for the internalized rage and sadism of her son. When Junior throws his mother's cat into Pecola's face, Geraldine's subsequent epithet for Pecola—"black bitch"—completes the sequence of events that leads to Pecola's deep psychic damage. But Morrison's exuberant typological set-up for Geraldine is about four times as long as Geraldine's own history and that of her relation to her child. Indeed, the narrative signals its nonchalance toward Geraldine at the very moment it pretends to be turning from typology to focus on a single character: "One such girl from Mobile, or Meridian, or Aiken [...]" (86). The text is supposedly narrowing the typology to a specific "One," but it clearly does not care about getting the facts of this "One" straight, since such facts are understood not to really count, or perhaps to threaten the very representativeness of the typology offered in the first place. In this feint from "They" to "One," then, we are not witnessing the cultural practices that give rise or meaning to the individual; rather, Morrison is describing a typology of cultural loss. Geraldine cannot change her race, but she can try to change her culture, and this process is described as loss rather than transformation or gain.

This typology is part of the novel's larger project of examining the grounds for group identity in the midst of a crisis of minority citizenship in the United States. Geraldine's typology and its conflation of race and culture must be heard not only within the novel's 1941 timeframe but also in the intellectual context of the composition of the novel: that of the philosophical struggle between the Black Arts movement and the Civil Rights movement. That Geraldine, like Pecola, does not hold that "black is beautiful" is the thematic center of the novel. "The reclamation of racial beauty in the sixties stirred these thoughts, made me think about the necessity for the claim," Morrison wrote in her 1993 afterword to the 1970 novel (210). Conceiving of this reclamation as one tactic in a larger decolonization, Black Aesthetician Hoyt Fuller wrote in 1968, "Across this country, young black men and women have been infected with a fever of affirmation. They are saying, 'We are black and beautiful,' and the ghetto is reacting with a liberating shock of realization which transcends mere chauvinism. They are rediscovering their heritage and their history" ("Towards" 8). This passage is from "Towards a Black Aesthetic," which was reprinted in Addison Gayle's Black Aesthetic the year after The Bluest Eye was published, where it joined other key documents that outlined the development of the movement. In that collection, Gayle considered the central project of the Black Arts movement to be the "de-Americanization" of black communities (xxii). The collection also reprinted Larry Neal's 1968 article "The Black Arts Movement," where he argued that "Black Art is the aesthetic and spiritual sister of the Black Power concept," both of which were to define and substantiate African American self-determination and nationhood. Neal noted that there are "two Americas—one black, one white" ("Black Arts" 272–73).

Black nationalism was contesting the newly official liberal consensus enshrined by Brown's overturning of Plessy's "separate but equal" segregationist logic, the ramifications of which were being worked out in the Civil Rights movement. Morrison repeatedly invokes *Brown* to critique its vision of the cultural assimilation of racialized minorities. Against this newly official liberal consensus on sociology's culture, black nationalism and the Black Aesthetic posed an alternative, separatist, racially essentialist model that imagined African American double consciousness as a problem to be solved not through unification (as Du Bois had hoped), but through a reclamation of racial pride.[2] As Neal put it, "Implicit in the Black Arts Movement is the idea that Black people, however dispersed, constitute a *nation* within the belly of white America" ("Black Arts Movement" 290). Insofar as *The Bluest Eye* understands Geraldine's cultural practices and values as inappropriate given her race, it is a Black Arts novel; in concurrence with Neal, it imagines a different kind of national belonging for African Americans than the sociological model approved in *Brown*.

Along with the passages from the Dick-and-Jane reader that begin each chapter and the Hollywood images that attract Pauline, Pecola's mother, Geraldine constitutes the 1940s white cultural norm that the novel critiques. She has largely assimilated into white society, assuming its waspy, middle-class trappings: lace doilies, "a large Bible in the front room," the making of "soufflés in the Home Economics Department"—a hygiene-cum-sterility of both house and person (84, 83, 86). Geraldine exemplifies Robert Park's thesis about the cultural assimilability of racialized minorities. Like Park's Hawaiian Asian American, Geraldine is an American in disguise, though this time the disguise is "brown" rather than yellow. Being "brown," in fact—which the novel's typology repeatedly emphasizes—likewise exemplifies Park's link between sociology and amalgamation: that cultural assimilation most speedily happens when there is intermarriage and miscegenation. Capping this series of links, Geraldine adopts the nomenclature of the liberal, sociology-using, integrationist NAACP: she and her son are "colored."

The Bluest Eye thus takes up the two competing models of culture in the 1960s. The official, liberal one was integrationist, was energized by the Boasian notion of racial equality, was extended to assimilable racialized minorities by Robert Park in the 1930s, was codified and made official with "the force-feeding of *An American Dilemma* to the American public by the press and the federal government" by the early 1950s (L. Baker 198), was the grounds for the LDEF's argument before the Supreme Court, was approved by the Supreme Court in its famous footnote 11 to *Brown,* and was consequently the grounds for the Civil Rights movements emerging in the next decade (L. Baker 207). The other flavor, submerged but now re-emerging, emphasized cultural relativism and cultural pluralism; it is perhaps best illustrated by

Hurston's own field work, her resistance to the discourse of black pathology and the pressures of assimilation, and her insistence on the vitality of African American culture and art, all of which would find strong, new, nationalist articulators in the Black Aesthetic and Black Power movements.

The debate between these two positions in the 1960s formed the intertextual ground for *The Bluest Eye,* which took up issues articulated in *Brown.* Most obvious is the pathology of self-loathing that its social science documented; Morrison invokes that pathology in Pecola, but here, as in so many things in the novel, invokes it in such a way that the process does not become more comprehensible but more complicated. (Both the narrator and the author believe that the novel's task has in some important way failed, we are told.) Pecola and Claudia go to an integrated school and the latter at least lives in an integrated neighborhood in Lorain, Ohio. But, in an ironic commentary on the premise of *Brown*—that black self-esteem is irreparably harmed when law sanctions social segregation, especially during the elementary education that is "the very foundation of good citizenship," as Chief Justice Warren put it—this pathology emerges forcefully in Pecola despite her partially integrated environment.

Besides these instances contesting *Brown,* the most interesting attention the novel gives the social science behind the decision is the dolls test developed by Kenneth and Mamie Clark.[3] In May 1951, Kenneth Clark accompanied Thurgood Marshall and Robert Carter to Charleston, where, while Marshall and Carter prepared argument, Clark interviewed sixteen black children in Clarendon County's segregated schools. Using his dolls test, in which children indicated preference for and identification with otherwise identical brown- and white-colored dolls, he discovered that "Ten of the sixteen children said they preferred the white doll. Eleven of the children referred to the black doll as 'bad,' while nine said the white doll was 'nice.' Seven of the children pointed to the white doll when they were asked to choose the doll most like themselves" (Williams, *Thurgood Marshall* 200). In the case that would become *Briggs v. Elliott* (1951), Clark testified, based on these tests, "that school segregation was distorting the minds of black youngsters to the point of making them self-hating" (202). Although the majority opinion rejected the introduction of what it called Clark's "sociology" into legal interpretation, it found the material conditions of the segregated schools unequal and gave the county six months to equalize the black and white schools.

Briggs v. Elliott was one of the four cases on appeal before the Supreme Court in 1952 and 1953, all of which ended together in *Brown.* In the decision's renowned footnote 11, the Court referenced Clark's work as one of the seven social science studies substantiating the psychological damage that attended school segregation.[4] A decade after *Brown,* toward the end of the Civil Rights movement that it had made possible, and as the Black Arts movement commenced, Toni Morrison turned to this figure of the black child's desire for the white beauty and subjectivity embodied in a doll. Unlike the black children in the Clarks' studies in the 1940s, who tended statistically to prefer white dolls, *The Bluest Eye*'s narrator, Claudia, thinks back to what she realizes is her atypical reaction, as an African American child in the 1940s, to the "blue-eyed" dolls received at Christmas (Clarks, "Racial Identification"). "From the clucking sounds of adults I knew that the doll represented what they thought was my fondest wish," Claudia recalls (*Bluest* 20), this being the Clarks' conclusion as well: "It is clear [...] that the majority of these Negro children prefer the *white* doll and reject the colored doll" ("Racial Identification" 175).

For Claudia, however, the white dolls, "which were supposed to bring me great pleasure, succeeded in doing quite the opposite" (*Bluest* 20). She can read the racial code, at least retroactively, understanding the white doll to be "beautiful" (21), but she lacks the spontaneity of many of the Clarks' subjects who chose a white doll " 'cause he's pretty" ("Racial Identification" 178). Instead of pleasure and desire, the doll elicits only revulsion from this atypical pupil:

> I had only one desire: to dismember it. To see of what it was made, to discover the dearness, to find the beauty, the desirability that had escaped me, but apparently only me. Adults, older girls, shops, magazines, newspapers, window signs—all the world had agreed that a blue-eyed, yellow-haired, pink-skinned doll was what every girl child treasured. (*Bluest* 20)

Indeed, Claudia seems unfazed by the move from preference to identification that, for the Clarks' subjects, appeared to initiate a crisis of "racial mental hygiene" ("Racial Identification" 175).[5] As the Clarks note, "some of the children who were free and relaxed in the beginning of the experiment [the phase of racial preference] broke down and cried or became somewhat negativistic during the latter part when they were required to make self-identifications. Indeed, two children ran out of the testing room, unconsolable, convulsed in tears" (178). Claudia, however, "could not love [the white doll]. But I could examine it to see what it was that all the world said was lovable. Break off the tiny fingers, bend the flat feet, loosen the hair, twist the head around" (*Bluest* 21).

Claudia somehow escapes the pathology that the Clarks identified, which was at the center of *Brown,* and which eventually engulfs Pecola, who shares with one of the Clarks' students the desire for a white doll "cause it's got blue eyes—cause it's got pretty eyes" (Clarks, "Emotional Factors" 348). Pecola, in fact, imagines that she has achieved the doll's blue eyes by the end of the novel. Her problem mirrors the conclusion that the Clarks came to in a 1950 study:

> The negation of the color, brown, exists in the same complexity of attitudes in which there also exists knowledge of the fact that the child himself must be identified with that which he rejects. This apparently introduces a fundamental conflict at the very foundations of the ego structure. Many of these children attempt to resolve this profound conflict either through wishful thinking or phantasy. ("Emotional Factors" 350)

Such fantasies of racial identity and preference—the grounds of the Clarks' studies cited in *Brown*—are at the center of *The Bluest Eye*. Claudia not only rejects the white dolls that she understands the world deems lovable, but she also hates Shirley Temple, whom Pecola and Frieda so adore: "I couldn't join them in their adoration because I hated Shirley. Not because she was cute, but because she danced with Bojangles, who was *my* friend, *my* uncle, *my* daddy" (19). Claudia rejects what Clark would see as a pathological racial preference, choosing instead a "healthy" racial identity, imagining racial belonging progressively as friendship, kinship, and then paternity. But this is only because Claudia, younger than her sister and Pecola, "had not yet arrived at the turning point in my development of my psyche which would allow me to love her" (19).

While *The Bluest Eye* thus suggests that the social construction of white beauty uncovered by the Clarks' study exists and exerts an overwhelming pressure on girls of any "race," it also portrays the application of this phenomenon as bumpy, incomplete, complicated, and resisted. *Brown*'s answer of integration is also rendered strangely problematic by the novel, whose semi-integrated setting seems not to have eradicated the pathologies of the past and, perhaps, to have created others. The assimilation that Park and Myrdal imagined as being the unavoidable and just end of the "race relations cycle" is represented by the sadistic Junior, who is only allowed to play with white boys, not the black boys he so desires (87). And Claudia, in an integrated school and an integrated neighborhood, transfers her violent impulses from the white dolls to her white neighbor Rosemary, whose face she scratches, and whose "fascinated eyes in a dough-white face" remind us of the dolls that Claudia detests (30). In these instances, being at school with or living next to white people is not imagined as the answer that *Brown*'s social science seemed to promise.[6]

The Bluest Eye details both the psychological violence of white norms of beauty and cultural citizenship *and* a black resistance to that violence in the form of Claudia's appropriate anger at them (Matus 43), thus revealing its affinity to the Black Arts movement that formed the novel's intellectual context. But beyond their common exploration and critique of "racial self-loathing," as Morrison puts it in her afterword (210), *The Bluest Eye* and the Black Arts movement also shared suspicion, even hostility, toward the social science discourse that underlay *Brown,* and to the minority citizenship model that *Brown* helped inaugurate. In short, they rejected the assimilationist trajectory of Park and Myrdal and the portrayal of Negro pathology—that black people need to be near or around whites in order to be spiritually, psychologically, and culturally healthy—implied in Clark. In this sense, the Black Aesthetic would seek a return to the concept of culture formed by Boas, embraced by Hurston, but denied by Chicago sociology—one that saw African American culture as healthy, slow to change, cohesive, and potentially continuous with African traditions.

While Morrison was writing *The Bluest Eye,* for example, Thurgood Marshall, then associate justice of the Supreme Court, was harassed by the Black Panthers as "an establishment voice" when he spoke at the University of Wisconsin in September 1968 (Williams, *Thurgood Marshall* 342–43), and Ralph Ellison was verbally confronted in April 1969 by black students at Oberlin College where he came to speak, being termed by them an "Uncle Tom" (Walling 128). Marshall, conversely, rejected the militancy of the younger black generation and their "separatism" in a confrontation that received widespread press (Williams, *Thurgood Marshall* 343–44). As Hoyt Fuller argued that same year in "Towards a Black Aesthetic," "black intellectuals have rejected the NAACP" just as they were rejecting "the Literary Establishment" (3). Morrison, having graduated in 1953 from Howard University—which had trained Marshall in its law school and Clark in its psychology department, and which had provided the legal muscle for the desegregation challenge— likewise questioned the wisdom of *Brown,* not understanding why "black children were going to learn better if they were in the company of white children." As she recalled, in a 1983 interview, "I was not in favor of integration. But I couldn't officially say that, because I knew the terror and the abuses of segregation. But integration also meant that we would not have a fine black college or fine black education" (Interview 51). Morrison's statements directly echo Hurston's 1955 letter to the *Orlando Sentinel* (widely reprinted in Southern papers), in which she questioned the premise that black children learn better while sitting next to white children and thought the ruling denigrated the "very good" black schools in existence (Kaplan 738–40). But Hurston's and Morrison's questioning of *Brown* was a marginal position in 1955; it was not part of the dominant integrationist politics in African American circles, though it would slowly grow to be. That it was marginal is indicated by Morrison's retrospective, in which she recalls not being able to talk about her unease with *Brown* even at Howard, which of all places should have been sensitive to a fear of losing African American excellence in education.

It is revealing to compare the fates of Wright and Ellison as the Black Arts movement grew in the 1960s, with Ellison's novel famously being called "the most distinguished single work published in the last twenty years" by an almost exclusively white "Book Week" poll in the *New York Herald Tribune* in 1965, and Wright being named as "the most important black American writer of all time" in a 1968 *Negro Digest* poll (Walling 125–27).[7] The ascendance of Wright's reputation in the Black Aesthetic was due to its portrayal of white liberal hypocrisy (as the quotation from Addison Gayle in the epigraph to this chapter suggests) and its promise of violence. This ascendance was also probably due to an emphasis on Wright's "Blueprint," which Gayle reprinted in *The Black Aesthetic* and which he approvingly invokes in the final paragraph of the final essay in the collection ("Function" 418). But Wright's being given virtually the last word in *The Black Aesthetic* is based on a reading of his Blueprint's prescriptive aesthetics and cultural politics that he pointedly did not enact in his own writing. The Black Aesthetic was not embracing *Native Son*'s realism or its status as protest literature, for, as Arthur P. Davis argued in response to *Brown,* protest literature, in view of the integration to come, was a passé form. "When the enemy capitulated," said Davis, "he shattered our most fruitful literary tradition. The possibility of imminent integration has tended to destroy the protest element in Negro writing" (142). Like *The Bluest Eye,* the Black Aesthetic eschewed both protest and the realism that enabled it, opting instead, as Larry Neal put it in 1968, for writing authentically and "directly to Black people" ("Black Arts" 273).

The Black Arts movement's rejection of the NAACP and "the Literary Establishment"—embodied perhaps in Marshall, now co-opted in the Supreme Court, and Ralph Ellison, now co-opted at the 1965 White House Arts Festival—was a cultural politics whose authenticity was grounded in race. As must be clear by now, *The Bluest Eye* is a Black Arts novel, and its themes of racial beauty and cultural oppression were received in the current terms of the Black Aesthetic. This is probably why the mostly male, Black Aesthetic critics did not criticize Morrison's novel as they did the novels of some other African American women at the time (Dubey, *Black Women* 33–34). Reviewers Liz Gant in *Black World* and Sharyn Skeeter in *Essence* recognized the themes of racial beauty and ugliness in *The Bluest Eye,* noting Pecola's ultimate inability to see "the beauty deep within herself" (Gant 52).

The novel's engagement with African American psychology was thus acknowledged through Black Aesthetic concepts. As Ruby Dee puts it in her review: "The author digs up for viewing deep secret thoughts, terrible yearnings and little-understood frustrations common to many of us. She says these are the gnawings we keep pushed back into the subconscious, unadmitted; but they must be worked on, ferreted up and out so we can breathe deeply, say loud and truly believe 'Black is beautiful'" (319).

In reviewing how the Black Arts movement situated itself in terms of realism and protest literature in the 1960s as Morrison was composing *The Bluest Eye,* my aim is to indicate this alignment with contemporaneous moves in citizenship law and the social sciences. To put that alignment most simply, the realist methodology that both the Black Arts movement and *The Bluest Eye* rejected was associated, directly and in spirit, with the empirical strain of sociology, and with the so-called legal realism or sociological jurisprudence whose era *Brown* was said to inaugurate.

It was Robert Park and his mentor Thomas who helped establish, borrowing from anthropology, a "fieldwork" model for sociology, whereby details were to be gathered by visiting the actual sites of ethnic urban difference. But the parallel between literary realism and sociology is not just an affinity of method—whereby an accurate picture of the real is established through patient observation of detail and accumulation of fact. Nor is it only a political trajectory that both shared in the 1930s and 1940s—with realist protest literature and sociological models of assimilation and psychopathology both leading toward *Brown*'s official model of integrated citizenship. There is also strong evidence that literary realism and the newly established social sciences recognized in one another a similar attentiveness to the facts of ethnic life, and that these discourses borrowed concepts and evidence from one another during this time period. Thomas and Znaniecki's *The Polish Peasant in Europe and America,* for example, helped pioneer "the use of personal documents, such as letters, diaries, and especially life histories or autobiographies written at the request of an inquirer" (Timasheff 155). The major figures of the Chicago school were sometimes trained in literature, or made use of literature in order to inspire or illuminate their work on the city.[8]

By the 1940s and 1950s, sociology used literary writing to verify empirical findings. Only a page after a reference to the Clarks' doll study, the Truman administration's 1950 *Personality in the Making: The Fact-Finding Report of the Midcentury White House Conference on Children and Youth* referred to Wright's *Native Son* as a "fictional case history" when making a point about the hostility that racial prejudice creates (Witmer and Kotinsky 143–44). Both "studies" are on the psychological effects of prejudice, but the problem here, of course, is that *Native Son* is being used as evidence in support of the very sociological findings that had greatly influenced Wright's thinking and the composition of *Native Son*. Werner Sollers sounds a similar warning, after noting how Robert Park misread a Jewish autobiography in his important "Human Migration and the Marginal Man":

> Even when the literary evidence is not so overtly misread, there are some problems with the way in which literature is viewed by the more theoretical analysts. Richard Wright's fiction, for example, is frequently invoked in sociological accounts of the ghetto. Yet it is—precisely in its depiction of psychological alienation and cultural deprivation—the partial product of Wright's immersion into Chicago school of sociology readings (Fabre 232). Such uses of literature as social evidence may be circular. (*Beyond Ethnicity* 9)

We confront a conceptual circuit here, in which social science findings—"culture," the pathology of the Negro family, the effects of race prejudice—in turn influence the composition of literary texts, which are then read as evidence of the original theory. Nor is this circuit finished indeed. Midge Wilson and Kathy Russell, in *Divided Sisters: Bridging The Gap between Black Women and White Women* (1996), use *The Bluest Eye* to answer the research question of "How is girls' cross-race play affected by dolls that are White instead of Black?" (43), but appear not to notice that Morrison's novel has as its intertextual source and inspiration the initial social scientific evidence about dolls and "cross-race play" (the Clarks' studies) that their book mentions only a few pages earlier (40). Such intersections of literature and social science raise important questions of discipline and method that I address in the conclusion.

This alliance between realism and sociology was joined by a third constituent at this key historical moment announced by *Brown:* legal realism, or "sociological jurisprudence," which was the self-conscious turn to "extralegal data" and fact-finding as substantiated in particular by the newly authoritative social sciences (Rosen 157). What we might call an alliance of the real among realist-based protest fiction, the sociology of racial pathology, and legal realism—summarized neatly when *Brown* cited the *Mid-Century White House Report,* which substantiated the effects of prejudice by referring to both Wright's *Native Son* and the Clarks' doll study—helped bring forth a new citizenship order for racialized minorities in the United States. They established an official national consensus on what African American culture was, and what would happen to it.

Toni Morrison's *Bluest Eye* and the Black Arts movement were, together, refutations of this mid-century alliance. Against the sociological model of culture approved by *Brown*—whereby integrated, assimilative childhood education was considered the "foundation of good citizenship"—*The Bluest Eye* posed a racial understanding of culture that concurred with the Black Aesthetic's call for pluralism and racial authenticity. This is what it means for Morrison, in the extended typology of Geraldine, to peel back the layer of cultural assimilation in order to reveal the racial truth that remains. "Brown girls" are learning "how to get rid of the funkiness" (*Bluest* 82–83), and though funk here seems like a species-wide quality, its etymology suggests a more specific set of associations. Indeed, to explain funk's roots in slavery in "The Black Arts Movement," Larry Neal had to footnote LeRoi Jones's *Blues People*, where Jones explained that in the 1950s

> Even the adjective *funky*, which once meant to many Negroes merely a stink (usually associated with sex), was used to qualify the music as meaningful (the word became fashionable and is now almost useless). The social implication, then, was that even the old stereotype of a distinctive Negro smell that white America subscribed to could be turned against white America. (219)

According to the *Oxford English Dictionary*, the seventeenth-century meaning of "funk" as a bad smell associated with tobacco became racialized in the early twentieth century as it was applied to African Americans; it was then applied to jazz in the 1950s and then contemporary music later on (the *OED* offers Mick Jagger as an example). In other words, the word has a racial history. It was adapted for use as a racist concept, and then, Jones notes, the stereotype was redeemed (perhaps after social psychologists went after it).[9] In one sense, Morrison invites us to consider funk to be human in general, in a way that might have us see, in accordance with Morrison's *Playing in the Dark,* that whiteness produces itself as non-funk, thus allowing Mick Jagger to rediscover something natural he has lost. But funk's history is one of fascination with the bodies of black people specifically—and it is this fascination that Morrison's typology returns us to, with its discussion of both Geraldine's sexual repression and the subversive body of her son Junior. *The Bluest Eye* thus understands, along with the Black Arts movement, that the question of who has or should have African American culture can be answered only by one's race. Larry Neal claimed "an African-American cultural tradition" was the basis for the Black Aesthetic ("Black Arts" 274), but, as with *The Bluest Eye,* that tradition could be appropriately practiced only according to racial group.

But *The Bluest Eye* betrays an anxiety about group ontology, as if it is casting about for an appropriate language for and model of the group. This anxiety is especially apparent in Geraldine's typology, where the type and the description of culture are seen to overlap and be, in fact, indistinguishable.

It is ostensibly an ethnographically sophisticated description of cultural practices, covering the major areas of anthropological detail: living conditions, housing, employment, education, hygiene, sexuality, gesture, and values. The voice is that of the field anthropologist, making notes on the natives ("They") and seeing meaning in their practices. In other words, what this passage is describing is culture. And yet what becomes apparent is that cultural description is not enough. Much of the passage describes practices—in other words, the situation and behavior that should make Geraldine who she is. Though she cannot pass for white because she is too colored (as she puts it), she is adopting the middle-class, Protestant values associated with whiteness. But the ground for the group in the passage is not performative culture, but rather race (and it does not really try to disguise this fact).

The novel exuberantly develops Geraldine's typology just as it does the literary stereotypes that cannot capture the "whores" who live above the Breedloves (55–57), even though such self-reflectively crafted formulations fail to get at the groups' ontologies. With such investigations, *The Bluest Eye* evokes similar accounts of the same problem in both Chicago sociology's development of types in the 1920s and 1930s and realism's use of types in 1840s and 1850s.[10] The novel's compulsive experiments with group definition—of sociological type, literary stereotype, culture, and race—display a kind of anxiety about the grounds for who "they" are. It thus rehearses its own hermeneutic disappointments as it constantly tries to fit people into one kind of group or another, and finds "them" to be inexact fits. "Were they real?" Pecola wonders of the "whores" (58). Nor is Claudia a real African American, exactly, as her rage at the white dolls exceeds the racial typology discovered/predicted by the Clarks' study. Geraldine is not really culturally white, though she practices dominant American white culture, but is sort of racially black, though she tries not to be. Thus, the intertextual dialogue between *The Bluest Eye* and *Invisible Man* involves not only Cholly's rape of his daughter, as Michael Awkward has shown, but also the hermeneutic anxiety of Ellison's narrator, who fears, as Trueblood tells his tale, that a particular act by a single individual will be understood to be a trait of the group (Awkward 57–68). What remains in *The Bluest Eye* as the limits of the group are probed is a systemic idiosyncrasy for her fiction's characters ("I chose a unique situation, not a representative one," Morrison recalls in her afterword [*Bluest* 210]), one frequently marked by the fantastic and the extraordinary. That idiosyncrasy comes as a relief because we have developed, like the novel itself, scheme fatigue.

The Bluest Eye stands at the beginning of third-phase literary multiculturalism, and its logic—that we have to figure out what culture we should have, a question answered racially—is representative of this multiculturalism, and the cultural nationalism out of which it came. Morrison's oeuvre has worked toward substantiating African American cultural presence, though that presence is often, according to many critics, rendered through tropes of loss, nostalgia, dispossession, and grieving.[11] But the typology of Geraldine suggests how even the description of the loss of one's proper culture can generate a content for African American culture that is both positive and positivist; it is, we might say, real. Thus in this politics of recognition beginning with *The Bluest Eye,* Morrison has advanced the Black Aesthetic's project, as Henry Louis Gates Jr. has put it, of making blackness into "a trope of presence" rather than absence (*Signifying* 237).

But while *The Bluest Eye*'s cultural pluralism is representative of our current paradigm of literary multiculturalism, its suspicion of group identity is not. Equally important to the emerging multiculturalism was the novel's strategy of imagining the description of Geraldine's culture as insufficient to get at who she really represents, and though Morrison does not use the word, this logic is an emerging notion of identity constructed by the eschewal of description that, we have seen, likewise characterized Okada, Ellison, and Paredes. These successful moves would become cornerstones of our current multiculturalism.

The Black Arts Movement and Zora Neale Hurston

> Zora Neal Hurston, anthropologist, throwing light on language. Open the way for today's freedom-wigged freaks. Stone-cold, bad-blood revolutionaries. Escapees from prisons of Anglo rhetoric. Frontiersmen in the lumbering netherlands of Black language. Medicine men schooled in witchcraft, black magic, the voodoo of words. Immortalized, subterranean, out-of-this-world travelers. Dutchmen. LeRois. LeRoi Joneses. Quick-change sleight-of-hand magicians. Dons. Don Lees. Changing. "Change your enemy change your change change change your enemy change change . . . change your mind nigger." Killens. Killens' chilluns. On their jobs. Taking care of business. "De-niggerizing the world." Voodoo cowboys. Loop Garoo Kids. Riding loose—cool ones—into the whirlwind of change; who, as they gallop into town, have a "posse of spells phone in sick." Ishmaels. Ishmael Reeds. Yeah. Yellow Back Radio Done Show Good Broke-Down. Up against the wall, Prospero.
>
> —Sarah Webster Fabio, "Tripping with Black Writing," *The Black Aesthetic,* 1971 (187–88)

In the genealogy of literary multiculturalism we find in *The Bluest Eye* a few key strategies that are exemplary of this inaugural multiculturalist turn. The first is a rejection of minority assimilation, not only abstractly, but by directly taking up and refuting the most contentious social science work of the sociological model of culture central to *Brown* and the Civil Rights movement. The second strategy is a turn to the anthropological principles of pluralism, relativism, and historical particularity. The third key strategy that exemplifies the multiculturalist turn is the reattaching of culture to race, in a move that both undoes Franz Boas's principle, and makes possible the treatment of culture as a kind of identity and the object of ambition. These three strategies are central to *The Bluest Eye* and to the multiculturalist paradigm that emerged with the Black Arts movement and other inaugural texts of third-phase multiculturalism, as revealed in the cultural nationalisms of its first decade (1965–1975).

The mere description of Geraldine's cultural practices is not enough to define who Geraldine is, and in this respect *The Bluest Eye* does not conform to the anthropological model of culture developed by Boas and passed on to the African American tradition largely through Zora Neale Hurston. Nevertheless, *The Bluest Eye*'s model of what African American culture is more closely resembles Hurston's model than Wright's model, or to put it another way, it is closer to Boas's understanding of culture than Robert Park's understanding of culture. Indeed, *The Bluest Eye* shows signs of having been influenced by Hurston's work, though Morrison's composition of the novel (1962–1970) substantially predates the generally recognized beginning of the Hurston "renaissance" in 1975. I would like to argue that we have yet to recognize the earliness of Hurston's influence on a generation of multicultural African American writers—those writers who emerged after the Wright-Ellison-Baldwin triumvirate's dominance that I date from between *Native Son* (1940) and Ellison's White House Arts Festival appearance (1965).

Two signs (at least) of what Zora Neale Hurston knew about African American culture are constitutive to *The Bluest Eye*. The first is the novel's use of and interest in black vernacular. The novel's very story is framed by the vernacular signal "Quiet as it's kept" (5), a "familiar phrase," Morrison later explained in her afterword, "familiar to me as a child listening to adults; to black women conversing with one another, telling a story, an anecdote, gossip about some one or event within the circle, the family, the neighborhood" (211–12). While the story that unfolds is certainly different from the Eatonville porch's tales collected in *Mules, The Bluest Eye* is nonetheless framed by oral communal telling, chosen "for how speakerly it is, how it speaks and bespeaks a particular world and its ambience" (212), the voice "mimicking the adult black women on the porch or in the backyard" (213). *The Bluest Eye* is thus framed by a traditional tale-telling signal of black vernacular—though its content is not a recognizable "lie" because Morrison "jus' made dat one up herself" as one of Eatonville's listeners might have put it (*Mules* 30)—and is likewise deeply interested in and attuned to African American speech. Hurston's complaint about *Uncle Tom's Children* that its author "does not write by ear unless he is tone-deaf" ("Stories" 913) could not be said of *The Bluest Eye*. Morrison's novel hears and celebrates African American speech, and the reader experiences it through the child narrator Claudia's ears with a sense of wonder, as with a tale of local philandering (13–15), the scolding of children (21), the prostitutes' banter and song (51–58), or (from Cholly's point of view) the story of Aunt Jimmy's death by peach cobbler (140–42). As in Hurston's work, orality itself is part of an African American cultural distinctiveness that is, already artful, to be reworked in turn in other art.

The second commonality between Hurston and Morrison's sense of African American culture is its historical rootedness in the rural South. It is perhaps not coincidental that the three most canonical post-Hurston integrationist African American writers, Wright, Ellison, and Baldwin, lived primarily in cities and set their novels primarily in Northern cities. The assimilation of African Americans or Asian Americans could be indexed, for Park, according to their urbanity and opportunities for social integration. Hurston's, Ellison's, and Wright's living places at the time *Brown* was handed down in 1954—in Eau Gallie, New York, and Paris—index their respective commitments to African American culture.

Furthermore, the Great Migration of hundreds of thousands of African Americans to large urban centers from the rural South in the second and third decades of the twentieth century is the background for *The Bluest Eye*. Much of this migration ended in New York (like Ellison's narrator), Chicago (as with Wright, and creating the urban ghettoes that Robert Park and other Chicago sociologists studied), Cleveland (outside of which lies Lorain, Morrison's home town and the setting for *The Bluest Eye*), Detroit, and other cities. In its effort to trace the destruction of Pecola, the narrator backs up to tell the stories of her parents and their migrations from the South. Pauline's family moves from rural Alabama to a Kentucky town around "the beginning of World War I" (111), and Cholly's family is from Georgia (133), and they move together to Lorain. While the rural South is not idealized as it sometimes is in Hurston (Georgia is the site of both intraracial and interracial violence, as the infant Cholly is left for dead by his mother and the teenage Cholly is rendered powerless by two white hunters during his first sexual experience), it becomes a source of nostalgia and regret for Pauline.

In fact, the occasion of their migration to Lorain is understood as part of the sequence in the psychic destruction of their daughter, for in Lorain Pauline begins to internalize images of white beauty she finds in movies, is ostracized by the town's other black women because of her backward dress, speech, and hairstyle, and it is partly her need to work that ushers along the family's descent (118). The novel makes clear that it is her separation from rural community, and Cholly's flight from his family following his Aunt's death, that move them toward the conviction of their own "ugliness," a conviction they pass on with devastating consequences to their daughter (39). As Trudier Harris has compellingly demonstrated, it is the unraveling of African American "folk culture"—beliefs, remedies, stories, speech, and customs—in their new setting that both indexes and partly causes the Breedloves' destruction (75). The rural South is understood by Morrison to be the site of an authentic black culture that is essentially healthy, inventive, resistant to white supremacy, and integral to the community.

Morrison articulates her vision of African American culture though a lens that is more anthropological than it is sociological, and part of that articulation probably came from Morrison's own reading of Hurston in the mid and late 1960s, before the Hurston revival is said to have commenced. In rejecting the presumed universalism of the dominant culture (in the person of Geraldine especially) for instance, Morrison adopts with some ambiguity a pose of cultural relativism, indeed, to the extent that she has even been criticized for it.[12] To see the South as the site and origin of lived African American culture, and to see that culture under wrenching transformation during a migration to the cities, is to likewise partake of the aspect of historical particularism central to Boas's model and Hurston's work. Like Hurston and Boas, Morrison sees the verbal life of a culture as just one component of a dynamic whole. But Morrison departs from Hurston's work—and Boas's model of culture—when she reattaches culture to race. It is not that Geraldine cannot be culturally white, it is just that it is unnatural for her. Hurston's criticism of the Haitian bourgeoisie's rejection of voodoo in Horse is different from Morrison's criticism of Geraldine's funklessness because, while the intersections of race and class are at stake in both moments, the Haitian bourgeoisie is not following a programmatic, social science–theorized extension of white cultural traditions to racialized minorities. Hurston's example is more precisely a postcolonial social class conflict than a question of assimilation, while Morrison is entirely concerned with the assimilationist politics imagined by the Civil Rights movement.

There are also hints in the novel that Morrison was specifically aware of, and writing back to, Hurston's work, beyond these two general aspects.[13] What I am suggesting here is that we need to push back the conventional date of the Hurston revival, said by both her biographer and her series editor to have begun in earnest with Alice Walker's 1975 *Ms.* magazine article "In Search of Zora Neale Hurston." Henry Louis Gates Jr. suggests that Hurston was "virtually ignored after the early fifties, even by the Black Arts movement in the sixties, an otherwise noisy and intense spell of black image- and myth-making that rescued so many black writers from remaindered oblivion" (Afterword 196). In particular, Gates says, Walker, Gayl Jones, Gloria Naylor, and Toni Cade Bambara all turned to Hurston's work for its "black vernacular speech and rituals," to "establish a maternal literary ancestry" (196). Valerie Boyd likewise suggests that Walker's "act of reclamation spurred a renewed interest in Hurston and her work" (437). But there are good reasons to push back the date of critical influence on a generation of African American writers by five to ten years. As we shall see in chapter eight, for example, Ishmael Reed's 1972 *Mumbo Jumbo* is infused with Hurston's work.

According to Walker, she discovered *Mules and Men* when doing research in 1970 for a story involving "voodoo practices among rural southern blacks of the thirties" (Foreword xi). In an astonishing account that comments on anthropology's primal scene, and also on McNickle's research for *The Surrounded* and N. Scott Momaday's research for his work, Walker continues:

> Here was this perfect book! The "perfection" of it I immediately tested on my relatives, who are such typical black Americans they are useful for every sort of political, cultural, or economic survey. Very regular people from the South, rapidly forgetting their southern cultural inheritance in the suburbs and ghettos of Boston and New York, they sat around reading the book themselves, listening to me read the book, listening to each other read the book, and a kind of paradise was regained. For Zora's book gave them back all the stories they had forgotten or of which they had grown ashamed (told to us years ago by our parents and grandparents—not one of whom could *not* tell a story to make us weep, or laugh) and showed how marvelous and, indeed, priceless, they are. *This is not exaggerated.* (xii)

Here at last Hurston's ironic commentary on salvage ethnography that opens *Mules*—

> "[The stories] are a lot more valuable than you might think. We want to set them down before it's too late."
> "Too late for what?"
> "Before everybody forgets all of 'em." (8)

—comes full circle, with *Mules and Men* becoming an antidote to cultural forgetting for Alice Walker's family four decades after the tales were collected.

These two important early multiculturalist African American writers, Ish-mael Reed and Alice Walker, doing their research around the time that *The Bluest Eye* was published (1970), simultaneously discovered Zora Neale Hurston as they researched voodoo. Importantly, Hurston's rehabilitation started when these two cultural nationalist writers began researching black culture: Hurston the anthropologist was discovered before Hurston the nov-elist. Hurston's anthropological work would be a clearer line of transmission for Boas's culture concept than even her anthropology-laced novels would.

So even though Wright was hailed in 1968 as "the most important black American writer of all time" (Walling 127), I am arguing here that it was in fact Zora Neale Hurston who was more important to a generation of cultural nationalist writers and intellectuals associated with the Black Arts movement beginning in the second half of the 1960s, the generation that properly began the third phase of multicultural American literature. Black Arts movement writers and intellectuals derived from Wright not his sense of African American culture—which Wright did not really care about—but rather his militancy, his warning of violence, and his devastating critique of white racism and liberal hypocrisy. The particular cultural nationalism of the Black Arts movement could emerge only from a genealogy that had a culture concept entailing longevity, coherence, integrity, historical endurance, and the health of its various parts. For these qualities Toni Morrison, Ish-mael Reed, Alice Walker and others of the post–Civil Rights nascent cultural nationalist generation turned to, as Reed called her, "our theoretician Zora Neale Hurston," the anthropologist-writer authority on African American culture ("Neo-HooDoo" 21).

As with Hurston's critical evaluation of Boasian anthropology—in which she resisted the implication of assimilation and cultural disappearance—so too did this multiculturalist generation critically take up Hurston's model of African American culture. And one of their innovations, as I have argued in this chapter and will further consider in chapter eight, is their undoing of the fundamental Boasian conceptual distinction between culture and race. While *Jonah's Gourd Vine* ultimately resolves the ambiguity as to whether African American difference is culturally or racially derived by the assertion of cul-ture, those two contrasting possibilities—they were fundamentally different for Hurston and Boas—are strategically joined by Black Arts critic Larry Neal in his introduction to the 1971 edition of *Jonah's*. As he summarizes the novel's importance,

> What makes all this so significant is that Miss Hurston is essentially exposing us to two distinctly different *cultural* attitudes toward the

concept of spirituality. The one springs from a formerly enslaved communal society, non-Christian in background, where there is really no clean-cut dichotomy between the world of spirit and the world of flesh. The other attitude is clearly more rigid, being a blend of Puritan concepts and the fire-and-brimstone imagery of the white evangelical tradition. Zora's preacher and his people were forced to accept Christianity, but it was impossible to accept it without bringing to bear upon it their own ethos and social modality. In accepting it, or at least in submitting to its main external tenets, they were yet able to shape out of it unique forms of expression that reflected the most retrievable, and hence the most important, aspects of pre-Christian cultural memory. (6–7)

Neal's introduction shows how the cultural nationalist turn signified a return to the lessons and language of anthropology. Neal is (ostensibly) talking about cultural difference and the processes of adaptation and diffusion. More directly still, he is citing the African retention thesis that Herskovits and Hurston helped to establish (as I show in chapter eight), but which was eclipsed between the time of their work and Neal's by the ascendance of sociology's thesis of the cultural erasure that took place during the Middle Passage. Like Ishmael Reed and N. Scott Momaday during this same time, Neal finds in Hurston the lesson that religious traditions were passed on, sometimes hidden beneath Christian ones, but nonetheless vibrant and present in contemporary communities. But also like Reed and Momaday, and unlike Hurston and Boas, Neal reconnects the cultural traits to race, not just in the historical particularist terms of Boas's cultural anthropology—which could explain without racial logic why African diasporic peoples retained African cultural traits—but in racially essentialist terms.

The logic of that move is displayed in this passage in a couple of key moments. First, while Neal says that Hurston's "preacher" was forced to accept Christianity, he is of course actually talking about John's ancestors. We could more correctly say that all Southern Christian folk are forced to accept Christianity, just as they are forced to accept other learned attributes like language or race signification taught to them as children. Christianity and English and what Richard Wright called "racial etiquette" in the South are learned attributes, and as elements of culture they can be changed by adopting other cultural traits and values. But that is evidently not what Neal is talking about. He conflates a character in a contemporary book (who is, like many African American and white Southerners in this period, brought up as a Christian but who then must make a personal commitment to the faith) with the fact that many captured African slaves were forced to adopt Christian worship. It is this generational conflation that counts: having one's ancestors forced to accept a religion that is not theirs is the same, for Neal, as being forced to accept a religion that is not one's own. But if John's religion is not the one he grows up with—the one he actually practices—then what counts as his religion? Neal's answer is that of his racial ancestors.

Second, Neal's all-important formulation of "pre-Christian cultural memory" describes culture as a kind of memory instead of a kind of non-pedagogical learning that is passed on between generations. This also racializes—or biologizes—what Boas and Hurston understood to be a cultural dynamic. Memory is a metaphor, of course, but what the metaphor does is to make a past experience that did not happen to you an experience that did happen to you; and since who we are must partly be a function of the memory of our experiences, it makes someone else's cultural idea or practice part of our own identity. Describing culture as a kind of memory allows one to skip the question of transmission in favor of imagined experience. Neal here productively misreads *Jonah's* by treating one's ancestors' paganism as part of one's own identity. One's identity is not based so much on what one actually believes or does (a culture), and we are to understand that this memory should be one's racially; there is a racial logic as to who should have this "cultural memory" and who should not. As we shall see in chapter seven, this is the exact logic at work in Momaday's multiculturalist texts between 1968 and 1976.

Neal's reading of Hurston reintroduces a natural rather than a historical connection between race and culture, thereby collapsing Boas's conceptual distinction. That rhetorical move is one that Hurston herself rarely makes because there is a certain disciplinary complexity in her notion of culture, which entails learned as opposed to inherited behavior. In the frame of *Mules,* for instance, in which Hurston returns to Eatonville in order to record tales before everybody "forgets" them, she is ironically taking up salvage ethnography's mission by questioning how people will forget and remember stories. Even Walker's family might be in the process of forgetting precisely because of their own Great Migration to Boston and New York, away from their Southern roots. Walker's is not a racializing metaphor of memory, since in her actual family, stories that were once told by actual grandparents and parents to children are now, because of a new geographical location and environment, not recirculating. But what Neal is suggesting by "cultural memory"—especially through reference to an African paganism underneath black Christianity that cannot really be seen but which has been extended for five to twenty generations—is a kind of identity. As we shall see, it is not coincidental that to imagine culture as a kind of memory as opposed to what a group learns to do or believe is to begin to construct a notion of identity that is necessarily racial and actively hostile to the anthropological project of description.

The point to be made here is that Neal—and, we shall see, Momaday, Reed, and Anzaldúa—share anthropology's interest in tracing particular practices and values through history and noting instances of longevity and adaptation; such is a fundamental gesture they would bequeath to literary multiculturalism. The problem is that they lack Boas and Hurston's rigor not only in their culture concept, but in the ethnographic practice of collection: of paying attention to what is happening on the ground. These moments of unearned longevity and unsubstantiated transmission, of preferring group prescription to lived description, they would also bequeath to literary multiculturalism.

Asian American Cultural and Literary Nationalism after 1965: Frank Chin and the *Aiiieeeee!* Group

> The gang council decides we're too controversial. They call me to a meeting. The leader of the China-town Red Guards taps me on the shoulder and says, "I want to talk to you." I turn around and just like in the movies, his fist is coming toward me. He knocks me down, my glasses go flying, he punches me in the stomach. . . .
> He says, "Identify with China!" I say, "Wait a minute. We're in America. This is where we are, where we live and where we're going to die. There's not going to be any revolution. That's crazy." He can't hit me anymore. He's already done that and it's not working. [. . .] He curls his lip and says, "You cultural nationalist!" I go, "*What?* What's a cultural nationalist?"
>
> —Frank Chin, 1992 (qtd. in Terkel 311)

Frank Chin's purported ignorance of the term "cultural nationalist" in the early 1970s notwithstanding, the Red Guardsman was correct in his diagnosis of Chin's politics. Of course, the Red Guardsman himself was a nationalist, as is suggested by his demand that Chin "identify with China" rather than, say, the international working class. The Red Guardsman seems to have shared America's Cold War strategy of supplementing the purported ideological conflict between communism and capitalism with a good dose of patriotism. The Asian American cultural nationalism that Chin helped articulate shared with African American cultural nationalism the dual strategy of rejecting the assimilative and integrationist Civil Rights era ethos, along with the sociology that helped form it, and of embracing a model of culture that was in many ways reminiscent of Boasian anthropology's culture. Indeed, it was reminiscent partly because the Asian American cultural and literary nationalisms could be—indirectly—traced back to practicing anthropologists. In the hugely influential anthologies of Asian American literature, the 1974 *Aiiieeeee!* and its 1991 successor *The Big Aiiieeeee!,* the editors singled out sociology and repudiated it, along with Christianity and the autobiography genre, as destructive and assimilationist forces in the Asian American literary tradition. While Asian America did not produce as nationalistic a program as its contemporaneous analogues in the Black Power movement, the American Indian movement, or the Chicano *El Movimiento,* its anti-assimilationist cultural pluralism, like those in the other three movements, took form through the explicit repudiation of the University of Chicago tradition of sociology.

Chin's early 1970s plays *The Chickencoop Chinaman* and *The Year of the Dragon* are two such literary articulations of an Asian American cultural nationalism. A post-realist and post-protest work like Morrison's *Bluest Eye, The Chickencoop Chinaman* is a surreal satire directed at opposite Asian American trajectories: model minority assimilative citizenship and the excessive longevity stereotype treating Chinese American or Japanese American cultures as equivalent to Chinese and Japanese cultures. These opposites are strangely united in the character of Tom, who is played by the actor also playing Tonto. Tom is "a very neat, tidy, uptight hip Chinese American" (52) who is writing a book called *Soul on Rice,* "a book about Chinese-American identity" (55). But Tom is less Eldridge Cleaver than Uncle Tom, since he has assimilated and is proud of the model minority status enjoyed by Asian Americans. As he tells the other characters, "Americans are proud to say we send more of our kids to college than any other race. We're accepted. We worked hard for it. I've made my peace" (59), though he knows that his antagonist, Tam, "is going to call me white" for such sentiments (60). Tam's anger at assimilation is the dramatic center of the play, as he resents having grown up "bustin our asses to be white" and "being 'Americanized'" (26).

The specter of "marrying white" is a preoccupation for both *Chickencoop* and *Dragon,* in which an Asian American female propensity to marry white men comes under special attack for both its sexual-cultural politics, and its effect of cultural assimilation through racial amalgamation. In *Chickencoop,* Tam has previously married white, and the white Lee—though accused of only passing for white since she has a supposed "bucket of Chinese blood in her" (59)—has conversely previously married Asian American. As Fred, the hero of *The Year of the Dragon,* explains to his white brother-in-law, "it's the rule not the exception for us to marry out white. Out in Boston, I might even marry me a blonde" (85). Fred's sister has married white and moved to Boston so she can "just be people" and "forget we're Chinamen" (110). For Chin, marrying white is a sign of "yellow" racial self-loathing in white supremacist America. Given the historical association between the sociologically modeled cultural assimilation of racialized minorities and the idea that this project is hastened by miscegenation, this preoccupation in Chin's literary work and literary criticism must also be understood in terms of a rejection of the cultural politics of assimilation.[14] As Dorothy McDonald makes clear in her introduction, the plays imagine "assimilation" as a form of "extinction" (xiii), a metaphor that clearly underscores the conflation of culture to race.

Like Chin's plays, *Aiiieeeee!* rejected assimilation and amalgamation. As the alarmed editors noted in the original preface, by 1972 "more than 50 percent of Japanese American women were marrying outside their race" (xii–xiii), and in their 1991 preface to the Mentor edition of *Aiiieeeee!* the picture appeared (to them) even bleaker, as "Upwards of seventy-five percent of all Japanese Americans marrying today are marrying out" (xl). While the original edition did not explicitly name sociology—in fact it suggests that the works of Pardee Lowe and Jade Snow Wong were received as "anthropological" (4)—the preface to the 1991 edition put the pieces together in linking sociology to assimilationist texts, the erasure of Asian American history and culture, and racial amalgamation (xxviii, xxxv). The editors quote critically the sociologist Daniel Okimoto—who had married white, calling it the "key to final assimilation" (qtd. in E. Kim 82)—and his inability to imagine a future Japanese American literary tradition, an absence they link to Okimoto's "contempt" for "yellow history" (xxv–xxvi). As with Paredes's anti-hero George Washington Gómez, cultural disappearance is intrinsically linked to sociology and to "marrying out" of one's race, though for the *Aiiieeeee!* group and in Chin's own plays the obsession becomes fevered.

Just as Morrison's cultural nationalism was articulated through the rejection of the crucial integrationist social science work of the Clarks' dolls study, so too do the *Aiiieeeee!* editors tackle what had become a fundamental social science trope for Asian American marginality, that of the "dual personality" said to especially afflict second-generation Americans of Asian descent. As they wrote in the preface to the 1974 edition,

We have been encouraged to believe that we have no cultural integrity as Chinese or Japanese Americans, that we are either Asian (Chinese or Japanese) or American (white), or are measurably both. This myth of being either/or and the equally goofy concept of the dual personality haunted our lobes while our rejection by both Asia and white America proved we were neither one nor the other. Nor were we half and half or more one than the other. Neither Asian culture nor American culture was equipped to define us except in the most superficial terms. (xii)

The editors' attack on the idea of the dual personality emerged in response to an earlier 1971 debate in the pages of *Amerasia Journal* between Stanley and Derald Sue on the one hand and Benjamin Tong on the other. Using Park's notions of the "marginal man" and the generation gap and his method of typology, the Sues' work investigated the Parkian question of the range and results of the intergenerational cultural assimilation of racialized minorities and the social barriers that slowed but could not stop it. The Sues developed three personality types: the traditionalist who stays close to parental values (they used Jade Snow Wong's autobiography as an example of parents' use of shame [36]); the "Marginal Man" who rebels against his parents and adopts Western values; and the "Asian-American" who rebels against his parents but tries "to formulate a new identity" (42) in a move that includes pan-Asian American alliances and a critique of institutional racism.

Tong's cultural nationalist response took the Sues to task for their finding of a "pseudoneurotic schizophrenia" among Chinese American men (Sues 46), and for imagining the solution to psychological problems of Chinese Americans as lying in the victim, not the racist American institutions (Tong 2). He argues that "the sickness of Chinese America, however, is *not* to be treated by psychotherapy. Something else is required. Something of a radical political nature that has yet to be seriously considered" (24). Anticipating the *Aiiieeeee!* group's historicism, Tong offers a historically particular explanation for the learned "meek-and-mild" behavior that has developed as a survival mechanism among Chinese American communities and since become the object of stereotype. "The truth of the matter," Tong says, "is that the majority of Chinese-Americans descended from the peasant stratum of Kwangtung (a province in southeastern China), a class which certainly was *not* the repository of thousands of years of sophisticated civilization" (4). Tong attributes the purported personality trait of Chinese American deference to a historical cultural retention of a struggle within Confucianism itself, in which the proper Confucian ethic of "harmony" is hijacked by the ruling class and perverted into total obedience. Confucian deference, argues Tong, emerged at the same moment as the "southern Yueh aborigines, the ancestors of Chinese America, were colonized and converted by [northern]

T'ang Chinese" (6), and this historical tradition of deference-as-obedience found new uses during the dynamic California racisms and white supremacy of the nineteenth and early twentieth centuries. Quoting Fanon, Tong argues that Chinese America has "a rich cultural sensibility—complete with folk-lore, language, art and social institutions—that has yet to be discovered and affirmed" (4), and that the politics of mental health care delivery cannot be premised on helping the victim to adjust to American racisms.

The *Aiiieeeee!* editors' rejection (shared with Tong) of the three options of wholly Asian, merely American, or schizophrenic dual personality goes some way to explaining their attraction to John Okada's *No-No Boy,* the assimilationist tendencies of which they otherwise ignore. The stereotype of the sojourner is one of several important racial meanings of the Asian that the editors of *Aiiieeeee!* engage with in the introduction to their anthology, and in this aspect, at least, their enthusiasm for *No-No Boy* makes sense, given its strategy of strongly summoning the stereotype and then refuting it. But the editors ignore its critique of ethnic enclaves in the United States, its hope to subsume disappearing ethnicities within a larger American patriotism, its politics of cultural assimilation, and its moral equivalency between America's "mistake" in interning almost 120,000 Japanese Americans and Ichiro's "mistake" in equivocating about serving in the war. They looked on *No-No Boy* in the same way that Black Arts movement critics regarded Wright's *Native Son:* in highly selective readings of both novels that ignored their authors' assimilationist cultural politics, the novels became inspirational to the two later movements. As critics have noticed in the last few decades, *Native Son* and *No-No Boy* have their heroes work through their existential woes through the use of caricatured female characters whose own existential anguish remains backgrounded. We should not underestimate the role this gender dynamic played when these 1970s African American and Asian American male critics looked back at these two paradigmatic masculinist novels, especially considering that in this decade, many of these same critics were critical of African American and Asian American women writers who, wrongly they thought, were depicting gendered divisions within the communities to readers outside the communities (see Dubey, *Black Women,* and Cheung).

The cultural pluralisms of the 1970s were indebted to anthropological notions of culture rather than sociological ones, but the distinctions between groups that led them to draw on different variations of sociology now meant they drew on different variations of Boasian culture. African American cultural nationalists drew on anthropological survivals to establish African cultural connections earlier denied by sociologists. Thus the question of African survivals was at stake in both the integrationist second phase (in which they were denied) and the nationalist third phase (in which they were explored, as we shall see with Ishmael Reed). For Asian American literary nationalists, the issue was the opposite: there was too much perceived connection between Asian Americans and ancestral cultures. This "strange continuity" was, in fact, one of the stereotypes to be refuted: "Thus, fourth-, fifth-, and sixth-generation Asian Americans are still looked upon as foreigners because of this dual heritage, or the concept of dual personality [...]" (*Aiiieeeee!* 7). As David Palumbo-Liu puts the problem, "This rupture [in cultural traditions between Asia and Asian America] takes place even as blacks, with whom many Asian American activists identified, sought to regain a sense of roots in Africa: it was precisely because Asia had historically been established as an abject realm within an orientalist discourse that Asian Americans were dubious about finding 'strength' in searching back" (*Asian* 304). Instead of the cultural blank slate rendered by the Middle Passage that animated second-phase African American sociology, sociologically inspired second-phase Asian American writers chose the generation gap and the marginal man, precisely to sever ancestral (and racial) connections. Conversely, when the Asian American literary nationalists of the 1970s turned to Boasian culture, they were not interested in the concept of survivals that so enthralled Reed and Gloria Anzaldúa. Rather, it was the idea of historical particularity that mattered: that Chinese American culture was not Chinese or white American, but had a specific legal, social, and economic history that made it identifiable. Chinese and Japanese Americans "have evolved cultures and sensibilities distinctly not Chinese or Japanese and distinctly not white American" (xi), declared the editors of *Aiiieeeee!* in their opening paragraph, and such was square one for their cultural nationalism. The idea that cultures are historically specific was an insight that helped disengage Asian America from the too-present and too-recent Asian cultures.

Like Paredes arguing for a border distinctiveness based in history against a false hispanophilia imagining border culture as (degraded) survivals and against an equally false notion that equated border culture with Mexican culture, the *Aiiieeeee!* group argued for Boasian historical particularism. Such is behind Chin's constant insistence on "yellow history." The fundamental gesture of the *Aiiieeeee!* critics was thus to insist on the centrality of a historical particularist account of Asian American cultures: in other words, the project of knowing the facts of yellow history was inextricably connected to a fourth option of seeing Asian American cultures as distinct from Asia, America, and dual personality. "Yellow history is still the great yellow mystery," the editors put it (xxiv–xxv). Thus the task of the African American cultural nationalist was slightly different from the Asian American cultural nationalist. We might say that the different perceived problems the cultural nationalists faced was that African Americans had too little African culture and that Asian Americans had too much Asian culture. Therefore, the Asian American nationalist impulse was a historical particularism that downplayed survivals and links with Asian cultures and emphasized instead the American-grown transformations, adaptations, and syntheses, whereas the African American nationalist impulse was a historical particularism that sought to establish possible cultural survivals across the Middle Passage and through the generations.

The Asian Americanist cultural pluralists of the 1970s were making a Boasian point about culture, but did not articulate it directly as Boasian or anthropological because there was almost no tradition or historical connection between anthropology and Asian American communities, as there had been for the African American community (with Hurston and others), the Chicano community (with Américo Paredes), and Native American communities (with the whole project of anthropology in some sense being initially formed around studying the Indian). Rather, the most important social science tradition for the Asian American community has been sociology and its cousin psychology, which is why the Asian American integrationist tradition has taken form through a sociological frame and its cultural nationalist tradition has taken form through a repudiation of sociology.

Nonetheless, I hypothesize that anthropologically derived concepts of culture entered Asian American cultural nationalism through the influence of other minority traditions. The *Aiiieeeee!* group was part of a lively pan-ethnic California sensibility that emerged partly around the work of Ishmael Reed in the late 1960s and early 1970s. The *Aiiieeeee!* editors thank Reed in the original preface (xxii), and, in fact, the four editors "met for the first time in San Francisco, at a party for Ishmael Reed's new book, an anthology of writing by Americans of many American races, colors, and cultures" (Chin, "Rashomon Road" 290). The lines of influence on these four editors thus might have been from Reed (influenced, as we shall see, by Hurston), from Momaday (influenced, as we shall see, by James Mooney and other anthropologists), whom they cite in the original introductory essay (25), and from contemporary Chicano writers (influenced by Paredes). That Asian American historically particular cultures were to be articulated through the anthropological model rather than the sociological one is suggested by the wider frame of loss and extinction, thus alluding to the primal anthropological scene of salvage ethnography:

A century's campaign of Christian conversion and years of American concentration camps and their yellow converts have successfully erased Asian American history. The loss of history means a loss of identity. With the loss of identity comes extinction. The loss of Chinese American and Japanese American literary integrity reflects the loss of a sense of yellow historical and cultural integrity. Extinction is all around us. (xl)

As we shall see, this invocation of identity—instead of, or as a supplement to, what they have been arguing is a culture—increasingly characterized 1970s and 1980s multiculturalism.

While the application of historical particularism to Asian American cultures was not always coherent, my point is that Asian American cultural nationalism did not only share a "tonal alliance with the black aesthetic movement" (Li 19) and explicitly craft its own nationalist literary and critical aesthetic through references to African American cultural nationalism, but that these parallels signal a deeper homological consensus whose shorthand was the turn from sociological culture to anthropological culture. The best example is the turn to Asian American vernaculars, in parallel with similar turns in the African American and Chicano traditions. Thus a few mid-century canonical Japanese American texts were praised by the *Aiiieeeee!* critics for their treatments of history and language, a fact that should not be taken as a sign of cultural pluralism in the texts. Toshio Mori's 1949 *Yokohama, California* and John Okada's 1957 *No-No Boy* paid attention to the facts of "yellow history" and to colloquial language, in a way that recalled Hurston's insistence on the cultural and literary legitimacy of the vernacular. William Saroyan had famously introduced Mori's *Yokohama, California* with the opening sentence, "Of the thousands of unpublished writers in America there are probably no more than three who cannot write better English than Toshio Mori" (1). For the *Aiiieeeee!* group, this implicit demand that minority authors write white needed to be combated by dethroning standard English as the American language. In Chin's plays, writes Dorothy Ritsuko McDonald in her introduction, "language abounds with slang, obscenities, and unusual grammar. The Cantonese terms may also make for difficult reading" (xviii). Invoking a pluralist account of language—that it is not to be merely measured against white proper English, but is to be recorded as it is spoken by a community, a descriptive project of which Hurston and Boas would have approved—the *Aiiieeeee!* editors write:

> The assumption that an ethnic minority writer thinks in, believes he writes in, or has ambitions toward writing beautiful, correct, and well-punctuated English sentences is an expression of white supremacy. The

universality of the belief that correct English is the only language of American truth has made language an instrument of cultural imperialism. The minority experience does not yield itself to accurate or complete expression in the white man's language. (23)

What begins as a cultural pluralist and relativist account of language in the beginning of this quotation assumes by the end the linguistic relativism of the Sapir-Whorf hypothesis: that only Asian American vernaculars are commensurate to lived Asian American lives and communities. Language accordingly becomes central in the emerging nationalist account of Asian American culture: "The deprivation of language in a verbal society like this country's has contributed to the lack of a recognized Asian American cultural integrity," the editors warn (24).

Because he is deprived of a language of his own, Tam Lum's "'normal' speech jumps between black and white rhythms and accents," according to the stage description of the character in *Chickencoop* (6). As Tam says in an opening soliloquy, "I am the natural born ragmouth speaking the motherless bloody tongue. No real language of my own to make sense with, so out comes everybody else's trash that don't conceive" (7). As Fred says to his father's Chinese wife, "Just because we're born here don't mean we're nobody and gotta go away to another language to talk. I think Chinatown Buck Buck Bagaw is beautiful" (*Year* 115–16). Like the Red Guardsman who demanded Chin "identify with China," China Mama's demand that Fred be Chinese instead of Chinese American with a particular language of its own—here and in *Chickencoop* called Buck Buck Bagaw—must be rejected, just as is the mode of assimilating and privileging standard English. Similarly, the *Aiiieeeee!* editors found in Mori and Okada two Asian American writers who "demonstrate, as did Claude McKay, Mark Twain, and N. Scott Momaday, that new experience breeds new language" (25). Okada in particular, the editors argue, "writes from an oral tradition he hears all the time, and talks his writing onto the page" (25).

As the invocation of N. Scott Momaday suggests, the *Aiiieeeee!* group explicitly understood the aesthetic turn to the vernacular and to oral traditions as part of a larger post-assimilationist multiculturalism that they shared with writers and intellectuals from the African American, Native American, and Chicano traditions. In the original preface the editors thank Ishmael Reed and Leslie Silko (xxii), and approvingly cite Malcolm X (xix). In a 1980 interview, Rudolfo Anaya acknowledged this kind of interethnic interest, citing "a great new generation of Asian American writers coming up in the Northwest, and California [. . . such as] Frank Chin, Lawson Inada,

Shon [*sic*] Wong, to name a few, all of whom are interested in what we're doing as Chicanos" (193). Published by Howard University Press, *Aiiieeeee!* not only acknowledged Native and African American writers, but praised them, with Chicano writers, for the turn to vernacular and non-standard English (32). As we shall see in chapter eight, Ishmael Reed's museum-raiding cultural nationalists—those who, in a critique of salvage anthropology, want to treat artifacts as part of lived cultures rather than dead ones—are made up of African Americans, Asian Americans, Mexican Americans, and Native Americans. These moments of cross-tradition intellectual awareness and influence in the early 1970s make clear that the cultural nationalist turn was a paradigm shift not metaphorically but descriptively: many minority writers and intellectuals understood themselves to be allied with some writers and intellectuals in other traditions. They understood their alliance in opposition to the assimilationist politics that underwrote the Civil Rights era and its literature. It is thus not accidental that Chin's Tonto/(uncle) Tom became the object of Chin's critique shortly after Ralph Ellison himself was named an "Uncle Tom" by black nationalist students in 1969.

As this chapter has made clear, the cultural and literary nationalism that was emerging in the decade 1965–1975 understood itself, as in *The Bluest Eye's* critique of the Clarks' work and the *Aiiieeeee!* editors' critique of the Sues' work, to be premised on the rejection of a model of culture that understood conflict to be caused by social barriers preventing cultural assimilation. This model was neither relativist nor pluralist, and it imagined minority cultures as entities that properly disappeared in the course of integration into urban modernity. The nascent multiculturalist reaction to this model entailed the construction of an alternative, one that shared key qualities with an earlier anthropological model of culture. Minority culture for these cultural and literary nationalists was understood under the auspices of relativism and pluralism, but also, as we have seen particularly with Morrison, Chin, and the critics in both *The Black Aesthetic* and *Aiiieeeee!*, in terms of historical particularism and with an emphasis on recording ethnic vernaculars in lieu of the false universalism of standard English. This was, in short, a Boasian model of culture. My argument is not that Morrison, Chin, and the critics of *The Black Aesthetic* and *Aiiieeeee!* were reading Boas or cultural anthropology. Rather, it is likely that Morrison and other black aestheticians were intensely reading Hurston, and that the "yellow" aestheticians of *Aiiieeeee!* were reading Chicano, African American, and Native American authors who, we know, had studied their Américo Paredes, their Zora Neale Hurston, and their James Mooney and D'Arcy McNickle. It is the argument of *A Genealogy of Literary Multiculturalism* that this return with a difference to anthropology also entailed an undoing of the Boasian conceptual distinction between culture and race. As I show in the next chapter, that undoing came with the development of a new tactic for reattaching culture to race and for separating who a group was from what it descriptively did: the new technology, which has since become central to our paradigm of literary multiculturalism, of identity.

CHAPTER 7

N. Scott Momaday: Blood and Identity

> Jealous of the wealth, power, and influence of the Jewish families who had converted, many of whom were using their new Christian identity to advance themselves in the civil or church hierarchies, some of the Christian leaders began to question the theological probity of some *conversos* [...] An Inquisition directed at heretics was established in 1478, sanctioned by the Catholic kings and the church. It was designed to weed out recalcitrant converts, or "secret" Jews, by investigating personal behavior and genealogies for evidence of Jewishness. Some of the seminal ideas that later became basic ingredients of a racial worldview were set into motion during this period of rising Christian intolerance and rampant persecution of Jews and Moors.
>
> —Audrey Smedley, *Race in North America,* 1999 (66)

> On the very day in 1492 that Christopher Columbus set sail from Palos for what turned out to be the New World, he noted in his log the shiploads of Jews and *conversos* leaving their Old World home of a millennium under threat of death.
>
> —Marc Shell, *Children of the Earth,* 1993 (26)

In N. Scott Momaday's *House Made of Dawn,* the Jemez Pueblo protagonist Abel returns to his grandfather's home in Walatowa, New Mexico, from fighting in the European theater in the Second World War. It is July 1945. The war in Europe is over and the war in the Pacific approaching its end. Ichiro is still in prison for saying No twice, and unreleased as yet are Ichiro's parents, and Monica Sone's parents from their concentration camp in Minidoka, Idaho. Jade Snow Wong is still working in the shipping industry, shortly to begin her pottery business in San Francisco's Chinatown. Ralph Ellison is recuperating from his service in the merchant marine, working on his story about a Tuskegee pilot and supposed spokesman for the other allied prisoners of war, some of whose racism is exploited by their German camp commander. He will shortly hear a "voice" speaking "so knowingly of invisibility" (*Invisible* xi). Richard Wright has just published

Black Boy, and it has been adopted as a Book of the Month Club choice—with the proviso that he drop the second portion of his autobiography, called *American Hunger,* which focused too much on Northern racism and segregation.

Eight days later, Abel has killed the monstrous white man—the character of the albino—who had earlier bested him in the town's fertility ritual. He goes to prison for five or six years and emerges into a different world in 1951 urban Los Angeles. The historical program of Relocation that sent thousands of Native American youths (like the fictional Abel) to urban centers directly echoed—and was in fact modeled on, as we shall see—the program giving early release to thousands of Japanese American youths from wartime concentration camps to Midwestern and Eastern cities, as well as the subsequent policy of Japanese American resettlement. The goal in both cases is assimilation. The world is different not just because one war is over and another begun, and not just because Walatowa is categorically different from Los Angeles, but because what culture means is changing, and thinking about racialized minorities is likewise under transformation.

The next year, 1952, is the year that Abel leaves Los Angeles to return to his dying grandfather in Walatowa, but also the year that Ralph Ellison publishes his *Invisible Man,* a novel which would, like *Fifth Chinese Daughter,* lay claim to America by denying racial difference and embracing Americanization. When Abel returns not just to Walatowa but to Jemez culture—his last act in the novel, perhaps ever, is to engage in the running, joining his ancestors at least figuratively if not literally—he is rejecting the very dominant American culture to which Ellison laid claim that same year. Under the policies of Relocation and Termination, the United States has sought to solve its Native "problem" by integrating Abel into an urban setting. While not exactly integrated, writing as he is from his hole in the ground, the invisible man pleads for integration through imagining an appeal to the founding principles of the nation, principles used by the NAACP in a series of cases ending in desegregation. Thus, in the middle of the Korean War, as McCarthyism reaches its patriotic climax, a Chinese American and an African American writer forcefully articulated a plea for integration and, perhaps, the cultural assimilation that would underwrite it, and at the same time, a Native American character turned his back on the promise of integration and assimilation, choosing instead a de facto segregated community and separate culture. What accounts for these two different trajectories?

Part of the answer is that, while the novel is set during and after World War II, its sensibility is the late 1960s turn to ethnic nationalism that was its context for composition. As with Morrison's *Bluest Eye,* published two years after *House Made of Dawn,* Momaday's nationalist novel is set during an earlier period—a period indeed in which both protagonists experienced personal destruction in partially integrated settings. Morrison's partially integrated Lorain, Ohio, of 1941 and Momaday's partially integrated and urbanized experience of Los Angeles of 1951 serve as fictional studies of what the cultural assimilation of racialized minorities looks like. In both cases, the conclusions the authors come to in the wake of the Civil Rights movement is that cultural distinctiveness is worth preserving. And while Momaday and Morrison embrace a cultural relativism inimical to the assimilationist ethic they critique, they ultimately ground the endurance and value of minority U.S. cultures in terms of racial appropriateness, not (only) by way of rejecting the dominant practices and values and their claims to universality.

Born in 1934, Momaday grew to intellectual maturity in the Civil Rights decade (1955–1965). Two scenes suggest how Momaday can be productively understood within that larger frame of racial politics. Briefly interrupting his University of New Mexico undergraduate study in political science and English, he enrolled in the University of Virginia Law School in 1956–1957. There he joined the Jefferson Debating Society, and met William Faulkner, who was a visiting reader (Schubnell 21). Faulkner by this time was enmeshed in desegregation debates initiated by the Supreme Court's order the year before to desegregate schools "with all deliberate speed." While condemning segregation in 1955 and 1956, Faulkner also opposed federal involvement, and was even quoted (while apparently inebriated) in early 1956 as saying that he would "fight for Mississippi against the United States even if it meant going out into the street and shooting Negroes" (qtd. in Singal 292). (That winter James Baldwin printed his famous response "Faulkner and Desegregation," arguing that after three hundred years of injustice, African Americans could hardly be asked to go slowly.)

The other scene occurred when, after dropping law, Momaday completed his Stanford Ph.D. in English in 1963; according to his dissertation's front page, the second reader at the defense was none other than Irving Howe. Howe published his famous article "Black Boys and Native Sons" that very year, attacking Baldwin and Ellison and praising Wright's protest tradition, which shortly elicited Ellison's famous response "The World and the Jug." These events indicate that N. Scott Momaday not only came to intellectual maturity during the Civil Rights period, but that, largely integrated and assimilated himself, he actually met some of the key players, and his own intellectual maturation should be understood as responding to the questions raised by these figures and these debates: the role of art and aesthetics, the political responsibility of the writer, the place of racialized minorities and cultures within the nation.

Like the matrix of literary and critical texts of cultural nationalism that I addressed in the last chapter, Momaday's novel, which slightly preceded them, is representative of the new paradigm of literary multiculturalism based on the embracing of cultural pluralism and the rejection of assimilation. It is not so much that formal segregation is to be embraced. Neither Momaday nor Morrison imagines that the white supremacist rules undergirding the separation of the "races" are a good idea. But on the other hand, living next to white people is not imagined as the solution that Clark and Park thought it might be: worse, it is actively imagined as part of the problem. Studying next to white children in a primary school in Lorain, Ohio (in Morrison's novel), or working next to white men in a box factory in Los Angeles (in Momaday's novel), is seen to be potentially damaging to the psychic health of the minority characters. Such damage is not absolute—Claudia has her own source of strength and resistance, and *House Made of Dawn*'s Ben Benally, while not without his problems, is also not crushed by the dominant society. But what is forcefully rejected in both books is the idea, as Ben puts it, that you need to "forget" (131) in order to get along in mainstream white American culture: that it is worth giving up the culture that should be yours—as Geraldine has done, and as Ben might be on his way to doing—by embracing the practices and values of the dominant culture. What is rejected in both books is precisely the cultural assimilation of racialized minorities made possible by Park's sociology, and embraced in *Brown* and Relocation.

Abel returns to Walatowa on July 20, 1945, after serving in the war. He is drunk when he gets off the bus to meet his grandfather, and in the days following he tries and fails to reincorporate himself into the town. His war experience has unsettled him, perhaps not only through the traumatic incident with the tank briefly narrated at this point and again later (21–23, 102–4). As several critics have pointed out, Abel's status in the town was already tenuous. His mother had died early, leaving him and his brother Vidal in the care of their grandfather Francisco. While his mother and Francisco were, like the other Walatowans, of the cultural group called Jemez Pueblo—or at least partly, as the novel will reveal—Abel's father was an outsider, perhaps "a Navajo, they said, or a Sia, or an Isleta, an outsider anyway, which made him and his mother and Vidal somehow foreign and strange" (11). This early frame indicates Abel's already problematic place, which is still further disturbed when he joins the army.

What is at stake is that which the novel will come to understand as not exactly Abel's culture, but rather, I will show, his identity—cultural identity, identity through birth, identity through his upbringing in Walatowa and through his knowledge of the outside world. Serving in the U.S. armed forces during the war is crucially seen by Momaday—and by other minority writers and intellectuals—as a form of integration with nationalizing effects. This is the effect for the Japanese American Kenji in *No-No Boy;* it is likewise the effect for the Mexican American Richard in José Antonio Villarreal's *Pocho.* The NAACP's efforts during the war were likewise aimed at desegregating the armed forces; the way the uniform integrates—or fails to integrate—a Native American is also central to Leslie Silko's *Ceremony.* As Paredes noted in *"With His Pistol in His Hand,"* many border Mexican Americans who served in the armed forces "began to think of themselves seriously as Americans" (106). It is thus not accidental that the already-precariously encultured Abel is further displaced by the integration of serving in World War II, moved further along the road toward possible assimilation.

On the day of his return after he awakes, "His mind turned on him again in the silence and the heat, and he could not hold still." It is only when he goes for a walk in the surrounding landscape that "for a moment everything was all right with him. He was at home" (27). But Abel's reintegration into Jemez Pueblo culture goes less well. He partakes in the festival of the Feast of Santiago, the town's hybridized Christian-Jemez fertility ritual (Scarberry-García 41). "For the first time since coming home he had done away with his uniform" (37), the novel tells us. But Abel is bested in the rooster pull after making "a poor showing" (38) and the victorious albino, "the white man," in what appears to be the conventional resolution of the rooster pull, flails Abel with the dying rooster (39). One week later, Abel slays the albino in a fashion that is described ritualistically, as a kind of sacrifice (73–74). The Jemez have a high incidence of albinism, and albinism frequently signals witchcraft in Jemez culture (Watkins 139–41; Scarberry-García 42–45). Accordingly, some critics have read Abel's murder of the albino as a non-Jemez attempt to exorcise a witch (Evers, "Words," Evers, "Killing," and R. Nelson 65–67), a failure of cultural reintegration that echoes his loss in the Feast of Santiago (Douglas, "Flawed"). At the murder trial that follows, Abel tells "his story once, simply" and then "refused to speak" (90). In an assertion of cultural relativism, the novel understands that the cultural meanings of the events are not explicable in court, and so Abel eschews (unlike Gregorio Cortez) an appeal before the potentially universalist law. The novel thus early on centrally frames its questions of cultural belonging and cultural incommensurability.

Released from prison into Los Angeles in 1951 under the auspices of Relocation, Abel is housed with a Navajo, Ben Benally, is given a job in a box factory, and his integration into American urban life is to be eased by a white social worker, Milly. Like the associated federal policy of Termination, Relocation was a coercive assimilationist Cold War policy made possible by the emerging sociologically enabled consensus about the cultural assimilability of racialized minorities. Congress's 1953 Termination Resolution "called for Indian equality under the law as well as the release of certain tribes from federal supervision" (Waldman 194). Between 1954 and 1962 Congress terminated the federal relationship with 61 tribes and bands. These two policies were reversals of the "Indian New Deal" under President Roosevelt (when D'Arcy McNickle worked for the Bureau of Indian Affairs). By the late 1940s, federal-Native relations were implicated in the Cold War for two reasons: first, in 1948 and 1949, there began to be Soviet and international scrutiny about the American handling of Indian affairs (Fixico 13), just as the South's segregation and disenfranchisement of African Americans was becoming a focus of propaganda efforts; and second, the communal holding of reservation lands, some of which had been retribalized during the Indian New Deal (Fixico xiii), was increasingly understood to echo communist practices. There were thus domestic and international reasons for the newly official policies of assimilation that emerged in the years before *Brown*.

Relocation and Termination were premised on a logical association between urbanization and assimilation, the lesson at the heart of Chicago sociology. But Park's ideas, crucial for mid-century African American and Asian American liberal consensus writers, could not quite work the same way for Native Americans because of very different histories. Theories of racial amalgamation and cultural assimilation had long animated white political thinking about Native Americans. As Ronald Takaki shows, Thomas Jefferson was an early proponent of "two views of the Indian's future in the new nation: He could be civilized and assimilated, or he could be removed and possibly exterminated," with both paths leading to a more homogenous nation (55). Jefferson believed that, while uncivilized, Indians were nonetheless the racial equals of white people, a theory he was unwilling to extend to African Americans (58). He envisioned a policy of cultural learning, whereby Indians were to "give up hunting and turn to agriculture and household manufacture" and intermarriage: as he put it, "we shall all be Americans; you will mix with us by marriage, your blood will run in our veins, and will spread with us over this great island" (qtd. in Takaki 59).

The "long and tortuous" development of federal Indian policy has been marked by "various stages and reversals" on this question of assimilation and, not always explicitly, the question of amalgamation (Waldman 190). When federal Indian policy swung away from some of the sovereigntist and culturalist principles of the 1930s Reorganization for national and international political reasons, it found an ally in the liberal sociological consensus. If the technology for Indian assimilation of the 1887 Dawes

General Allotment Act was to make individual property out of what had been communal land—as Senator Dawes put it, without greed there is no civilization—the technology for Indian assimilation of the 1952 Voluntary Relocation Program was sociology's discovery of the power of the urban space to dissolve minority cultures into the national fabric. By working with, living next to, and going to school with the children of members of the dominant culture, one would soon lose one's cultural distinctiveness. Momaday's emphasis on the placedness of culture is in logical agreement with Park's sociology. "He had lost his place," the novel tells us: "He had been long ago at the center, had known where he was, had lost his way, had wandered to the end of the earth, was even now reeling on the edge of the void" (92).[1] But that agreement is superficial compared to their deeper disagreement about culture.

Momaday rejects sociology's model of culture by rendering Abel's relocation a failure in *House Made of Dawn*. Teased by whites at work, taunted by other Native men, bored and stressed by his boxcutting job, drawn to drink, and maddened by the interference of the Relocation agents, Abel's assimilation into L.A. culture does not work. Like the social worker Mary Wirth, who helped Richard Wright and his family settle into Chicago, Milly is charged with easing the transition of relocated Native men into the economy and culture of urban Los Angeles. As Ben later tells it, "The parole officer, and welfare, and the Relocation people kept coming around, you know, and they were always after him about something. They wanted to know how he was doing, had been staying out of trouble and all. I guess that got on his nerves after a while" (139). Narrating Abel's downfall in Los Angeles and his eventual return to Walatowa, Ben says that Milly "used to bring a lot of questionnaires and read them to us, a lot of silly questions about education and health and the kind of work we were doing and all, and she would write down a lot of that stuff" (127). Abel dislikes these social work tools, and after Milly abandons them she becomes a friend to Abel and Ben. Milly the social worker and other Relocation agents instantiate the social science of assimilation as the danger to be avoided in *House Made of Dawn*. But Milly might not just be the midwife of social science assimilation, but maybe the wife too, as she becomes Abel's lover. The possibility of sociological assimilation through amalgamation—echoing the sociologists Horace Cayton, St. Clair Drake, Daniel Okimoto, the sociologically enabled writers Richard Wright and Pardee Lowe, and the fictional George Washington Gómez—that Milly represents is raised carefully, and then just as carefully closed when Abel leaves Los Angeles for Walatowa. In Momaday's understanding, Abel is sick precisely to the extent that he is separated from his culture and is losing his culture. *House Made of Dawn* is thus a study of why the cultural assimilation of Native people into the dominant white culture is bad—why cultural distinctiveness should be preserved, and more particularly, why the Jemez Pueblo culture is the one appropriate to Abel.

❧ The Tenured and the Sojourning

As a child, especially, my features belied the character of my ancient ethnic origin. (There are early photographs of me which might have been made thirty thousand years ago on the Bering Strait land bridge; just wide of the prehistoric camera's eye there stands a faithful dog of the chow strain, dragging a travois. My mother recalls that one day in Bayou le Batre, a pretty moppet was heard to say in my defense, "Well, I don't care if he *is* a Chinaman. *I* like him anyway." And as recently as my undergraduate days someone sitting next to me on the side of a swimming pool asked me from what part of Asia I had come. "Northern Mongolia," I replied.) In Hobbs, New Mexico, in 1943, I was suspected of that then dreadful association. Nearly every day on the playground someone would greet me with, "Hi'ya, Jap," and the fight was on.

—N. Scott Momaday, *The Names*, 1976 (85–86)

The residents, of course,
regard me for what I am:
a man, one of them.
. . . .

they know about me;
they've seen me before;
they've been there
more or less,
in dreams, in prophecies,
through what comes
drifting back,
washed ashore
on the benevolent banks...

—Lawson Fusao Inada, "Ainu Blues," 1991
(*Big Aiiieeeeee!* 610)

When Momaday says that Abel has lost his "place," he means this metaphor in a complicated way. Abel and his grandfather have a spiritual relation to the landscape, a cultural and political idea *House Made of Dawn* develops as "tenure in the land." In a long passage famous for expressing this idea,

Momaday describes the animals who inhabit the Southwest, some of whom, as he puts it, "have tenure in the land" in contrast to other arriviste species. "There is a kind of life that is peculiar to the land in summer," the narrator says, naming road runners, quail, russet hawks, rattlesnakes, coyotes, foxes, bobcats, mountain lions, wolves, and eagles (50–51). The narrator names a specific relation between these animals and the land they inhabit:

> These—and the innumerable meaner creatures, the lizard and the frog, the insect and the worm—have tenure in the land. The other, latecoming things—the beasts of burden and of trade, the horse and the sheep, the dog and the cat—these have an alien and inferior aspect, a poverty of vision and instinct, by which they are estranged from the wild land, and made tentative. They are born and die upon the land, but then they are gone away from it as if they had never been. Their dust is borne away in the wind, and their cries have no echo in the rain and the river, the commotion of wings, the return of boughs bent by the passing of dark shapes in the dawn and dusk. (52)

Momaday then extends this idea to humans as well:

> Man came down the ladder to the plain a long time ago. It was a slow migration, though he came only from the caves in the canyons and the tops of the mesas nearby. There are low, broken walls on the tabletops and smoke-blackened caves in the cliffs, where still there are metates and broken bowls and ancient ears of corn, as if the prehistoric civilization had gone out among the hills for a little while and would return; and then everything would be restored to an older age, and time would have returned upon itself and a bad dream of invasion and change would have been dissolved in an hour before the dawn. For man, too, has tenure in the land; he dwelt upon the land twenty-five thousand years ago, and his gods before him. (52)

The narrative tells the story of this invasion of the tenured by the untenured, in a tale of imperialism and resistance:

> The people of the town have little need. They do not hanker after progress and have never changed their essential way of life. Their invaders were a long time in conquering them; and now, after four centuries of Christianity, they still pray in Tanoan to the old deities of the earth and sky and make their living from the things that are and have always been within their reach; while in the discrimination of pride they acquire from their conquerors only the luxury of example. They have assumed

the names and gestures of their enemies, but have held on to their own, secret souls; and in this there is a resistance and an overcoming, a long outwaiting. (52–53)

Momaday insists on a spiritual relation to the land that the long-standing animals and Native peoples have, as opposed to the superficial life of the colonizing white Christians. This ongoing spiritual relation should be heard to imply an ongoing legal title to the land, no matter if official paper shows white ownership.

Momaday's particular metaphors for tenure—to have "dust" and "echoes" that remain after death—are, strangely, echoes challenging Nathaniel Hawthorne's formulation of spiritual relation to landscape. In "The Custom-House," the 1850 preface to *The Scarlet Letter,* Hawthorne imagines that he has a greater claim to belonging in the land than his fellow citizens because his ancestors have been there longer. Hawthorne's dead and buried ancestors are part of the landscape, and Hawthorne's account anticipates the imagery and language that Momaday uses. Hawthorne's feeling for "old Salem," he hypothesizes, "is probably assignable to the deep and aged roots which my family has struck into the soil" (11). His ancestor was among the first settlers, Hawthorne says, "And here his descendants have been born and died, and have mingled their earthy substance with the soil; until no small portion of it must necessarily be akin to the mortal frame wherewith, for a little while, I walk the streets" (11). Not merely "akin" *to* the soil, but literally a kin *of* the soil, Hawthorne imagines that these corpses have become part of the local particulate ecology; it is as if he and others are breathing, drinking, and eating the matter that has passed through the dead bodies of his ancestors. "In part, therefore, the attachment which I speak of is the mere sensuous sympathy of dust for dust. Few of my countrymen can know what it is" (11). Hawthorne anticipates Momaday's logic—one belongs in a place because the land carries the bodies, the ongoing presence, of one's ancestors; their "dust" indeed "echoes" in the landscape's "soil."

John Okada, like Hawthorne and Momaday, also linked spiritual title to the "soil" with the death of a blood relative, though in *No-No Boy*'s case it is through the agency of a son's death in war that the Kumasakas were "finally sinking roots into the land" (26). Okada's intervention, then, is to claim precisely the kind of tenure that had been denied to Asian Americans because of American law premised on (but also producing) the ongoing "sojourner" image in American consciousness.

I would like to hypothesize that one way the dominant culture has historically dissolved the anxiety about an enduring Native presence in and title to the land (of the kind imagined by Momaday) is through the production and maintenance of the Asian sojourner stereotype. Of course, this sojourning image of seeking "not nourishment but only gold," refuted by Okada, could describe a great many European settlers, especially if we start our American mythology with the Virginia Colony rather than Plymouth Rock. This comparison suggests the real, and ongoing, ideological work that the stereotype of the Asian sojourner has performed in American culture over the last century and a half or so. This stereotype establishes a difference between traveling through and belonging to the land. By the mid 1800s, Robert Lee shows, popular songs were already suggesting that Chinese do not adapt to American ways, and were sojourners (44). California, as free soil, was imagined as the opportunity to recreate a white republic (45). "By the end of the 1850s, the 4,000 black residents of the state seemed a lesser threat, to the apostles of a white Mechanics' Republic, than the 47,000 Chinese residents of California" (47). We can understand Denis Kearney, the Irish anti-Chinese agitator in California, as crafting white identity through his vilification of Asians; but more than this, we can see that he was performing an early version of what would become the dominant thinking about Asians in America: that through Asian non-belonging to the land (not just the nation), white belonging to—spiritual relationship with—the land was established.

Certainly taking "nourishment" from the land was not the experience of the land by the early Puritan settlers, as William Bradford, Mary Rowlandson, and Nathaniel Hawthorne's imaginary conceptualization of that time show. Bradford and Rowlandson identified the land as hostile, and for them part of that hostility was the presence of what seemed like Satanic Native peoples along the East Coast. Native people were understood to have been a kind of terrestrial effect emerging from a hostile wilderness.[2] Since then, this complementary image of the peculiar relation between the Indian and the land and white anxiety at taking land that was not theirs has endured.[3]

There are various ways to deal with this anxiety. One is a kind of denial performed by imagining an empty continent, a denial famously articulated in Robert Frost's poem "The Gift Outright," which retroactively establishes a spiritual connection between the land and the European settlers through, or perhaps leading to, the war of independence. Besides Frost's and Hawthorne's strategies (namely, to see the land as empty and to breath the molecules that previously constituted one's dead ancestors' bodies, now part of the land), another strategy in the white imaginary has been to project anxiety about a non-relation to the land onto another racial group: the Asian. If "Asian Americans have historically functioned as a peculiar kind of Other (among other Others) in the symbolic economy of America" (S. Wong, *Reading* 5), we can begin to see that the Asian sojourners' transience and non-belonging are projections of the white American imaginary's own sense of these things. This Asian racial stereotype performs ideological work inextricably linked to the Indian. This is what it means for General DeWitt, somewhat like Kearney 140 years before him, to insist that there can be no tie between the Japanese and American soil.

What I am claiming here—that racial meaning accrues through structuralist opposition—is not news to literature, criticism, or recent social science. *Invisible Man* understands whiteness to emerge in a complicated way from a contradistinction with blackness, an understanding that Toni Morrison develops in *Playing in the Dark*. Similarly, Ronald Takaki notes that part of the Chinese racial image in the late nineteenth century emerged from comparisons with black people, a social construction of race responding to new needs for mechanical factory labor (219). This process of racialization is often not merely binary in the United States, because it has resolutely engaged with several "racial" groups at once. I am hypothesizing, in short, that the racial meaning of the Asian sojourner is established not in a binary, but in a triangular relation with whiteness and the Indian, and that its ideological and historical currency would not have been so strong—perhaps it would not have occurred at all—were it not for the enduring actual presence of Indians on the land, and the imaginary presence of dead Indians in the land.

Thus Momaday's and Okada's arrivals at the same kind of Hawthornian logic of "tenure in the land" being attained by the ongoing presence as dust, soil, and dirt of one's ancestors (or one's sons) likely signals their response to a larger Asian-Native inverse relation in the white American historical imaginary. The irony of one nineteenth-century yellow peril cartoon registered this, and cut in several different ways (see Figure 1). Most superficially, it is a warning that history might repeat itself: whites should exclude Chinese so that they do not become more powerful than American whites. A second-level irony is premised on the first: whites do not want to be driven off their rightful land by the Chinese who do not belong, which is now recognized as the very process enacted by whites on Native populations for a few hundred years. But a third level of irony hinges on the return of the repressed: that the Chinese who will drive us out of our land are in some identifiable way the same people that we drove off hundreds of years before. This third level is premised on the suspicion that the Native people are in fact Asians here before us, the very suspicion that motivated Boas's formation of the Jesup expedition to substantiate the hypothesis of human migration and cultural transmission across the Bering Strait. But finally, this third level can be undercut by yet another move that sees the Bering Strait hypothesis as

1620 Plymouth Rock. A weary traveler begs a little footing

1879 The "weary travelers" Descendant "There, you infernal redskin: I've driven you from the Atlantic to the Pacific, now git!"

1879 Chinese Immigrant. "Mellican man lettee Chinaman landee,—me washee, washee, and me workee cheapee!"

1979 "Mellican man must git!"

WILL HISTORY REPEAT ITSELF?
EASTWARD THE STAR OF CHINA TAKES ITS WAY!—POPULATION OF THE UNITED STATES, 40,000,000; OF CHINA, 400,000,000.

FIGURE 1. History Did Repeat Itself. From *McGee's Illustrated Weekly,* March 6, 1880. Courtesy of Hesburgh Library, University of Notre Dame

signaling that the old ones here before Europeans are alien after all, having arrived from another place entirely epochs before. Such is the solution to the problematic Native prior presence in the land conceived in the work of H. P. Lovecraft, whose nativist Cthulhu stories in the 1920s imagined the terrifying "Old Ones" as somehow still here "inside the earth," but with their spiritual precedence deactivated by virtue of the fact that they are aliens who ages ago came from the stars ("The Call of Cthulhu" 153, 154).

The Cthulhu stories suggest the ways in which nativism sometimes formed itself through a refutation of the emerging tenets of Boas's anthropological concept of culture. The protagonist of "The Call of Cthulhu" wants to be an "anthropologist" (159), and he is a skeptic rationalist who denies the supernatural as an explanation for the unlikely reoccurrence in widely different global cultures of an image depicting the Old Ones. But the story's point is that the anthropological tenets of historical particularism and dynamic holism, deployed by Boas to counter racial accounts of group behavior, are inadequate explanations of the racial dreams that afflict peoples as culturally diverse as voodoo practitioners in Louisiana, Eskimos in Greenland, and Melanesians in the Pacific. Nonwhite peoples are somehow attuned to the dormant Old Ones: Professor Angell dies after being "jostled by a nautical-looking negro" (140); the New Orleans voodoo cult is made up of "mixed-blooded [. . . with] a sprinkling of negroes and mulattoes" (153) in a forest "untraversed by white men" (151), and out of which they question a "mestizo" (154); one cult is composed of "Esquimaux" (149); the *Alert* is manned by Melanesians and other "half-castes" (161); Johansen is helped (or possibly killed) by two East Indians after he has a bundle of papers dropped on him (164).

The "European witch-cult" is not allied with the cult of the Old Ones (156), and in fact Europeans are largely unaffected, unless they are artists. One such artist is Wilcox, who comes from "an excellent family" (142)—which in the 1920s meant he did not have Jewish, Mediterranean, or Alpine ancestry; he was a Saxon. He is, the story tells us, "New England's traditional 'salt of the earth'" (145). Lovecraft, a nativist committed to biological race, has his budding anthropologist character confounded by the story's events. But as a nativist, Lovecraft is also working out the problem of the Natives: how they could have priority but not indigeneity. The story's various references to Roger Williams suggest that Indians are indeed behind Lovecraft's terror of the Old Ones. The narrator and his uncle are descended from a companion of Roger Williams (140, 394n5), and Wilcox lives in the shadow of the church founded by Williams (157, 397n35). As related in John Winthrop's journal, Roger Williams's heresy—which ultimately caused his expulsion from the colony, from which he leaves to found Providence—is that "he disputes their [the Plymouth council's] right to the lands they possessed here, and concluded that claiming by the King's grant they could have not title, nor otherwise except they compounded with the natives" (61). In other words, according to Williams, the Europeans do not have a right to Indian land; Indians have a spiritual tenancy—Momaday's tenure—and must be negotiated with. But Lovecraft arrives at an ingenious solution to the problem of the Old Ones' precedence by imagining them as alien sojourners after all, in a manner that symbolically rereads the Native as a permanent alien—that is, as a kind of Asian.

If the Asian and the Native occupy inverse positions in the white American imaginary, that symbolic fantasy has nonetheless been historically produced by real events and structures of power. One aspect of the inverse relation is that there has in general not been an anthropological tradition in Asian America or a sociological tradition in Native America. Such is not just the historical reality that American anthropology was formed through an encounter with the Indian and American sociology reached some of its answers (as with Park) about race and assimilation when researching on the West Coast's Asian American communities. This inverseness of symbol and social science history also suggests that, Lovecraft's superficial conflation of non-white racial groups notwithstanding, it is not an accident that the assimilationist Okada arrives at the same images of soil, dust, and dirt and presence in the land that for Momaday is the mark of Native distinction. In other words, Okada repeats the solution of claiming title and spiritual presence that white American writers like Hawthorne and Lovecraft have also done. What for Momaday is distinctiveness is thus for Okada a method of inclusion and assimilation. Momaday refutes the second-phase liberal consensus that does not distinguish among the different racialized groups and their histories and imagines minority cultures disappearing into the American melting pot. This is thus also why, despite the inverseness of symbol and social science history between the Asian and the Native, the logical continuity of this consensus had it that the man who was charged with wrapping up the internment of Japanese Americans through a technology of cultural dispersal was likewise, seven years later, the man charged with assimilating Native Americans through the same technology of cultural dispersal.

In *Keeper of Concentration Camps*, Richard Drinnon suggests that "as head of the WRA (1942–46) and of the BIA (1950–53), Dillon S. Myer was director and commissioner of twin calamities. His career enables us to bring together vast bodies of evidence on the treatment of Native Americans and of Japanese Americans—materials too often studied separately—and trace these to their common matrix" (xxvi–xxvii). Myer was appointed to head the War Relocation Authority after John Collier's Bureau of Indian Affairs, for which D'Arcy McNickle was still working, had been contracted to run the Poston Internment camp on the Colorado River Reservation (Parker 88). But Myer, says McNickle's biographer Dorothy Parker, "had had almost no contact with any ethnic group other than his own, and he was totally committed to the melting-pot concept of American society. He was unfamiliar with the idea of cultural pluralism, and he would have rejected it had he known about it" (99). Against Collier's policies that encouraged retribalization and used "applied anthropology" to substantiate the cultural specifics that might underwrite renewed tribal constitutions, Myer represented the increasingly dominant sociological vision between 1940 and 1965 of the demise of minority cultures. As Parker puts this difference,

> Underlying the conflict between Collier and Myer was a basic philosophical difference. Myer was convinced that communities that differed culturally from mainstream society were inherently "un-American," and that their existence weakened the fabric of American life. Initially, he and Collier had agreed that most of the evacuees, especially those born in America, were loyal to the United States. They had also agreed, at least theoretically, that the nation would be best served by releasing these loyal citizens from the relocation centers as quickly as possible, not, of course, back to the coastal areas, but to scattered locations throughout the country. Families could be moved to cities and farms throughout the nation's interior, where they would be free to find jobs and become part of the local population. (100)

By March 1946, "about 57,000 'evacuees' had moved back to the West Coast, but about 50,000 had settled eastward in new homes" (Drinnon 9). Myer's approach to Native America was the same: he declared he wanted to put the BIA out of its business, and Indians were now to be driven away from communities and into "welfare rolls and the slums where Myer had already scattered so many of the Japanese Americans" (Drinnon 192). If Collier had been called by some congressmen "communistic" for the measure of tribal sovereignty and communal ownership entailed in Reorganization (168), there were also, no less important than such Cold War international reasons, real economic benefits (for whites) resulting from Termination, with many Western state senators enthusiastic about the land to soon be opened up (209). Despite the fact that there was no equivalent to the NAACP or JACL among the Native American communities demanding integration, Myer pursued the coercive policy on behalf the of federal government, even couching the program in terms of desegregation and "assimilations" (236).

Myer's solution to the question of what to do with the interned Japanese Americans during and after World War II was to try as much as possible to relocate them away from the West Coast and to integrate them into white communities. The War Relocation Authority's policy of resettling Japanese Americans away from Japanese American communities on the Coast had its theoretical roots in Chicago sociology, as I established in chapter four, and Dillon Myer is the causal link that connects sociology's culture to the policy of Relocation. Myer, in other words, was selected to head the BIA precisely for his instantiation of sociology as the basis for government policy toward minority groups—a connection that has not yet been recognized in historical accounts of Native Relocation, the political context for Momaday's *House Made of Dawn*.

If Collier was an applied anthropologist, Myer might have been termed an "applied sociologist." Whereas Boas and Park resisted using social science to formulate government programs, both Collier and Myer believed in social engineering projects on a massive scale. But their key differences derived from their social science models of culture. As Drinnon argues,

> An accident of chronology has masked the underlying meaning of Myer's termination policy. Had he been commissioner of the BIA *before* he became director of the WRA, then the continuities stretching from the reservations to the camps could hardly have been missed and the fundamental sameness of his treatment of Native Americans and Japanese Americans would have elicited close analysis long ago. Just as his *termination* of Native Americans meant their *relocation* in ghettos, so his *relocation* of Japanese Americans across the country meant the *termination* of their communities (Little Tokyos) on the West Coast and the breakup or attempted breakup of their subculture. In both instances he and his staffs energetically grubbed up the roots of their charges and gave them one-way tickets away from their places of shared recollections. (265)

Myer represents the gradual emergence of the liberal consensus during World War II and the Cold War. Myer was no liberal himself, steeped as he was in a historically constitutive American racism, but the ethic of the programs that he administered was nonetheless the integration and assimilation of racial minorities into the nation, an emergent official federal policy that would have been an anathema to nativists (like Lovecraft) of the first two decades of the century.[4] Hence, when the recently retired secretary of the interior, Harold Ickes, wrote to President Truman in 1946 recommending Dillon Myer for the Medal for Merit based on his administration of the War

Relocation Authority, "Ickes did no more than express this liberal consensus in his high praise of Myer for converting one of the most 'locality-bound' minorities into a 'widely distributed one'" (Drinnon 267). Four years later, Myer was selected by Truman to head the BIA precisely for this partly achieved resolution of dispersal.

Remarking on Myer's graduate degree in education at Columbia, Drinnon observes, "No Franz Boas or any other teacher ever set his imagination ablaze" (18). While this is an indicator for Drinnon of Myer's ordinary, gray unreflectiveness, what Boas might have taught Myer in 1925, perhaps seated next to Hurston, was an understanding of what minority culture was and what would happen to it in the United States totally different from the understanding implicit in the programs that Myer went on to administer. While John Collier resigned from the BIA in 1945, eventually to become an anthropologist at the City College of New York (Drinnon 169), D'Arcy McNickle hung on, continuing "to write about the need to incorporate the insights of anthropology and the other social sciences into Indian policy" and being elected to honorary membership in the American Anthropological Association (Parker 120). But by the late 1940s, anthropology's culture concept and its applicability to federal Indian policy were already in decline, and were over by the time Myer was appointed to head the BIA in the spring of 1950. As McNickle's biographer suggests,

> In the face of a growing national consensus that looked askance at cultural diversity, Chapman gravitated toward Myer's position that Indian reservations, like Japanese relocation centers, served only to isolate those who lived there. He had observed Myer's management of the War Relocation Authority and his efficient (some called it ruthless) dismantling of the relocation centers after the war, and he believed that under Myer's guidance Indian reservations could be terminated as well. (127)

McNickle left the BIA shortly after, but his interest in anthropology endured: he founded the anthropology department at the University of Saskatchewan in 1966.

When N. Scott Momaday turned to anthropology in the late 1960s, that constituted a turn away from the sociological connection between internal migration and assimilation that animated both the resolution of internment and the program of Relocation. Momaday's critique in 1968 in *House Made of Dawn* of the government policy of Relocation was enabled by an older anthropological notion of culture. In fact, a closer examination of Momaday's idea of "tenure in the land" suggests that it is not people but only culture that can have tenure, or placedness. There are a couple of ways that the tenure in the land idea might be established. The first does not bear much scrutiny: it is the idea that certain animals persist in the land even when they die, and that they are the ones, unlike the newer animals introduced by European and American settlers, whose echo persists in the landscape. But dust is dust, Hawthorne's mysticism notwithstanding. What really is going to be the difference between the dust of a rattlesnake and the dust of a horse? How could the planet or this landscape treat these corpses differently? Will it take longer for the alien animals to decompose? New World bacteria that break down bodies are surely not so choosy; besides, Old World species-specific bacteria would have accompanied the new species across the Atlantic.

But this distinction between tenured and untenured animals might be metaphorically true in that native fauna evolved in local ecological niches, whereas the various domesticated mammals, brought by European and American colonizers, did not. In this sense, there might be a biological outwaiting akin to the cultural outwaiting of which Momaday speaks: after these white sojourners have passed from the land, perhaps taking with them the animals they brought, the landscape will return to the animals that were there in the first place. But even if this disappearance were largely to occur, the people remaining might still choose to retain some of the imported animals. What would it look like, for instance, for the horse to disappear from the continent? That might have a striking effect on the various Plains cultures, such as the Kiowa.

The other way tenure in the land might be established is again an adaptive one, but this time cultural rather than biological. It is, in fact, the tenure and placedness of culture (rather than people) that Francisco, in a hallucinatory moment on his death-bed, recalls teaching Abel and his brother:

> They were old enough then, and he took his grandsons out at first light [...]. He made them stand just there, above the point of the low white rock, facing east. [...] They must learn the whole contour of the black mesa. They must know it as they knew the shape of their hands, always and by heart. The sun rose up on the black mesa at a different place each day. [...] They must know the long journey of the sun on the black mesa, how it rode in the seasons and the years, and they must live according to the sun appearing, for only then could they reckon where they were, where all things were, in time. [...] But his grandsons knew already [...] the larger motion and meaning of the great organic calendar itself, the emergency of dawn and dusk, summer and winter, the very cycle of the sun and of all the suns that were and were to

come. And he knew they knew, and he took them with him to the fields and they cut open the earth and touched the corn and ate sweet melons in the sun. (172–73)

The lesson of place and cyclical time, the "organic calendar," for these Jemez Pueblo children is punctuated by another kind of life-giving violence, the "cutting open of the earth," as the cessation of vegetal life sustains the lives of the humans that live there—returning us thematically to the feast of Santiago and its symbolism of violence, death, and new life. This reference to the organic calendar establishes a more specific endurance in a more specific landscape, so long as there are individuals who learn it. But in this case, it is not individuals who have tenure in the land, but culture. The culture has a relation to the landscape (the town's festivals are timed according to local climate, and that "organic calendar" is indexed on the landscape itself), and the only way people can attain that relation is through cultural learning. Learned culture is what might bind people to place, giving them a kind of belonging—as Francisco teaches his grandsons. But despite this scene of cultural instruction, Momaday's novel and his other work during this first decade of multicultural American literature reattached culture to racial descent in a way that undid—and made theoretically unnecessary—the process of cultural learning.

❧ N. Scott Momaday and the Culture of Anthropology

> But Indians have been cursed above all other people in history. Indians have anthropologists. [...] Over the years anthropologists have succeeded in burying Indian communities so completely beneath the mass of irrelevant information that the total impact of the scholarly community on Indian people has become one of simple authority. Many Indians have come to parrot the ideas of anthropologists because it appears that the anthropologists know everything about Indian communities. Thus many ideas that pass for Indian thinking are in reality theories originally advanced by anthropologists and echoed by Indian people in an attempt to communicate the real situation.
>
> —Vine Deloria Jr., *Custer Died for Your Sins*, 1969 (78, 82)

House Made of Dawn is an inaugural novel of American literary multiculturalism because of its simultaneous gesture of rejecting the politics of sociologically informed Relocation and its embrace of the anthropological model of culture that animated the work of Hurston, McNickle, and Paredes. The cultural nationalisms developing at the end of the 1960s signified the reemergence and reinvigoration of a Boasian notion of culture as resistant to external pressure, slow to change, historically particular, and inwardly complex.

According to Matthias Schubnell, 1963 marks the year that Momaday defended his dissertation at Stanford and began his research into Kiowa culture. That search for his Kiowa origins was inaugurated by two events in 1963: first, his viewing of the Tai-me bundle, the most sacred Kiowa medicine, with his Kiowa father Al and his paternal grandmother Aho; and second, shortly after, visiting Aho's grave on Rainy Mountain in Oklahoma. As Schubnell puts it, "The driving forces behind Momaday's search for Kiowa oral expressions and retracing of the migration route of his forefathers from the Yellowstone to the southern plains were his fear of the impending loss of much of Kiowa culture and his conviction that without a conscious exploration of his racial past he would forsake much of his human potential" (30). Accordingly, Momaday, even as he was preparing his dissertation for publication, also spent time researching the Kiowa oral tradition. "Like many contemporary American Indians," asserts Schubnell, "Momaday had to take recourse in written materials compiled by anthropologists, folklorists, and translators of Kiowa oral tradition" (144). Because he could not speak Kiowa himself—his family had left the Kiowa community when he was two years old because his non-Kiowa mother did not get along with his father's Kiowa family—Momaday's father Al had the "crucial role of interviewing informers and translating the recorded material" for his son (144). The earliest publication of two of these tales appears to be in 1964 in Momaday's article "The Morality of Indian Hating"; more were published privately in the not so well-known *Journey of Tai-me* of 1967.

But by the time most of these stories from the Kiowa oral tradition were reprinted in his 1969 memoir *The Way to Rainy Mountain*, they were accompanied, in one of the three voices of that text, by historical and ethnographic information from the anthropologist James Mooney. Momaday used Mooney's *Calendar History of the Kiowa Indians*, published in 1898, which was also a source for the 1967 article published in *The Reporter* that became the basis for Tosamah's monologue in the 1968 novel *House Made of Dawn* and that became the introduction to *The Way to Rainy Mountain*. Additionally, Momaday made use of other ethnographers like Mildred Mayhall, Alice Marriott, and Wilbur S. Nye. Anthropology was thus the academic supplement to Momaday's own "fieldwork" (Schubnell 144) in researching the Kiowa oral tradition in the early-mid 1960s.

It is not always clear in *The Way To Rainy Mountain* which material derives from the oral tradition and which from anthropology; Schubnell has tracked down perhaps a half dozen instances, but his work is not exhaustive on this point. Between the prologue and the epilogue are twenty-four two-page sections (with some occasional illustrations between sections as well). Each section is broken into three voices, which Schubnell likens to "the mythical-legendary, the historical-anthropological, and the personal" (157). On the left page in italics is a voice that sounds like transcribed verbal tradition speech. On the right page at the top is anthropological-sounding discourse in regular type; below it in slightly cursive script is presumably Momaday's own personal voice that speaks frequently about his family. In general, the anthropological voices on the top right have their source in Mooney's *Calendar,* although occasionally Mayhall is the anthropological source.[5] Less frequently, the top right voices are not anthropological at all (the top right voice of the last three sections speak of Momaday's father and paternal grandmother), and sometimes the left voice of the oral tradition has an anthropological source, or at least a corroboration, in Mooney (compare section I [*Way* 16] with Mooney 152–53).

A single instance will suffice to show the general tenor of *The Way to Rainy Mountain*'s use of Mooney's anthropology, aside from instances in which Momaday merely quotes Mooney directly with attribution (*Way* 25, 37, 61), and likewise suggests the way in which Momaday often uses anthropology as a means to his own aesthetic ends—in this case, advancing his lifelong theme of the creative power of language. In section VIII, the second voice reads:

A word has power in and of itself. It comes from nothing into sound and meaning; it gives origin to all things. By means of words can a man deal with the world on equal terms. And the word is sacred. A man's name is his own; he can keep it or give it away as he likes. Until recent times, the Kiowas would not speak the name of a dead man. To do so would have been disrespectful and dishonest. The dead take their names with them out of the world. (33)

This unattributed paragraph has its partial source in Mooney's description of a warrior society (which Momaday had previously described [21], using Mooney):

Sometimes an old warrior, having outlived the need of a name and not regarding any younger man as worthy to bear it, deliberately "throws it away" and is henceforth nameless. Should he die without having bestowed his name upon a successor, the name dies with him and can not be revived. The name of the dead is never spoken in the presence of the relatives, and upon the death of any member of a family all the others take new names—a custom noted by Raleigh's colonists on Roanoke island more than three centuries ago. Moreover, all words suggesting the name of the dead person are dropped from the language for a term of years, and other words, conveying the same idea, are substituted. (231)

Occasionally, the three voices group information that is surprisingly found within a page or so of the same Mooney source, suggesting that the primary source has been Mooney's anthropology, perhaps supplemented with actual oral tradition gathered by Momaday and his father.[6]

Mooney met Franz Boas at the 1893 Columbian Exposition in Chicago, five years before his *Calendar History of the Kiowa Indians* was published by the Bureau of American Ethnology (Moses 76). Mooney's role at the fair was to help prepare the display of some "Navajo and Hopi costumes, foodstuffs, and native crafts" that he had collected in the Southwest (Moses 74). Boas was organizing the anthropometry exhibit at the fair, the science that was to become in the following decades the cornerstone of his attack on the concept of race. They carried on an on-again-off-again correspondence that lasted for more than three decades, between 1888 and 1920,[7] but Boas never had the mentoring and supervisory role with Mooney that he had with Hurston, Deloria, and Herskovits. Mooney's work was implicated in some of the earliest challenges that Boas was making to the "evolutionist" and racial anthropology entrenched in the last two decades of the nineteenth century. He was already an ethnographer doing fieldwork before Boas fought for its importance, and his supervisor at the BAE, W. J. McGee, thought his fieldwork among the Kiowa excessive and wanted him to wrap it up and "stop wasting the bureau's money" (Moses 106). In the 1890s, writes Mooney's biographer, "as McGee expounded theories of cultural development and the effect of environment on human society, Mooney returned repeatedly to the Kiowas to learn just a little more about a specific Indian tribe" (Moses 106). His interest was historical like Boas's, in that he tried to trace the cultural developments and transformations of the Kiowa as they adapted and adopted cultural elements from other groups. He presented part of his research on the Kiowa at the Tennessee Centennial Exposition in 1897:

> The bureau's exhibit represented another example of the detailed, individual tribal displays that had become the fashion beginning with the ethnological exhibits at the Columbian Exposition. Most museum-quality displays before 1893 had reflected the developmentalism favored by Mason and Powell at the time of the argument with Franz Boas in

the pages of *Science* in the mid-1880s. Since that time Boas's emphasis on what came to be called "historical particularism" had become the norm. (Moses 110)

Mooney was part of the earliest challenges to "developmentalism" that aligned him with Boasian cultural anthropology.

Boas invoked Mooney's 1896 *The Ghost-Dance Religion and the Sioux Outbreak of 1890* in his *Mind of Primitive Man* as evidence of the continual creative power of individuals within cultural systems, thus illustrating his central antiracist argument (136). Mooney paid attention to the whole of culture and emphasized the interlocking parts of culture, as when he described the dynamic religious whole in which myth, different Kiowa medicine bundles, and peyote use are inseparable parts. While there are occasional comparativist statements in the *Calendar,* such as his likening of the Sun god's wife's refusal to heed his warning against digging up a bush to Eve and Pandora (238), they are brief thematic connections akin to Hurston's comparison of John to Daniel, rather than analytical units to be the basis for a universal approach to mythology. Citing Boas's famous 1896 article "The Limitations of the Comparative Method in Anthropology," published the same year as the *Calendar History,* Mooney's biographer writes that "Mooney also knew" that the linear evolutionist scheme and the comparativist method were shaky grounds for anthropology, "and had known it long before he ever read Boas's address" (Moses 112).

One aspect that Mooney did not clearly share with the paradigm of cultural anthropology in its nascent development was the idea of racial equality and the strong distinction between culture and race. Mooney describes the Kiowa's "character" thusly:

In character the Kiowa are below the standard. Having been intimately associated with them for some years, the author would be better pleased to make a different showing, but truth compels the statement. Tribal traits are strongly marked among Indians. The Sioux are direct and manly, the Cheyenne high-spirited and keenly sensitive, the Arapaho generous and accommodating, the Comanche practical and business-like, but the Kiowa, with some honorable exceptions, are deficient in all these qualities. They have the savage virtue of bravery, as they have abundantly proven, but as a people they have less of honor, gratitude, and general reliability than perhaps any other tribe of the plains. The large infusion of captive blood, chiefly Mexican, must undoubtedly have influenced the tribal character, but whether for good or evil the student of heredity must determine. (233–35)

Needless to say, Momaday does not make use of Mooney's ethnography of the Kiowa "character." Accuracy aside, what begins here as a description of probable cultural traits shades off into racial ones with the assertion of "blood" affecting character, and to be sure, in the 1890s these ways of thinking about group behavior were not so distinct as Boas was to make them. So while I am not claiming that Mooney was a Boasian before Boas, he was nonetheless arriving at some of the same answers about culture as Boas. Boas did not invent all these traits about culture; he merely helped synthesize and systematize them into a dominant paradigm that he then taught to a couple of generations of important anthropologists. Momaday's *Way to Rainy Mountain* borrows not just the content of Kiowa culture from Mooney, but the thinking about culture in terms of a history of adaptation and a dynamic holism, terms of Boasian anthropology *avant le mot*.

While Momaday's primary anthropological source was thus too early to have been fully formed by the paradigm of cultural anthropology Boas was to put in place in the first four decades of the twentieth century, the same is not so for the ethnographers Mayhall, Nye, and Marriott, who were doing their anthropology late enough to be working fully within the anthropological culture concept established earlier in the century by Boas. Like Américo Paredes, Mayhall, Nye, and Marriott imbibed, to a greater or lesser extent, the Boasian anthropological tenets of racial equality, historical particularism, dynamic holism, cultural relativism, and the disengagement of culture from race. Mayhall, for instance, frames her chapter titled "The Evolution of a Civilization" in terms of Clark Wissler's "culture area" (Mayhall 106). Wissler was a colleague of Boas's who challenged and extended the tenet of historical particularism by showing how cultural traits were sometimes regionally grouped, suggesting both historical diffusion and some measure of environmental determinism; this was the idea that Herskovits drew on for his own dissertation work applying it to the "cattle complex" in East Africa ("Cattle" 239). Mayhall frames her history of Kiowa culture by suggesting that archaeological records do not precisely support the application of the "culture-area concept" to the Plains cultures:

> The culture-area concept is a neat way of cataloguing and dividing Indian material for museum display, conceived by Clark Wissler. As such, it has served admirably. Not so neat is the actual geographic division, or a sequential basis upon archaeology. Some culture areas typify the concept nicely—for example, the Southeast. The Plains culture, of historic growth and development, the last culture to evolve in North America, cannot show a definite archaeological sequence. It was a complex of many tribes of varied ancestry, language, and culture. (106)

When Momaday describes his grandmother Aho as belonging "to the last culture to evolve in North America" (6) in an unattributed quotation from Mayhall, he thus narrows to the Kiowa what for Mayhall had been a point about the culture area in which the Kiowa later developed.[8] For Mayhall and Momaday, what is at stake is the Kiowa adoption of a culture complex (horses, Sun Dance, nomadism, warrior societies [Mayhall 110–11; Momaday, *Way* 6–7]) particular to the culture area of the Plains.

Mooney's tracing of Kiowa culture's debts to elements of Crow culture that had been borrowed during their migration implied that the Kiowa could not have the same kind of "tenure in the land" that the Tanoan cultures had, since their migration into Oklahoma from the Rockies was no older than many European settlers' migration to North America. Beneath this theoretical problem lies a similar but deeper one about Momaday's use of anthropological sources in his "process of self-fashioning as a Kiowa that Momaday had begun in the Spring of 1963" (Ransom 83). To put the problem most bluntly, what does anthropology have to say about how the Kiowas could still be Kiowa, and what does it have to say about how Momaday could be Kiowa? Momaday's work in *House* and *Way,* as in *The Names,* is most concerned with how to fashion, or claim, identities. Both the Kiowa oral tradition and the anthropology of Mooney show how the Kiowa emerged from the headwaters of the Yellowstone River around 1700 and moved "eastward to the Black Hills and south to the Wichita Mountains" (*Way* 4). Along the way, this tribe of mountain hunters adopted the Plains culture of the Crows as they migrated southward. As Momaday puts it in *The Way to Rainy Mountain,*

> Along the way the Kiowas were befriended by the Crows, who gave them the culture and religion of the Plains. They acquired horses, and their ancient nomadic spirit was suddenly free of the ground. They acquired Tai-me, the sacred Sun Dance doll, from that moment the object and symbol of their worship, and so shared in the divinity of the sun. Not least, they acquired the sense of destiny, therefore courage and pride. When they entered upon the southern Plains they had been transformed. No longer were they slaves to the simple necessity of survival; they were a lordly and dangerous society of fighters and thieves, hunters and priests of the sun. (6–7; see also *House* 114)

This account is amplified in the anthropologist Mildred Mayhall's history, where she writes that the Kiowa also received from the Crows the use of the "buffalo-skin tipi," an "annual summer Sun Dance," and warrior societies (11). Given that the Kiowas were thereby culturally "transformed," as Momaday calls it (*Way* 6), how does it make sense to call them Kiowas instead of, say,

Crows? What kind of concept of culture does one need, in other words, to consider the Kiowas still to be Kiowa after this wholesale transformation of the way people actually lived? This is related to another question: what does it mean for Momaday to be able to imagine himself as Kiowa, even though he did not quite grow up among the Kiowas and he does not speak their language and presumably does not practice many of the cultural traditions that he cites as giving historical definition to the Kiowa? We can see that one possible answer to the first question—that the Kiowas are still Kiowa even though they have adopted Plains culture because they speak Kiowa—would trouble an answer to the second, since Momaday did not grow up speaking Kiowa, and still does not. What kind of notion of culture does one need, in other words, to consider the Kiowas still to be Kiowa after their transformation, and to consider Momaday to be Kiowa—and, to extend the question to *House Made of Dawn,* to consider Abel to be Jemez and Bahkyush?

Much of the material for the anthropological voice in *The Way to Rainy Mountain* corresponds to sections from Mooney's *Calendar History.* Even some of the oral tradition voice may have come from Mooney rather than from Momaday's expedition with his father to hear Kiowa stories, a speculation unconfirmable until we can examine Momaday's records from his own ethnographic fieldwork. Establishing Momaday's general debt to anthropology in terms of its model of culture and its ethnographic collections should not surprise us, Deloria's claim in the epigraph notwithstanding, since as Schubnell notes (144), many Native Americans have been supplementing cultural learning with anthropological sources, as was the case with D'Arcy McNickle's *Surrounded.* But despite the obviously laborious process by which he learned these cultural traditions—the oral tradition doubled by book learning, or perhaps vice-versa—Momaday has seen fit to describe such learning processes in terms of memory, and cultural processes in terms of race. Momaday's oeuvre-wide trope for this process—rendered variously as "memory in the blood" and "blood memory"—joins these two aspects together, thus reattaching culture to race in a way that departs from the Boasian anthropological tradition through which his work between 1967 and 1976 was otherwise framed.

One example of blood memory in *House Made of Dawn* is the idea that since Abel carries Bahkyush blood in his veins, he is somehow attuned to the vision of the eagles and the snake he sees one day, and is granted permission to come with the Eagle Watchers Society on the eagle hunt. This Society, according to the novel, is descended from the remnants of the Bahkyush (otherwise known as the Pecos Pueblo), whose population was demolished by disease in the nineteenth century. The novel hints that "the ancient blood of this forgotten tribe still ran in the veins of men" (15), and we are invited through genealogical hints to understand that Abel is at least one-eighth Bahkyush, since Francisco, his grandfather, appears to be the son of the Priest Frey Nicolás and a Bahkyush witch called Nicolás *teah-whau* (11, 45–46, 179).[9] Similarly, Tosamah describes his grandmother as having the Kiowa's migration from Yellowstone to the Plains as "lay[ing] like memory in her blood" (114). This is the section of *House Made of Dawn* taken from a prior article in which Momaday described his own grandmother, Aho, and which is used again in *The Way to Rainy Mountain* (7). In *The Names,* Momaday says that he was taken to Tsoai, the Devil's Tower, "so that by means of the child the memory of Tsoai should be renewed in the blood of the coming-out [Kiowa] people" (55), and later writes "that I am a Kiowa, that therefore there is in me, as there is in the Tartars, an old, sacred notion of the horse. I believe that at some point in my racial life, this notion must needs be expressed in order that I may be true to my nature" (155).

As with *The Bluest Eye,* invocation of bodies and blood are generally appeals to race and not to familial descent. In some sense, it looks as if what should be Abel's culture can be decided on the relatively contingent facts of family: though he is partly white, partly Jemez, and possibly partly Navajo, it is his Jemez grandfather—or at least the grandfather who while racially mixed himself is practicing Jemez culture—who is bringing him up. In this sense, the land, and the culture, and his family bonds with his grandfather might form a powerful affect for Abel, all of which call him back away from the possibility of cultural transformation in Los Angeles. Here is nostalgia, but also the memory of culture (which is different from "cultural memory"), belonging, and placedness. However, affect based in his life's experience cannot be the basis for his attunement to the Bahkyush, and in the novel's assertion that the "ancient blood of this forgotten tribe still ran in the veins of men," blood can only be a technology for what is inherited as opposed to what is learned.

The trope of blood memory has been extensively commented on in Momaday criticism (see Allen), but I would like to make a couple of points about it in relation to anthropology. The first is that this racial metaphor undoes the paradigm shift inaugurated by Franz Boas. Boas's central intervention in anthropology was to draw it away from racial thinking toward cultural thinking, eventually winning the argument that group-based differences were acquired—learned through culture—rather than innate. But as Chadwick Allen has pointed out, Momaday has developed "the signature trope" of "memory in the blood," which he sometimes calls "blood memory" and "racial memory," throughout all his work (93). And, Allen continues, the "connotative possibilities of his trope have been developed" by other contemporary Native writers like Leslie Silko, James Welch, Joy Harjo, Linda Hogan, and even Gerald Vizenor (94). But the problem with "blood memory" is that it describes learned things—acquired things—as being inherited and natural. Momaday researched the Kiowa tradition— which took the form of interviewing, through his father, Kiowa elders, and of reading anthropologists' books about the Kiowa—but he then redescribed that learned information as information that was in his blood, in his racial makeup. It is thus no accident that for Momaday and his chief interpreter, Matthias Schubnell, there is not a clear distinction to be made between race and culture, since they regularly describe as racial what Boasian anthropology would understand as cultural.[10]

This critique connects to my second point: that this trope of memory in the blood is a way of answering by race the question which culture one should have. As Walter Benn Michaels argues, "any notion of cultural identity that goes beyond the description of our actual beliefs and practices must rely on race [...] in order to determine which culture is actually ours. Hence the idea of cultural identity—despite the fact that in recent years it has customarily been presented as an alternative to racial identity—is in fact, not only historically but logically, an extension of racial identity" ("Response" 121). Momaday's work is deeply interested in answering the question of which culture is his, and which culture is that of his characters. This is in part how Momaday counters the politics of Relocation, which was, after all, another way (the liberal consensus's way) of answering the question of which culture should be Abel's. Abel needs to return to Walatowa because he is Jemez; likewise, he is drawn to Bahkyush practices because of the racial memory he shares with other Bahkyush. We could go even further than this to say that Abel is actually already Bahkyush even before he does Bahkyush things; similarly, Momaday himself can be Kiowa even before he has adopted Kiowa practices and values.

It might be protested that Momaday here is only using the trope of blood memory in the service of imagining and fashioning his identity as a Kiowa (Allen). He has constantly emphasized, in his writing and in interviews, the imaginative process of identity construction, an event that takes place through language. In this sense, the concept of identity that runs throughout his work might be considered postmodern, in that it explicitly acknowledges language's creative role in identity construction, and the fact that identity is above all an act of imagination. Momaday's commentators, especially Schubnell, have followed him in this lead. But if one's identity is an act of imagination, the problem that remains is deciding which culture one should imagine having. And this seems to me precisely the point: it is not without consequence that in the process of imagining and self-fashioning his identity, he answers the question of which culture he should have, and which culture his Native characters should have, by first determining which race they already are. What first appears to be a concession to postmodern habits of identity construction is actually grounded in a deeply essentialist, and explicitly anti-existentialist, account of being.

Both *House Made of Dawn* and *The Way to Rainy Mountain* are full of examples of cultural acquisition, cross-cultural transmission, and the adaptation or adoption of wholesale ceremonies, religious practices, and ways of life. Francisco does Jemez things and also Catholic things; Abel does Bahkyush things and Jemez things and even Navajo things; Tosamah is a member of the Native American Church that synthesized Native religious practices like peyote with Christian theology; Angela tells Native stories; the Chicken Pull appears to be a Spanish custom adopted by some Southwestern peoples like the Jemez (Schubnell 114); the Pecos Bull Run was introduced by another Pueblo people, the Pecos/Bahkyush; and as Mooney shows, the Kiowa adopted the Sun Dance, Plains culture, horses, and the Tai-me bundle from the Crows, and then adopted peyote use, and then agriculture after Dawes, and then lost their horse culture. Both books are packed with examples of people changing their cultural practices and values. Moreover, these examples and their source in anthropology or in the oral tradition underline culture as being learned and acquired, not biologically based. How strange it is then, for Momaday to redescribe such obviously learned characteristics with a racial conceit like "blood memory." I wonder if, because the cultural acquisition was so self-conscious—Momaday actually set out in his early thirties to gather material that he had not quite grown up with—there was an anxiety about cultural authenticity. What better way to combat that suspicion, that he is researching a culture that has not really been his culture exactly, but by affirming an ancestral, familial, and indeed racial tie to that culture? The model of identity here, developed partly through the use of the trope of blood memory, is to imagine that what one actually does and believes does not confer one's identity; rather, one's identity pre-exists and awaits discovery in a process that is then retroactively described as already "laying like memory in the blood," that is, in one's racial descent. Anthropology's labor and concepts provided opportunities for Momaday's work, but also theoretical problems that have been problematically contained through the reintroduction of race by this inaugural multiculturalist writer.

❧ The Identity Supplement

> A MESSAGE OF CONSOLATION TO GREEK BROTHERS IN
> THEIR PRISON CAMPS, AND TO MY HAITIAN BROTH-
> ERS AND NICARAGUAN BROTHERS AND DOMINICAN
> BROTHERS AND SOUTH AFRICAN BROTHERS AND SPAN-
> ISH BROTHERS AND TO MY BROTHERS IN SOUTH VIET-
> NAM, ALL IN THEIR PRISON CAMPS: YOU ARE IN THE
> FREE WORLD!
>
> —E. L. Doctorow, *The Book of Daniel,* 1971 (236–37)

According to Matthias Schubnell, Momaday "is concerned with a native identity which manifests a compromise between the extremes of traditionalism on the one hand and complete cultural assimilation, that is, the rejection of a tribal heritage, on the other" (9). He continues, quoting Momaday, that "the Indian" can "take advantage of the possibilities" and "opportunities" of the modern world even as he "retain[s] his identity," and must reconcile with the modern world "without sacrificing his being and identity" (9–10). While there is a contradiction between these two uses of "identity"—what Schubnell imagines as a "compromise" but Momaday says is "retain[ed]" and not "sacrifice[ed]"—the promise of what identity can do for multiculturalism has most generally been fulfilled by Momaday's usage. We can begin to see, then, that identity works as a kind of supplement to an anthropological notion of culture, and that it is, in fact, invoked precisely to perform a labor that mere cultural description fails to do. This point can be put more finely by saying that the notion of identity is generally deployed against the work of description. The question for *A Genealogy of Literary Multiculturalism* is: if this genealogy is, as I contend, at its most basic level the sequence of an anthropologically enabled culturalist literature displaced by a sociologically enabled assimilationist and integrationist literature in turn disrupted by a cultural nationalism enabled by a return to anthropology, at what point and for what reasons did identity become a central component in that development?

The answer begins to become clear when we see that the most effective way for Momaday to imagine himself as Kiowa is to treat Kiowa as an identity and not a culture. Because the actual description of Momaday's cultural practices and values might not render him part of the group known as the Kiowa, the supplement of identity becomes the basis for that act of imagination. Identity is not only indifferent to the question of what is actually taking place (in terms of national identity or ethnic identity), it is theoretically hostile to the question of what is actually taking place. The whole point of a notion of identity—as opposed to a notion of culture—is that it is a supplement: because one's culture (in the anthropological sense) is based on the description of the things a group does and believes, identity allows one to derive being not from those things but rather, when necessary, in spite of those things. There are moments in Momaday's work when cultural description joins identity and works to authorize it. But identity's tendency is toward an account of being—who you are or who a group is—that is essentialist rather than existentialist. In this sense, identity is generally deployed as an antidote to description, and its tendency is against historical particularism and toward an ahistorical essentialism: it is a supplement to the labor of anthropological description which in itself can have no affect, and can do no ideological work. It is thus not surprising that identity has an instinctual return to nature as opposed to nurture, to use the terms of the popularized social science debate; likewise, it is not surprising that identity tends (as in Momaday's work especially) to conceptually collapse culture back into race. Identity instinctively wants to see being as natural and not learned or environmentally determined: thus Momaday's redescription of things learned as things in the blood.

I have argued in this book that the writers in the first two phases—the anthropologically enabled culturalism c. 1920–1940 and the sociologically enabled assimilationism c. 1940–1965—turned to rival social science concepts of culture. Such representative writers as Hurston, McNickle, Wright, Wong, and Okada did not use the word "identity," and generally did not have a concept of identity. They exemplify my argument that cultural description does not have to entail an ambition toward an identity. Although their concepts of minority culture were different, we might say that what united them was a labor of description, in that they saw culture as something that was real and could be observed. That labor was undertaken by different formal strategies—a vernacular-influenced one for Hurston and a set of ethnic realisms for Wright, Wong, and Okada—but it was a labor born of seeing the group as constituted by actual practices and values. Cultural description was one way of combating the damaging essentialism of biological race theory. It was the mystical essence of race and blood which Momaday finds so compelling as the basis for identity that these earlier writers, in their different ways, were writing against.

How identity became a way to distract from description can be seen in the few identitarian gestures in this earlier generation of writers who generally eschewed it. Hurston's "my country, right or wrong" is a declaration of national identity as patriotism, one that grew troublingly during the Cold War. It was precisely the description of American practices at home and abroad, critiqued by Hurston during World War II, that she became willing to suspend in her embrace of Cold War patriotism. The call of national identity during the Cold War was likewise deployed by John Okada in order to leave behind the moral muddle of internment and continued American racism: what was to be dissolved by "that feeling flooding into your chest and making you want to shout with glory" (Okada 96) was the complex account of national being as encompassing *both* democracy and freedom *and* the internment and historical racisms and oppressions. Patriotism, right feeling, and national belonging are the antidotes to the moral complexity of actual national practices and values. Such was likewise the formulation of Ellison's "American identity," which had the virtue of redescribing not actually instantiated universally good practices and values as nonetheless part of the identity of the country. Another early instance of identity's antidote to description came at the end of Paredes's *"With His Pistol in His Hand,"* where it named the ambition of the "Border Mexicans" to remain distinct even as they began to recognize themselves (and began to be recognized by the dominant society) as increasingly Americanized (106).

But it is only with the nascent multiculturalism of Toni Morrison and N. Scott Momaday that the promise of identity comes to full fruition. What remained a marginal strategy for Hurston, Okada, and Paredes became central with the multiculturalist turn, the third phase in *A Genealogy of Literary Multiculturalism*'s scheme. As we have seen, Morrison's account of Geraldine carefully upends the description that *The Bluest Eye* has itself performed of this character's cultural practices and values. What Geraldine actually does and actually believes is untrue to who she really is. Likewise, Abel can be Bahkyush and Momaday can be Kiowa precisely because what had been cultures to which they might or might not belong are now reimagined as identities that cannot be lost. That both writers' turns to the structure of identity are made possible by concomitant turns to race is not accidental, but central to the developing logic of a multiculturalism that took the Boasian model of what culture was but carefully separated it from Boas's method of cultural description and his conceptual separation of culture from race. As we shall see with Ishmael Reed and Gloria Anzaldúa, the multiculturalist turn to identity is often (but perhaps not always) accompanied by the rejoining of culture to race.

To return to the question I thus posed above—why was this multiculturalist turn accompanied by a notion of identity in addition to (and sometimes instead of) anthropological culture?—part of the answer is the already ongoing work of national identity as patriotism during the Cold War in which the multiculturalist turn took place. The cultural nationalism at the end of the 1960s embraced identity partly in reaction to the national embrace of national identity during the Cold War and its liberal consensus: the nationalists' rebellion against the oppressive conformity of national culture entailed pluralism but also, paradoxically, the very strategy of identity that made patriotic right feeling possible. The cultural nationalists' use of the word "nation" should not just be heard in terms of Frantz Fanon's insistence that the nation was the necessary foundation of culture (Palumbo-Liu, *Asian* 307) and in terms of the contemporaneous decolonizations of the 1950s, '60s, and '70s. What was equally important to the cultural nationalists between 1965 and 1975, I contend, was that the nation of America was already understood as having an identity distinct from practices and values that might be described. The nation—especially national character—was already something that floated free from any need to describe what it actually did, what its actual values were.

Internally and externally, mere description of actual national practices and values could not do the heavy lifting that the Cold War required: because, after all, the United States was only ambivalently for democracy at home or abroad. America was democratic in the 1950s in that most of its adult citizens had a role in choosing the government and in that it opposed a totalitarian system that, in Europe for instance, had imposed autocratic regimes; America had democratic values (which is different from saying that democracy is a culturally specific American value) in that it helped to protect Western European democratic nations in the 1950s. But America was not democratic in the 1950s in that it supported the systematic disenfranchisement of a portion of its own citizens, African Americans in the South; likewise, it did not have democratic values when it supported right-wing autocratic regimes in the places ironically mentioned in this section's epigraph from E. L. Doctorow's critical Cold War novel *The Book of Daniel*. Such is the complicated descriptive picture of America policy in the 1950s: it is, descriptively, both democratic and not democratic. How much easier it is—existentially more soothing—to turn to a notion of identity in order to supplement a very blurred ideological power struggle. The nation can be good—and its citizens like Ellison, Okada, and Hurston proud—not because of the things it does (because, descriptively, it is committed to both good things and bad things), but because of its identity. It is the power of national identity to answer the question of national character without reference to—and even in the face of—the facts of actual national practices and values that made it a central part of the Cold War struggle. America could still be about democracy and freedom even if it did not actually do democracy and freedom.

Hurston's Cold War commitment to national identity is instructive on this point. *Dust Tracks* includes a trenchant critique of Western hypocrisy during World War II, as the West preached democracy but did not practice it in India or in America (259–61). Democracy is a good practice according to

Hurston, though not part of any country's identity. It is constitutive of any critique of hypocrisy to empirically describe actual practices and values. As such, the impetus to description goes against the grain of any essentialist or a priori notions of national identity or patriotism. But it was on this question of national identity—as opposed to the invocation of identity in other realms like culture or race—that Hurston became unbalanced by the Cold War, when she failed to raise in the 1950s the same kind of trenchant critique of what the nation was actually doing. Perhaps Hurston's loathing of communism, and the increasing introduction of the notion of national identity into the second grand ideological struggle of the century, led to what one biographer sees as her hardening of positions (Hemenway 336).

I submit that it was precisely this function in precisely this field of international struggle that was the precedent for the turn to identity for multiculturalist writers c. 1970. As the Civil Rights movements failed to generate substantial material change for minorities, there was a turn to identity as a kind of compensation, just as its patriotism had already functioned as compensation for the nation that was not doing racial justice at home or supporting democracies abroad. Such was the available psychic material—an increasingly powerful lingua franca of the Cold War—at the moment at which the Civil Rights movements stumbled and minorities increasingly called attention to the lack of economic improvement. National identity was already a group ontology with a powerful affect, available as an organizing principle to which the cultural nationalists turned at the beginning of the third phase. Although some black nationalists used the word "nation," and some Chicano nationalists used the word "raza," or race, it was the concept of identity that gradually displaced other keywords as third-phase multiculturalism consolidated its gains in the 1980s. Multiculturalism increasingly borrowed a group ontology from the Cold War arena of national identity, where it worked to provide a way of thinking about a group without necessary reference to what the group actually did or believed.

How identity helps construe continuities in a group despite discontinuities in practices became the center of a fascinating debate in the 1990s inaugurated by James Clifford's account of the 1977 Mashpee land claims trial. His 1988 essay "Identity in Mashpee" was trying to answer a question entirely parallel to the one I posed above as to how the Kiowa could still be Kiowa after all the profound cultural changes they had undergone. How the Mashpee could still be Mashpee was the philosophical question underlying the trial's legal question of whether the Mashpee "tribe" had been in continuous existence for the almost two hundred years between the trial and the 1790 Federal Non-Intercourse Act ("Identity" 333). The jury answered no, and Clifford himself finally hedged his bets, saying, "The Mashpee 'tribe' had a way of going and coming; but something was persistently, if not continuously, there. The testimony I heard convinced me that organized Indian life had been going on in Mashpee for the past 350 years. Moreover a significant revival and reinvention of tribal identity was clearly in process" (336). While Clifford problematizes the notions of culture, tribe, and identity, this sentence—and the title of the essay—suggest that identity is the medium of continuity even as practices and values change.

While space does not permit me to give a full account of Clifford's complex work, I want to suggest that this turn to identity is generally consistent with an emerging technology of the multiculturalist period beginning in 1965. Much of the trial seemed to be about the existence and continuity of Mashpee culture, and accordingly the Mashpee "plaintiffs depended more on anthropologists" (317). Anthropological expertise promised continuity and other elements of the model of culture that the Mashpee needed to substantiate. And while "the trial can be seen as a struggle between history and anthropology" (317), Clifford also notes that the defense (as the reader of *A Genealogy of Literary Multiculturalism* will by now be expecting) "relied on a sociologist, Jean Guillemin" (318), who "had no hesitation in affirming that Mashpee Indians never had a distinct culture and never were a tribe" (324). And yet what becomes clear in the trial is that culture itself is not quite the issue, but rather the related notions of tribe and identity. The tribe is a legal-historical notion with wide ramifications for the Mashpee, and while much of the trial focused on the culture and the legal existence of the tribe—what practices and values characterize the Mashpee as a group—Clifford's essay itself turns on the notion of "identity."

This notion is deployed in the way that we have come to expect: against the work of cultural description, as a way of solving—or at least short-circuiting—the almost impossibly complex cultural mixings that characterize the historical and contemporary Mashpee. Clifford deploys identity as Momaday deploys it: it is what stays the same, what he calls in his summary of the plaintiffs' case the "core of Indian identity" (302), even as peoples' cultural practices and values are transformed through contact and interpenetration with other groups. Identity is not so much the compromise that emerges from the complexities of existence (as Schubnell momentarily imagined it) but rather the thing that pre-exists cultural transformations, and is not altered by changes in what the group actually does or believes. Identity, in short, is something that is not learned and that pre-exists the individual's (or nation's) existence. Although Clifford appears to be calling at the end of the essay for more complicated notions of culture and identity (344), is not identity the thing that, unlike culture, can never be lost or even changed? Whether it is a tribe or not, and whether this tribe's cultural practices and values have changed to a greater or lesser extent, their identities as Mashpee are not touched. Identity, in Clifford's account of the Mashpee trial, is the thing that works against registering discontinuities, ruptures, radical cultural breaks, and transformations.

This kind of critique of Clifford's account was offered by Walter Benn Michaels in an essay (that turned into a section of *Our America*) which was in turn contested by several later critics in an ongoing debate about identity, race, and culture. Michaels argued that while Clifford found claims of cultural continuity to be problematic, the notion of identity that he turned to instead was no less problematic, since Clifford's terms of "reinvention" and "remembering" could succeed only via a suppressed notion of biological—that is, racial—continuity. While Michaels's critique of Clifford was framed within a larger questioning of the notion of cultural survivals and cultural continuity—notions I defend in chapter eight in theory, if not always in anthropological practice—his critique of Clifford's use of identity follows largely the outline I have suggested here. Michaels, for instance, argued that identity provided a non-existentialist account of group ontology:

> Clifford rejects culture as a mark of identity because culture tolerates no discontinuities. But he himself can tolerate discontinuity only if it is grounded in a continuity that runs much deeper than culture: drumming will make you a Mashpee not because anyone who drums gets to be a Mashpee but because, insofar as your drumming counts as remembering a lost tradition, it shows that you already *are* a Mashpee. The point here is not that Clifford is secretly depending on some notion of racial identity but that his rejection of cultural identity gets him no further away from racial identity than does the more usual insistence on cultural identity. The problem, in other words, is with the claim for identity. ("Race" 681n36)

In the *Critical Inquiry* debate two years later, Daniel Boyarin and Jonathan Boyarin on the one hand, and Avery Gordon and Christopher Newfield on the other, contested Michaels's critique of Clifford and his argument against identity; Michaels also printed a response to both articles.

Recognizing Michaels's essay's "extraordinary theoretical importance" both to their own project of analyzing "the ancient dialectic between Paul and the Rabbis on the status of Jewish ethnicity" and for American debates about race and ethnicity (702), the Boyarins make the excellent point that Michaels's argument sometimes lacks a "model of *learning* or *transmission*"

(704). The Boyarins insist on the aspects of generational transmission and early learning as a non-racial logic for cultural continuity, for nostalgia for early childhood practices, and for the joining of affect to practices and values that may be partly remembered (704–5). Their argument appears entirely valid so far as it goes: intergenerational transmission and cultural learning are obviously non-racial (and entirely Boasian) accounts of culture and its continuities and affects.

The problem is that these points do not really qualify Michaels's original critique of Clifford's use of identity, or of his more general argument that race frequently continues to ground our sense of cultural appropriateness. Clifford, after all, invokes identity precisely *because* intergenerational transmission and cultural learning were frequently discontinuous among the Mashpee. It is precisely these same qualities of cultural discontinuity between generations and in terms of early learning that characterized Momaday's life as Kiowa and his protagonist Abel as Jemez and Bahkyush: while there are clearly some aspects of childhood nostalgia and intergenerational transmission and affect at work for both author and character, Momaday's turn to identity, "blood memory," and "racial memory" unapologetically reinvokes race in the form of identity. And it is precisely not intergenerational transmission and early cultural learning that can save Morrison's "brown girls," whose assimilationist school learning continues "the rest of the lesson begun in those soft houses with porch swings and pots of bleeding heart: how to behave" (83), from an ultimately racial grounding of cultural identity.

Avery Gordon and Christopher Newfield's response to Michaels is framed by their reading of him in terms of a dominant "liberal racism," a socialized position in "white philosophy" that he shares with (he might be surprised to learn) Arthur Schlesinger Jr.[11] Gordon and Newfield are often as concerned with the effects of this liberalism's individualism, dehistoricization of cultures and identities, and purported "color-blind outcome" (744) as they are with Michaels's actual argument. The most trenchant elements of their critique of Michaels's contentions are, I think, that Michaels ignores antiessentialist accounts of identity, and that Michaels misreads Clifford's account of Mashpee culture, history, and identity, especially by employing the "simplistic culturalism" of stereotyped drumming as the index of what it takes to make someone Mashpee or not (743–44, 748). While Gordon and Newfield believe that Clifford "traces the Mashpee's defeat to the court's demand for an essential group *identity*," but later say that "*culture* comes up as the demand of the court" (745; emphases added), in my reading it is the latter that is true, not the former, and the court's method of answering the legal question of tribal status through reference to *cultural* continuity is replaced by

Clifford himself later as the question of Mashpee *identity,* not culture. There is, indeed, a certain terminological slippage about what identity and culture mean in their critique.[12] It may be true that the criterion of drumming simplifies too greatly the question of what counts as culture. Is the unit of culture a single practice, an entire tribally distinct way of life, or something in between, as John B. Gatewood has productively asked ("Reflections")? But Gordon and Newfield's disinterest in any performative criteria for culture seems to me to support the argument that identity is a way of transforming the question of who you are away from existential cultural description toward essence, Gordon and Newfield's disavowals of ahistorical essentialism notwithstanding. As for the question of antiessentialist accounts of identity, I will suggest that one of the "pioneers" of antiessentialist identity named by Gordon and Newfield, Gloria Anzaldúa (744), actually had a fairly essentialist notion of identity.

Gordon and Newfield, like the Boyarins, thus fail, in my estimation, to undermine Michaels's primary argument that race continues to underwrite claims of cultural identity, and that identity is always an essentialist account. While I have argued against Michaels that we can have forms of cultural pluralism that do not depend on race or identity, my argument that identity first emerged as a language for national character, and then for cultural nationalist literary expression as a way to counter the insufficient group ontology of mere cultural description, supports his more general thesis that identity solves the problems of cultural continuity and appropriateness by ascertaining first what one's race is. In his response, Michaels takes the opportunity to emphasize that cultural identity should be "crucially dependent precisely upon one's actual experience" and that the Boyarins' example of the converted Jew "reiterates rather than refutes the primacy of actual practices and experiences" ("No-Drop" 760–61). He tangentially addresses what I take to be the most probing questions of the Boyarins' essay, that "their discussion of cultural and linguistic transmission does suggest the possibility in their view of a certain discrepancy between at least the language children actually speak and the language that will count as theirs" (761n3). But here again, Michaels emphasizes that one's actual culture (he continues to use the word "identity") must depend on what one actually does, not on (if it is different) the culture that one was raised in.

The Boyarins' suggestion that we need to pay attention to issues of intergenerational transmission and early childhood learning is a valid complication of Michaels's argument rather than a refutation of it. These two questions, coupled with a more complete anthropological account of what the smallest unit of culture is (and therefore at what level "cultures" can be said to mix and be learned), are the only cracks in this argument so far. But these cracks do not open the door for identity: rather, they open the door for further and finer-grained historical particularism. Such intricacies suggest that Michaels's argument generates a powerful set of questions—how are the terms "race," "culture," "identity" being used, and are culture, history, and memory being learned or understood as inherited?—that must be asked anew of each situation in which the concepts are in play.

I have argued that Toni Morrison and N. Scott Momaday ground their post-assimilationist third-phase inaugural multiculturalist novels in a model of being that, while paying some attention to actual cultural practices and values of characters, also grounds African American and Native American identities in race, and that this structure holds true generally for much literary multiculturalism. While Momaday bases his work on significant anthropological research on Kiowa and Jemez cultures, Native *identity* is upheld even when problems like intergenerational transmission and childhood learning are precisely the very *cultural* processes in question. We need to assess claims about culture, race, and identity on case-by-case bases: the word "identity" might hide actual cultural description and learning, but conversely, the word "culture" might conceal an identity-based notion of racial continuity and appropriateness. While identity began as a supplement to the work of cultural description in the genealogy of literary multiculturalism, it frequently ends up a substitute for the work of cultural description in providing multiculturalism's account of group ontology.

CHAPTER 8

Ishmael Reed and the Search
for Survivals

The [Bandung] conference called for a renewal of
the ancient Asian and African cultures and religions.
Privately, Wright considered such resolutions
"pathetic exultations of past and dead cultures."

—Hazel Rowley, *Richard Wright,* 2001 (466)

A spectre is haunting america—the spectre of
neo-hoodooim. all the powers of old america have
entered into a holy alliance to exorcise this spectre:
allen ginsberg timothy leary richard nixon edward
teller billy graham time magazine the new york review
of books and the underground press. may the best
church win. shake hands now and come out conjuring.

—Ishmael Reed, "Black Power Poem," *catechism
of d neoamerican hoodoo church,* 1970 (3) [qtd. in
Fontenot 20]

Part of what was at stake for N. Scott Moma-
day's work between 1967 and 1976, roughly coterminous with the cultural
nationalism marking the first decade of the emerging paradigm of multiculturalism, was the problem of formulating a model for and substance of
cultural continuity across many generations. That search for continuity was
at stake for Momaday as a Kiowa, for his characters Abel as a Bahkyush and
Ben as a Navajo, and it was no less true for the Mashpee trial that James
Clifford examined in his essay in a decade in which multiculturalism was
consolidated, even as it faced challenges from the right (and the left). Identity
promised to solve the unimaginable actual complexity of cultural learning,
adaptation, translation, and mixing, a complexity always present in human
experience, but whose speed and intensity increased with modern migrations. Momaday turns to race as the grounds for thinking about cultural
continuity, describing things obviously learned—learned sometimes quite
laboriously—as lying like "memory" in peoples' "blood."

Like the third-phase Momaday, the first-phase Hurston had also been concerned with theorizing continuity. One theme common to both Hurston's

ethnography and fiction in the 1930s was her search for cultural survivals, or retentions, across many generations of African Americans and Afro-
Caribbeans, transversing the violent diaspora of the Middle Passage. How to
formulate that kind of cultural continuity without slipping into a racial basis
was a key problem with which Boasian anthropology struggled. Inaugural
multiculturalist writers in the 1970s and 1980s sometimes turned to this
anthropological account to formulate cultural continuity through the model
of cultural longevity and endurance, and sometimes the substance of that
continuity, as established by a previous generation of anthropologists. Such is
the case in Ishmael Reed's work in the late 1960s and early 1970s culminating
in the 1972 *Mumbo Jumbo,* and Gloria Anzaldúa's work in the 1980s culminating in her 1987 *Borderlands/La Frontera: The New Mestiza.* Reed looked
back explicitly to Zora Neale Hurston's 1930s work, and Anzaldúa looked
back (less explicitly) to Américo Paredes's 1950s work. Reed and Anzaldúa
were deeply interested in what these two anthropologists (and other ones)
had to say about the possibilities for cultural survivals in otherwise mod-
ernizing and assimilating populations. What makes them exemplary of the
third phase of multiculturalism is their turn against the liberal-consensus
sociologically modeled assimilationism, and their turn to anthropology for
both the model of minority culture and the substance of what was in that
culture. But like Momaday, Reed and Anzaldúa ultimately ground African
American and Chicano cultural retentions in race, thus erasing the hard-won
conceptual disengagement of culture from race that had been the orthodoxy
for Hurston and Paredes.

Walter Benn Michaels, however, has argued that the earlier search for
retentions undertaken by Hurston and Herskovits was no less racial than the
kind of survivals hypothesized by Reed and Anzaldúa. Herskovits's exploration of the possibilities of retention was inseparable from race, according to
Michaels, "for in his identification of the Negro 'people' and, more particularly, in his characterization of African customs as part of that people's past,
Herskovits turns out to lean more heavily on the concept of racial identity
than his culturalist rhetoric suggests" (*Our America* 126). Herskovits, says
Michaels, wants to "guarantee an unbroken chain of (cultural) Africanisms
and so avoid any appeal" to race, but is ultimately unable to do so: "For the
fact that some people before you did some things that you do does not in
itself make what they did part of your past. To make what *they* did part of
your past, there must be some prior assumption of identity between you and
them, and this assumption is as racial in Herskovits as it is in [Countee] Cullen or [Oliver] La Farge" (127). For Michaels, Herskovits's theorization of
African cultural retentions culminating in his 1941 *Myth of the Negro Past*

was always underwritten by an unacknowledged logic of race and identity, thus suggesting that the anthropological project of understanding cultural continuity was always already grounded in the racial ideas that it sought to repudiate.

When Boasian anthropology began to theorize cultural continuity, race was always a risk. Historical particularism could explain in a non-biological way how a specific culture might overlap a phenotypically distinct descent population. Indeed, the development of rural Southern African American culture could be seen to be one such development of a culture that, while not entirely separate from the larger dominant culture and sharing many traits with it, was nonetheless for historical reasons such as slavery and segregation a *relatively* distinct descent population with *relatively* distinct cultural practices and values. Historical particularism was an approach to the culture of a descent population that recognized cultures as creative and under constant transformation, both from within and from contact with other cultures. Cultural anthropology's answer to the question I posed in the last chapter—why does it make sense for the Kiowa to be still Kiowa after their cultural transformation?—is that the Kiowa are still Kiowa after adopting most of the facets of Crow culture because they formed a somewhat continuous descent population and spoke the same language. For the Kiowa there has been considerable continuity—traceable through language, family ancestries, and calendars—even amid more considerable discontinuities in how people actually lived, such that, for Momaday, it became advantageous to think of Kiowa as an identity instead of (or in addition to) a culture.

When the idea of cultural continuity is extended across an even greater time period with less traceable historical evidence, the theory of cultural continuity as retentions runs an even greater risk of racial logic. The question of African retentions across the Middle Passage was more abstracted because of the lack of specific family genealogies and historical records. Because specific continuities had to be assumed (or reconstructed) rather than traced through historical records or archaeological evidence, the group becomes abstracted to the point where, as Michaels suggests of Herskovits, it becomes a race, with individuals not actually sure of the cultural practices and values of their ancestors. Thus the question of African cultural retentions in the Americas is, for these reasons of the historical record's contingencies, already close to being racial.

But the empirical question of African retentions in the Americas need not be racial. Conceptually, one could hypothesize cultural continuities by examining similar cultural practices in different regions when a known historical population has traveled the distance between them. Such was

Hurston's work in the 1930s as she examined voodoo and hoodoo's religious origins in West Africa. Hurston was especially interested in African deities' transformation into the Haitian loas, which might be outwardly symbolized in Catholic iconography, but whose worship and traits retained qualities associated with African origins. Hurston's *Mules* and *Horse* established such continuities, but once she finished her ethnographic research, she did not carry on with these practices—that is, there is no evidence that she imagined her exploration of hoodoo as an exploration of her own past or heritage. Unlike Momaday, Hurston did not imagine Haitian voodoo as part of who she was, or as an ambition toward which she should appeal. The African survivals that she found were not part of her identity, her past, or a kind of memory awaiting discovery. She did not regard the religion that might possibly have been practiced by some of her ancestors as her proper religion.

Herskovits, however, sometimes slides from documenting cultural continuities to prescribing appropriate cultural traditions based on one's race. Describing learned rather than innate behavior, Herskovits nonetheless sometimes implies who should learn the behavior. This was not an intrinsically anthropological move. Hurston imagined the white houngan as a fully realized voodoo practitioner, despite the fact that this cultural practice was (presumably) not done by his ancestors, and would not be considered (by Herskovits) as part of his past. It is one thing, in other words, for Herskovits through "fieldwork in Suriname, Dahomey, Haiti, Trinidad, and Brazil" to conclude "that black cultures throughout the Americas were strongly influenced by African cultures" especially in the areas of music, religion, and folklore (Gershenhorn 59). That is merely an empirical question of cultural description without affect, the claims and evidence of which might be evaluated, as some of Herskovits's peers did. It is then another thing to recommend to a population that may or may not currently have that culture an affective stance toward it. While one might find evidence of African culture in the cultures of some African American populations, the mistake is imagining specific influences as an entire racial group's past. That amounts to noticing that some specific people do voodoo, and then reasoning about others who do not that it is nonetheless part of their African past. Herskovits's skid from cultural description to racial prescription suggests how dynamic the first phase of culturalist development was in the 1920s and 1930s. For all their differences, nativism and anthropology imagined culture in terms of continuity, but second-phase sociology imagined culture in terms of migrational discontinuities and intergenerational ruptures.

We should understand Herskovits's changing ideas between his 1925 article in *The New Negro* and his 1941 book *The Myth of the Negro Past* in terms of these contesting forces. As Jerry Gershenhorn notes, Herskovits in the mid–1920s

> minimized the differences between the cultures of blacks and whites. Toward that end, he argued that American blacks had absorbed mainstream American culture and that there was no distinct black culture. [...] Herskovits's assimilationist position paralleled the views of most mainstream sociologists, including the leading specialist on race relations, Robert Park of the University of Chicago. (62)

Herskovits's agreement with Chicago sociology's thesis on the absence of distinct African American culture suggests the anti-racist politics that anthropology and sociology shared. But by the late 1920s, "perhaps nudged by the work of Zora Neale Hurston and Arthur Huff Fauset" (Hutchinson 76), Herskovits had begun to question whether African cultural influences might account for distinctly African American speaking and singing styles (Gershenhorn 67). By 1928 he formulated a research program around this question, which over the next decade took him to Suriname, Dahomey, Haiti, Trinidad, and Brazil.

It was specifically in contest with sociology, which Herskovits in 1925 counted as authoritative on this question at least, that he formulated his most polemical account of African survivals in the United States in *The Myth of the Negro Past,* the research for which was requisitioned by Gunnar Myrdal for possible inclusion in *An American Dilemma.* This research pitted the sociological model of culture against an anthropological one. Myrdal's co-chair was Guy B. Johnson, a sociologist at the University of North Carolina, and the final 1944 research report reflected his, Frazier's, and Howard University political scientist Ralph Bunche's conception of African American assimilability much more than the African cultural retentions championed by Herskovits. Myrdal was irritated with Herskovits's interest in African cultural heritage (Gershenhorn 98), and agreed instead with Frazier that differences between white and black populations were pathological results of systemic racism (101). These parties understood the political dynamics of their different positions on African survivals: for Herskovits, "knowledge of the dynamism and strength of African cultures would improve African Americans' self-respect" (107), whereas for Myrdal and Frazier, seeing difference in terms of racist barriers buttressed the need for progressive antiracist legislation. Herskovits lost this battle between anthropological culture and sociological culture, though he eventually won the war, to use the same metaphor I previously used to describe the similar dynamic of Hurston's eclipse in the second phase. But this historical snapshot shows Herskovits, fighting a losing battle against the newly triumphant sociological model of culture, occasionally slipping into, as Michaels has suggested, a not very well disguised nativist (and thus racial) account of cultural continuity.

I thus disagree with Michaels's critique that the search for cultural survivals is intrinsically racial, because it was not so for Hurston, though it was sometimes so for Herskovits and, we shall see, Ishmael Reed. That Reed was not reading Herskovits but Hurston suggests that Reed's affective leap and transformation of survivals into a facet of racial identity was not a component of the anthropological discourse with which he worked, but possibly the result of the influence of "national" identity, or the result of like cause having like effect. Third-phase inaugural multiculturalist authors were not influenced by the nativist writing of the 1920s, despite the fact that they grew to share some qualities with its authors. What Herskovits, Clifford, and Reed show is that once we start talking about continuity, the notion of race is not so much built into it as it is an ever-present danger. It is a danger insofar as description slips on the grounds of actual immense complexity and becomes prescription instead: the labor needed is far less, and the affective product much greater. The question of cultural continuity need not be the same as the question of which past is yours, but in multiculturalism it would tend to become so.

Ishmael Reed, Zora Neale Hurston, and Religious Survivals

> A careful study of Negro churches, *as conducted by Negroes,* will show, I think, that the Negro is not a christian, but a pagan still.
>
> —Zora Neale Hurston to Franz Boas, "The Florida Expedition," probably Fall 1927

Hurston's interest in African cultural survivals in the Americas was primarily about religion, and to a much lesser extent music and dance. In the last section of *Mules* on hoodoo, and in most of *Horse,* she substantiates the continued cultural presence and creativity of West African religious traditions and gods. This focus on religion and voodoo deeply influenced Ishmael Reed in the late 1960s and early 1970s, becoming a central part of his inaugural multiculturalist novels as well as the theoretical and cultural ground for his critical essays of this period (his essay subtitled "The New Literary Neo-HooDoo" is included in Gayle's *Black Aesthetic*). As with Momaday during the same phase, the sources for thinking about cultural continuity were specifically anthropological, but, again as with Momaday, the logic for that continuity became racial rather than cultural. Reed transforms learned processes into biological ones; whereas for Momaday the key metaphor is memory in the blood, for Reed the key metaphor in *Mumbo Jumbo* is epidemiology.

Mumbo Jumbo is a hilarious satire of the Harlem Renaissance "in black and white," to use the subtitle of George Hutchinson's book. And while Hutchinson's recent revaluation is intended to break up the monolithic "white" power and cultural structures that in criticism either make the New Negro Renaissance fail or against which it succeeds (20), Reed turns the screw by conceiving of the Renaissance as merely one episode in a millennia-old struggle for power. "Someone once said that beneath or behind all political and cultural warfare lies a struggle between secret societies," Reed teasingly writes (18). On the one side is the "Jes Grew epidemic," a Dionysian "anti-plague" that moves the body to dance, song, and the pagan worship of nature; it is "the delight of the gods" (6). Against it is a better-organized society aimed at defending "the cherished traditions of the West"; as one character describes it,

> At the foundation of the aesthetic order which pervades this country is a secret society—an ancient society known as the Atonist Path which is protected by its military arm the Wallflower Order, those to whom no 1 ever asked, "May I have this 1?" (132)

Mumbo Jumbo recasts the Jazz Age's Harlem as one historical crisis in the epochal struggle between the two forces, and sees the New Negro Renaissance as a challenge to Western Civilization. While it makes reference to historical people, including New Negro authors of the period, the novel's characters are inventions; as a period satire rather than a roman à clef, its characters are sometimes types or composites.[1]

Reed's *Mumbo Jumbo* (1972)—as well (to a somewhat lesser extent) as his first two novels, *The Free-Lance Pallbearers* (1967) and *Yellow Back Radio Broke-Down* (1969)—is fundamentally enabled by the anthropological and fictional work of Zora Neale Hurston. Though Reed acknowledged "our theoretician Zora Neale Hurston" in his "Neo-HooDoo Manifesto" (21), the strength of this line of influence has not yet been sufficiently recognized.[2] Hurston's model of culture at first seems to allow Reed to understand Jes Grew as a set of cultural retentions in contemporary African American life that trace back to African origins. *Mumbo Jumbo*'s bibliography—part of the novel's paratextual apparatus, which includes footnotes and internal editorial comments—references two books by "Hurston, Zoran." Whether this is a typographical error or a playful attempt to throw us off the scent is not entirely clear. But his listing of *Mules and Men* and *Tell My Horse*[3] acknowledges the novel's debt to Hurston's substantiation of African American and Afro-Caribbean religion (as hoodoo and Vodun, respectively), folktales, music, and dance. In *Mumbo Jumbo,* these aspects are parts of a dynamic whole of a pagan system of nature worship. Hoodoo is the cultural survival, through voodoo, of West African paganism.

Introducing Pa Pa LaBas, whose name recalls that of the loa Papa Legba, the guardian of the crossroads between the material and spirit worlds (*Horse* 128–29; see also Gates, *Signifying* 23–25), Reed explicitly invokes anthropology's cultural retentions thesis, writing, "Whoever his progenitor, whatever his lineage, his grandfather it is known was brought to America on a slave ship mixed in with other workers who were responsible for bringing African religion to the Americas where it survives to this day" (23). LaBas is a root doctor and conjure man; his practices recall the hoodoo men Hurston apprenticed with in the second part of *Mules,* the formula and paraphernalia of rootwork at the end of *Mules,* and the service of the loas described (in their Rada aspects) in *Horse.* Also important is Hurston's account of how loas can possess or "mount" practitioners, which Reed uses for his own version of an inadvertent mounting of one character by Erzulie, "the pagan goddess of love" whose "husband is all the men of Haiti" (*Horse* 121). Reed uses the episode to show how "The Blues, Ragtime, The Work" are aspects of continual adaptation and creativity that "Jes Grew here in America among our people" (*Mumbo* 130, 128), and that are as powerful and authentic as Haitian voodoo.

Thus Hurston's ethnographies provide the content of African American religious and musical culture for Reed. Reed's work constitutes, as with Momaday's most obviously and Morrison's to a less obvious extent, an explicit turn to anthropological sources in order to fill out the practices and values— the content—of the minority culture that is the new object of a nationalist claim. Reed draws from Hurston not just the hoodoo and African content of some African American and Afro-Caribbean religion, dance, and music, but also the model of culture, with some important differences. The most obvious characteristics of culture shared by Hurston and Reed are longevity, endurance, and continued vital creativity. Thus while the Haitian envoy who is an ally of LaBas and Black Herman acknowledges that he is "closer to Africa than yourselves" (198), he nonetheless recommends that they serve those loas that Jes Grew in America. Unlike the Atonists, Jes Grew finds its roots in Africa but does not have a fixed creed or catechism; it is the medium of cultural continuity as adaptation and creativity.

Reed's treatment of hoodoo is a cultural relativist one, as was true of Hurston's Boasian defense of voodoo as "a religion no more venal, no more impractical than any other" (*Horse* 204). The aesthetic-religious struggle between Jes Grew and Atonism features the rejection of Western "universal" standards, now revealed in all their ethnocentricism as forces of intolerance and cultural imperialism. Jes Grew manifests in several different areas of a dynamic whole, including religion, dance, music, and literature. *Mumbo Jumbo* implies a contingent but historically particular relation among religious practices and the Ragtime of the 1890s and the Blues and jazz of the 1920s; these are elements of a common culture that began, to use LaBas's shorthand, in New Orleans, moved on to Chicago, and is coming to New York (25). African American culture is not something that ruptures easily even during the Great Migration, as Wright and Park thought it did. Like Hurston, Reed rejects Boas's implication that minority cultures gradually assimilate, the cultural transformation central to Chicago sociology and the integrationist paradigm of the second phase.

But Reed, like Momaday and Morrison, undoes one of the fundamental qualities of Boas's culture concept: that of its difference from, and irreducibility to, race. There is an ambivalent hint of this in Reed's description of LaBas, of whom "Some say his ancestor is the long Ju Ju of Arno in eastern Nigeria, the man who would oracle, sitting in the mouth of a cave, as his clients stood below in shallow water. [...] His father ran a successful mail-order Root business in New Orleans. Then it is no surprise that PaPa LaBas carries Jes Grew in him like most other folk carry genes" (23). The explicit invocation of genes here is resolved (for the moment) by the fact that Reed is referring to familial ancestry, not racial culture.

But when Reed introduced a 1990 edition of *Tell My Horse*—the anthropology that had been so enabling for him—with this argument, a racial, not familial, claim takes place:

> It is interesting to note that a growing number of psychiatrists and physicians are beginning to trace the mental and physical health problems of many blacks—in particular the lack of self-esteem—to the symbolic annihilation to which their culture is subjected by the white-pride school curricula and media. Perhaps another cause of this depression is the severance of any link to the images of their ancient religion. (xiii)

Here one could acknowledge the plausibility of the (unnamed) studies linking "white-pride school curricula" to "the lack of self-esteem" among African American students, and see the pluralist ethos at the heart of multiculturalism as a positive force to combat it. But how can anyone have an "ancient religion"? To have a religion is to have a certain set of cultural practices and values, but Reed's "ancient religion" proposes a pre-existing connection to a group of people who lived long ago, a connection that is racial instead of (as with LaBas) familial. Hurston investigated voodoo and defended it on the grounds of pluralism and relativism, but she never regarded it as her "ancient religion." On the contrary: Larry Neal's introduction to the 1971 edition of *Jonah's Gourd Vine* conflated her character's religion with that of his ancestors, and redescribed learned culture as practices to be "remembered." It is characteristic of what I will term the "multicultural complex" to treat cultures that one's ancestors had (or people who were possibly one's ancestors) as one's own culture, to treat culture as a kind of memory, and to stake identity claims not on description of what people do, but, as is done by Reed and Neal, on racial prescription.

In *Mumbo Jumbo,* 1920s America can be the site of an age-old struggle between the Atonists and Jes Grew because of Hurston's and Herskovits's anthropological retention thesis. "Jes Grew carriers came to America because of cotton," Reed explains early on (16). But what the novel proceeds to call "Jes Grew carriers," or "J.G.C.s," is at the center of the novel's ambivalence about whether African Americans "carry" a set of cultural traditions or a racial trait. As with Momaday's Francisco, who is representative of the idea that Jemez Pueblo, despite "four centuries of Christianity [...] still pray in Tanoan to the old deities of the earth and sky" (52), the J.G.C.s may only have made superficial concessions to dominant cultural practices that conceal a deeper cultural endurance. As with Hurston's voodoo practitioners who have appeared to embrace the Catholic saints, the Jemez Pueblo "have assumed the names and gestures of their enemies, but have held on to their own, secret souls; and in this there is a resistance and an overcoming, a long outwaiting" (*House* 52–53). As opposed to the syncretic tradition of Tosamah's Native American Church, Francisco continues to practice Tanoan religion, which he must do secretly in the 1880s (46) but can do openly in 1945.

Thus the question for this genealogy of multiculturalism is, does *Mumbo Jumbo* imagine the holding on to one's "secret soul" to be a cultural continuity or racial essence? The virus which has historically been "carried" by people of African descent might, after all, threaten people not of African descent—just as, to pursue the epidemiological conceit central to *Mumbo Jumbo,* smallpox and other Europe-developed diseases went on to ravage other parts of the world, including other "races." In fact, this is what happens in the novel's opening scene, with an early "outbreak" of Jes Grew (Ragtime in New Orleans in the 1890s) threatening white people—including someone who should have substantial immunity, a priest, of whom it is reported that

"He said he felt like the gut heart and lungs of Africa's interior. He said he felt like the Kongo:'Land of the Panther.' He said he felt like 'deserting his master,' as the Kongo is 'prone to do.' He said he felt he could dance on a dime" (5).

The epidemiological conceit might evoke what happens in *Seraph on the Suwanee*, where Hurston shows how African American music affects/infects white music, and her parallel observation about white Southern speech. Hurston fictionally inscribes the African American rural folk culture influences on white Southern rural folk culture and national music culture. This was, after all, another model of what assimilation looks like: not just one culture adopting that of the other, but an ongoing process of mutual interpenetration and influence. When Hurston has her white characters in *Seraph* share with her black characters a set of wide-ranging cultural practices that include vernacular expressions, religion, labor, and music, she is acknowledging such interpenetration and cultural diffusion. And when she finally has Arvay's son Kenny, who has learned to "pick a box" from the white family's black employee and friend, travel to New York to perform this music, she is inscribing the historical influence of African American music on national culture. The white bands in New York and New Orleans are "taking over darky music," one character protests, but this music is "not considered just darky music and dancing nowadays. It's American, and belongs to everybody" (176).

With Hurston's seeming approval, white people are adopting black cultural ways in music and dance, a process made possible by the Boasian understanding that such music and dance for reasons of historical particularism developed in a rural group characterized by cultural difference, but which, as learned material, could be learned by other groups. And so, to jump ahead to *Mumbo Jumbo*, Jes Grew is regarded as dangerous by the Atonists precisely because it can be caught by white people, whether in the form of Ragtime in New Orleans in the 1890s, or in the form of jazz in New York in the 1920s. To this extent, at least, Reed confirms Hurston's reading of the direction of cultural influence in American music and dance, and the historical particulars of how that process worked in New York's Harlem in the Jazz Age.

❧ Ishmael Reed's Clash of Civilizations

> Well anyway, the Pope continued, when African slaves were sent to Haiti, Santo Domingo and other Latin American countries, we Catholics attempted to change their pantheon, but the natives merely placed our art alongside theirs. Our insipid and uninspiring

saints were no match for theirs: Damballah, Legba and
other deities which are their Loa.

—Ishmael Reed, *Yellow Back Radio Broke-Down,*
1969 (153)

We can see that the movement from the clash of ideologies to the clash of civilizations should be understood as a movement from the universalist logic of
conflict as difference of opinion to the posthistoricist
logic of conflict as difference in subject position.
From this perspective, the rise in the United States of
racial and cultural difference as emblems of difference
as such might be understood as a rehearsal for the end
of ideological difference.

—Walter Benn Michaels, *The Shape of the Signifier,*
2004 (33)

While *Mumbo Jumbo* was written during the Cold War, the central struggle it portrays is organized around identities rather than ideologies. In this
sense, it anticipates the post–Cold War conflict between civilizations and
cultures, in the accounts of Samuel Huntington and Francis Fukuyama,
who argue that history has ended insofar as there is no serious ideological
contender to capitalism (Michaels, *Shape* 26). Huntington sees international
conflict as being organized around civilizations; anticipating him by about
twenty years, Reed sees the clash of civilizations as being the key structure
of world history. On this point, Reed agrees with his character Hinckle
Von Vampton, the head of the Knights Templar and organizer of the Wallflower Order's attempt to destroy Jes Grew before it can find its "text." Von
Vampton is impatient with the Marxism of Woodrow Wilson Jefferson,
the man he is trying to train to be a Negro spokesperson who will undermine Jes Grew from within. As he muses, *"W. W. would be all right if he'd
just avoid those Marxist-Engelian and sociological clichés. Economics, integration,
separation…capitalism. No one took this seriously. Why, this Soviet business would
blow over"* (78). Woodrow Wilson Jefferson, a refugee from poverty and religion in the South, is not unlike Richard Wright in his joining of the project
of integration with Marxism and sociology. From Von Vampton's point of
view, Woodrow Wilson needs to get over ideology and get with identity, the
authentic struggle that goes deeper than any momentary political conflict.

In one episode, W. W. is not allowed into a Harlem speakeasy (he is too
dark) with Von Vampton, who, flipping him three cents, tells him instead
to wait outside and buy an "August Ham." When W. W. asks what that is,
the exasperated Von Vampton replies, "Dammit, W. W.! An August Ham is a
watermelon. Don't you know your own people's argot? Get with it, Jackson,
maybe it will enliven your articles a bit. You still haven't made a transition

from that Marxist rhetoric to the Jazz prose we want" (100). One of the many ironies here is that the novel in general shares Von Vampton's analysis of where the struggle lies. To undermine the burgeoning Harlem Renaissance, Von Vampton sponsors a sleazy magazine called the *Benign Monster;* it is intended, with W. W.'s article contributions, to undermine the New Negro Movement from within by *"confus*[ing] *the state of Black letters"* and by *"pitt*[ing] *1 writer against the other"* (78–79). Von Vampton's strategy is to muddy the artistic and intellectual waters of the Harlem Renaissance by sapping its energy and undermining its artistic purpose, printing its poems and literary criticism between "acres of flappers' tits" (69) and using a critical idolatry of any flavor *"as long as it is limited to 1"* (76). His "2nd phase of the Wallflower plan" is a refinement of the first: the creation of a "Talking Android," a "'spokesman' who would furtively work to prepare the New Negro to resist Jes Grew and not catch it" (190), a *"pet zombie he could use any way he wanted to undermine Jes Grew. Tell it, it was promising but flawed. Tell it that it had a long way to go"* (139).

Von Vampton's plans for the Talking Android, the enemy within, fails when he cannot find a willing candidate, and his back-up plan to use skin lightener on W. W. likewise fails when the latter's preacher father arrives at Von Vampton's Long Island hideout and forcibly takes his son back to Mississippi "to heal yo' soul" (143). The last-ditch effort is to paint his Templar associate in blackface and represent him as "the dominant figure in Negro letters today" who recites bad Harlem poetry:

O Harlem, if you are a sea, why... why
Dat makes Lenox Ave. one of your many
Swift currents, grappling me as I
Beckon to big Black bucks—lifeguards
On de sho. Up on de sho O Harlem
Where jazz is a bather writhing in de
Sand and claw-snapping crabs do dey
Duty. Where dippermouthed trumpets
Summon de tides
Root-t-toot! Root-t-toot! Root-t-toot!
And de tom toms play in sea shells
Da-bloom, Da-bloom, Da-bloom-a-loom (158)

The imposter is exposed by LaBas and Herman, who, with Haitian help, have figured out the Wallflower plan.

Though himself an object of satirical critique in *Mumbo Jumbo*, Von Vampton (whose name and status as a white sponsor of the new Harlem writers suggest some affinity to Carl Van Vechten, friend of Hurston, Hughes, and others) as the leader of the Knights Templar, newly in charge of the Wallflower Order's defense of the Atonist Path against the Jes Grew epidemic, nonetheless correctly understands the stakes of "civilization" in this central conflict. He is the novel's villain, but he is dangerous and effective precisely because he comprehends (more than does W. W.) the Harlem Renaissance's challenge to Western Civilization.

In this clash of civilizations, one cannot authentically change sides. W. W. is understood to be a dupe of the Marxist rhetoric he employs, arriving from Mississippi with a bagful of clippings, "all the 487 articles written by Karl Marx and Friedrich Engels" (76). Three other characters try to change sides in this identity-based struggle, and, significantly, they are all dead by the end of the novel. Charlotte is a French apprentice to LaBas at the "Mumbo Jumbo Kathedral." She leaves for a stage career at the Plantation House (51), which sexualizes voodoo themes for an audience of *"bankers, publishers, visiting Knights of Pythias and Knights of the White Camelia, theatrical people, gangsters and city officials,"* thus pursuing the novel's theme that the Atonists constitute themselves through a suppression of the body (43). Her apartment is also a place where select white clientele are *"initiated into certain rites* [...] *of a sexual nature"* (44), among them Biff Musclewhite, who is "Curator of the Center of Art Detention" (42).

In a side plot, Biff is abducted by the *Mu'tafikah,* "art-nappers" who "were looting the museums [and] shipping the plunder back to where it came from" (15), possibly (it is not quite clear) with Charlotte's intentional help. When Biff later discovers Charlotte's association with one of the *Mu'tafikah,* he kills her. But the novel understands that Charlotte has cheapened what LaBas calls "The Work" in her decision to teach for money "diluted versions of the dances I have observed" (52). Charlotte paints her decision in terms of universal beneficence, saying to LaBas, "I want to take the benefits of all of the beautiful things you and Earline and Berbelang have taught me and give it to everyone" (52). LaBas is worried that the "Haitian aspects of The Work" might not be translatable in New York, but tepidly consents. Charlotte is not understood to have "Africa" in her "tones" like Hurston's white *houngan* Dr. Reser (*Horse* 257), but is a fraudulent practitioner of The Work that she does not authentically understand.

The second self-chosen traitor to white civilization is Thor Wintergreen, whose father is a rich benefactor and trustee of the very museums that Thor has pledged to help the *Mu'tafikah* raid. The *Mu'tafikah* is a pan-ethnic alliance of "Black Yellow and Red" and Brown (15), and the inclusion of Thor in the group is a point of contention, for some fear that he will betray them.

They discuss him in his presence in their hide-out, which serves as a way-station for the collection and return of cultural artifacts from First World museums to peoples in Nigeria, the Gold Coast, Upper Volta, the Ivory Coast, the Pacific Islands, the Cayuga and Onondaga Reservations, Central America, Egypt, South America, and elsewhere.[4] The brown Fuentes and the yellow Yellow Jack doubt the white Thor's sincerity, but he is defended by the black Berbelang. As Fuentes warns him about their museum-raiding plans, "We wouldn't tell you anyway, gringo. You just joined the group and how do we know that you won't tell. Your father is on the board of several museums, you might squeal on us" (85).

A similar declaration of doubt prompts this exchange:

> Look, if you don't trust me now, you never will, Fuentes. I've tried to prove myself. Make sacrifices.
> Sacrifices, huh? Liar like Cortez, Pizarro, Balboa and the rest of your "virile" Conquistadors who raped our motherlands.
> But what have Cortes and Pizarro or the others to do with me?
> You carry them in your blood as I carry the blood of Montezuma; expeditions of them are harbored by your heart and your mind carries their supply trains. You've changed your helmet for a frontier hat while I have changed my robes for overalls and a black leather jacket. The costumes may have changed but the blood is still the same, gringo. (86)

The danger in interpreting a satire like *Mumbo Jumbo* is to take its pronouncements too seriously. But through the novel's humor, Reed has his cake and eats it too: it is a send-up of the Jazz Age and its cultural politics, but it is also a novel of ideas that turns particularly on questions of culture, race, and identity. According to Fuentes at least, blood functions as Momaday suggests it does, as a kind of memory in which other people's experience and actions are latent, waiting to be recalled. The blood in question is not genealogical (Thor's ancestors were not conquistadors) but racial—that is, European blood. And while Robert Park had redescribed race as a kind of a "mask" that falsely signaled someone's culture instead of as a "uniform" that signaled inner loyalties, Fuentes's "costume" sees someone's cultural practices (what kind of clothes they wear) as something that will fail to conceal the essence of blood. Fuentes fears that blood will tell.

Berbelang's faith in Thor is pragmatic—"He's the only 1 among us who's able to enter a museum without arousing suspicion," he tells Fuentes (86)—but it is also investigative. "I'm just 1 man," Thor protests Fuentes's racial profiling to Berbelang. "Not Faust nor the Kaiser nor the Ku Klux Klan.

I am an individual, not a whole tribe or nation" (92). This becomes Berbe-lang's wager, as he explains: "That's what I'm counting on. But if there is such a thing as a racial soul, a piece of Faust the mountebank residing in a corner of the White man's mind, then we are doomed" (92). The question *Mumbo Jumbo* thus dramatically sets up is whether Thor can choose his own political and cultural affiliations—which side he is on in this clash of civiliza-tions—or whether he has a "racial soul" whose "blood" will demand to be heard. To answer this question, Berbelang has Thor guard Biff Musclewhite after he has been kidnapped by the group.

In a hilarious scene, Biff tries to talk Thor out of his support for the multiethnic *Mu'tafikah*. And as in other scenes, the humor does not so much subvert the ideas as help the medicine go down. Biff begins with a disquisi-tion on race and class in Europe versus America. "I know you look down on me because I come from one of the European countries under domination by stronger Whites than my people," Biff tells Thor. "We were your niggers; you colonized us and made us dirt under your heels" (111–12). He continues, "But in America it's different. [. . .] Only money counts": money transforms the European ancestries into matters of wealth (112). Class becomes no longer a matter of genealogies in America, because whites without pedigree (but with cash) can aspire through imitation to the white elites they would have been shut out of in Europe. Biff speaks the novel's truth that America transforms class differences into purer racial differences:

> Look, son, we are trying to save you. Your class. We used to run along-side your carriages in barefeet when you drove through our neigh-borhoods, and you would splash mud in our faces violate our sisters, flog our fathers; but we kept coming for more because we loved your beautiful clothes, your clean hair, the charming ladies riding beside you, the way you talked. (112)

America makes possible the whitening of the lower classes, transforming those who had been class "niggers" into white elites. "You are all we had," Biff pleads with Thor, "Against them. Against the Legendary Army of Marching Niggers against the Yellow Peril against the Red Man" (112). Biff articulates the alliance between dispossessed whites and aristocratic whites against dispossessed blacks, the nationalizing difference of race so central to the 1915 *Birth of a Nation*.

Against this language of identity Thor fights back, arguing that "this looting of the world's art treasures can't go on" (113). For Thor, the actual practices and values entailed in such robbings are indefensible: "I believe in their ways and reject yours. I can't sleep at night for the thoughts of your foul deeds" (113). But when Biff brings their struggle back to the terms of civilization and identity, such are the terms that not only he prefers, but that the novel prefers as well. And so he ratchets up the pressure on Thor:

> Son, this is a nigger [Berbelang] closing in on our mysteries and soon he will be asking our civilization to "come quietly." This man is talking about Judeo-Christian culture, Christianity, Atonism whatever you want to call it. The most noteworthy achievements of anybody anywhere. [...]
>
> I've seen them son, in Africa, China, they're not like us, son, the Herrenvolk. Europe. This place. They are lagging behind, son, and you know in your heart this is true. Son, these niggers writing. Profaning our sacred words. Taking them from us and beating them on the anvil of BoogieWoogie, putting their black hands on them so that they shine like burnished amulets. Taking our words, son, these filthy niggers and using them like they were their god-given pussy. Why... why 1 of them dared to interpret, critically mind you, the great Herman Melville's *Moby-Dick*!!
>
> [...] They're the 1s who must change, not us, they... they must adopt our ways, producing Elizabethan poets; they should have Stravinskys and Mozarts in the wings, they must become Civilized!!!! (114)

It is the aesthetic order of the civilization that must be defended at all costs; Jes Grew's rival aesthetics do not sufficiently imitate "Judeo-Christian culture, Christianity, Atonism." In one sense, Biff does not believe in biological racial superiority—it is not race that makes white people better but rather culture—and so the colored peoples of the world can and "must become Civilized." One could say that, like the normative sociologists, Biff is extending the model of cultural assimilation to racialized minorities, but underlining the direction of change that must take place. If Thor's friends the *Mu'tafikah* are cultural pluralists who join the first and third phases of multiculturalism, Biff represents the second phase's liberal consensus that racial minorities must "adopt our ways."

The point I am making here is not that Biff is not a racist, but that his argument with Thor does not turn on racial superiority. It is cultural superiority that counts; or rather, given that Thor has already criticized the cultural *practices* of Western Civilization (including imperialism, looting, and violence, a list to which *Mumbo Jumbo* rightly adds several other indictments), what counts is a notion of cultural *identity*. The pull of this identity is in the end too strong, and Thor, weeping, unties Biff Musclewhite and betrays his friends and the values he holds dear. In consolation, Biff gives him a charm with the

"Crowned Head of Charlemagne done in gold," which Thor kisses and fondles (115). Fuentes has turned out to be correct: Thor's "blood" has told, and his "racial soul" has finally declared its allegiance, despite Thor's purported conversion. Atonism is Thor's proper civilization, and his momentary opposition to it is understood to be a betrayal of who he really is. Race determines which side one is on in the clash of civilizations, and as if in repentance for his betrayal of who he really is, Thor commits suicide in prison.

The third convert in the clash of civilizations—who also must die—is a black Muslim named Abdul Hamid. With Abdul, what becomes clear is that the clash of civilizations imagined by Reed has a different shape from that imagined by Samuel Huntington. That shape assumes detail when Abdul debates LaBas and Herman at an anti-lynching fundraiser. Abdul opposes the latest Jes Grew outbreak, condemning the dancing: "that's just a lot of people twisting they butts and getting happy. Old, primitive, superstitious jungle ways. Allah is the way" (34). To Abdul, LaBas and Herman are aligning themselves with forces that hold back African American "progress" (34). But LaBas responds, "We've been dancing for 1000s of years [...]. It's part of our heritage"; Herman likewise follows up, asking Abdul, "Why would you want to prohibit something so deep in the race soul?" (34).

As with the extended debate that comes between Biff and Thor, the debate between Abdul on the one hand and LaBas and Herman on the other is laden with humor, but is also, in this novel of ideas, Reed's way of detailing the essential struggle he sees as characteristic of the African American cultural challenge to white America in the 1920s (and in the 1970s). What emerges is Abdul's essential similarity to the Atonists he pretends to oppose. "You are no different from the Christians you imitate," LaBas informs him: "Atonists Christians and Muslims don't tolerate those who refuse to accept their modes" (34–35). Like other Atonists, *Mumbo Jumbo* contends, Muslims live in fear of the body, and the novel symbolically links Abdul with the Wallflower Order when it describes him against "the wall where he has been standing watching the other people dance" (32). Like Atonism, Muslim insistence on monotheism is a form of theological intolerance: "where does that leave the ancient Vodun aesthetic: pantheistic, becoming, 1 which bountifully permits 1000s of spirits, as many as the imagination can hold," LaBas asks Abdul (35). Abdul appoints himself as the "arbiter for the people's tastes" (35) as the editor of a literary magazine, but also of what people should wear and whether they should dance. "Sounds as if you've picked up the old Plymouth Rock bug and are calling it Mecca," LaBas responds (36).

LaBas and Herman understand Christianity and Islam as forms of the same mania for unity and fear of nature that manifest as intolerance. The clash of civilizations, then, is not Islam versus Christianity, an opposition central to Huntington's hypothesis, but rather monotheism versus pantheistic paganism. (We should understand Abdul not only in the timeframe of the novel's 1920s setting, but also in the timeframe of its composition's recent history, that of the rise of the Nation of Islam in the 1960s and the assassination of Malcolm X in 1965: what is wrong for Reed with the black nationalism of the Nation of Islam is that it is premised on sexual self-repression and theological intolerance, like Christianity.) Abdul more or less concedes their critique but questions their political strategy:

> Look, LaBas, Herman. I believe that you 2 have something. Something that is basic, something that has been tested and something that all of our people have, it lies submerged in their talk and in their music and you are trying to bring it back but you will fail. It's the 1920s, not 8000 B.C. These are modern times. These are the last days of your roots and your conjure and your gris-gris. (38)

However, Abdul has gotten hold of the ancient Book of Thoth, the "liturgy" of Osiris's ancient dances, toward which the Jes Grew epidemic advances. This is the text that Von Vampton seeks to destroy lest Jes Grew achieve dominance, and the Wallflower Order kills Abdul to get it, though they do not find it. By the end of the novel, we discover that Abdul has translated its hieroglyphics, and the manuscript translation, rejected by a publisher, has been lost in the mail, though "maybe it will turn up someday" (200). But we also find out that Abdul has burned the original, linking him to the Atonist opposition to all that the Book stands for. "I have decided that black people could never have been involved in such a lewd, nasty, decadent thing as is depicted here. This material is obviously a fabrication by the infernal fiend himself!! So, into the fire she goes!! It is our duty to smite the evil serpent of carnality" (202). "Censorship until the very last," muses LaBas after reading the letter. "He took it upon himself to decide what writing should be viewed by Black people, the people he claimed he loved" (203), thus performing a function akin to the homogenizing of experience and expression the Talking Android was to effect. With the Book of Thoth burned (and the spread of music disabled by a Wallflower plan triggering the Great Depression to make radios too expensive), Jes Grew dies away—for now.

Reed thus collects a series of psychological forces on the side of Atonism—fear of the body, sensuality, and sexuality; intolerance of difference and the love of the monolithic, found in both its theology and its aesthetics; and a tyrannical will to power. Opposed to them are a pagan polytheistic love of nature; a celebration of the body and sexuality; and an openness to the manifold experience of lived life. To an important degree, Reed is talking about what Toni Morrison called "funk" in her novel published only two years before *Mumbo Jumbo*. And as with Morrison's funk, it is imagined as both a species-wide quality that everyone shares and a quality that is more specifically black, "something that all of our people have," as Abdul concedes, and which is suppressed by black people when they try to act white (as does Geraldine) or Atonist (as with Abdul). Thus Abdul, like Thor, tries to change his culture, and *Mumbo Jumbo* understands that in doing so they are mirror-image traitors to their identities. Like Geraldine, they ultimately cannot practice cultures that are not racially theirs.

It is worth commenting here that *The Bluest Eye* and *Mumbo Jumbo,* like Momaday's *House Made of Dawn,* do pose universalist (and not just pluralist and relativist) critiques of Western and Christian cultural practices and values. *House Made of Dawn* poses a devastating critique of Christian theology,[5] and its critique of modern forms of urban alienation and the desacralization of language can be understood to be posed not just from the point of view of another (Kiowa or Jemez) culture, but on universalist grounds. Likewise, the Western ascetic fear of the body and sexuality comes under universal critique in both *The Bluest Eye* and *Mumbo Jumbo:* this fear is a pathology for white people, not just the black people who try to imitate them. But the fundamental operation of these inaugural multiculturalist novels is to double that universal critique with an account of cultural pluralism that transforms their portrayals of the weaknesses and anxieties of white cultural practices into accounts of how these practices are (especially) not good for their characters Geraldine and Abdul (and Abel).

✄ The Moses Retention in Reed and Hurston

> It is my habit as a born-again pagan to lie on the earth in worship.
>
> —Alice Walker, *Same River Twice,* 1996 (25)

One of Reed's fascinating adaptations of Hurston's question of cultural survivals is his use of the Moses mythology. If Reed's misprinting of Hurston's name in his bibliography is accepted as evidence for the way he acknowledges but evades Hurston's critical importance for his work, his outright omission of Hurston's not very well known 1939 novel *Moses, Man of the Mountain* from his bibliography would seem to close the case. Its absence suggests a kind of anxiety of influence that Henry Louis Gates Jr., following Harold Bloom, sees at work in the African American literary tradition (see *Signifying*

113–21). *Mumbo Jumbo* has been seen as a kind of postmodern detective story (Swope), and the climactic explanatory whodunit—in this case, who Von Vampton and the rest of the Wallflower Order are—involves an explanation of the aesthetic-religious struggle that finds its roots in ancient Egypt. It is a struggle that involves the biblical and legendary Moses, and so involves the Moses of Hurston's novel. But Reed's crucial revision to Hurston's story is to go on beyond Moses to a pre-Mosaic Egyptian ancient mythology.

In Hurston's introduction to *Moses, Man of the Mountain,* she describes the novel's premise about Moses' life, which departs from Judeo-Christian orthodoxy:

> There are other concepts of Moses abroad in the world. [...] Africa has her mouth on Moses. All across the continent there are the legends of the greatness of Moses, but not because of his beard nor because he brought the laws down from Sinai. No, he is revered because he had the power to go up the mountain and to bring them down. (337)

Whereas anyone might have brought down the laws, Moses is conceived in this set of unorthodox legends as having magical power in his own right, power "to command God to go to a peak of a mountain and there demand of Him laws." This and Moses' ability over nature "calls for power, and that is what Africa sees in Moses to worship. For he is worshipped as a god." Hurston goes on to see these legends as cultural survivals:

> In Haiti, the highest god in the Haitian pantheon is Damballa Ouedo Ouedo Tocan Freda Dahomey and he is identified as Moses, the serpent god. But this deity did not originate in Haiti. His home is in Dahomey and is worshipped there extensively. Moses had his rod of power, which was a living serpent. So that in every temple of Damballa there is a living snake, or the symbol.
>
> And this worship of Moses as the greatest one of magic is not confined to Africa. Wherever the children of Africa have been scattered by slavery, there is the acceptance of Moses as the fountain of mystic powers. (337)

To make sure that the Moses legends and symbols are understood as cultural, not racial, retentions, Hurston points out, "This is not confined to Negroes. In America there are countless people of other races depending upon mystic symbols and seals and syllables" understood as Mosaic (337–38).

Moses, Man of the Mountain has nothing to do with Haiti or America; Hurston's introduction is intended to make the case why her fictional account of Moses' life matters for a contemporary audience. In many respects, her account closely follows the biblical Moses who is raised by the Pharaoh's daughter away from his brother Aaron and sister Miriam; who kills an Egyptian overseer and who must flee the Pharaoh's wrath; who is befriended by Jethro and who marries his daughter Zipporah. The key difference between the biblical Moses and Hurston's Moses—indicating possible debts to Mosaic legends—is an extended apprenticeship to Jethro and his natural magic before he meets God on Mount Horeb. Hurston's Moses is a pagan worker of "hoodoo" first (443), and the famous monotheist later. Like Jethro, he learns from nature how to work nature, eventually becoming more powerful than Jethro is; Moses' power is understood to be his own, not God's.

Moses, Man of the Mountain does not resolve its tension between Moses the wielder of natural magic and power in his own right, and Moses the consolidator of monotheism who draws his miraculous abilities directly from God. Jethro somehow sees their natural magic as evidence that "we done found out about the one true God" (449), and certainly the source of this tension may lie with the biblical record itself, where God appears to teach Moses the magic of the serpent-staff, the leprous hand, and the water turned to blood, which become "wonders that I have put in your power" (Exodus 4:21). After apprenticing with Jethro, Hurston's Moses goes to the "temple of Isis at Koptos" (447) to retrieve "the book of Thoth" (387), which,

> if you read it, will bring you to the gods. When you read only two pages in this book you will enchant the heavens, the earth, the abyss, the mountain, and the sea. You will know what the birds of the air and the creeping things are saying. You will know the secrets of the deep because the power is there to bring them to you. And when you read the second page, you can go into the world of ghosts and come back to the shape you were on earth. You will see the sun shining in the sky, with all the gods, and the full moon. (387)

As this passage makes clear, Moses' power after reading the book of Thoth is a kind of pagan "hoodoo" in a polytheistic natural world. This seems (somewhat uneasily) subsumed at the end of the Moses' life, when he climbs Mount Horeb because "He wanted to ask God and Nature questions" (592). Hurston's Moses, though "He's a two-headed man" (543), seems ultimately resolved as the monotheist of traditional Judeo-Christian theology.

But in Reed's revision of *Moses, Man of the Mountain* at the end of *Mumbo Jumbo,* he takes the two strains of Hurston's Moses and separates these out clearly, so that the first becomes a kind of pose in the service of the second. Reed rewrites some of Hurston's episodes to make Moses out as a charlatan. In doing so, Reed's account brings back this fundamental tension, undermining this important religious moment in which one tribal god among others becomes the Supreme God and object of the monotheistic tradition in Western civilization. This happens in particular as Reed investigates the book of Thoth, which, in fact, becomes in *Mumbo Jumbo* the very "text" that Jes Grew is seeking as its continuously creative "liturgy."

Mumbo Jumbo's dénouement occurs when LaBas and Herman arrive at the Hudson party to unmask Von Vampton and his sidekick. The struggle between Atonism and Jes Grew "all began 1000s of years ago in Egypt" as a difference between the brothers Osiris and Set, LaBas begins, commencing a thirty-page exegesis of the mythological origins of the struggle (160–90). Osiris, though a prince, is "allergic" to power, and prefers instead the "agricultural celebrations" involving "dancing and singing," which "was known as the Black Mud sound" (161). Reed links these fertility rituals to the ones detailed in Sir James Frazer's *Golden Bough,* though he rejects Frazer's characterization of the rites as "lewd" (161). Osiris becomes a master of the singing, dancing, and natural magic associated with the pagan worship, while Set was "the 1st man to shut nature out of himself. He called it discipline. He is also the deity of the modern clerk, always tabulating" (162).

As the power struggle between the two brothers develops, an artist named Thoth illustrates Osiris's dance steps, and the resulting Book of Thoth is a "litany to feed the spirits" by which "Osirian priests could determine what god or spirit possessed" someone; it is "the 1st anthology written by the 1st choreographer," to which people "could add their own variations" (164). Set plots against Osiris and his nature worship, eventually slaying him, and his wife Isis and followers Thoth and Dionysus are scattered. *Mumbo Jumbo* thus suggests an Egyptian origin for the pagan nature worship of West African and European religious rites (173). Unable to squelch the ongoing pagan rites, Set develops an alternative religion based on "Aton (the Sun's flaming disc)" (174); it becomes the world's first monotheism, deployed against the pantheism of Osirian tradition. From this religion, Atonists of all flavors develop; likewise, from Osiris's original pagan rites come the voodoo and hoodoo of Jes Grew, against which the Wallflower Order fights. When Constantine converts to Christianity centuries later, it marks the growing success of Atonism in putting down "the mystery Dionysus had brought from Egypt" (170). Jesus becomes the Atonists' most powerful development, since "They made him do everything that Osiris does, sow like a farmer, be a fisherman among men but he is still a *bokor,* a sorcerer, an early Faust" (170).

Reed's revision of Hurston's version of Moses places him in this epochal struggle between Atonism and Osirian religion, a struggle entirely absent in Hurston's Moses, for whom monotheism and natural magic exist in tension only from an orthodox Judeo-Christian theological perspective. Reed's Moses is at first drawn to Osirian mysteries, and eventually travels to Jethro to apprentice. He marries Zipporah to get at the "family secret" that Jethro holds, and uses both father and daughter for his own selfish ends (177). On Mount Horeb, Moses meets the specter of Set (instead of God, as in Hurston's version) who instructs him how to get the hidden Book of Thoth, but who also tells him he must revive the cult of Aton in Egypt. Reed's account of Moses' power reflects the quasi-authoritative sources of his 104-item bibliography that makes *Mumbo Jumbo* a work of serious research and fantastic legend:

> The VooDoo tradition instructs that Moses learned the secrets of Voo-Doo from Jethro and taught them to his followers. H. P. Blavatsky concurs: "The fraternity of Free Masons was founded in Egypt and Moses communicated the secret teaching to Israelites, Jesus to the Apostles and thence it found its way to the Knights Templar." But this doesn't explain why he received the Petro Asson instead of the Rada. My theory is that it was due to the fact that he had approached Isis at Koptos during the wrong time of the Moon and stirred her malevolent aspects thus learning this side of the Book. (186–87)

Moses, in any case, repudiates the Book and hides it in the Temple of Solomon, where it is found by Von Vampton centuries later during the Crusades.

As this passage makes clear, Reed's playful-but-suggestive account of Atonism and Jes Grew makes use of legend, history, and scholarship both dubious and uncontroversial. *Mumbo Jumbo* works like other conspiracy theories: by connecting the dots and weaving the true but little-known (the invasion of Haiti, the actual development of Atenism in fourteenth-century BC Egypt, and the founding of the Knights Templar c. 1118 AD in the Holy Land) with the painfully falsifiable legends and paranoid connections (that Moses' monotheism was a version of Egyptian Atenism and that President Harding was poisoned by the Knights Templar). Developed from this pseudo-scholarly apparatus is Reed's account of cultural survivals in the Americas, about which I would like to make two points.

First, *Mumbo Jumbo* stretches the hypothesis of cultural survivals geographically and temporally. If Hurston's oeuvre, as I have shown, worked to substantiate the verifiable and anthropologically factual retention of West African religious traditions in the Caribbean and the American South, Reed extends voodoo's sources all the way to the ancient Egypt of fourteenth century BC. Hurston's survivals work across several centuries—she is concerned with only one to four centuries before her ethnographic labors in the late 1920s and early 1930s. Reed's survivals need roughly another twenty centuries before the four Hurston's ethnography requires. Hurston's survivals work within a single migratory network across the Atlantic. Reed's retentions, meanwhile, encompass three or four continents. His is the more ambitious project; it is thus no accident (and this is my second point) that his account of cultural survivals, thus stretched, slides into a racial explanation. It is also the reason that his aesthetic-cultural contest is recast as a religious struggle, one that is essentially racial in its shape. Thus, while Osiris, Set, and Thoth are understood to be African and while Dionysius and Moses are understood to be Caucasian (more or less), the religious difference they set in motion eventually becomes matters of inherited identity. As Reed's central epidemiological metaphor shows, it is possible for white people to catch Jes Grew, but it is not exactly natural to them. And while black people like Abdul can suppress what is naturally theirs, that procedure of repression—understood, appropriately, as religious conversion—is critiqued at some length by LaBas and Herman, reflecting Reed's own Black Aesthetic in third-phase multiculturalism.

Another aspect of how Reed reconstellates the clash of civilizations and its cultural politics is his imagining, as I have noted, of the pan-ethnic alliance of the *Mu'tafikah,* the "art-nappers" (15). As we have seen, this alliance's members are African American, Chicano, and Asian American; while there is no Native American member, the *Mu'tafikah* does serve Native groups by returning their sacred relics from Western Centers for Art Detention. It is impossible for white Americans (like Thor) to join this group, however sympathetic they may be, since *Mumbo Jumbo* understands real membership to reflect a biological truth. This group somewhat reflects an actual set of publishing and literary alliances that Ishmael Reed developed during the third phase of the genealogy of literary multiculturalism in the late 1960s and 1970s, an alliance that eventually grew into the Before Columbus Foundation in 1976. The Foundation is "devoted to the task [*sic*] of redefining our notion of mainstram [*sic*] American literature to reflect this ocuntry's [*sic*] milticultural [*sic*], multiethnic, and multiracial diversity,"[6] and its poetry anthology, published by Norton, can be said to represent part of the growing official status of literary multiculturalism after the first decade of the third phase. The editors of the 1974 *Aiiieeeee!,* for example, thank Ishmael Reed and Leslie Silko in their preface, and one of the editors, Shawn Wong, became one of the co-editors, with Reed, of *The Before Columbus Foundation Poetry Anthology.*

There are interethnic connections among writers of this generation, many of them centering around Reed and Frank Chin. Such connections and interrelations are too numerous to account for completely in this study, and must await a more detailed literary history of this phase of literary multiculturalism, when writers became self-consciously pluralist, nationalist, and frequently interethnic in their literary politics. What I want to point out is that, by the third phase of the genealogy of literary multiculturalism, a number of the writers became self-conscious of the interconnections among different ethnic and racialized American groups in a way that was more profound and deeply influential than Hurston's momentary reference to the "Indian" to define her defiance of *Brown*. This awareness seemed to center on the West Coast and the Southwest, involving writers like Reed, Chin, many Chicanos, Silko, and others, and not Eastern and Midwestern writers like Morrison. Many of these writers shared with Reed a consciousness of a "trend" that "you are going to get other ethnic groups into the ballgame," as Reed put it in 1971. "I'm interested in what the Asians out here in California are doing. They combine their experience with that of other ethnic groups. A person like Frank Chin is influenced by black and white culture but in addition has an identity of his own. That engenders a hybrid that really fascinates and amazes me" (qtd. in John O'Brien 23–24). One such "hybrid" and (like Reed) transplanted Californian was Gloria Anzaldúa, whose 1980s *Borderlands/La Frontera* represented a culmination of third-phase multiculturalism.

⚘ CHAPTER 9

Gloria Anzaldúa, Aztlán, and Aztec Survivals

> [...] They had rushed
> across an ocean, swifter than the swift, numerous
> in loud migration as the African swallows
>
> or bats that circle a cotton-tree at sunset
> when their sight is strong and branches uphold the
>   house
> of heaven; so the deities swarmed in the thicket
>
> of the grove, waiting to be known by name; but she
> had never learnt them, though their sounds were
>   within her,
> subdued in the rivers of her blood. Erzulie,
> Shango, and Ogun [...]
>
> —Derek Walcott, *Omeros,* 1990 (242)

> The short time he had been in Tucson, Sterling had
> begun to realize that people he had been used to call-
> ing "Mexicans" were really remnants of different
> kinds of Indians. But what had remained of what was
> Indian was in appearance only—the skin and the hair
> and the eyes. The cheekbones and nose like eagles and
> hawks. They had lost contact with their tribes and
> their ancestors' worlds.
>
> —Leslie Silko, *Almanac of the Dead,* 1991 (88)

Although Ma Kilman, "sibyl," has not learned the names of the African gods who crossed the Atlantic with the enslaved Africans, she nonetheless carries their sound in "the rivers of her blood," and it is through their continued presence in the Caribbean that she finds the cure for Philoctete's wound, a metaphor in Walcott's poem for the ongoing destruction and (incomplete) cultural erasure wrought by historical slavery. The cure is enabled by a cultural survival somewhat like Reed's—the enduring presence of African gods in the New World—and that is, again like Reed's, manifested not so much historically but as something in the "blood." Walcott, the St. Lucian poet who wrote (and set) part of *Omeros* in the United States, thus contemplates such survivals and their destiny in the Caribbean and in North America. Such becomes apparent when one character witnesses the Sioux "waltzers in their ghost dance" (181), the religion (examined by Mooney) premised on the prophesied disappearance of white people and white cultures from North America.

Like Walcott's *Omeros*, Leslie Silko's *Almanac of the Dead* was another famous work of multicultural literature of the early 1990s that imagined cultural survivals from Africa in terms of the African gods that crossed the Middle Passage. This theme is developed through a series of vignettes about Silko's African American character, Clinton. Clinton is a black nationalist, but not an Afrocentric one because he feels connected to the North American continent, a "connection the people had, a connection so deep it ran in his blood" (414–15). The connection to the land comes not just from his few Cherokee ancestors, but also from "the realm of the spirits" (416). As the narrator describes Clinton's views, he "wanted black people to know all their history; he wanted them to know all that had gone on before in Africa; how great and powerful gods had traveled from Africa with the people" (416). Escaped slaves and indigenous Indians had together "discovered a wonderful thing: certain of the African gods had located themselves in the Americas as well as Africa: the Giant Serpent, the Twin Brothers, the Maize Mother, to name a few" (416). While the Europeans had left their God behind in Europe—the Christian God, after all, is he who exiled Adam and Eve, the first forced migration—the African gods had arrived to make a home in New World soil. "Ogoun, Eurzulie, and Damballah" arrive, and are changed, in the Americas (417). African religion is his even before he consciously embraces it: the "cutting metal edge of the knife was Ogou's favorite dwelling," and Clinton feels its power "long before he studied African religions in black studies and realized his family's regard for knives was a remnant of old African religion" (413). As with Larry Neal's interpretation of Hurston's preacher and as with Walcott's Ma Kilman, one worships one's ancestor's gods unconsciously, even if one does not know their names: such is what counts as one's "history," which is what happens not to a person, but to that person's ancestors and, more broadly, to that person's race.

Walcott alludes to Wovoka's prophesy about the disappearance of white people from the continent, but this prophecy becomes the premise of Silko's novel. It is because "slavery joined forever the histories of the tribal people of the Americas with the histories of the tribal people of Africa" (428) that indigeneity is extended by the Laguna Pueblo Silko to African Americans and the ancient African gods. Silko thus sees the alliance between Native people and African Americans—and Mexicans on either side of the border, two of whom are forcefully told, "*You* are Indians!" (114)—as part of a hemispheric tribal alliance that is moving toward a clash of civilizations that, as with Reed's struggle between Atonism and Jes Grew, mirrors the structure of Huntington's thesis even if the content is not quite what Huntington imagined. As Walter Benn Michaels puts it,

> Books like *Beloved, Maus,* and *Almanac of the Dead* imagine societies organized by identity. The injustices against which they protest fundamentally involve disrespect for difference; their murdered bodies (six million Jews, sixty million and more African-Americans, another sixty million Native Americans) died, as these novels understand it, for their cultures, the victims of genocide and Holocaust. (*Shape* 150)

When Wilson Weasel Tail, a Lakota "poet lawyer" (713) invokes the Paiute prophet's ghost dance prophecy, the disappearance of things white from the Americas is understood to be the culmination of this struggle of identity:

> "Moody and other anthropologists alleged the Ghost Dance disappeared because the people became disillusioned when the ghost shirts did not stop bullets and the Europeans did not vanish overnight. But it was the Europeans, not the Native Americans, who had expected results overnight; the anthropologists, who feverishly sought magic objects to postpone their own deaths, had misunderstood the power of the ghost shirts. [...]"
>
> Moody and the others had never understood the Ghost Dance was to reunite living people with the spirits of beloved ancestors lost in the five-hundred-year war. (722)

Weasel Tail's criticism of "Moody" (which I read as Mooney, another slightly suppressed anthropological enabler like Reed's "Zoran") is a correction rather than a repudiation of anthropological culture. It is after all true, Clinton reflects, that "a lot of the African-American studies classes had been bullshit honkie sociology or psychology. Having a black professor didn't make it the gospel" (420), and it is sociology's discontinuities that are bullshit, rather than anthropology's cultural continuities and survivals. Like Reed, Silko concedes the abstract possibility of people switching sides in the apocalyptic battle of identities, and the tribal alliance adopts the policy that "Europeans were welcome to convert, or they might choose to return to the lands of their forebears to be close to Europe's old ghosts" (737). But when the dust settles after 750 pages—and as the main event is about to begin—the characters still living, as with Reed's *Mumbo Jumbo*, are true to their race's proper religion.

Thus one of the tropes of the pan-ethnic multicultural alliance in this third phase of the genealogy of literary multiculturalism—imagined by

Reed in *Mumbo Jumbo* and instantiated by him and Chin and others in the 1970s—was the fundamentally anthropological notion of minority cultural continuity, a continuity often rendered as a kind of cultural retention bridging migrations. And one way of imagining those cultural survivals was to suggest that African gods traveled to the Americas, as do Reed, Walcott, and Silko, as well as Hurston before them. Hurston's anthropology enables this move, and not, Silko's Clinton knows, the sociology which, even when mouthed by black professors, saw rupture and discontinuity across the Middle Passage. Sociology had no language for this kind of cultural continuity, a fact revealed by Richard Wright's confusion in Ghana when he witnessed dancing that echoed Southern practices: "What did that mean? He had always insisted that race was a social myth, not a biological fact, and that the very word 'race' should be put in quotation marks" (Rowley 423). Wright correctly intuited how such continuity was dangerously close to a racial logic. Anthropology's historical particularism provided the alternative logic that Wright did not possess.

Third-phase multiculturalism envisioned returning to one's true gods as an identitarian project. Like Silko's *Almanac* and Walcott's *Omeros,* Gloria Anzaldúa's *Borderlands/La Frontera* was a third work composed in the 1980s that envisioned not just the endurance of pagan gods in the Americas, but the pluralist politics of discovering their names. *A Genealogy of Literary Multiculturalism*'s decade-and-a-half jump from the 1972 *Mumbo Jumbo* to the 1987 *Borderlands/La Frontera* in this last chapter is meant to gesture at the themes and politics that third-phase multiculturalism consolidated and intensified in the 1980s. It is with *Borderlands* that the group ontology of identity, implicit and emerging in Morrison, Momaday, and Reed, becomes the explicit organizing principle for the group.

What Means Aztlán to Me?

> Part of the blood that runs deep in me / could not be vanquished by the Moors. I defeated them after five hundred years, / and I endured. / Part of the blood that is mine / has labored endlessly four hundred / years under the heel of lustful / Europeans. / I am still here!
>
> —Rudolfo "Corky" Gonzales, *I Am Joaquín,* 1967 (82)

Like Reed, Silko, and Walcott, Gloria Anzaldúa imagined cultural continuity and the continued presence of the old gods; for Reed and Anzaldúa at least, this continuity is achieved through the mediation of cultural anthropology.

Anzaldúa's debts to (and feminist revision of) Américo Paredes have been widely recognized,[1] but the extent of her use of anthropology's culture and its contents has not received much attention. Like Paredes, Anzaldúa was born in the Rio Grande Valley, and as with Paredes, her understanding of the border turns on its function as both the site of a particular culture with a specific history and a larger metaphor for cultural conflict. *"With His Pistol in His Hand"* and *Borderlands/La Frontera* start with history, including the history of American imperialism in the Southwest (also formative to Momaday's *House* and Silko's *Almanac*). Central to both Paredes's and Anzaldúa's accounts is the 1848 treaty that placed an artificial border through the middle of a culture, inaugurating the Mexican-influenced border culture that was not identical to Mexican culture. The border is both a historically specific geography and a broader metaphor for postcolonial politics and identities. As Anzaldúa famously puts it, "The U.S.-Mexican border *es una herida abierta* where the Third World grates against the first and bleeds" (25).

But if Paredes's history starts with the Spanish settlement of Nuevo Santander in 1749, Anzaldúa's history begins roughly 35,000 years before with the Bering Strait migration into the Americas. Importantly revising Paredes's account of the border, Anzaldúa makes central indigenous peoples' historical and ongoing presence. "In the Southwest United States," says Anzaldúa, "archeologists have found 20,000-year-old campsites of the Indians who migrated through, or permanently occupied, the Southwest, Aztlán" (26). Mexican people were thus the original inhabitants of Aztlán:

> In 1000 B.C., descendents of the original Cochise people migrated into what is now Mexico and Central America and became the direct ancestors of many of the Mexican people. (The Cochise culture of the Southwest is the parent culture of the Aztecs. The Uto-Aztecan languages stemmed from the language of the Cochise people.) The Aztecs (the Nahuatl word for people of Aztlán) left the Southwest in 1168 A.D. (26)

When the "Spanish, Indian, and *mestizo* ancestors explored and settled parts of the U.S. Southwest as early as the sixteenth century" (27), it was for some a return to a homeland: "For the Indians, this constituted a return to the place of origin, Aztlán, thus making Chicanos originally and secondarily indigenous to the Southwest" (27). If Paredes's counter to the racist Anglo charge that Mexicans should "go back to Mexico" (Anzaldúa 75) was the historical argument the U.S. Southwest *was* where they came from (beginning in 1749), Anzaldúa doubles this indigeneity by suggesting that the "new hybrid race," *"una nueva raza, el mestizo, el mexicano"* settling in the Southwest in the sixteenth to eighteenth centuries were returning to the ancient home of their ancestors (27). Even late twentieth-century Mexican immigration into the U.S. Southwest is part of *"El retorno* to the promised land" of Aztlán that has been ongoing for the past four or five centuries (33), argues Anzaldúa, and it is a return whose acceleration Silko for her part imagines as hastening Wovoka's apocalypse, an idea Anzaldúa shares (85–86).

In *The Lost Land: The Chicano Image of the Southwest*—a key source for Anzaldúa's *Borderlands,* quoted heavily in its first chapter—John R. Chávez writes, "Over the last 130 years [since 1848] the myth of the lost land has served as a focus for Mexican nationalism in the Southwest" (4–5). In the late 1960s, Chávez notes, Chicano cultural nationalism took the form of "repeated Chicano allusions to the ancient Aztec homeland of Aztlán," and the adoption of the term was encouraged by Rudolfo "Corky" Gonzales, though "in modern times the term was first applied to the Chicano home-land in 1962 by Jack D. Forbes, a Native American professor who argued that Mexicans were more truly an Indian than a mestizo people" (5, 141). Thus one difference between the second-phase Paredes and the third-phase Gonzales and Anzaldúa is the former's anticipatory, non-nationalist nostalgia for the disappearing border culture which itself previously subsumed dis-appeared "Indian" cultures, and the latter two writers' embrace of a cultural nationalism articulated through the discovery of Aztec ancestors (Oscar Zeta Acosta also spoke of himself as an "Aztec lawyer" in his 1972 *Autobiography of a Brown Buffalo)* and the reconceptualization of the Chicano Southwest as the mythic Aztlán.[2]

Anzaldúa's Chicano culture is like Paredes's Mexican American culture in that it is historically particular, but it is a history with a difference. The other Boasian principle informing their work is dynamic holism, that different facets of social life are interdependent and mutually constitutive. Paredes's anthropology centered on the oral tradition as a way of accessing the cul-ture itself, and Anzaldúa likewise attends to the oral tradition (Saldívar-Hull, Introduction 10), citing *corridos* (82–83), contemporary music (47), folk-tales (87) and sayings (77, 84). As Anzaldúa says, in words that might well have come from *"With His Pistol in His Hand,"* "The everpresent *corridos* narrated one hundred years of border history, bringing news of events as well as entertaining. These folk musicians and folk songs are our chief cultural mythmakers, and they made our hard lives seem bearable" (83).

The oral tradition, as Boas understood, encodes cultural values, or, to update the point, contested cultural terrain. One example Anzaldúa offers is *"En boca cerrada no entran moscas.* 'Flies don't enter a closed mouth' is a saying I kept hear-ing when I was a child," and its lesson is a cultural one about gender: *"Hocicona, repelona, chismosa,* having a big mouth, questioning, carrying tales are all signs of being *mal criada.* In my culture they are all words that are derogatory if applied to women—I've never heard them applied to men" (76). Her account of Chicano oral tradition is holistic, understanding its role in conveying sexual mores and gender relations.

Anzaldúa's analysis of Chicano culture develops through her investigation of language, which takes on the peculiar hue, at times, of the Sapir-Whorf Hypothesis. The complex linguistic situation on the border is described by eight distinct languages and dialects available to border Chicanos, and "Chicano Spanish," of which there are regional variations, is a "living language," "*un lenguaje que corresponde a un modo de vivir*" (77). Chicano Spanish reflects a way of life and grounds the primary group concept of identity: it is "a language which [Chicanos] can connect their identity to, one capable of communicating the realities and values true to themselves" (77). Distinct language differences marking Chicano culture were generated by historical factors, such as the "250 years of Spanish/Anglo colonization" (79).

One of Anzaldúa's most important revisions of Paredes's construction of border culture is her critique of its patriarchal elements. For Paredes, the "natural equality among men" (10) in border culture and *El Corrido de Gregorio Cortez*'s celebration of manly courage and insistence in his right were seemingly neutral cultural observations, but ones which Anzaldúa and other feminists have interrogated in the last two decades.[3] Anzaldúa recalls her own rebellion against misogynist gender roles while growing up: "Instead of ironing my brothers' shirts or cleaning the cupboards, I would pass many hours studying, reading, painting, writing. Every bit of self-faith I'd painstakingly gathered took a beating daily. Nothing in my culture approved of me" (38).

Like her contemporaries Alice Walker and Maxine Hong Kingston, Anzaldúa critiques patriarchal practices of her minority culture and the way that those cultural practices are sometimes passed on and enforced by "male-identified women," as Sonia Saldívar-Hull calls them (Introduction 3):

> Culture forms our beliefs. We perceive the version of reality that it communicates. Dominant paradigms, predefined concepts that exist as unquestionable, unchallengeable, are transmitted to us through the culture. Culture is made by those in power—men. Males make the rules and laws; women transmit them. How many times have I heard mothers and mothers-in-law tell their sons to beat their wives for not obeying them, for being *hociconas* (big mouths), for being *callejeras* (going to visit and gossip with neighbors), for expecting their husbands to help with the rearing of children and the housework, for wanting to be something other than housewives? (*Borderlands* 38)

While the first three sentences are anthropological orthodoxy, the critique of male power constituted by culture signals Anzaldúa's forceful evaluation of the cultural traditions and values with which she grew up. As with Walker and Kingston, that ethical evaluation necessitates a confrontation not just with the men whose interests are served by such practices and values, but with other women who have been conditioned by it and enforce it on the younger generation of girls.[4]

Part of what is at stake in *Borderlands/La Frontera* is thus Anzaldúa's need to "leave home so I could find myself," an act that draws her away from "the Valley" and toward "entering the world by way of education and career and becoming self-autonomous persons" (38, 39). Her reading of Chicano border culture rereads male "protection" of women as fear of their physicality and sexuality (39). Her critique of misogyny in Chicano border culture is, importantly, joined to her critique of its homophobia, which it shares with other cultures (40). "Though I'll defend my race and culture when they are attacked by non-*mexicanos*," Anzaldúa declares, she is nonetheless willing to sort through her culture's values, particularly its gender roles: "I abhor some of my culture's ways, how it cripples its women, *como burras*, our strengths used against us, lowly *burras* bearing humility with dignity. The ability to serve, claim the males, is our highest virtue. I abhor how my culture makes *macho* caricatures of its men" (43). Anzaldúa's account of Chicano border culture is grounded in history, is composed of dynamic and mutually constitutive elements like gender roles, religion, language, and oral traditions, and is non-assimilative and pluralist.

✺ The Palimpsest Religions of *Borderlands/La Frontera*

> They destroyed our gods and made us bow down to a dead man who's been strung up for 2000 years.... Now what we need is, first to give ourselves a new name. We need a new identity. A name and a language all our own.... So I propose that we call ourselves... what's this, you don't want me to attack our religion? Well, all right....
>
> —Oscar Zeta Acosta, *The Autobiography of a Brown Buffalo,* 1972 (198)

If Reed's identity-based clash took place between two cultural continuities that were each more or less homogenous, Anzaldúa's clash is both intercultural (Anglo vs. Chicano) and intracultural (a masculinist Aztec warrior ethos vs. an embodied Indian women's tradition of resistance). "My Chicana identity," states Anzaldúa, "is grounded in the Indian woman's history of resistance."

Female resistance to patriarchy is thus as indigenous to the culture as the border Chicanos are to the Southwest: "I feel perfectly free to rebel and to rail against my culture. I fear no betrayal on my part because, unlike Chicanas and other women of color who grew up white or who have only recently returned to their native cultural roots, I was totally immersed in mine. [...] Not me sold out my people but they me" (43). Anzaldúa grounds her critique of Chicano patriarchy not through reference to abstract universal ideals of equality (for instance, women and men should share political and social power), but through a cultural archaeology that reads Indian women's resistance to Aztec and then Western patriarchy as a cultural survival. It is a picture that is developed through reference to the endurance of the old gods under the guise of the new, thus returning us to the dynamic established anthropologically by Hurston, feared by the nativist Lovecraft, suggested by Momaday, re-envisioned by Reed, and, after Anzaldúa, embraced by Silko and Walcott. One such prominent god is "*la Víbora,* Snake Woman" (48). If Hurston had established that the apparent Haitian worship of the Virgin Mary was a cover for the pagan African loa Erzulie (*Horse* 121), Anzaldúa establishes the similarly anthropologically imagined point that beneath Mary's currency in Mexican culture is Coatlalopeuh, the Snake Woman. While Acosta's humorously imagined nationalist speech, quoted in the epigraph to this section, backs off from rejecting Christianity, Anzaldúa's innovation is to uncover the Aztec palimpsest beneath the Christian form. She explains: "My family, like most Chicanos, did not practice Roman Catholicism but a folk Catholicism with many pagan elements. *La Virgen de Guadalupe*'s Indian name is *Coatlalopeuh.* She is the central deity connecting us to our Indian ancestry" (49).

Anzaldúa's cultural archaeology of the gods is central to both her feminist and her Indian revisions of Paredes's conception of Mexican American culture:

> *Coatlalopeuh* is descended from, or is an aspect of, earlier Mesoamerican fertility and Earth goddesses. The earliest is *Coatlicue* [...] mother of the celestial deities, and of *Huitzilopochtli* and his sister, *Coyolxauhqui* [...]. Another aspect of *Coatlicue* is *Tonantsi.* The Totonacs, tired of the Aztec human sacrifices to the male god, *Huitzilopochtli,* renewed their reverence for *Tonantsi* who preferred the sacrifice of birds and small animals.
>
> The male-dominated Azteca-Mexica culture drove the powerful female deities underground by giving them monstrous attributes and by substituting male deities in their place, thus splitting the female Self and the female deities. (49)

Coatlicue was split, so that Tonantsi became "the good mother," separated from "her dark guises" (49). This already-existing theological-cultural struggle was renamed under Spanish imperialism: "After the Conquest, the Spaniards and their Church continued to split *Tonantsi/Guadalupe.* They desexed *Guadalupe,* taking *Coatlalopeuh,* the serpent/sexuality, out of her" (49). Thus *"la Virgen de Guadalupe/Virgen María"* became "chaste virgins," while the sensual and sexual aspects left behind became "Beasts," "the work of the devil" (49–50).

As with Reed's religious palimpsest in *Mumbo Jumbo,* Anzaldúa describes processes whereby the Church takes the sexually repressive side of an already-existing pagan struggle (Set's Atonism vs. Osiris's fertility cults; the newly desexualized Virgen de Guadalupe vs. Coatlicue), and lays on top of the repressive side new names for older structures, in their respective cases, Christianity and Mary. The first part of this development occurs when Guadalupe appears to Juan Diego in 1531 on the very site of the former temple to Tonantsi, and, "speaking Nahuatl," announces her name as *"María Coatlalopeuh,"* a name "homophonous to the Spanish *Guadalupe"* (50–51). The second development is the Church's 1660 equation of this figure with "la Virgen María," and her canonization as the patron saint of Mexico (51). Her image retains political viability, Anzaldúa notes, as it was called upon in one formative moment of Chicano political activism, the 1965 farmworkers' strike in Delano, California, led by César Chávez and others. The Virgen de Guadalupe remains "the single most potent religious, political and cultural image of the Chicano/*mexicano,*" one that summarizes the cultural synthesis of "the old world and the new" that Anzaldúa repeatedly calls "hybridity" (52).

In *Borderlands/La Frontera,* the aspect of Our Lady of Guadalupe as cultural survival makes her the site of productive cultural struggle. She is a symbol of resistance, but an ambiguous one, since her official Catholic status repudiates the deity upon which she was overlaid. The "true identity" of Guadalupe and her aspects have been obscured, Anzaldúa says, resulting in a *"virgen/puta* (whore) dichotomy" (53), but "we have not all embraced this dichotomy. In the U.S. Southwest, Mexico, Central and South America the *indio* and the *mestizo* continue to worship the old spirit entities (including *Guadalupe*) and their supernatural power, under the guise of Christian saints" (53). Like Momaday's Jemez Pueblo, who, "after four centuries of Christianity, [...] still pray in Tanoan to the old deities of the earth and sky" (52), Anzaldúa's *indios* and *mestizos* still pray to the old deities, though their names have changed and the language of prayer may no longer be Nahuatl. "Like the ancients, I worship the rain god and the maize goddess, but unlike my father," and, we might add, unlike Walcott's Ma Kilman, "I have recovered their names" (112).

This pre-Christian Aztec cultural struggle between its female and male forces, manifested in the theological changes among their gods, is the ground for Anzaldúa's feminist challenges to Chicano cultural formations. "Before the Aztecs became a militaristic, bureaucratic state where male predatory warfare and conquest were based on patriliniel nobility," she says, "the principle of balanced opposition between the sexes existed" (53). Anzaldúa dates the decline in this balance to 820 AD, when the Aztecs left Aztlán for their migration south. Social changes accompanied religious ones, and the past was revised to reorder Aztec society into a patriarchal and militaristic one (54). In further parallels to Reed's mythic history, the new patriarchal order commences warfare on its neighbors and represses the fertility and agricultural deities, who (unlike in the account in *Mumbo Jumbo*) are female ones (55).

Turning to these occluded female deities, Anzaldúa adopts a cultural relativism to clear the space for their acceptance by first rejecting the "white rationality" that denies such supernatural existence as "mere pagan superstition" (58). But her turn also entails the archaeological work of going beneath the ossified Catholic structures to the indigenous deities below. For Anzaldúa, the Church "fails to give meaning to my daily acts" and it "impoverish[es] all life, beauty, pleasure" (59). Agreeing centrally with Reed, Anzaldúa says, "The Catholic and Protestant religions encourage fear and distrust of life and of the body" (59). Anzaldúa's forensic approach to Chicano religious life features a discovery of the original Aztec female deities such as Coatlicue, who becomes (through a citation of Jung [118n6]) not just a god but a "powerful image, or 'archetype,' that inhabits, or passes through, my psyche" (68).

In her archaeology of the Aztec-Christian palimpsest at the heart of Chicano border culture, Anzaldúa relies not only on the anthropological concept of culture, but on specific anthropological research providing the content of the struggle she finds in the palimpsest. Two anthropological accounts provide the backbone of her third chapter's description of how a struggle between Aztec deities was transmuted into the Catholic triumph of the Virgin Mary. The first is Geoffrey Parrinder's 1971 *World Religions: From Ancient History to the Present,* an undergraduate textbook whose chapter "Aztecs and Mayas" is a standard history of religion and social anthropology developed through archaeological records of central Mexico and the Aztec codices. The second is anthropologist June Nash's 1978 article "The Aztecs and the Ideology of Male Dominance," a feminist revision of the standard account of the transformations of Aztec gods. While Parrinder gives some notice to how changes in theology worked in tandem with the culture's power struggles, these are not, for him, gendered (e.g., 77). Nash's feminist anthropology rereads this traditional account of the Aztec gods as a record of pre-Columbian gender struggles.

Though she cites neither Boas nor Parrinder, Nash poses a historically particular account of Aztec society and its gods against a supposedly universalist, biological account of "the origin of male dominance [...] [in] the female experience of bearing and rearing children" (349). From Nash's account, Anzaldúa derives her own history of the ascendance of the militaristic, male god Huitzilopochtli, a transformation that meant, in Nash's words, "a shift from a tribe based on clans to a kingdom based on classes" in which women lost political, social, and economic power (352). As Nash says, "Theological doctrines paralleled the structural changes in Aztec society. First, there was the emergence of a single god at the apex of a hierarchy of male gods, and second, the eclipse of female deities related to fertility, nourishment, and the agricultural complex" (359). Neither Nash nor Parrinder treats the issue of Aztec cultural survivals in Mexican culture, as both address solely the ancient Aztec world. Anzaldúa's innovation is to suggest a cultural survival by looking at Guadalupe.[5]

By uncovering the retention of Aztec elements in contemporary Chicano culture, Anzaldúa performs her most powerful revision of the forebear who helped establish the particularity and endurance of that culture, Américo Paredes, whose account Anzaldúa understands to be insufficiently multicultural, or to put it more finely, insufficiently Indian. Paredes began his historical account of border culture in 1749, and suggested, "In succeeding generations the Indians, who began as vaqueros and sheepherders for the colonists, were absorbed into the blood and the culture of the Spanish settlers" (8–9). In Paredes's account of border culture, Indians disappear, a total assimilation by amalgamation that leaves no distinct cultural traces. Anzaldúa's powerful rereading asserts continued Indian cultural contributions, an interpretation of Chicano culture rendered most vivid by the cultural survivals of Aztec religious struggles beneath the seemingly Catholic society.

Like Reed's novel, *Borderlands* advances its thesis on survivals through research that is partly anthropological: both texts contain extended academic apparatuses such as footnotes and (for Reed) a bibliography, and while this might be part of a joke on the reader of *Mumbo Jumbo,* it cannot be so for the relatively (compared to Reed) humorless Anzaldúa. These texts want to have their survivals theses taken seriously. Continued African American and Mexican American cultural distinctiveness is partly a function of the endurance of more ancient religious traditions. But Anzaldúa's substantiation of cultural survivals is authenticated by a no less racial and essentialist logic than Reed's. This racial logic is intimately tied to the dominant concept of identity, the productive blurring of race and culture, and the treatment of history as though it were a form of memory—a co-occurring set of qualities common to our current third-phase paradigm of multicultural literature and criticism.

❧ Culture, Race, Identity

> I don't know what impelled me to go down.
> ....
> I heard footsteps in the basement,
> an intruder breaking in.
> ....
> I had to go down.
> ....
> A gnarled root had broken through
> into the belly of the house
> and somehow a shoot
> had sprung in the darkness
> and now a young tree was growing
> nourished by a nightsun.
> Then I heard footsteps again
> making scuffling sounds
> on the packed dirt floor.
> It was my feet making them.
> It had been my footsteps I'd heard.
>
> —Gloria Anzaldúa, "I Had To Go Down,"
> *Borderlands/La Frontera,* 1987 (189–91)

For Anzaldúa, representative like Morrison, Chin, Momaday, and Reed of post-1965 third-phase multiculturalism, mere culture is understood to be not quite enough, and to require a more metaphysical anchor for its pluralism and relativism. That anchor function is performed by two related concepts, race and identity. Anzaldúa, like the other three multiculturalist authors already examined in detail, actually does pay a great deal of attention to cultural description and to the incredibly complicated patterns of cultural adoption, adaptation, mixings, and transformations that accelerated in the twentieth century. But what marks third-phase multiculturalism is the sense that the ontology of the group (and the nation) cannot be defined solely through the description of its existence—that is, its current and historical experiences, its values, its practices.

Of all the third-phase multiculturalist authors discussed, Anzaldúa is most unapologetic in productively blurring the conceptual distinction between race and culture. This too is in some degree representative of multiculturalism as a paradigm: we have lost our sense of the difference between race and

culture, between biology and learning, between inheritance and environment. It is not only through the biological metaphors saturating *Borderlands*
that Anzaldúa reintroduces race and reattaches culture to it. It also occurs
through the constant swerving between the concepts in her book. A good
example comes in her account of Guadalupe:

> Today, *la Virgen de Guadalupe* is the single most potent religious, politi-
> cal and cultural image of the Chicano/*mexicano*. She, like my race, is a
> synthesis of the old world and the new, of the religion and culture of
> the two races in our psyche, the conquerors and the conquered. She
> is the symbol of the *mestizo* true to his or her Indian values. *La cultura
> chicana* identifies with the mother (Indian) rather than with the father
> (Spanish). (52)

As an aspect of a culture and a religion, the *Virgen* is learned, and it is certainly
true that the symbol has been historically associated with the "racial" group
known as Chicanos and Mexicans. There is no doubt that for historically
particular reasons, there has been considerable overlap between a culture (what
Anzaldúa calls folk Catholicism, with its palimpsest of Guadalupe/Coatlicue)
and a race (the amalgamation of Central American Aztecs and other Indians
with Spanish people). As with the distinct body of folklore that Hurston and
others associated with Southern rural African Americans, reasons of history
account for why a culture might be shared across a racial group.

But such is not Anzaldúa's formulation. What she calls Aztec and Spanish
"religion and culture" are not just historically tied to the two racial groups,
but intrinsically and essentially connected to the two racial groups. It is
because *mestizos* are racially mixed, according to this logic, that they are also
culturally mixed, with Guadalupe/Coatlicue as the symbol of that mixing.
The *mestizo* thus faces the choice of whether or not to be "true to his or her
Indian values" because (and this is an identitarian account of what counts as a
value) those values are racially hers even though they might not be culturally
hers. And in a further complication, *mestizas* must choose the proper cultural
values based not only on their racial identity but on their gender identity:
Guadalupe is a racial and matrilineal inheritance. The slide from culture to
race and back again becomes apparent in Anzaldúa's critique of Chicano
self-naming, when she says, "As a culture, we call ourselves Spanish when
referring to ourselves as a linguistic group and when copping out. It is then
that we forget our predominant Indian genes. We are 70 to 80% Indian" (84).
Boas's revolution was to argue that there could be no natural relation between
"culture" and "genes"—that any culture or language could be attached to
any race. It is thus possible that no matter how genetically Indian someone

was, they could be entirely culturally and linguistically Spanish. But for
Anzaldúa, self-naming one's culture or linguistic group "Spanish" is to "forget" one's racial genes.

Américo Paredes, like other second- and first-phase authors, had to conceptually separate culture from race in order to dismiss the latter as an onto-
logically true description of the group, as Boas had done. "*El Corrido de
Gregorio Cortez,* then, is a Border Mexican ballad, 'Mexican' being understood in a cultural sense, without reference to citizenship or to 'blood,'" Paredes warned in the introduction to his study (xi). But a similar clarification
of terms in Anzaldúa produces the opposite effect: "(by *mexicanos* we do not
mean citizens of Mexico; we do not mean a national identity, but a racial
one)" (84). Against Paredes's refusal of blood and race, Anzaldúa embraces
both. Paredes, like Wright, Okada, Wong, and even Hurston, almost never
used biological metaphors to talk about culture. These writers of the first and
second phases were too close to the original Boasian paradigm shift of replacing race with culture. For this reason, they never invoke racial metaphors
like "blood" to characterize what is now, properly, understood to be cultural
differences between groups. It was, after all, Walter Prescott Webb's notion
of Indian "blood" that Paredes countered by his cultural understanding of
Mexican American border society (17–18). Thus when Anzaldúa, revising
Paredes, invokes blood and other biological metaphors (like "hybridity") in
order to talk about culture, she is strangely reverting to Webb's biologism.

Her work constantly repeats these three keywords, "culture," "race," and
"identity," treating them synonymously, as different terms for the same group
ontology. Thus Mexican, Indian, Chicano, and white refer simultaneously
to both racial groups and cultural groups. "What I want is an accounting
with all three cultures—white, Mexican, Indian," Anzaldúa says in one summary that both homogenizes, and, by homogenizing, treats the three terms as
descriptions of races as well as cultures (44). As she continues shortly after,

> *Guadalupe* unites people of different races, religions, languages: Chi-
> cano protestants, American Indians and whites. "*Nuestra abogada siem-
> pre serás* / Our *mediatrix* you will always be." She mediates between
> the Spanish and the Indian cultures (or three cultures as in the case of
> *mexicanos* of African or other ancestry) and between Chicanos and the
> white world. She mediates between humans and the divine, between
> this reality and the reality of spirit entities. *La Virgen de Guadalupe* is
> the symbol of ethnic identity and of the tolerance for ambiguity that
> Chicanos-*mexicanos,* people of mixed race, people who have Indian
> blood, people who cross cultures, by necessity possess. (52)

As becomes clear here, culture and race are the very same thing in *Borderlands/La Frontera*. One's race is what one's culture is; mixed blood confers *mestizo* culture "by necessity"; one's ancestry is the same as one's ethnic identity; to genetically "cross" a culture is not different from crossing a religion or a race. Anzaldúa invokes her biological metaphors when she writes, in the final chapter to the essay portion of *Borderlands/La Frontera:*

> At the confluence of two or more genetic streams, with chromosomes constantly "crossing over," this mixture of races, rather than resulting in an inferior being, provides hybrid progeny, a mutable, more malleable species with a rich gene pool. From this racial, ideological, cultural and biological cross-pollinization, an "alien" consciousness is presently in the making—a new *mestiza* consciousness, *una conciencia de mujer.* (99)

Anzaldúa's "blood" functions much the same way as in Reed and Momaday, and her much-discussed notion of cultural "hybridity" likewise biologizes cultural learning. Hybridity is at the heart of what Anzaldúa's subtitle calls "the new mestiza," which means both the complicated cultural mixings of border Chicano culture and the centuries-old processes of racial mixing between Indians and Spanish. When Anzaldúa, describing the hybridity of the *mestiza,* writes, "Indigenous like corn, like corn, the *mestiza* is a product of crossbreeding, designed for preservation under a variety of conditions" (103), such biological metaphors are not accidental but part of an ongoing biological conceit for processes of culture.

Anzaldúa is an extreme example of a general and productive indistinction between race and culture in our current paradigm of multiculturalism. In Anzaldúa's work, this indistinction is partly produced by the fact that there are not different terms for racial and cultural groups. "Chicano," "Mexican," "white," "Indian," and "Spanish" are words that describe cultures and races. With that equivalence, it is impossible for someone of the Mexican race to have white culture or someone of the white race to have an Indian culture, and so on. Of course, it is not really impossible—Anzaldúa calls people in the first example "*agringado*": "In the 50s and 60s, for the slightly educated and *agringado* Chicanos, there existed a sense of shame at being caught listening to our music" (83). Thus while the liberal assimilationist consensus of the second phase could, as we have seen, allow (or compel) racial Chicanos to adopt culturally mainstream Anglo music, Anzaldúa must introduce a new term at the moment when someone's culture does not match her race. The default position in *Borderlands/La Frontera* is that Chicano describes both a culture and a race; just as, in multiculturalism generally, African American refers to a culture and a race, Asian American refers to a culture and a race, and Native American refers to both a culture and a race.

This linguistic indistinction in terms—we must, as does Anzaldúa, make an extra explanation at the moment someone's culture does not match their race—is part of multiculturalism's built-in racial prescriptivism. What were historically particular reasons for why a racial group generally shared a culture are now replaced by a default language that assumes that races and cultures are coterminous. Thus multiculturalism's "difference discourse describes social identities such as race as a manifestation of underlying differences—a racial culture—while at the same time generating those very differences," suggests Richard Ford (28).[6]

The productive blurring and indistinction between race and culture are nicely captured by the term "identity." Of all the texts examined in *A Genealogy of Literary Multiculturalism*, *Borderlands/La Frontera* is the most thoroughly saturated by the term and notion of identity, and is a good example of its culmination and triumph in literary multiculturalism and the criticism that has grown around it. Occasionally using it in reference to herself, and many times substantiating it by reference to personal practices or actual Chicano traditions, Anzaldúa most generally deploys it in the fashion that I have critiqued in this book: as a way to think about being that is an antidote to a descriptive and existential account of who or what a person, nation, or culture is. Anzaldúa is frequently credited with developing a postmodern, nuanced, and fluid notion of identity through metaphors of hybridity and borderlands. In her original preface, for instance, she writes, "Living on borders and in margins, keeping intact one's shifting and multiple identity and integrity, is like trying to swim in a new element, an 'alien' element" (19). But as one recent critic, Linda Martín Alcoff, has usefully reminded us, Anzaldúa's experience of "hybridity" was painful, not celebratory, and her concept of identity was not antifoundational, but oriented toward coherence and an essentialism of a sort, which Alcoff thinks is good (256). It is likewise useful to remember Walter Benn Michaels's critique, that the problem with identity is not that we use essentialist concepts of identity instead of dynamic and fragmentary and provisional ones, but that there is no non-essentialist account of identity.

Speaking of her own psychological and spiritual growth as she explores "the *Coatlicue* state," Anzaldúa seems to repudiate the square one of identity, writing "I am no longer the same person I was before" (70). But this transformability and self-alienation are in turn called into question in a later chapter, where she quotes in an epigraph a psychologist of shame, Gershen Kaufman, as saying, "Identity is the essential core of who we are as individuals, the conscious experience of the self inside" (84). As I suggested in

chapter seven, it is somewhat extraordinary that the notion of national identity (from which developed multiculturalism's notions of cultural and ethnic identities) emerged from a psychology that, coming after Freud, should
have been well aware of the ways in which the subject is neither coherent
nor the same as itself, but is marked by self-alienation and the lack of self-
knowledge. But Kaufman's rendering of personal identity as "the essential
core" of our experience of inner continuity and coherence more accurately
describes Anzaldúa's notion of identity than her earlier claim to not be the
same person she was before. As Alcoff points out, *Borderlands/La Frontera* is
mistakenly used to support "a current trend that celebrates hybridity as the
political and theoretical antidote to essentialism" (256).

For Anzaldúa, identity is fundamentally concerned with consolidation
and return. That is why she performs a cultural archaeology that recovers
the Indian gods beneath the Catholic ones; it is why she is not to forget her
Indian "genes" beneath her mixed Mexican and Anglo culture; it is why
eighteenth-century and contemporary Mexican migrations to the border
area are actually Aztec returns to Aztlán; female resistance is also that which
is discovered beneath the patriarchal elements of Chicano culture that are to
be repudiated; it is likewise why the footsteps in the basement in her poem
"I Had To Go Down" are discovered to have been her own all along. "My
Chicana identity is grounded in the Indian woman's history of resistance,"
Anzaldúa suggests, and so her feminist politics are actually returns to what
Kaufman calls "the essential core" of pre-warrior Aztec culture. What is
complicated and fluid is the unravelings of culture that Anzaldúa must perform; what is not fluid but is rather deeply essentialist is the notion of iden-
tity that guarantees her genealogical and forensic labors.

Like Anzaldúa's *Borderlands,* Reed's *Mumbo Jumbo* has also been read in
terms of its indeterminant, postmodern identity, a dynamic of cultural mixings also represented by borders and "crossroads" like the one presided over
by Legba (see, for instance, Swope 619). But as with Anzaldúa, while the
mixings have been historically fluid, the notion of identity *Mumbo Jumbo*
advances is not. For Reed and Anzaldúa, Egypt and Aztlán are the sites of
the original struggles between fertility/femininity and power/patriarchy, and
while the dynamic struggles originated in these homelands, one side of the
struggle has temporal and moral priority—that of the natural. Such is the
"core" of essential identity that is anything but fluid and indeterminate; it
is this core that the anthropology of cultural survivals promises to uncover
beneath the religious palimpsests that characterize the clash of civilizations.

Reed's 1972 novel and Anzaldúa's 1987 mixed-genre of autobiography,
poetry, and essay are synecdoches of third-phase literary multiculturalism.

Insofar as these two texts are representative, the decade and a half between them signals the consolidation of third-phase innovations in the genealogy of literary multiculturalism in the United States. *Mumbo Jumbo* and *Borderlands/La Frontera* are grounded in anthropological (and archaeological/historical) research and in an anthropological model of culture entailing pluralism, relativism, holism, historical particularism, and a theory of cultural continuity contained not just in what is passed from generation to generation but in a theory of cultural survivals through which subterreanean cultural features might be retained through the radical discontinuities of forced migrations and violent imperialisms.

But those cultural survivals are supplemented by the guarantor of race for both Reed and Anzaldúa. In a move that the relatively orthodox Boasians Hurston, Herskovits, and Paredes were unwilling to make, Reed and Anzaldúa reintroduce racial difference into their account of historically particular communities of cultural difference, and in doing so reattach culture to race, not in a historically particular way but in the natural, organic way that Boas had contested. Race had always been a tidier concept for thinking about continuity, since establishing learned continuity was an especially arduous labor that anthropologists have struggled to perform, sometimes failing. Thinking about cultural continuity as intrinsic rather than historical—as racial rather than contingent—was not confined to these two authors, however. One of the most famous critical debates in Asian American literature in the 1970s also revolved around this issue: that of Frank Chin's criticism of Maxine Hong Kingston's rewriting of the ancient Chinese *Ballad of Fa Mulan* in her 1976 fictionalized memoir *The Woman Warrior.* While Kingston insisted that myths and stories have to change and adapt in a new culture, suggesting that her version of Fa Mulan has "become American" ("Personal" 24), Chin has criticized her version for its changes, which he regards as revealing ignorance of the original. To Chin, Kingston and her "literary spawn" Amy Tan and David Henry Hwang "boldly fake the best-known works from the most universally known body of Asian literature and lore in history" ("Come All" 3); in particular, argues Chin, "Losing touch with China did not result in Chinese Americans losing touch with 'The Ballad of Mulan.' It was and is still chanted by children in Chinatowns around the Western hemisphere" (3). But in an analogy suggesting that what might have been a historical particularist account of cultural continuity is actually a notion of racial continuity, Chin adds, "Losing touch with England did not result in English whites losing touch with the texts of the Magna Carta or Shakespeare" (3).

It is easy to see how a notion of cultural continuity and endurance can slide into a formulation in which learning is assumed rather than demonstrated, and so becomes the object of racial essence. As Chin claims,

> the shape, content, and moral values preached in the Holy Bible have not gone through this natural process between the languages and nations of Europe. Whites, settled in America for hundreds of years, have not lost track of the plots, the characters, or the authors of the most cherished fairy tales and adventures told in Western childhood. The values of Chinese fairy tales, the form and ethics of the classics of the heroic tradition, the names of the heroes, and the works themselves are written into the bylaws of the tongs and associations that run Chinatown to this day. The characters of the fairy tale and the heroic tradition are found in figurines, statues, and calendar art. Their stories are told through toys, on flash cards, and in comic and coloring books throughout the country, in Chinese American homes and in Chinatowns—in the restaurants, on the walls, in the windows. . . . At no time in Chinese American history was the real Fa Mulan obscure or inaccessible to a Chinese American girl or boy. (3–4)

It is by now a well-worn truism in the pedagogy of English literature that we can not assume students' knowledge of the events or characters of the Bible, and, given patterns of evangelization in the United States, this knowledge is as likely to come from Asian American students as from white students. (For Chin as for Reed, Christianity is the racially inappropriate religion for Asian Americans and African Americans, as Chin's dismissal of Jade Snow Wong's "Christian autobiography" reveals.) Conversely, while one could imagine many Chinese American children knowing the chant of Fa Mulan, one could also imagine many—maybe most?—Chinese American children growing up without testable knowledge of it. Again representative of our current multiculturalism, Chin's terms "white" and "Chinese American" are descriptors of someone's race and someone's culture, and because of the indistinction between them, their sameness is assumed. To be racially white is to know the Bible and to be racially Chinese American is to know Fa Mulan; and while both are framed as examples of cultural continuity and learning, the very willful disinterest in actually trying to figure out how many white Americans (in which cultural segments of the population) know their Bible and how many Chinese Americans know their Mulan—the determined agnosticism on the question of describing actual practices and learning—makes the question of cultural continuity into a racially prescriptive assumption.

Thus what anthropology understood as culture has been transformed into a question of identity. Our current paradigm of literary multiculturalism has been profoundly shaped by cultural anthropology—sometimes self-consciously so—even as it has gone beyond its Boasian purview to embrace some aspects of racial discourse that Boas understood himself to be struggling against. Ishmael Reed tips his hat to the Boas-Hurston dynamic central to the New Negro Renaissance and the stage it set for the Black Arts movement forty or so years later. At the end of *Mumbo Jumbo,* even as Jes Grew is unraveling, Earline tells PaPa LaBas about her interest in "The Work":

> I want to learn more, pop. I'm thinking about going to New Orleans and Haiti, Brazil and all over the South studying our ancient cultures, our HooDoo cultures. Maybe by and by some future artists 30 to 40 years from now will benefit from my research. Who knows. Pop, I believe in Jes Grew now. (206)

In this brief wink, Reed acknowledges his own research and intellectual debts to Hurston and her mentor—here PaPa LaBas instead of Papa Franz. And indeed, multiculturalism's theoretical debts to anthropology and its model of culture are equally important. But as *A Genealogy of Literary Multiculturalism* has shown, multiculturalism's anthropological culture was a culture with a difference. It must be clear by now that Walter Benn Michaels's central argument, that identity is a way of retaining racial technology as the guarantor that tells us which culture we should have, is true of third-phase multiculturalism in a way that it was not true of first-phase anthropology and the multiethnic writing it influenced. It must also be clear by now that Franz Boas's fear of generalization has been borne out: Chin's, Anzaldúa's, and Reed's easy generalizations about races and cultures assume far too much continuity and homogeneity in what have actually been vastly complicated cultural mixings, migrations, adaptations, and transformations. They are representative of a multicultural literature and criticism that, uninterested in the rigorous demands of historical particularism, reattach culture to race by treating their relation as organic and natural rather than contingent and historical. Representative too is their turn to identity as a guarantor of that relation, and to identity's constitutive hostility to the collecting of facts, to description as such. These qualities are part of what I call the "multicultural complex," which I describe in more detail in my conclusion.

❧ CONCLUSION

The Multicultural Complex and the Incoherence of Literary Multiculturalism

> THE NATURALIST: Thus behave our subjects naturally. Thus behave our subjects when they believe we cannot see them when they believe us far far away when they believe our backs have turned. Now. An obvious question should arise in the mind of an inquisitive observer? Yes? HHH. How should we best accommodate the presence of such subjects in our modern world?
>
> —Suzan-Lori Parks, *Imperceptible Mutabilities in the Third Kingdom,* 1995 (29)

In *Imperceptible Mutabilities,* the Naturalist sets loose some giant fake cockroaches, equipped with hidden cameras, in the kitchen of two African Americans. Gathering data about his subjects, he imagines the act of observation as itself invisible to his research group. The point of such knowledge will occur to "an inquisitive observer": how do these minority subjects fit into American modernity? Problematically, "our subjects" devote a good deal of their "natural" conversation to discussing the abnormal size of the cockroaches, and how they strangely do not run when threatened. Parks captures the modern social science fantasy of being able to "observe the object of study—unobserved" (27) while the minority object acts "naturally," as though the observer were not there. "Wonder what I'd look like if no one was lookin,'" one such object wonders (28).

While a certain vein of postmodern social science no longer imagines the observing act as having no effect on the observed culture or its subjects, *A Genealogy of Literary Multiculturalism* has established the constitutive observational feedback loop between the social sciences and the multicultural literatures of the United States. Literary authors read, studied, and sometimes wrote the very social science concerned with cultural others—ethnography, anthropology, and sociology—that, like the Naturalist, has imagined itself, as an act and as a discipline, to be invisible to its subjects. Likewise, that social science has sometimes used literary texts as though they were "natural" acts by the objects of study, as happened with Morrison's *Bluest Eye* and Wright's *Native Son*. But even when the very circularity of use is not so evident, I have shown that social science ideas were always part of the intellectual fabric of race and culture that helped constitute American literary multiculturalism as it developed in the twentieth century. It is therefore deeply problematic for the social sciences and ethnic studies to use the literary texts that they helped make conceptually possible to substantiate either an idea about "culture," or what minority cultural values or practices might really be or—worse—mean. Social science and ethnic studies may use literary texts as evidence for particular conceptions of culture or as the content of culture, but this data sample is thoroughly muddied. Literary writers, especially racialized or ethnic ones, have long been using social science research as an intellectual resource.

What I have offered here is not only a theory of influence—whereby African American, Asian American, Native American, and Mexican American authors read and so were shaped by social science ideas—but also a theory of articulation within a feedback loop, whereby authors seemed to take up ideas that already spoke to them, and then powerfully changed, and sometimes misread, those ideas which then sometimes became the fodder for further social science. They took, in other words, what they needed, and sometimes that formal or informal training conferred powerful benefits for their work. When we try to figure out what drew these writers to anthropology or sociology, what is at stake is not merely biographical sequence and in which phase the writers wrote, but that there were personal, aesthetic, and political reasons that drew the writers into productive relationships with social science discourse, such that it gave them, as Hurston put it, a "spyglass" with which to look at the self and at one's community. The feedback loop describes the individuals and the trajectory of multicultural American literature in the twentieth century as a whole: that mid-century writers used and were energized by social science concepts of culture that were in turn partly invented or inspired by social scientists' exploration of "literary" texts like folklore, myths, life writing of immigrants, or novels about urban life. Recognizing this circuit delegitimizes the contemporary social science–based ethnic studies practice of treating literary work as a kind of data set for proving, illustrating, or disproving social science theory about cultures and their content.

It is not that anthropology's "spyglass" was a pair of false spectacles for Hurston or that the visions of Hurston, McNickle, Wright, Wong, Okada, Paredes, Morrison, Chin, Momaday, Reed, and Anzaldúa were impaired by white social science in the middle of the century—though that sometimes happens. Rather, it is that many of these writers took the Naturalist's project as their own. But that made the project itself untenable: there would never be a moment in which "our subjects" believed that "we cannot see them," because the subjects began to see themselves, as Jade Snow Wong put it (in yet another ocular metaphor for what social science does) "with two pairs of eyes": from within the studied group as a member of the group, and as a social scientist studying the group from without.

✤ Dis-Orientation

> I found Jade Snow Wong's book myself in the library, and was flabbergasted, helped, inspired, affirmed, made possible as a writer—for the first time I saw a person who looked like me as a heroine of a book, as a maker of a book.
>
> —Maxine Hong Kingston, Letter to Amy Ling, 1988 (qtd. in A. Ling 120)

Suzan-Lori Parks's repudiation of social science's modern dream of unobserved observation came in the 1990s, the decade that consolidated and extended the gains of the third phase of literary multiculturalism developing since the mid 1960s. But literary anxiety about social science models of, and ways of reading, culture had been around for some time, and was perhaps latent in third-phase multiculturalism. One famous display of this anxiety was Maxine Hong Kingston's 1976 fictionalized memoir *The Woman Warrior.* Kingston's book, wrongly read (and sometimes publicized) as autobiography,[1] took up the question of cultural authority that had been so central to the social science–authorized *Fifth Chinese Daughter* by Jade Snow Wong, whom Kingston later called "the Mother of Chinese American literature" (qtd. in A. Ling 120). Reading the two books beside one another indicates the extent to which Kingston felt it necessary to repudiate social science knowledge of ethnic culture, in a fashion not typical of other third-phase multiculturalist writers.

The conditions for Wong's status as authoritative autoethnographer and her politics of ethnic assimilation are laid bare retrospectively through the intertextual allusions to *Fifth Chinese Daughter* in Kingston's *Woman Warrior.* Kingston's revisions to specific episodes in Wong's autobiography not only highlight Kingston's rejection of any authorial status as ethnographic authority, but also suggest some of the problematic consequences of the circuit between literature and social science that is constitutive of the genealogy of American literary multiculturalism. Several allusions to *Fifth Chinese Daughter* seem reminiscent homage rather than revisionist critique: the daughters' resistance to their parents' perceived attempt at arranging a marriage (Wong

227–32; Kingston 193–94), the experience of school baseball as a child (Wong 20; Kingston 173), the tale of the parent who spent a night in a haunted room (Wong 52; Kingston 67), the general childhood project of acquiring an American personality through books and learning (Wong 92) and through speech at school (Kingston 180), and the climactic verbal argument with parental authority around the dinner table (Wong 129–30; Kingston 201–4).

In other moments, Kingston's text produces gently ironic echoes when read in conjunction with Wong. Wong's "straight A's" reflect her Americanized sense of self-determination in the face of resistance, but Kingston's narrator's report of "straight A's" to her mother produces only further confusion about "her" culture, a confusion ("I could not figure out what was my village") that she cannot settle for her readers (Wong 111; Kingston 45). In another episode, Wong reacts with calm condescension to a schoolmate's racial slur "Chinky, Chinky, no tickee, no washee, no shirtee!" (Wong 68), whereas a customer's "No tickee, no washee, mama-san?" (Kingston 105) produces a more ambivalent reaction of embarrassment and counter-naming ("Noisy Red-Mouth Ghost," the narrator's mother writes on the laundry package). In another telling example, against Wong's careful tourist-guide descriptions of Chinese foodways (we get, for instance, four pages on how to buy and cook rice and later a recipe for egg foo young), Kingston offers only an in-your-face catalogue of icky things the narrator's mother has cooked for her family (Wong 57–60, 159; Kingston 90–92). *Fifth Chinese Daughter* and *The Woman Warrior* share narrator outrage over gender inequalities in traditional Chinese culture; but even if it is Wong's father who appears as a Christian to believe "that women should be freed from certain oppressive rules" (Palumbo-Liu, *Asian* 139), and so is already placed as progressive, it is Kingston's book that does not let American culture off the hook for its own patriarchal systems, with its child-narrator imagining that the field of future vocations for girls includes only the sequence pom-pom girl, cheerleader, and housewife (Kingston 180).

Other intertextual instances do more to articulate the way Wong claims, and Kingston rejects, the social science pose of authority about minority culture in their texts. Wong's childhood paintings are understood as early experiments in self-expression, an American mode condemned initially by her father (18), that she eventually embraces through writing and pottery in "the convergence of two narrative strands: the imperative of highly individualized self-expression meets the need for a cultural representative" (Palumbo-Liu, *Asian* 143). Kingston's parallel self-expression, childhood paintings covered in layers of black ink like a "stage curtain [. . .] the moment before the curtain parted," suggest mere potential rather than actual cultural expression "(so black and full of possibilities)" (Kingston 165), or, reflective of the crucially palinodinal structure of Kingston's cultural authority,[2] the impossibility of cultural or self-representation. Both Wong and Kingston's narrator, as children, speak of their parents' unwillingness to explain culture and its traditions (Wong 3; Kingston 5, 121), but the way their texts work out this cultural ignorance is vastly different. Wong takes it upon herself to discover and represent Chinese culture to her ignorant readership; far from remaining unknowing, she learns at home, trains as a sociologist at school, and reports her fieldwork in the written word. On the other hand, Kingston's book again and again undercuts her status as cultural authority.

In one parallel instance, Wong and Kingston's narrator are forced to consult dictionaries as a way of obtaining cultural information. Wong's lesson is framed by her father, who commands that she look up the word "slippers" in an English dictionary so that she will learn that "bedroom attire" is not tolerated in the kitchen, where the result is "chaos" (83). Kingston's narrator, however, is driven to a Chinese-English dictionary to try to make sense of the Cantonese phrases "Sit Dom Kuei" and "Ho Chi Kuei" because "I don't know any Chinese I can ask without getting myself scolded or teased, so I've been looking in books" (88, 204). In relaying the findings of her research, Kingston's text thematizes and declares outright its own status as radically unauthoritative ethnography:

> So far I have the following translations for *ho* and/or *chi:* "centipede," "grub," "bastard carp," "chirping insect," "ju-jube tree," "pied wagtail," "grain sieve," "casket sacrifice," "water lily," "good frying," "non-eater," "dustpan-and-broom" (but that's a synonym for "wife"). Or perhaps I've romanized the spelling wrong and it is *Hao* Chi Kuei, which could mean they are calling us "Good Foundation Ghosts." The immigrants could be saying that we were born on Gold Mountain and have advantages. (204–5)

Here the very plurality of possible meanings breaks down any social science project: our field-guide—our cultural insider—has admitted her own inability to sort among the possibilities. Our only recourse is to turn, with the narrator, to the English-Chinese dictionary: we must, as Frank Chin has commanded, do our homework ("Not an Autobiography" 125).

The politics of anti-autoethnographic representation are underscored best through Kingston's parody of Wong the field-observer, done through the narrator's aunt, Moon Orchid. Moon Orchid arrives from Hong Kong to visit her daughter (and perhaps reclaim her wayward bigamist husband), but becomes an anthropologist in the new world, studying the children who had "many interesting savage things to say, raised as they'd been in the wilderness," "raised away from civilization" (133, 134). Kingston's parody returns us to the primal scene of anthropology's constitution through an encounter with the Indian. Thus Moon Orchid imagines that the children's behavior and dress must be "Like an Indian" (134). Herself now "roughing it in the wilderness" (135), she makes several important cultural discoveries about her American nieces and nephews: "She saw them eat undercooked meat, and they smelled like cow's milk. At first she thought they were so clumsy, they spilled it on their clothes. But soon she decided they themselves smelled of milk" (134). Later, the participant-observer conducts a running commentary on the acts of the children as they bake or get ready for school, and her rendering of an electric beater as a "machine" with "two metal spiders" used to mix eggs and "cow oil" (140–41) begins to suggest the actual difficulties of cross-cultural observation, translation, and authority. Her ethnographic fieldwork is a humorous treatment of cross-cultural misreading, but its serious corollary is the difficulty—even impossibility—of naming and identifying "American" culture as a whole, in the same way that Kingston's narrator seems unable to get to the bottom of "Chinese" culture in order to represent it to her readers. Here, as elsewhere, Kingston refuses the mantle of social science cultural expertise, either as outside expert or as inside informant, that Jade Snow Wong assumes.

Unlike Wong, whose 1938–42 college career marked the beginning of what I call the second phase in the genealogy of literary multiculturalism, Kingston's college career happened in Berkeley in the 1960s—when African American and Chicano students were challenging the way that race and ethnicity were disciplined, and, they charged, pathologized by sociology. The consequence of this challenge was the creation of black studies programs and departments, and then ethnic studies programs and departments. We can see a generational change between Wong's 1950 autoethnography and Kingston's 1976 anti-autoethnography in respect to the way they consume social science discourse. Far from signifying the generation gap between her American self and her Chinese parents, Kingston's confusion about Chinese culture highlights the problems with autoethnographic authority undertaken by Wong. Kingston's strategies go against the grain of ethnography—she makes it difficult for us to derive ethnographic knowledge from her literary texts. And indeed, her rejoinder to her ethnographic-minded critics—"why must I represent someone other than myself?" ("Cultural Mis-readings" 63)—is part of her resistance to representing culture, or to having her books read for their cultural knowledge—as opposed to, Sau-ling Wong has shown, Amy Tan ("Sugar Sisterhood"). It is not just a problem of epistemology and method for Kingston; it is the ontology of "culture" that here comes into question. Her response to the constitutive circuit between social science and multicultural literature is the literary project of cultural dis-orientation: not only an anti-orientalist portrayal of Chinese America, but, more important, the disavowal of expertise in, and a thematic ontological uncertainty about, the cultures of Asian America.

🍏 Is Margaret Atwood an African American Writer?

What these shared episodes between Wong and Kingston constitute, of course, is a possible series of tropes for a Chinese American literary tradition that rests not on biological "race" or essential ethnic-cultural identity, but on a formal repetition and revision of the kind Henry Louis Gates Jr. has identified as the African American literary tradition (*The Signifying Monkey;* "Master's"). Gates's important theory of the African American literary tradition—which can be extended by analogy to the Asian American, Native American, and Mexican American literary traditions—developed in print in the 1980s and can be considered a culmination of the movement that I have identified as the arc of the genealogy of literary multiculturalism. The African American tradition, Gates argued, is "not defined by a pseudoscience of racial biology, or a mystically shared essence called blackness, but by the repetition and revision of shared themes, topoi, and tropes" ("Master's" 108). Gates proposes a cultural and formal conception of the tradition—an artistic continuity that must be learned instead of inherited—rather than one depending on the biological accidents of birth, and in this way his theory at first seems to be at odds with the third phase of multicultural literature that used anthropological culture but regrounded it in racial identity.

It is thus no accident that *The Signifying Monkey* emphasizes the Hurston—Reed—Walker line of cultural continuity, Southern vernacular, pluralism, relativism, and dynamic holism rather than (though he does get some space) Richard Wright's sociologically articulated literary vision. It is also no accident, according to *A Genealogy of Literary Multiculturalism*'s thesis, that Gates's book begins with a chapter on African cultural survivals of the kind explored by Hurston and Reed, indeed using Herskovits's field research in Dahomey to substantiate the central deity of Legba (25–28). Boasian anthropological culture and the Herskovitsian-Hurstonian extension of its model to include cultural retentions across the Middle Passage form the central dynamic by which Gates argues that the Signifying Monkey is the "cousin" if not the "heir" of Esu-Elegbara (20). Both figures encapsulate "black theories about formal language use" (21), including the formal "repetition and revision" that Gates identifies as fundamental to the literary tradition to come. That tradition includes standard topoi like the journey north and double consciousness, but also what he calls "speakerly texts" that comprise both the tropes of the talking book found in early slave narratives and the representation of vernacular in the written tradition. Gates's brilliant *Signifying Monkey* is advanced wholly within this anthropological notion of culture, and is posed against a biological and essentialist account of the literary tradition. His theory has become so important that it has itself been the source of literary inspiration for Suzan-Lori Parks, whose Becketian plays in the 1990s were often structured around the dynamic of "Rep & Rev," as Parks shortened Gates's signal phrase ("Elements" 9).

The obvious question that Gates never quite addresses, however, is, given the formal and performative criteria for inclusion in the African American canon according to his theory, are we ready to include in that canon racially non-black writers who meet those cultural criteria and to exclude from that canon racially African American writers who do not meet those cultural criteria? By such textual and non-biographical criteria, would it not be better, for example, to include Hurston's *Seraph on the Suwanee* in a tradition of fiction about poor white evangelical Southern women that extends from such writers as Flannery O'Connor to Dorothy Allison (not one of whom was evangelical herself, of course), a tradition constituted in part through repeated and revised scenes of born again experiences, sexual awakenings, and fears of apostasy? Is *Seraph*'s anthropological insight about the interpenetration of black and white Southern vernaculars still within Gates's model of "a black difference that manifests itself in specific language use" known as "the black English vernacular tradition," or does the evidence of that interpenetration and interdependence subvert the key source of difference grounding the tradition (*Signifying* xxii–xxiii)?

To use another example, what are we to make of the work of Richard Wright? While Gates notes that Wright tended to deny African American literary antecedents, we could nonetheless say that the journeys north in *Black Boy* and *Uncle Tom's Children,* and the forging of his own library pass in *Black Boy* (reminiscent of Douglass's forging of a travelling pass in his *Narrative*), constitute revisions of standard tropes in the African American tradition. But what are we to do with *Native Son,* which "Reps & Revs" none of these tropes, and which is utterly indifferent to black vernacular except as an index of its own project of urban realism and sociological accuracy? Can *Native Son* still count as African American fiction if it does not use these learned textual and cultural criteria? Or, to ask the same question of a few more examples that have not been central to this book, what of Charles Chesnutt's *The Marrow of Tradition,* Nella Larsen's *Passing,* and George Schuyler's *Black No More*? Do we expand the series of tropes that can be repeated and revised to include, for example, black people pretending to be white people or vice versa (which would then include all three of these novels)? If we thus expand the tradition, must we then not count Philip Roth's *Human Stain*?

That is the flip side of this problem: what of literature by non-African American authors that meets these learned textual and cultural criteria? Does William Styron's 1967 novel *The Confessions of Nat Turner* sufficiently repeat and revise elements from more traditional slave narratives, such that it can count as within the African American literary tradition? What of Margaret Atwood's 1985 novel *The Handmaid's Tale,* which, according to strictly formal criteria, is clearly and self-consciously repeating and revising standard African American tropes from the slave narrative like the journey north (including the existence of an "underground femaleroad") and the talking book, as well as being told in the "oral" voice in a way that Gates has identified as so important to Hurston's *Their Eyes Were Watching God*? Like Douglass's *Narrative of the Life of a Slave* on which it is clearly modeled, *The Handmaid's Tale* thematizes the prohibition against reading and the authority of the written word, especially the role of the talking book of the Bible in substantiating what Douglass always insisted on calling "Christian slavery." Such would be a conclusion we would be forced to concede were we to take seriously Gates's argument that

> Ralph Ellison, onto whose ideas of Signifyin(g) and formal critique I have grafted my theory of critical Signification, rightly argues, against Irving Howe, that "the notion of an intellectual or artistic succession based upon color or racial background is no less absurd than one based upon a common religious background." Literary succession or influence, rather, can be based on only formal literary revision, which the literary critic must be able to demonstrate. These discrete demonstrations allow for definitions of a tradition. (120)

If we are willing, then, to include *The Confessions of Nat Turner* and *The Handmaid's Tale,* along with *Beloved,* in a canon formally defined as repeating and revising nineteenth-century slave narratives but not as African American literature even though we can "demonstrate" their "formal literary revision," then there must be some other unspoken criteria for texts' inclusion or exclusion in African American literature. That other criterion might be lived experience in addition to learned culture—in other words, we might make the argument that while Atwood and Styron and Morrison can read slave narratives and so learn their literary conventions and then repeat and revise them, they themselves did not experience life as slaves and so cannot write authentic slave narratives. Or we could alternatively say—and this is probably more accurately the sense whereby multiculturalist canons form themselves through attention to questions of authenticity based not only on one's race but also on one's lived experience—that Morrison's experience of growing up black in America underwrites her African American literary conventions and provides her with a kind of experiential continuity with actual slave narrative authors like Frederick Douglass and Harriet Jacobs who also grew up black in America. Such would be an argument about experiential/environmental (and not just cultural) continuity that would permit Morrison's inclusion in African American literature but exclude Styron and Atwood, and, to take other examples, Carl Van Vechten and other white writers of the Negro Renaissance who, George Hutchinson has argued, were investigating many of the same themes of race, urbanity, art, and sexuality as their black compatriots (202–3).

But this argument about shared experience is rejected—rightly, I think— by Gates as he elaborates his theory:

> Has a common experience, or, more accurately, the shared sense of a common experience, been largely responsible for the sharing of this text of blackness? It would be foolish to say no. Nevertheless, shared experience of black people vis-à-vis white racism is not sufficient evidence upon which to argue that black writers have shared patterns of representation of their common subject for two centuries—unless one wishes to argue for a genetic theory of literature, which the biological sciences do not support. Rather, shared modes of figuration result only when writers read each other's texts and seize upon topoi and tropes to revise in their own texts. (128)

We should give credit to the ambition of *The Signifying Monkey,* for it is nothing less than the culmination of the paradigm shift from race to culture: against biology, Gates wants to pose an exclusively cultural—that is, learned—explanation for the African American literary tradition. He raises the question of an additional experiential criteria (which would include how one's race is socially constructed by forces beyond the individual) for writing black literature, but dismisses it, in a move that probably not all literary critics of the African American tradition would be willing to make.

A slightly different alternative might be a criterion of actual cultural transmission within a descent population: as Gates writes earlier about black vernacular's spread during the Great Migration: "There can be little doubt that Signifyin(g) was found by linguists in the black urban neighborhoods in the fifties and sixties because black people from the South migrated there and passed the tradition along to subsequent generations" (71). (Generational transmission was precisely that which was severed by the generation gap Park elaborated for Asian American communities, and was likewise central to the anthropological notion of cultural continuity.) But there are some problems with using intergenerational transmission to authenticate which cultural practices and values are the individual's: as we have seen, N. Scott Momaday did not quite grow up with Kiowa language and culture transmitted to him (nor did D'Arcy McNickle with Salish/Metis languages and cultures), and Alice Walker (re)discovered African American folklore from Hurston's book, thereby fulfilling anthropology's dream that texts be recorded before they were "forgotten." If lived experience and intergenerational transmission more particularly are the unspoken additional criteria necessary for literary writers to really repeat and revise the formal conventions of the traditions that the paradigm of multiculturalism routinely puts them in, then Alice Walker and N. Scott Momaday and many other multicultural writers might not count as African American and Native Americans writers. The only way we routinely get around this requirement of cultural transmission in a historical descent population is by assuming it rather than demonstrating it, in a maneuver exactly like Frank Chin's proposition that "Chinese Americans" all grew up with the Ballad of Fa Mulan. That argument was no less racial than multiculturalism's routine assumption that racialized minority people practice the appropriate minority culture.

Thus we see that despite the proper ambition of the brilliant *Signifying Monkey,* Henry Louis Gates too must collapse his carefully constructed cultural definition of African American literature back into the very racial basis of the tradition that he has fought so hard and so explicitly to avoid. And in doing so, he is part of our paradigm of literary multiculturalism that grounds purported cultural differences and identities in race. Though he tries hard to hew to the Boasian theoretical distinction between culture and race, his theory does not really permit the phrase "African American" to refer to either a race or a culture—rather, the phrase refers to both simultaneously, just as the analogous phrases "white," "Chicano," and "black" refer to both cultures and races in Anzaldúa's *Borderlands/La Frontera.* Thus while Margaret Atwood, neither black nor American, cannot count as an African American novelist, she appears to have written an African American novel, albeit one without any black characters. That is what it means to clearly distinguish between race and culture in the way that Gates says we must.

Thus it is that our current conceptual grounds for minority literary traditions are incoherent.[3] We collectively pretend that multicultural literature coheres around distinct cultures, with the possible addition that there is a continuity of African American/Asian American/Chicano/Native American "experience," one based on the shared historical environmental formation of different subjects. I am not claiming that our most famous and canonical multiculturalists are racist. We (and they) know we are not supposed to believe in race in a biological sense anymore, but instead as a social construction. Probably these authors do not quite believe in such a thing as old fashioned race (though their biological metaphors of blood, genes, and hybridity suggest that at least sometimes some of them do). Indeed, the rhetorical stance of multiculturalism in the last three decades or so has been to generally see through the biological fantasies that help generate the social construction of race. There is much evidence in Morrison's work, for example, to suggest a theorization of the social construction of racial symbolism in the United States that is at least as sophisticated as that of Omi and Winant's (as in, for example, her essay *Playing in the Dark*).

Nevertheless, even when our paradigm of literary and critical multiculturalism is most disenchanted about race—seeing it as a social construction rather than as a biological reality—it continues to ground cultural identity in a racial prescription. We erroneously fold into the social science truth that our races are socially constructed the dubious assumption that this construction includes the learning of racially appropriate cultures—such that, somehow, society's construction of the social reality of race out of its biological delusions *is the same thing as* or *happens simultaneously with* the learning by children of distinct African American or Chicano or Asian American or Native American cultures. Contemporary multiculturalism conflates these two distinct processes of social learning, distinct not only as lessons but as sites of learning and as audiences. Racialization's lessons are the social significance of "race" in America—its signs, its hierarchies, its forms of racial etiquette that apply differently to differently raced citizens—and these things are learned to different degrees by all citizens. But minority cultural transmission has a much wider content: it includes such things as vernaculars, oral traditions, religious beliefs, food practices, music, and so on. Racialization occurs as a national learning process, with regional pockets of difference cross-hatched by the usual catalog of identity-complicators like gender, class, sexuality, and religion. But minority cultural transmission occurs in local/familial neighborhood settings and in particularized segments of national media. As Kingston's narrator insightfully asks a portion of her readership at the beginning of *The Woman Warrior*—again announcing her project of dis-orientation, her lack of cultural expertise—"Chinese-Americans, when you try to understand what things in you are Chinese, how do you separate what is peculiar to childhood, to poverty, insanities, one family, your mother who marked your growing with stories, from what is Chinese? What is Chinese tradition and what is the movies?" (5–6). Racialization is a kind of cultural tradition in America, but it is not the cultural transmission of minority cultures to specific minority groups.

The primary example where these two processes overlap, of course, is the idea that racialized minority groups' experiences of social race and racism become part of a cultural tradition that is passed down to younger generations. This is certainly true: Hurston's work in African American folklore revealed stories constituting part of a minority cultural tradition that encoded black responses and understandings to the process of racialization and the facts of racism. But African American parents teaching their children how to deal with racism is a learned cultural trait that cannot count as an entire and distinct minority culture. This is only to say that, while all African Americans may be raced in America—heterogeneously according to gender, economic status, region, sexuality, and so on—such does not always or usually include the transmission of a distinctive culture. Alice Walker, for instance, was raced as black before she discovered (or rediscovered) the distinctive African American folklore in Hurston's *Mules*. To use another example, Americans of Chinese descent may all be raced (in similar but uneven ways), but that racialization is a process distinct from the learning of Chinese American cultural heritage such as the Ballad of Fa Mulan oral tradition. We have perhaps been laboring under the erroneous conflation, since Omi and Winant, that the social construction of race implied the social construction of cultural difference: in other words, that distinct cultures get attached to different races during the process of "racialization"—as if the social formation and signification of race somehow included the transmission of cultural traditions. This confusion has produced what Richard Ford calls our "racial cultures." Warning that "the degree and salience of cultural differences between the races is much less dramatic than between insular aboriginal groups and urbanized cosmopolitans" (8), Ford nonetheless finds that "the slippage between quite insular groups defined by 'societal cultures' and fairly diffuse groups with only mild and relatively superficial cultural distinctiveness is characteristic of multiculturalist argumentation" (11).

As will surely be clear by now, my argument largely concurs with (and has been influenced by) the theses about race and identity forcefully articulated by Walter Benn Michaels in *Our America* and *The Shape of the Signifier*. There have been some reasonable challenges to both his method and his conclusions, and these deserve to be carefully worked through.[4] But multicultural literary studies has more or less ignored his most important theoretical challenge, that our current notions of culture and identity depend theoretically (and for historical reasons) on an unacknowledged turn to race. My contribution to this debate has been to show that culture has itself not always been (and need not be) grounded in a race or turned into an identity, and that a more complex historical account of the genealogy of multiculturalism reveals the series of challenges and confrontations among rival conceptions of culture (anthropological, sociological, and nativist) that structured the literary history of multiculturalism in all four minority traditions. Marjorie Perloff famously asked of Michaels's account, what happened between the nativist twenties and the multiculturalist nineties (100), and I have demonstrated that the path between them was a tortuous one, with many of the most important and canonical multiculturalist writers turning not to nativist forebears but instead to the anthropological conception of culture that had (in the twenties) been the very concept to challenge nativist racial "culture," but that when such writers regrounded cultural difference in race they collapsed the conceptual distinction that Boas had fought so hard to establish.

✆ The Multicultural Complex

The racial grounds for culture is one aspect of what I would like to call a "multicultural complex" generally characterizing the way multicultural literature is written, researched, and taught. I am borrowing the notion of the "complex" from the history of anthropology, a notion which was itself the object of intensive debate within the discipline, becoming perhaps most widely known when Melville Herskovits adapted it for his dissertation (supervised by Boas) titled "The Cattle Complex in East Africa." The notion of the culture complex tried to answer a question of diffusion: why, in different cultures, did many of the same or similar cultural traits appear together rather than spread randomly across different cultural entities? Mooney's, Mayhall's, and Momaday's accounts of the Kiowa, for example, showed that they shared a pattern of cultural traits with other Plains cultures: horses, the Sun dance, warrior societies, and nomadic seasonal hunting (and sometimes agricultural) practices. While I am not so concerned with the anthropological debate about what the complexes meant and how they formed,[5] I am borrowing the notion of the culture complex for my interrogation of why certain characteristic gestures and strategies tend to co-occur in multiculturalism, suggesting a logic of common historical factors (such as diffusion) and of internal design (like causes have like effects). Our current multicultural complex is constituted by the following propensities, a pattern of co-occurring characteristics, strategies, and rhetorical moves by virtue both of the historical development in the genealogy of literary multiculturalism through engagement with social science ideas, and of certain kinds of inner logics. Tendencies and not laws, they are not representative of all literary multiculturalism and our literary criticism of it all the time; nevertheless, they co-occur frequently enough to be a discernable and historically meaningful pattern across the four different minority literary traditions. This delineation of the multicultural complex should be treated as an evaluative array: a set of questions to be asked rather than assumed of the literature and criticism that is interested in questions of race, culture, identity, pluralism, and nation.

1. First is the *productive indistinction between culture and race,* reflected in our lack of distinct terminology. Matthias Schubnell's unwillingness or inability to distinguish between culture and race is a trait he shares with his subject, N. Scott Momaday, but Robert Hemenway's unwillingness or inability to distinguish between them is one pointedly not shared by his subject, Zora Neale Hurston. Writers of phases one and two took up anthropology and sociology precisely because it produced a rigorous conceptual distinction between them, but phase three literary writers in general abandoned it. This productive blurring appears with the earliest forms of cultural nationalisms, such as in Addison Gayle's Black Aesthetic work. Multiculturalism's productive indistinction between culture and race is intricately connected to

2. The *grounding of appropriate culture in race,* as we have seen in the literary and critical work of Morrison, Chin, Momaday, Reed, and Anzaldúa. Multiculturalism's productive indistinction between culture and race frequently means that multiculturalist description becomes racial prescription. One way multiculturalist writers and critics frequently ground appropriate culture in one's race is through

3. The *relatively recent triumph of the category of identity.* Identity has worked as a supplement to, and frequently becomes a substitute for, the work of cultural description. Identity is in tension, in this sense, not with difference, but with description. As a supplement to the existentialist description of what people (or nations) do and believe, it is always essentialist: it develops a group ontology that does not derive from the facts of existence. First- and second-phase writers generally did not

322	A GENEALOGY OF LITERARY MULTICULTURALISM

have a concept of or interest in identity; those who momentarily did, like Ellison, Paredes, and Okada, did so in the midst of Cold War patriotism, the context within which a strong notion of national identity originally developed. Cold War national identity appears to have been the source of the word and idea of identity for the cultural nationalisms of the third phase, which eventually and gradually (for the most part) turned to identity and simultaneously abandoned the word and idea of the nation and nationalism. Identity's ascent as a concept that does more affective and ideological work than mere culture is in turn linked to

4. The *treatment of learned history and learned culture as innate.* History and culture are learned in ways that are not always explicit, named, or obviously pedagogical, but they are not inherited, and they cannot be forms of "memory." Our multiculturalist critical paradigm's treatment of learned culture as things that we are born with and of the history (or trauma) of things that happened to other people as one's own experience logically supports (and is supported by) identity's formation not through existentialist description but through essentialist ontology, and the racial grounding of appropriate culture. This can include, as we have seen, the collapse of a possible ancestor's religion, culture, or experience, into one's own religion, culture, and experience, a process as true of Neal's "cultural memory" as it is of Momaday's "memory in the blood." In *Beloved,* Toni Morrison tropes and transforms racialized history into a kind of racial memory—slavery is something that she, and the characters, and white and black readers, "don't want to remember."[6] Slavery and the Middle Passage become things that cannot quite be learned about, but rather must be reexperienced—even for contemporary readers—by a memory transference whose continuity is race, not culture. When Dorothy Ritsuko McDonald writes of Frank Chin's "sense of Chinese American history as a valiant, vital part of the history of the American West, a history he believes his own people, under the stress of white racism, have forgotten or wish to forget in their eagerness to be assimilated into the majority culture" (Introduction ix), she imagines Chinese American history not as something to be learned but as something, already possessed somehow "by his own people," that is threatened with "forgetting." This quote nicely summarizes the mutually supportive qualities of the multicultural complex, wherein innate history is understood to be the property of an undifferentiated cultural-racial group threatened by assimilative pressures.[7]

❧ Identity Is Not Progressive

As will no doubt be clear by now, I view this multicultural complex, espe-cially its emphasis on identity, as deeply conservative in politics instead of (as it is usually assumed to be on the left and the right) as progressive. In a 2006 debate about immigration, for instance, Senator Lamar Alexander said, "English is part of our national identity. It's part of our spirit. It's part of our blood,"[8] thus using the same metaphor to describe learned things as innate things that, we have seen, has been widely used by canonical multicultural-ist writers like Reed, Momaday, and Anzaldúa. Likewise former President George Bush and former Senator Bill Frist invoked the ideal of cultural "diversity" to justify the inclusion in public school curricula of the teaching of Intelligent Design, a sectarian-based nonscientific hatchet job on the cor-nerstone of modern biology, evolution. I do not view these deeply regressive political uses of the discourse of identity as cynical manipulations by politi-cians who know better. Rather, they suggest to me that the multicultural left has come to share a powerful set of conceptions and rhetorical strategies about identity with those on the religious and non-pluralist right.

I am, of course, not alone in this conclusion: there has been in the last decade a robust progressive-articulated critique of identity from theorists, cited in my introduction, as different as political philosopher Nancy Fra-ser, legal theorist Richard Ford, and literary critics Hazel Carby, Ross Posnock, and Walter Benn Michaels. I agree especially with Carby's, Fraser's, Ford's, and Michaels's arguments that identity and the politics of recognition work to distract us from material conditions and questions of redistribution. Iden-tity as a classic organizing principle distracting us from material conditions was impressively exemplified in *Birth of a Nation*'s political alliance between dispossessed whites and aristocratic whites against disenfranchised African Americans during and after Reconstruction: as David Roediger reminds us, following Du Bois's lead, such "wages of whiteness" are the psychological compensation for being poor (12).

Appeals to culture and pluralism can themselves conceal identitarian log-ics that are apparent in moments when they become racially prescriptive or collapse past peoples' practices and values with current ones. It is in such a vein that I interpret Kenneth Warren's observation that "One strange effect of this cultural turn has been the way that across the political spectrum many individuals who expressed concern about the economic and social plight of black urban populations in the 1980s and 1990s began to find it rhetorically compelling to contrast the post-segregation present unfavorably with the Jim

Crow and slave pasts" (76). Warren cites Cornell West on this point, but also Toni Morrison's mourning of a disappearing rural culture. He concludes,

> So as they surveyed the social scene from Princeton University in the late 1980s and early 1990s, writers like Morrison and West added their voices to the growing consensus that perhaps the most important political project facing black academics and writers in the waning decades of the twentieth century was to preserve and revitalize the village culture that had existed in the past, possibly among African societies but most certainly during the slave era in the U.S. south. (77)

As we have seen with writers like Neal, Reed, Momaday, Clifford, and Anzaldúa, this kind of imagined revivalism is based not so much on a pluralism of actual lived cultures as on the hope that identity itself will be a progressive answer to social oppression and economic poverty. "I worry," writes Richard Ford, "that multicultural rights will distract attention from the most pressing contemporary social ills that, by and large, concern disparities of wealth and income" (6).

Thus the critical multiculturalism of which David Palumbo-Liu speaks would entail, crucially, the kind of evaluation of cultural practices and values that Gloria Anzaldúa forcefully argues for in *Borderlands/La Frontera*. The *mestiza's* "first step," says Anzaldúa, is "to take inventory." "She puts history through a sieve, winnows out the lies," a process that represents "a conscious rupture with all oppressive traditions of all cultures and religions" (104). While I have been critical of Anzaldúa's cultural politics, this drive toward the critical evaluation of cultural traditions and ideas, imagined as a sieve, seems urgently needed. Anzaldúa, as we have seen, partly grounds her critique of Chicano patriarchal traditions by way of a pre-warrior Aztec cultural ethos—that is, she critiques a certain set of cultural practices partly through values generated from within (though at a different time) that same culture. But that such cultural relativism cannot do the job Anzaldúa needs it to do is reflected in her more universalizing language in this and other moments: that oppression itself is to be recognized, analyzed, evaluated, and rejected on universal grounds, grounds that claim to stand outside of culture. And while I have not emphasized this thread of critical, universal sifting of cultures in this book, much multiculturalist literature correctly takes the stance that to challenge the purported universalism of the West entails uncovering its ethnocentricism, not abandoning the ideal of the universal. But when such multicultural critiques are articulated through tropes of blood and memory or logics of disrespect and identity, we are witnessing a kind of failure of nerve, an undeserved retreat. Many of the values and practices constitutive of pluralist societies do not require critical evaluation. But we should not shy away from the processes of description and evaluation, based on ideals that aspire toward universal ones.

This critical and progressive multiculturalism can be used to read (and teach) against the identitarian grain of much of what our multicultural literature shares with deeply conservative politics in the United States today. We must, as Frank Chin has ordered, do our homework. We can enthusiastically answer Gloria Anzaldúa's call for critical evaluation and cultural sifting. And after doing our homework, that critical evaluation need not be limited to our own culture (as in Kingsolver's *Poisonwood Bible*) but can include that of other cultures (as in Alice Walker's *Color Purple*)—so long as we are willing to put up for critical analysis, *by cultural outsiders,* cultural values and traditions we hold dear. But we can also, recognizing the constitutive circuit between social science ideas and literary multiculturalism, approach culture with a proper sense of wonder and strangeness instead of authoritative expertise, as Kingston has taught us. And, finally, we should surely be nervous, as was Toni Morrison, about groups and what we think we know about "them." Constitutively infected by social science ideas about culture, multicultural U.S. literature no longer gives us pristine images of cultures—in fact, it never did.

🍂 Notes

Introduction

1. The citation is from *Dust Tracks,* 165.

2. As will become clear, many of the social science questions about race, culture, and identity centered around Jewish people, as inquirers, examples, and objects of study. Boas and Herskovits were important Jewish American anthropologists, and Robert Park first formulated his theory of the "marginal man" through the archetype of the Jew caught between two cultures. But while the transformation of Jewish difference from being racial to being cultural is included in this history of social science, I do not examine Jewish American writers in its critical genealogy of literary multiculturalism because social science did not crucially provide them with the enabling concept of culture that it provided to the other racialized minority writers. It may be that the reconceptualization of Jews as racially white meant that such social science concepts of culture had less appeal than they did to their still-racialized contemporaries. Many canonical postwar Jewish American writers (e.g., Bellow, Mailer, Roth) have been seen to be able to write not only about Jewish experience but also about "universal" experience supposedly rendered particularly in white protagonists in a way that some racialized writers have not (e.g., Hurston): the scandal that attended *The Human Stain* was not that Roth was writing about a gentile but that he was writing about a black man (passing for white). I accordingly concentrate on the circuit between social science and the literary traditions of four groups whose members continue to be racialized, though questions of Jewish culture and identity remain relevant to the genealogy that here unfolds.

3. This unanimity could be seen in the recent invocation, by conservative evangelical Christian leaders like President George Bush and Senate Majority Leader Bill Frist, of the ideals of "diversity" and cultural difference in their call to teach Intelligent Design alongside evolution in high school classrooms. That their language was multiculturalism's language is another sign of the success of multiculturalism as an official national paradigm.

4. Boas suggested that what looks like murder to us is a result of our "juridical concept of murder," but the psychologies behind taking lives may entirely vary from culture to culture. So a murder-revenge is entirely different from sacrifice (*Mind* 188).

5. Boas, *Mind* 49. Unless otherwise noted, in-text references to *The Mind of Primitive Man* are to the 1938 edition.

6. Legend said the link between his physics dissertation and his cultural anthropology career was that he had heard that Inuit have different categories for colors, and had to go investigate (Herskovits, *Franz Boas* 9).

7. Hyatt makes much of Boas's experience of anti-Semitism in Germany and the United States, arguing that much of the liberal politics of Boas's research was a proxy fight against anti-Semitism. Another biographer, Vernon Williams Jr., argues that the relationships Boas developed with African Americans suggest a deeper commitment than using them as "camouflage" (37). More accurate still is Hutchinson's conclusion that "believing that culture, not race, was the operative category of group identity, Boas did not consider himself Jewish, for he did not practice the Jewish religion and did not feel himself to have been raised in a Jewish culture" (69).

8. Herskovits writes, "The challenge to current biological thought was even more far-reaching. At that time, the doctrine of the autonomy of genetic determinants of physical type received almost unquestioned acceptance. [...] Such results could not but argue for the immediate effect of environmental factors on physical type, of a kind and to a degree held impossible by the biologists and physical anthropologists of the day" (*Franz Boas* 39–40).

9. Boas makes the point in the 1911 edition of *Mind*, as a way of arguing that race and culture are not connected, that "certain survivals of African culture and language are found" among African Americans, but that they are, "in culture and language, however, essentially European" (127–28). As he continues in the final chapter, "The tearing-away from the African soil and the consequent complete loss of the old standards of life, which were replaced by the dependency of slavery and by all it entailed, followed by a period of disorganization and by a severe economic struggle against heavy odds, are sufficient to explain the inferiority of the status of the race, without falling back upon the theory of hereditary inferiority" (272).

Chapter 1

1. See the table of contents in Herskovits, *The Anthropometry of the American Negro*, for a list of the physical traits Hurston and other assistants measured. See Gershenhorn for an analysis of the argument and receptions of Herskovits's anthropometric studies.

2. Hurston's arrival in New York is instructive of the feedback circuit between social science and literature constitutive of the Renaissance itself, which would refashion the understanding of race and culture, as Hutchinson has shown. Hurston moved to New York in January 1925 from Howard—with her studies only partly finished—after being urged by Robert Park–trained African American sociologist Charles S. Johnson, editor of *Opportunity* (Hutchinson 173), which had published her story "Drenched in Light" in the previous month's issue. *Opportunity*, a major periodical of the developing Renaissance, was devoted to publishing social science work by black social scientists (like Franklin Frazier and Ralph Bunche) and white social scientists (like Herskovits and Boas) as well as Renaissance writers (like Jean Toomer, Langston Hughes, Countee Cullen, Gwendolyn Bennett) (Boyd 89).

3. To clarify: both anthropology and sociology argued against racial thinking, even as, Boas noted in 1938, racial thinking continued to animate common opinion in America and Europe (*Mind* 253–54). The robust difference between them arises from their culture concepts, although there is some latitude for intellectual borrowing and adaptation: of two African American sociologists trained by Robert Park, Charles Johnson praised folk culture (which was nevertheless was contained by the ultimate co-assimilationism of Park's theory) but Franklin Frazier, like Wright, saw

that culture mostly as evidence of pathology. These are different accents on the general Parkian account of the origins and destiny of African American culture; both are different in turn from the Boas-Herskovits-Hurston line that would ultimately be interested in cultural longevity and survivals. Another Park student, the anthropologist Robert Redfield, became a key witness for the NAACP in arguing the school desegregation cases, but as we shall see, Redfield was an anthropologist in name only, owing most of his intellectual debts to the tradition of his mentor (and father-in-law) Robert Park. *A Genealogy of Literary Multiculturalism* thus fundamentally agrees with Lee Baker's conclusion about the different political implications of Boasian anthropology and Parkian sociology.

4. See Houston Baker, "Workings of the Spirit." Baker argues that Hurston breaks free of the formal, academic requirements of 1930s ethnography and provides an account of folklore and voodoo which, partly because they are offered together, does not just relay information about African American cultural practices but somehow instantiates the soulful essence of conjure. But Hurston did not so much slip Boas's yoke as willingly (yet critically) assume it, especially its paradigm of culture. (See Manganaro, *Culture* 196, for a concurring opinion regarding Hurston's rejection of formal ethnography.) Valerie Boyd likewise downplays (mistakenly, I believe) the way Boasian anthropology helped formulate Hurston's project (162, 285), thus adopting Hemenway's contention of a "vocational schizophrenia" resolved only by Hurston's final turn to literature. But what Boas represented was more than just a set of "techniques" or a formal method for transcribing the results of fieldwork: it was rather the culture concept itself that would become so useful to Hurston in the decades that followed.

5. Boas in 1911 thought there might be a few African survivals in an otherwise Americanized black population. Hurston posited some kind of African retention before her study of anthropology. In a 1925 story, "Black Death," which Hurston never published, one character seeking a hoodoo doctor sees lights in the swamp, and "three hundred years of America passed like the mist of morning. Africa reached out its dark hand and claimed its own. Drums. Tom, Tom, Tom, Tom, Tom, Tom, beat in her ears" (qtd. in Hemenway 74–75). In the years that followed, Hurston's theorization of retentions became more thoroughly and disciplinarily cultural than (as is true of "Black Death") ambiguously racial. Her folklore collection and her work on voodoo suggested that African cultural content was itself retained in significant ways, but the extent to which what Hurston (and Herskovits) found may have changed Boas's mind is unclear. Both Hurston and Herskovits played a role in establishing the anthropological idea that historically particular cultural traditions might have survived the Middle Passage (see Hutchinson 76).

6. In a mock-review of *Jonah's Gourd Vine,* Hurston wrote, "The characters in the story are seen in relation to themselves and not in relation to the whites as has been the rule.... To watch these people one would conclude that there were not white people in the world" (qtd. in Boyd 256).

7. The principle of cultural relativism was especially important for fieldwork. As Stocking notes, "Relativism, in the sense of the withholding of judgment by any external or a priori standard, thus came in Boas' work to be a fundamental premise of anthropological method, a necessary basis for accurate observation and sound interpretation" ("Franz Boas" 230).

8. As is well documented, one of the differences between Hurston and other Renaissance artists was the latter's belief, represented perhaps by Alain Locke's introduction to *The New Negro,* that the talented tenth had to speak for the inarticulate masses, crafting art out of folk material (Hemenway 42, 50). The Renaissance writers were at least "one generation of removal from the 'racy peasant undersoil'" of the folk whose work some claimed as inspiration—except for Hurston (51). Hurston knew from her own life that the folk tales and music were already art and "proof of psychic health" (51), and it was anthropology that helped her articulate her resistance to this Renaissance model of the conscious artist rendering pre-artistic folk material into finished and sophisticated art.

9. Hemenway suggests that the mule scene is from the unpublished *Mule Bone,* the contested play cowritten by Hurston and Langston Hughes that eventually broke their friendship (234). The contention was based partly on how much of the play was whose creation, though it is almost certain that the thin mule story was an Eatonville tradition supplied by Hurston. It was this kind of anthropological inclusion that Alain Locke bemoaned when he reviewed the novel for *Opportunity,* complaining that folklore became the novel's main point, at the expense of "motive fiction and social document fiction" (Hemenway 241), presumably of the kind that had begun to be written by Richard Wright in 1936, and was collected as *Uncle Tom's Children* in 1938. Already by the mid-late 1930s, then, the social science disciplines of anthropology and sociology were aligning distinctively with "folklore fiction" about culture on the one hand and "social document fiction" about the "Negro problem" in American society on the other.

10. Other examples of African retentions are found in *Horse* 116, 142, 148, 205, and 238.

11. B B61. Boas Papers. Zora Neale Hurston correspondence. American Philosophical Society.

12. Michaels represents Boas as more of a universalist than he typically was. Indeed, Boas was sometimes a "universalist" who did not refuse evaluation (173n199): he never treated the values and practices of racial supremacy in America or Germany as cultural traditions that needed to be respected as merely different. To Boas, these cultural traditions were not only morally wrong; they were also scientifically incorrect. Science was a privileged practice, not just another cultural position (Herskovits, *Franz Boas* 99). But while there was an underlying universalism to Boas's science, that science repeatedly argued for a form of cultural pluralism that Michaels suggests Boas was against. Boas's universalism and the evaluation it promised were rarely invoked in the anthropological program of descriptive pluralism and cultural difference. That is what it means, to return to Hurston's work, for voodoo to take its place beside Catholicism as only culturally different, not better or worse morally or as systemic theology (*Horse* 204), an observation that entirely leaves aside (as Boas would) the question of the truth claims of either religious tradition, and for her to briefly compare the African American folk hero John to the Hebrew hero Daniel (*Mules* 247). What is "basal for all culture[s]" (Stocking, qtd. in *Our America* 173n199) is religion and hero tales, but what is pluralist in both Hurston and Boas is the refusal to treat one cultural set as a standard of universal measure by which other cultural religions or stories could be evaluated.

13. Hutchinson's own evidence seems to show that James's antifoundationalism and denial of universals is an epistemological point, not the Boasian cultural point

that what we see and the way we interpret the real is determined largely by our cultural vantage point. In other words, the pragmatist argument since Charles Sanders Peirce, that we apprehend the real only through experience confirmed by a linguistic community, implies the existence of some kind of group, but to call the shape of that group a culture (instead of a "province" or a race) comes into sharp focus only with the Boasian renovation of the culture concept.

14. After *Mules,* Hurston may have seen herself in these Chaucerian terms. As she wrote to a black newspaper on December 29, 1934, she urged other African Americans to consider Chaucer, "who saw the beauty of his own language in spite of the scorn in which it was held" by the Norman English (qtd. in Boyd 265).

15. Letter from Charles Pearce, April 6, 1929, in Box 18, Folder 157, D'Arcy McNickle Collection.

Chapter 2

1. Included in *The New Negro* are two tales collected by Fauset from Cudjo Lewis, who would later tell Hurston of the Palace of Skulls (245–49).

2. Omi and Winant 10. This mistake is repeated by Tolentino (378). See also Bulmer 59 for Boas's influence on Thomas. In *From Caste to a Minority,* Vernon Williams Jr. likewise argues that Thomas was "the conduit between sociologists at Chicago and Franz Boas and his followers," citing specifically Thomas's use in 1912 of Boas's scholarship to substantiate an anti-racial environmentalist model (85).

3. Park outlined and drafted among other things some of Washington's life-writing: his *My Larger Education,* a sequel to *Up from Slavery* (Harlan 291). His subsequent participation in the Chicago School of Sociology, which advocated the use of life-writing as data collection, begins to outline the problematic circuit of articulation between literature and social science that I address in the conclusion to this volume.

4. Park wrote in the introduction to sociologist Charles Johnson's 1934 *Shadow of the Plantation* (reprinted as "The Negro and His Plantation Heritage," *Race and Culture* 66–78) that anthropologists were unlikely to approve of Johnson's book because of these disciplines' difference on the question of what culture was: "the study starts with a different tradition [than anthropology]—the tradition, namely, of the rural sociologist, who conceives his community rather as a statistical aggregate than as a cultural complex" (71).

5. Boas offers the example of personality differences between Italian immigrants and their American-born children (*Mind* 128), the generation gap that would become such an important trope for Asian American literature. But that trope had to first pass through the sociology of Robert Park, who extended to Asian Americans what Boas here figures as something that happens to European Americans.

6. Wright even directs doubters of *Native Son* and *Black Boy* to "study" *Black Metropolis* for confirming evidence (Introduction xx).

7. Richard Wright, "Bibliography on [the] Negro in Chicago," Box 53, Illinois Writers Project/"Negro in Illinois" Papers, Vivian G. Harsh Research Collection of Afro-American History and Literature, Chicago Public Library.

8. Wright and Myrdal personally desegregated the Hôtel de la Cloche in Beaune, France, in 1954, which, sensitive to white American tourist sensibilities, was going to deny them rooms. Myrdal crashed his cane on the front desk, shouting at the attendant, "You've gotten goddammed sophisticated, haven't you?" They were let

rooms, and Myrdal later lectured the full but silent dining room, a public display of white liberalism that left his friend uncomfortable (Rowley 454–55).

9. This is a key difference between Wright and Ellison: Ellison's narrator fears the white-dominated society's disposition to treat Trueblood's crimes as what "all Negroes do" (58), and for Ellison it is this extrapolation of the type that is itself the problem. For Wright, the reading for type should occur, since, according to Park (as I show in chapter six), what the urban environment produced was types. Wright's point was that the type was no longer racial, but, as with Park's understanding, a result of conditioning in specific urban ecological niches.

10. Though she opposed forced desegregation, Hurston basically lived an integrated life. She had, after all, moved from all-black Howard University to study at all-white Barnard College: as Valerie Boyd points out, "Zora was poised to step into a miniscule circle: of the thirteen thousand or so black people enrolled in college nationwide in the mid-1920s, fewer than three hundred of them attended white schools" (101). Being in the Renaissance itself and at Columbia basically meant that Hurston moved among African American, white, and black/white worlds. In opposing forced desegregation and opposing Jim Crow laws, Hurston's concern was not only for individual self-determination, but also for the preservation of cultures that individuals could move among. Hemenway points out that "Zora's [mainstream] journalism between 1942 and 1945 usually spoke favorably of an integrated society" (293), and that she stated clearly that she wanted Jim Crow laws overturned (295).

11. That concept of culture in turn would be opposed by the integrationists. Hurston instantiated her understanding of African American culture partly through putting on musical shows that combined folk tales, music, and dance. Hemenway notes that some African Americans resented the shows, seeing them as primitive and "counterproductive in the fight against segregation" (206). But, says Hemenway, "Hurston was not afraid to challenge the assimilationist politics of the era by emphasizing the cultural difference of black America" (206).

12. Hemenway misprints Szwed as saying "cultural procedures" instead of "cultural processes" (Szwed 158).

13. Hurston too was keenly aware of the disciplinary difference between her project and sociology. "Of course I am not interested in Sociology," she wrote regarding her *Mules* material on June 15, 1932 (Kaplan 260), as she was editing her folklore manuscript—a denial that Boyd links to Hurston's similar distaste for writing on "the Negro problem" (Boyd 241). She would later write to Fannie Hurst about *Jonah's*, "So I tried to deal with life as we actually live it—not as the Sociologists imagine it" (Kaplan 286).

Chapter 3

1. Much of this chapter was previously published in my article "Reading Ethnography: The Cold War Social Science of Jade Snow Wong's *Fifth Chinese Daughter* and *Brown v. Board of Education.*" I am here refining its argument in a couple of directions. First, I draw a sharper distinction among different social science disciplines here than I did in "Reading Ethnography." Second, I offer here a more nuanced view of the benefits and pitfalls that social science work offered early multi-ethnic writers.

2. See, for example, Elaine Kim 66–72, Jinqi Ling, *Narrating* 140–46, and Palumbo-Liu, *Asian/American* 138–46.

3. The term "generation gap," however, appears not to have been coined by Chicago sociology. I have been unable to trace the origin of the term, but Internet searches suggest that it was coined, alternatively, by sociologists or by advertising firms in the 1960s (also the decade of its earliest appearance in the *Oxford English Dictionary*), with reference to the baby boomers' rejection of their parents' values.

4. As Fred Matthews concludes of Park's work on the Pacific Coast,

> Two major conclusions emerged from the Carnegie and Pacific Coast race relations studies. The first was a confirmation of the earlier insight of Thomas and others, including Franz Boas, that differences in human behavior could be explained better by studying the environment and especially the culture of a group, than by resorting to biological explanations. The other major insight was one which has since become hackneyed in studies of immigration—the crucial importance of the second generation, the children of immigrant parents who grew up in the United States. (163)

5. And, not incidentally, echoing Américo Paredes's criticism (which I discuss in chapter five) of some Anglo ethnographers investigating Mexican American communities, whose marginal grasp of Spanish likewise created misrepresentations.

6. At the same time, sociology has obviously helped sharpen Wong's written sense of cultural authority. We can thus see Wong's four-page description on buying and cooking rice (57–60), her description of cooking a meal for her friends at Mills College (which is an actual recipe; 159–60), her description of Chinese holidays (chapter 5) and how Chinese get married (chapter 16) as partaking as much in the sociological tradition of recording urban ethnic practices as it is in the tradition of the tourist guide.

7. *Brown v. Board of Education*, 347 U.S. 483 (1954).

8. Kluger mistakenly reverses this impact (310). See Lee Baker 179–82 and 276n48, in which there is some suggestion that Herskovits was made to feel more of an influence than the resulting publication would justify.

9. As Williams makes clear, Herskovits's position was "a minority position in the social sciences for approximately thirty years" but was "revised and modified" during "the 'Black Power' revolt in the late 1960s [...]. Herskovits, in essence, provided the cultural foundation for nation-based theory" (Williams 100), or what I will more accurately call the culturalism of the literary multiculturalism that emerged in the late 1960s and early 1970s.

10. Except in those moments when it was seen to conflict with commonsensical definitions of race as in the important Asian American citizenship case of *United States v. Bhagat Thind* (R. G. Lee, *Orientals* 142–44).

11. "*An American Dilemma*: A Review," *Shadow and Act* 303–17. This review was originally written in 1944 for the *Antioch Review* but went unpublished until *Shadow and Act*.

12. Ellison correctly hypothesized that Chicago sociology's "timidity" was directly linked to Booker T. Washington's accommodationism through Park's friendship with, work for, and support of Washington (306).

13. Ralph Ellison Papers, Library of Congress, Box 146, Folder 16, page 167 "Novels—*Invisible Man*—Drafts—Episodes 'Woodridge'." Future references to the Woodridge chapter are in parenthesis.

14. My reading is thus different from Kim's, who sees Ellison's reaction against sociology return in *Invisible Man* in its critique of certain white men who, despite their apparent benevolence, want to place black men "in a position analogous to the one conventionally occupied by women in a patriarchal culture," where they can be used as erotic objects (312).

15. In turning the Constitution into a "living document," *Brown* famously (and controversially) helped move Supreme Court interpretation away from originalism and intention (see Karst 55–56).

Chapter 4

1. The narrow definition of a "no-no boy" is someone who answered no to the two so-called loyalty questions on the 1943 Leave Clearance Application Form administered to interned Japanese Americans. Question 27 asked, "Are you willing to serve in the armed forces of the United States on combat duty wherever ordered?" and question 28 asked the candidate to swear allegiance to the United States and to "forswear any form of allegiance or obedience to the Japanese emperor." Both questions were confusing. Many thought that if they answered yes to the first question, they were in fact signing up for the army and not just indicating their abstract willingness to join; others, given the injustice of internment itself, were refusing to serve. Question 28 similarly implied to many a false assumption that the candidate had actually sworn allegiance to the Japanese emperor, to which one might answer no merely to reject the question's premise, seen by many to be a trap. See Chin, Emi, Kuromiya and Inada, "Introduction." The wider sense of a "no-no boy" is developed in the novel to mean someone like Ichiro who has said no to both Japan and America.

2. My reading of Ichiro's mother's logic is suggested by Walter Benn Michaels's reading of Oliver La Farge's *Laughing Boy*: "Biology is an essential but not a sufficient condition of an identity that here requires a relatively autonomous set of practices to complete its constitution: *autonomous* because they don't simply follow from the biology (they can be embraced or rejected); *relatively* autonomous because the determination of which practices are the right ones can only be made by reference to biology" (*Our America* 119).

3. American music threatens not just the cultural contamination of Japanese racial identity, but is likewise possibly destructive of racial descent, since, in an interesting echo, the Supreme Court litigant Fred Korematsu would meet his white American bride at such a dance (Irons, *Delayed* 6).

4. Fred Korematsu, a ship welder, refused to report for "evacuation" in San Leandro, California, in May 1942, and after his arrest he was convicted for evading the order, a decision upheld by both the Court of Appeals and the Supreme Court. In *Korematsu,* the Court decided that though the racially based exclusion was constitutionally suspect, it was justified by the government's assertion of national emergency. Interestingly for this account of the assimilability of racialized minorities,

Korematsu's reason for resisting evacuation was that he didn't want to leave his Italian American girlfriend. In fact, he had had deorientalizing plastic surgery (before the evacuation order) so that he and his girlfriend would not be ostracized when they moved to Nevada together (Irons, *At War* 97). Korematsu's surgery anticipated D. R. Millard's postwar technology of eyelid surgery, an emergence that David Palumbo-Liu links to the sociological questions of assimilation and racial amalgamation: "If Park was impatient about the pace of racial 'enlightenment' in the United States during the thirties, if Stonequist could only see intermarriage as performing that necessary modification of racial markings [. . .] after the Second World War technology stepped in with something more immediate" (*Asian* 94). Korematsu was thus situated at the center of the question of the cultural assimilation of racialized minorities, which sociology was imagining as perhaps requiring, in the end, amalgamation as a way to end phenotypical distinctions. Sixty years later, Korematsu filed a friend-of-the-court brief in the case of *Rasul v. Bush,* 542 U.S. 466 (2004), linking the U.S. government's stance on Guantánamo prisoners to the internment's rush to sacrifice civil liberties in the name of military necessity.

Gordon Hirabayashi was a student at the University of Washington who purposefully defied the curfew ordered by General DeWitt. He turned himself in in 1942 to challenge the curfew order, which was ultimately upheld by the Supreme Court in 1943. Hirabayashi later became a sociologist, completing his Ph.D. at the University of Washington in 1952 on the Doukhobor community in British Columbia, and joining the faculty at the University of Alberta in 1959. He later reviewed Okada's *No-No Boy.*

5. This is to oversimplify the issue, of course. *Brown* is a cottage industry today for many reasons, and one of the major debates about it is the extent to which social science evidence was used, or should have been used, in reaching its decision. Richard Kluger called all of the famous footnote 11 "gratuitously obnoxious" (710). Justice Jackson, who dissented on *Korematsu* and criticized its racial logic—though he was part of the unanimous *Hirabayashi* decision—is reported to have seen as dubious the "extra-legal sociology and psychology that the black lawyers had introduced into" *Brown* (Kluger 607). Chief Justice Earl Warren of the unanimous *Brown* was the very California attorney general and then governor who warned against releasing the evacuated Japanese Americans because "no one will be able to tell a saboteur from any other Jap" (qtd. in Kluger 664). The distance between the two cases can be understood as part of a larger paradigm shift; like all paradigm shifts or attempts to periodize complicated intellectual and social developments, the transformation was neither smooth nor thorough. Law was, nonetheless, a kind of textual practice within a larger arena that included social science discourse and literature, in which the problems of real social difference were rearticulated as being aspects of cultural variation rather than genetic-based unalterable facts. Historical events and struggles had obviously also played their part in this transformation, with African Americans fighting for rights and recognition in the war years and after, and the genocidal brand of racial supremacy of the Nazis implicating similar kinds of supremacy abroad (Kluger 693).

6. As Werner Sollors points out, Park partly misreads these autobiographies (*Beyond Ethnicity* 9). But even this misreading indicates that theories of culture and race in the early and mid twentieth century were produced by a circuit of articulation

and influence between literature and social science, such that social scientists themselves viewed stories and life documents as data for hypotheses about culture and its transformations.

7. See Palumbo-Liu, *Asian/American,* chap. 9, for an excellent discussion of these social science tropes and how, once deployed to talk about racialized and Asian American citizens, they became contested terrain in Asian American cultural politics.

8. Wong also structures the more introspective moments of her autobiography according to the language of the second-generation marginal man who is between the cultures of her parents and America. Reflecting on her father's inability to pay for her college tuition, for instance, Wong muses, "She was trapped in a mesh of tradition woven thousands of miles away by ancestors who had had no knowledge that someday one generation of their progeny might be raised in another culture. Acknowledging that she owed her very being and much of her thinking to those ancestors and their tradition, she could not believe that this background was meant to hinder her further development either in America or in China" (110). Much of the autobiography's cross-cultural musings have this same structure of a kind of privileged agony at being caught in the middle of two cultural traditions.

9. For a fascinating critical account of the JERS, see Peter Suzuki's contribution to *The Big Aiiieeeee!,* an inclusion suggestive (among other things) of how important the repudiation of sociology became for the *Aiiieeeee!* group's cultural nationalist politics.

10. Robert Redfield, letter to Dillon S. Myer, April 12, 1943, Box 3, 1943–1944, Personal Correspondence File, Dillon S. Myer Papers, Harry S. Truman Library.

11. Letter from Robert O'Brien to President Wilkins dated March 26, 1942, Correspondence Series, 2/7 Ernest H. Wilkins, Box 58, Nisei folder, Oberlin College Archives. Accessed online at http://www.lib.washington.edu/exhibits/harmony/interrupted_lives/text/wil.html.

12. House Select Committee Investigating National Defense Migration. Part 30: Portland and Seattle Hearings: Problems of Evacuation of Enemy Aliens and Others from Prohibited Military Zones, 77th Cong., 2nd sess., 2 March 1942. Exhibit 3— Statement by Robert W. O'Brien, Assistant to the Dean, College of Arts and Sciences, University of Washington [p. 11598–11599]. Accessed online at http://www.lib.washington.edu/exhibits/harmony/interrupted_lives/text/tolan.html. Future quotations from the Tolan Committee hearings are in-text.

13. While Kenji's note of racial amalgamation is a sociological idea strictly traceable to Park and not one that was publicly voiced in the resettlement logic of Myer (Drinnon 56) or University of Washington sociologist Robert W. O'Brien ("Selective Dispersion"), it could safely be assumed (though not publicized) that the administrators and their sociological theorizers understood this would be the end-game.

Chapter 5

1. See José Limón, *Return,* José David Saldívar, "Chicano," and Héctor Calderón and José David Saldívar, Introduction to *Criticism,* for analyses of Paredes's deep influence on Chicano literature (particularly the work of Tomás Rivera and Rolando Hinojosa), the Chicano movement, and Chicano cultural studies.

2. The fact that Paredes covered the war crimes trials in Tokyo for the U.S. Army *Stars and Stripes,* spent considerable time in Japan, China, and Korea in the late 1940s, and married a "Japanese national who had grown up in Latin America" (see Limón, "Américo" 3) suggests that he might have been attentive to Asian American political issues.

3. Paredes published two short articles and nine book reviews in the *Journal* between 1958 and 1969, as well as an introduction to a set of papers, "The Urban Experience and Folk Tradition," in the April 1970 issue and a foreword to a set of papers titled "Toward New Perspectives in Folklore" in the January 1971 issue on folklore theory in the United States and Latin America.

4. This is not to say, of course, that there were not many sociologists engaged with the development of ethnic studies programs in the 1970s and after. It is only to say that the ascendant Park-Myrdal conception of a minority culture gradually abandoned for the dominant culture had to be replaced by one which imagined culture as something characterized by longevity, endurance, relative worth, and resistance to assimilative pressure—that is, Boasian and anthropological, even if unrecognized as such by sociologists themselves.

5. See Rosaldo, *Culture and Truth,* 150–55, and Saldívar-Hull, "Feminism," 215.

6. On the other hand, Paredes's student José E. Limón suggests that Paredes's ongoing mentoring of him was a separate intellectual experience from his exposure to "a relatively new and disturbing concern then at the margins of anthropology with issues of reflexivity and textuality in ethnographic writing," a concern represented for Limón by the work of Clifford, Marcus, Michael Fischer, and James Boon ("Dancing" 229).

7. And in fact, identity would also become a way of thinking about how one could keep getting "Americanized" and still not be American. The title makes it sound as if identity will be a supplement to thinking about cultural continuity in a single descent population (unlike Anglos taking their cowboy image from Mexican vanqueros): in other words, to possess identity one needs not only continuity but genetic descent. It is a short step from this idea to abandoning the idea of cultural continuity entirely—which is essentially what Momaday does with the Kiowa, as I show in chapter seven. The logic of what it means to deploy identity against an anthropological culture concept is not really worked out in the essay, though it is hinted at. Paredes ends the essay with a consideration of a recent 1969 lecture by Octavio Paz at the University of Texas at Austin in which Paz mused that recent violence in Tlatelolco had "correspondences with the Mexican past, especially with the Aztec world" (qtd. 46). While such "correspondences" could be theorized as cultural survivals (as Hurston had done, as Anzaldúa would do, and as even Webb had done in improbably attributing ostensible Mexican cruelty to the Inquisition), Paredes interprets Paz's comments to his mostly Anglo audience as biologism, that "Mexican biology was to blame" (46), an idea that Paredes shows animated the police response to the so-called *pachuco* riots in 1942 and 1943 in Los Angeles (45). This interpretation shows that even as late as 1978 identity remained a marginal concept for Paredes, and that he was attuned to the ways in which notions of identity threatened to reinvoke race and inheritance as the grounds for social characteristics instead of the hard-won cultural account of which he was a part.

8. For instance, Ramón Saldívar interestingly summarizes one of Paredes's arguments as "After 1835, this sense of being caught in the middle intensified and became a hallmark of Mexican-American identity" ("The Borderlands of Culture" 275). Drawing on Raymond Williams's idea of "residual culture," Saldívar suggests that the *corrido* nevertheless was an aspect of "subjective and collective identity construction" (275), again turning into a question of identity problems that both Paredes and Williams understood as questions of culture.

Chapter 6

1. Much of this section was previously published as "What *The Bluest Eye* Knows about Them: Culture, Race, Identity," *American Literature* 78.1 (March 2006): 141–68.

2. In fact, Gayle says Du Bois's problematic was abandoned when "the old master resolved the psychic tension in his own breast by leaving the country" for Africa in 1961 (Gayle xxii).

3. Kenneth Clark was a social psychologist who had done his Ph.D. at Columbia University under the supervision of Otto Klineberg, an anthropology student and "disciple of Boas at Columbia" (Kluger 309). Robert Carter of the NAACP had first turned to Klineberg as a possible social science authority for the case, and Klineberg (whom Hurston had helped study African American music in New Orleans) had directed Carter to Clark. While most of the social scientists put on the stand by the NAACP were anthropologists and psychologists (instead of sociologists, though there were some), according to Kluger's account of the struggle, it was nevertheless the sociological model of culture rather than the anthropological one that lay behind the case. The anthropologists were mostly asked to demonstrate the starting point of Boas's cultural revolution: the equality of the races. The anthropologist Robert Redfield became one of the key social science experts for this purpose, and his background is instructive. Redfield studied the Mexican village of Tepoztlan, but his approach was motivated not so much by questions of ethnography as it was by questions of modernization and cultural change as folk societies urbanized and industrialized. His work later influenced the so-called rural sociology. Though he was an anthropologist, his concept of culture was more akin to that of his dissertation supervisor and father-in-law Robert E. Park than it was to Boas's culture concept. The psychology experts for the NAACP tended to attest to the psychological damage caused by segregation, as with the Clarks' doll studies. They investigated the psychological effects of segregation, and their model of social forces preventing accommodation and assimilation derived from Park's model.

4. See Mody for a critique of this "conventional narrative." Even if Mody's argument is correct—that the Court was "seduced" but not influenced by mid-century social science as it sought intellectual cover for overruling the established juridical constraints of precedent and intention—the Court nonetheless officially approved of the project of the cultural assimilation of racialized minorities central to sociology.

5. Questions 1 through 4 in the Clarks' test were: "Give me the doll that you like to play with"; "... is a nice doll"; "... looks bad"; "... is a nice color." Questions 5 through 8: "Give me the doll that looks like a white child"; "... a colored child"; "... a Negro child"; "... like you" ("Racial Identification" 169).

6. Morrison may be referring to some troubling results produced by the Clarks' doll tests, which, it seemed, showed that African American children in the South's segregated setting were sometimes less inclined to reject the brown doll than those in the North's semi-integrated setting (see Kluger 356 and Monahan and Walker 185).

7. My discussion of Ellison here is indebted to Walling's account of how the reception of *Invisible Man* registered the growing cultural nationalism of the 1960s.

8. Cappetti, *Writing* 20–23. For instance, Thomas was trained as a philologist and throughout his career he emphasized the written record of diaries, letters, and autobiography; Park was influenced in his conception of industrial urban life by modern European and American writers; and Burgess offered courses and assignments on the sociology of the city as seen through literary texts.

9. Notes Kluger, reviewing the antiracist science in the years before *Brown,*

> it was the social psychologists who finally reached the not very profound conclusion that white belief in powerful Negro bodily aroma was inspired— to the extent that the phenomenon may have existed at all—not by a natural-born funk that ran with the genes but by the lack of bathing facilities and laggard sanitary habits among poor people living in warm climates who also tended not to have very large wardrobes or much chance to wash the clothes they owned. (309–10)

10. See Douglas, "What *The Bluest Eye* Knows," for an account of how Morrison's novel echoes the experimental use of the "type" made by Parkian sociology and Balzacian realism.

11. See, most recently, Rody; Nowlin; Dubey, "Narration"; Rushdy; Peach; McBride; and Dubey, *Black Women Novelists.*

12. Cynthia Dubin Edelberg takes *The Bluest Eye* to task for its negative portrayal of black people like Geraldine who choose education, hard work, and Christianity. As she argues, the assimilated Geraldine is poorly portrayed, and while Pauline appears somewhat funky, she is not a model to be emulated. Edelberg criticizes the novel's ironic use of biblical names, and its implication that Christianity is inappropriate for black people.

13. "M'Dear," the local folk healer brought in to diagnose and treat Aunt Jimmy (136–37), seems reminiscent of some of the root doctors and conjurors Hurston had discussed in the second part of *Mules and Men* (see "Prescriptions of Root Doctors" 281–85). (Houston Baker has also pointed to the root-working women in Morrison's 1973 *Sula* and in Alice Walker's 1970 *The Third Life of Grange Copeland,* attributing both to the influence of *Mules and Men* [304].) Morrison's rejection of the mix of romantic and religious discourse (the romantic partner who will complete you, the savior imagined sensually) (*Bluest* 113–22) seems like an outright critical revision of the same mix in *Their Eyes Were Watching God*—just as its portrayal of domestic violence, which in Hurston's novel is a sign of passion, is reversed in the brutal portrait of Cholly and Pauline's fights (as it also is in Alice Walker's *The Color Purple*).

14. The gendered and historical dynamic of Asian American women marrying white American men is wrapped up for Chin in a fear of the stereotype of effeminate or homosexual Asian men, a fear that responds to but does not reject the homophobia of the stereotype. *Chickencoop*'s triangulation of Asian American masculinity (see 18, 20, 23, 41, and 48) may account for the otherwise inexplicable repetition of the fact

that one character, Kenji, has twice peed next to a black man, an act that strangely recalls Morrison's Junior's desire to pee with the black boys.

Chapter 7

1. See R. Nelson, Watkins, and Evers, "Words," for extensive analysis of the importance of place in *House Made of Dawn.*

2. Douglas, "'You Have Unleashed a Horde of Barbarians!'"

3. As in, for example, *Poltergeist* or *The Blair Witch Project.*

4. Or rather, according to Drinnon, this racism was constitutive of American liberalism. Drinnon does not mean that Myer and others were motivated by a programmatic ideology of the biological racial inferiority of Asians or Indians (though some of them might have had some racist beliefs, and others clearly did not). He means rather that the "liberal consensus" expressed by Ickes, Myer, Roosevelt, and others entailed the liberal "absolutism" of making "everyone alike through 'Americanization,' 'assimilation,' 'integration,'" and dispersion (266–69).

5. The sources are generally as follows: section I (*Way* 17) is Mooney 148–50, 402, 413, 425; section II (19) is Mooney 154, 287–88; section III (21) is Mooney 161, 230, 284 and Mayhall 12–13; section V (25) is Mooney 153 and 238; section VIII (33) is Mooney 231; section IX (35) is Mooney 238–39; sections X and XI (37, 39) are Mooney 240; section XII (45) is Mooney 336; section XIV (49) is Mayhall ix; section XV (53) is Mooney 171; section XVII (59) is Mooney 281 and 294; section XVIII (61) is Mooney 161; section XIX (67) is Mooney 206 and 344; section XX (71) is Mooney 310; and section XXII (77) is Mooney 295. The anthropological part of section XIV (49) has its source in Mayhall ix, and the oral tradition part of section II may have its source, according to Schubnell, in John P. Harrington's *Vocabulary of the Kiowa Language* 252–53 (Schubnell 283n57). Several of these tracings are from Schubnell.

6. In section II, for instance, the first voice speaks the story of an ancient split between the present Kiowa and another band who departed after a fight about antelope udders and the second voice speaks of "reports of a people in the Northwest who speak a language that is similar to Kiowa" (18–19). The implicit (by proximity) connection of the two stories in *Way* is explicit in their probable source, as they both are details on the same page of Mooney's *Calendar History* (154). See also section V (Momaday 24–25) and Mooney 238.

7. American Philosophical Society B:B61 Boas Papers. James Mooney correspondence.

8. He appears to correct this in *The Names,* where he calls "horse culture" "the last culture to evolve in North America," another unattributed but more accurate quotation from the anthropologist Mayhall (155).

9. I have been unable to discover what *teah-whau* means, if anything; it is presumably in the Towa sub-dialect of Tanoan. Most critics regard the name Nicolás *teah-whau,* coupled with the evidence that Francisco is at one point teased that he is the son of the "consumptive priest" Frey Nicolás (179) as evidence that the witch is Francisco's mother.

10. As Allen notes, "Throughout his works, Momaday employs the term 'racial memory' to refer to the collective memories of a people passed down the generations

through the oral tradition" (114n16), thus joining the blurring of race/culture to the idea of memory. Ironically, it was through Native oral traditions that Boas partly formed the idea of culture in the first place; Momaday's innovation is to redescribe this classic instance of cultural transmission as something that is a kind of memory whose medium is race.

11. Here Michaels is himself, somewhat amusingly, made the object of the homological method that he frequently employs to show how apparently antithetical arguments share certain logical commitments, structures, or outcomes.

12. At one point they write, "*Culture* is one word for group agency," a definition loose enough to encompass all kinds of entities (like corporations) that the traditions of anthropology and multiculturalism would not consider to be cultures at all (746), and at another point they suggest that Clifford is moving toward "some conjuncture like historical socioculture," a new but undefined concept (750).

Chapter 8

1. Richard Swope is more precise, interpreting the character Nathan Brown as Countee Cullen (619) and the character Major Young as Langston Hughes (624).

2. For an important exception, see Lindroth, "Generating." Lindroth focuses on the link between their treatments of voodoo religion, and I frame these treatments within a larger context of anthropological theory allowing endurance and survivals.

3. The reference to "*Voodoo Gods: An Inquiry into the Native Myths and Magic in Jamaica and Haiti.* London: Dent, 1939" (221) is to the British edition of *Tell My Horse.*

4. This is, not incidentally, *Mumbo Jumbo*'s critique of anthropology and archaeology's historical participation in Western imperialism through museum-making. It is likewise Gloria Anzaldúa's critique of anthropology's historical relation to imperialism and museums; and like Reed, Anzaldúa suggests that the collection of non-Western art was a way of spiritually disempowering nonwhite peoples (*Borderlands* 90). These two multiculturalist writers were profoundly shaped by anthropology, but were nonetheless critical evaluators of it who shared a rejection of anthropology's historical role of art stealing and spiritually neutralizing colonized peoples. Included in this critique is Von Vampton's colleague Gould, who collects African American tales, songs, and dances in Harlem speakeasies and neighborhood streets, later using them to craft his own fraudulent New Negro poetry. One should hear in this instance and elsewhere a critical awareness of early twentieth-century anthropology's ethnographic situation, in which native informants were taken advantage of by white anthropologists. Franz Boas's relation with one informant and collaborator, George Hunt, has been the basis of a similar critique (see Briggs and Bauman).

5. See Douglas, "Flawed Design."

6. See http://www2.wwnorton.com/catalog/backlist/030832.htm. One can only read the number of typographical errors in this description of the multicultural anthology as evidence of what Papa LaBas knows is "the fate of those who threatened the Atonist Path [. . .]. Their writings were banished, added to the Index of Forbidden Books or sprinkled with typos as a way of undermining their credibility" (47).

Chapter 9

1. For example, Handelman 25; see also Saldívar-Hull, Introduction 1, 3.

2. In one departure from Chávez's study, Anzaldúa declines to note that imagining the Southwest as the Aztlán homeland was based on the erroneous conflation of an Aztec history of an actual Aztlán four hundred miles northwest of Mexico City and later Spanish imaginary fantasies of a golden land to the north, in what is now the Southwest (Chávez 8–9).

3. See Rosaldo, "Fables," Rosaldo, *Culture and Truth* 150–55, and Saldívar-Hull, "Feminism."

4. See Cheung, and Anzaldúa, Interview 229.

5. Anzaldúa's use of Parrinder and Nash is instructive: part of chapter three depends so heavily on these two sources that, were this an academic essay, its unacknowledged quotations would count as plagiarism (compare, for instance, Anzaldúa 54–55 with Parrinder 78 and Anzaldúa 55–56 with Nash 361). This was no less true of Momaday's use of James Mooney. Part of the reason we have not yet recognized the extent to which the most canonical multicultural literature has been developed through a dialogue with anthropology may be because there are different conventions for attributing others' words and ideas in academic and literary writing, a fact that has tended to obscure the constitutive circuit between multicultural literature and social science.

6. Multiculturalism's tendency to treat cultures and races as coterminous or causal entities was strengthened, Ford intriguingly argues, by the 1978 *University of California Regents v. Bakke* decision, which permitted "diversity" as the sole remaining avenue for affirmative action college entrance policies. Various universities and the decision itself used "ethnic" and "racial" interchangeably, as *Bakke* "silently analogized racial diversity to ethnic diversity" (45). In response, progressive admission policies now encourage students "to internalize the equation of racial difference with inherited cultural difference and incorporate it into their self-conceptions" (48). *Bakke* and the diversity rationale reaffirmed recently in *Grutter v. Bollinger* (2003) helped solidify the "cultural difference conception of race" (54) at the expense of an affirmative action policy based on students' actual experience of racism: "Post-*Bakke* universities want to know all about the unique culture of the ancestors of their minority applicants, but ignore the discrimination suffered by the applicants themselves" (52). If *Brown* affirmed the second-phase liberal and assimilationist consensus, it appears that *Bakke* has enshrined a third-phase multiculturalist consensus treating races and cultures as coterminous entities that we might call, following Ford, "racial cultures."

Conclusion

1. See S. Wong, "Sugar"; S. Wong, "Autobiography"; Douglas, *Reciting,* 104–46.

2. *The Woman Warrior*'s "governing rhetorical trope is the palinode, or the taking back of what is said" (S. Wong, "Sugar" 195).

3. It should be clear from this argument's logic that I find traditional grounds for "national" literary traditions, which also ultimately depend on accidents of birth, to be equally incoherent.

4. Besides those who take issue with his critique of identity (such as the Boyarins and Gordon and Newfield), other critics have legitimately focused on questions of

Michaels's methodology, questioning his use of logic rather than the conclusions his logic leads him to. Such was the case of Lindsay Waters's critique in *The Chronicle of Higher Education* ("Literary Aesthetics: The Very Idea"), where he chided Michaels for flattening literary texts into logical propositions. It was likewise the focus of Wai Chee Dimock's questioning of the "speed" with which Michaels's logical argument takes place in her paper for a special session on Walter Benn Michaels at the 2005 MLA meeting. Perloff provocatively argued, "Just as literary texts seem to have no historical determinants, so they have, in Michaels's specialized, structuralist paradigm, no authors" (102), again suggesting that his propositional criticism and argument by analogy were methodologically suspect. These criticisms of Michaels's method seem accurate for the most part. And yet in the service of a periodization hypothesis (the goal of which Fredric Jameson has recently and persuasively defended [*Singular*]), Michaels's method allows us to see the forest even if the trees do not get as much attention as they singly deserve (as is the case with his reading of Zora Neale Hurston). My method has been built on traditional literary historical practices (like biography and questions of influence) rather than logical deduction, but since the writers examined in *A Genealogy of Literary Multiculturalism* wrote books that had to do with ideas and cultural politics, I have taken their ideas and politics seriously, which has sometimes meant taking their authors (logically) to task.

5. See Herskovits's dissertation and Gatewood. The debates here are entirely pertinent to the history and use of the culture concept in multiculturalism because they examine the basis for the naming of distinct cultures when those entities share traits with others and have interpenetrated and intermingled.

6. See Michaels, *Shape* 135–39.

7. Another potential candidate trait of the multicultural complex is to imagine assimilation as a specific kind of group death (itself a complicated echo of the salvage ethnography ethic that Hurston parodied in the opening pages of *Mules and Men*). I do not find it quite widespread enough to label it as such, even though it works within the logic of the complex. The *Aiiieeeee!* group, like McDonald, link losing history to losing identity to the "extinction" (*Aiiieeeee!* xl) of what McDonald, quoting a Chin character, calls the "endangered species" of Chinese Americans (xii). The conflation of possible cultural disappearance into racial or species disappearance needs no comment. Another example is the opening pages of Sherman Alexie's *Indian Killer*, in which a helicopter taking a newborn Native infant to his adoptive white Seattle parents strafes the reservation with machine gun fire—"this is war"—as it takes off (6).

8. Qtd. in Griffin and McFarland 124.

✎ Bibliography

Acosta, Oscar Zeta. *The Autobiography of a Brown Buffalo.* 1972. New York: Vintage Books, 1989.

Alcoff, Linda Martín. "The Unassimilated Theorist." *PMLA* 121.1 (2006): 255–59.

Alexie, Sherman. *Indian Killer.* New York: Atlantic Monthly Press, 1996.

Allen, Chadwick. "Blood (and) Memory." *American Literature* 71.1 (March 1999): 93–116.

Anaya, Rudolfo, A. Interview with Juan Bruce-Novoa. *Chicano Authors: Inquiry by Interview.* Austin: University of Texas Press, 1980. 183–202.

Angelou, Maya. "Introduction." In *Dust Tracks on a Road* by Zora Neale Hurston. New York: Harper Perennial, 1995.

Anzaldúa, Gloria. *Borderlands/La Frontera: The New Mestiza.* 1987. 2nd edition. San Francisco: Aunt Lute Books, 1999.

———. Interview with Karin Ikas. In *Borderlands/La Frontera.* 227–46.

Arac, Jonathan. "Toward a Critical Genealogy of the U.S. Discourse of Identity: *Invisible Man* after Fifty Years." *Boundary 2* 30.2 (2003): 195–216.

Atwood, Margaret. *The Handmaid's Tale.* Toronto: McLelland & Stewart, 1985.

Awkward, Michael. "Roadblocks and Relatives: Critical Revision in Toni Morrison's *The Bluest Eye.*" In *Critical Essays on Toni Morrison,* ed. Nellie McKay. Boston: G. K. Hall, 1988. 57–68.

Baker, Houston A., Jr. "Workings of the Spirit: Conjure and the Space of Black Women's Creativity." In *Zora Neale Hurston: Critical Perspectives Past and Present,* ed. Henry Louis Gates Jr. and Anthony Appiah. New York: Amistad, 1993. 280–308.

Baker, Lee D. *From Savage to Negro: Anthropology and the Construction of Race, 1896–1954.* Berkeley: University of California Press, 1998.

Baldwin, James. "Faulkner and Desegregation." In *Nobody Knows My Name.* 1961. New York: Vintage International. 1989. 117–26.

Barbeau, Marius. *Indian Days in the Canadian Rockies.* Toronto: Macmillan Canada, 1923.

Bellow, Saul. *Henderson the Rain King.* 1959. New York: Penguin, 1976.

Bercovitch, Sacvan. *The American Jeremiad.* Madison: University of Wisconsin Press, 1978.

Birth of a Nation. Dir. D. W. Griffiths. Castle Hill Productions, 1915.

Blair Witch Project. Dir. Daniel Myrick, and Eduardo Sánchez, Artisan Entertainment, 1999.

Boas, Franz. Boas papers. Zora Hurston correspondence. American Philosophical Society. B B61. Philadelphia.

Boas, Franz. "Human Faculty as Determined by Race." In Stocking, ed., *The Shaping of American Anthropology 1883–1911*. 221–42.

———. "The Instability of Human Types." In Stocking, ed., *The Shaping of American Anthropology 1883–1911*. 214–18.

———. "The Limitations of the Comparative Method in Anthropology." *Science* 4 (1896): 901–8.

———. *The Mind of Primitive Man*. Rev. ed. 1911. New York: Macmillan, 1938.

———. *Tsimshian Mythology*. Based on Texts Recorded by Henry W. Tate. Washington: Bureau of American Ethnology, 1916.

Boyarin, Daniel, and Jonathan Boyarin. "Diaspora: Generation and the Ground of Jewish Identity." *Critical Inquiry* 19.4 (Summer 1993): 693–725.

Boyd, Valerie. *Wrapped in Rainbows: The Life of Zora Neale Hurston*. New York: Scribner, 2003.

Bradford, William. *Of Plymouth Plantation, 1620–1647*. Ed. Samuel Eliot Morison. New York: Knopf, 1952.

Briggs, Charles, and Richard Bauman. "'The Foundation of All Future Researches': Franz Boas, George Hunt, Native American Texts, and the Construction of Modernity." *American Quarterly* 51.3 (1999): 479–528.

Brown v. Board of Education. 347 U.S. 483 (1954). Reprinted in "Appendix: Text of the Decisions," in Kluger, *Simple Justice*. 790–96.

Bruce-Novoa, Juan. "José Antonio Villarreal." *Chicano Authors: Inquiry by Interview*. Austin: University of Texas Press, 1980. 37–38.

Bulmer, Martin. *The Chicago School of Sociology: Institutionalization, Diversity, and the Rise of Sociological Research*. Chicago: University of Chicago Press, 1984.

Calderón, Héctor, and José David Saldívar, eds. *Criticism in the Borderlands: Studies in Chicano Literature, Culture, and Ideology*. Durham: Duke University Press, 1991.

Camus, Albert. *The Myth of Sisyphus and Other Essays*. New York: Vintage Books, 1955.

Cappetti, Carla. "Sociology of an Existence: Richard Wright and the Chicago School." *MELUS* 12.2 (Summer 1985): 25–43.

———. *Writing Chicago: Modernism, Ethnography, and the Novel*. New York: Columbia University Press, 1993.

Carby, Hazel. "Can the Tactics of Cultural Integration Counter the Persistence of Political Apartheid?: Or, the Multicultural Wars, Part Two." In *Race, Law, & Culture: Reflections on Brown v. Board of Education*, ed. Austin Sarat. Oxford: Oxford University Press, 1997. 221–27.

———. "The Multicultural Wars." *Radical History* 54 (Fall 1992): 7–18.

———. "The Politics of Fiction, Anthropology, and the Folk: Zora Neale Hurston." In *History and Memory in African-American Culture*, ed. Geneviève Fabre and Robert O'Meally. New York: Oxford University Press, 1994. 28–44.

Chan, Jeffery Paul, Frank Chin, Lawson Fusao Inada, and Shawn Wong, eds. *The Big Aiiieeeee!: An Anthology of Chinese American and Japanese American Literature*. New York: Meridian, 1991.

Chávez, John R. *The Lost Land: The Chicano Image of the Southwest*. Albuquerque: University of New Mexico Press, 1984.

Chen, Fu-jen. "John Okada." In *Asian American Novelists: A Bio-Bibliographical Critical Sourcebook*, ed. Emmanuel S. Nelson. Westport, CT: Greenwood Press, 2000. 281–88.

Chesnutt, Charles. *The Marrow of Tradition.* 1901. Ann Arbor: University of Michigan Press, 1969.

Cheung, King-Kok. "'Don't Tell': Imposed Silences in *The Color Purple* and *The Woman Warrior.*" *PMLA* 103.2 (March 1988): 162–74.

Chin, Frank. Afterword: "In Search of John Okada." In Okada, *No-No Boy.* 253–60.

———. *The Chickencoop Chinaman* and *The Year of the Dragon: Two Plays.* Seattle: University of Washington Press, 1981.

———. "Come All Ye Asian American Writers of the Real and the Fake." In Chan et al., eds., *The Big Aiiieeeee!* 1–92.

———. "Rashomon Road: On the Tao to San Diego." In *MultiAmerica: Essays on Cultural Wars and Cultural Peace,* ed. Ishmael Reed. New York: Viking, 1997. 286–308.

———. "This Is Not an Autobiography." *Genre* 18.2 (Summer 1985): 109–30.

Chin, Frank, Frank Emi, Yosh Kuromiya, and Lawson Inada. "Introduction to a Conversation on John Okada's *No-No Boy.*" http://www.resisters.com/study/okada_no-no-boy.pdf.

Chin, Frank, Jeffery Paul Chan, Lawson Fusao Inada, and Shawn Hsu Wong. "An Introduction to Chinese and Japanese American Literature." In Chin et al., eds., *Aiiieeeee!* 3–38.

Chin, Frank, Jeffery Paul Chan, Lawson Fusao Inada, and Shawn Hsu Wong, eds. *Aiiieeeee!: An Anthology of Asian American Writers.* 1974. New York: Mentor, 1991.

Clark, Kenneth. *Prejudice and Your Child.* Boston: Beacon Press, 1955.

Clark, Kenneth B., and Mamie P. Clark. "Emotional Factors in Racial Identification and Preference in Negro Children." *Journal of Negro Education* 19.3 (Summer 1950): 341–50.

———. "Racial Identification and Preference in Negro Children." In *Readings in Social Psychology,* ed. T. M. Newcomb. New York: Henry Holt, 1947. 169–78.

Clifford, James. "Identity in Mashpee." In *Predicament of Culture: Twentieth-Century Ethnography, Literature, and Art.* Cambridge: Harvard University Press, 1988.

Clifford, James, and George Marcus, eds. *Writing Culture: The Poetics and Politics of Ethnography.* Berkeley: University of California Press, 1986.

Cox, Ross. *Adventures on the Columbia River.* New York: J. & J. Harper, 1832.

Davis, Arthur P. "Integration and Race Literature." *Phylon* 17. 1/4 (1956): 141–46.

Davis, Peggy Cooper. "Performing Interpretation: A Legacy of Civil Rights Lawyering in *Brown v. Board of Education.*" In *Race, Law, and Culture: Reflections on Brown v. Board of Education,* ed. Austin Sarat. New York: Oxford University Press, 1997. 23–48.

Dee, Ruby. Rev. of *The Bluest Eye* by Toni Morrison. *Freedomways* 11.3 (1971): 319.

Deloria, Ella Cara. *Dakota Texts.* 1932. New York: AMS Press, 1974.

———. *Waterlily.* Lincoln: University of Nebraska Press, 1988.

Deloria, Vine, Jr. *Custer Died for Your Sins: An Indian Manifesto.* 1969. Norman: University of Oklahoma Press, 1988.

De Smet, Pierre Jean, S. J. *Life, Letters and Travels of Father Pierre-Jean de Smet, S.J., 1801–1873.* New York: Harper, 1905.

Dimock, Wai Chee. "Against Race: Walter Benn Michaels and Paul Gilroy." Walter Benn Michaels's *Our America* Ten Years Later Session. MLA Convention. Grand Marriott Hotel. Washington, DC, December 27, 2005.

Doctorow, E. L. *The Book of Daniel*. 1971. New York: Vintage, 1991.

Douglas, Christopher. "The Flawed Design: American Imperialism in N. Scott Momaday's *House Made of Dawn* and Cormac McCarthy's *Blood Meridian*." *Critique: Studies in Contemporary Fiction* 45.1 (Fall 2003): 3–24.

——. "Reading Ethnography: The Cold War Social Science of Jade Snow Wong's *Fifth Chinese Daughter* and *Brown v. Board of Education*." In *Form and Transformation in Asian American Literature*, ed. Zhou Xiaojing and Samina Najmi. Seattle: University of Washington Press, 2005. 101–24.

——. *Reciting America: Culture and Cliché in Contemporary U.S. Fiction*. Urbana: University of Illinois Press, 2001.

——. "What *The Bluest Eye* Knows about Them: Culture, Race, Identity." *American Literature* 78.1 (March 2006): 141–68.

——. "You Have Unleashed a Horde of Barbarians!: Fighting Indians, Playing Games, Forming Disciplines." *Postmodern Culture* 13.1 (2002).

Douglass, Frederick. *Narrative of the Life of Frederick Douglass, An American Slave*. 1845. New York: Penguin, 1982.

Doyle, Bertram S. *The Etiquette of Race Relations in the South: A Study in Social Control*. Chicago: University of Chicago Press, 1937.

Drinnon, Richard. *Keeper of Concentration Camps: Dillon S. Myer and American Racism*. Los Angeles: University of California Press, 1987.

Dubey. Madhu. *Black Women Novelists and the Nationalist Aesthetic*. Bloomington: Indiana University Press, 1994.

——. "Narration and Migration: Jazz and Vernacular Theories of Black Women's Fiction." *American Literary History* 10.2 (1998): 291–316.

Du Bois, W. E. B. *The Souls of Black Folk*. 1905. New York: Penguin, 1989.

Dudziak, Mary L. "Desegregation as a Cold War Imperative." *Stanford Law Review* 41.61 (November 1988): 61–120.

Edelberg, Cynthia Dubin. "Morrison's Voices: Formal Education, the Work Ethic, and the Bible." *American Literature* 58.2 (May 1986): 217–37.

Elliott, Michael A. *The Culture Concept: Writing and Difference in the Age of Realism*. Minneapolis: University of Minnesota Press, 2002.

Ellison, Ralph. "*An American Dilemma*: A Review." In his *Shadow and Act*. 303–17.

——. *Invisible Man*. 1952. New York: Vintage Books. 1989.

——. *Juneteenth*. Ed. John Callahan. New York: Random House, 1999.

——. *Shadow and Act*. 1953. New York: Quality Paperback Book Club, 1964.

——. "Some Questions and Some Answers." In his *Shadow and Act*. 261–72.

——. Unpublished draft of "Woodridge" episode chapter. Ralph Ellison Papers, Library of Congress, box 146, Folder 16.

——. "The World and the Jug." In his *Shadow and Act*. 114–43.

Evers, Lawrence J. "The Killing of a New Mexican State Trooper: Ways of Telling a Historical Event." *Wicazo Sa Review* 1.1 (Spring 1985): 17–25.

——. "Words and Place: A Reading of *House Made of Dawn*." *Western American Literature* 11 (February 1977): 297–320.

Fabio, Sarah Webster. "Tripping with Black Writing." In Gayle, ed., *The Black Aesthetic*. 182–91.

Fabre, Michel. *The Unfinished Quest of Richard Wright*. Trans. Isabel Barzun. New York: William Morrow, 1973.

Fauset, Arthur Huff. "American Negro Folk Literature." In Locke, ed., *The New Negro*. 238–44.

Ferguson, Roderick. *Aberrations in Black: Toward a Queer of Color Critique*. Minneapolis: University of Minnesota Press, 2004.

Fixico, Donald Lee. *Termination and Relocation: Federal Indian Policy, 1945–60*. Albuquerque: University of New Mexico Press, 1986.

Fontenot, Chester J. "Ishmael Reed and the Politics of Aesthetics, or Shake Hands and Come out Conjuring." *Black American Literature Forum* 12.1 (Spring 1978): 20–23.

Ford, Richard T. *Racial Culture: A Critique*. Princeton: Princeton University Press, 2005.

Fraser, Nancy. "Introduction: The Radical Imagination Between Redistribution and Recognition." http://www.newschool.edu/GF/polsci/faculty/fraser/.

Frazer, Sir James. *The Golden Bough: A Study in Magic and Religion*. 1950. Abridged ed. New York; Macmillan, 1951.

Frazier, E. Franklin. "Durham: Capital of the Black Middle Class." In Locke, ed., *The New Negro*. 333–40.

———. *The Negro Family in Chicago*. Chicago: University of Illinois Press, 1932.

———. *The Negro in the United States*. Toronto: Macmillan, 1949.

Frost, Robert. "The Gift Outright." In *Complete Poems of Robert Frost*. New York: Holt, 1949. 467.

Fukuyama, Francis. *The End of History and the Last Man*. New York: Free Press, 1992.

Fuller, Hoyt. "Towards a Black Aesthetic." In Gayle, ed., *The Black Aesthetic*. day 3–12.

Gant, Liz. Rev. of *The Bluest Eye* by Toni Morrison. *Black World* 20 (May 1971): 51–52.

Garrow, David. "From *Brown* to *Casey:* The U.S. Supreme Court and the Burdens of History." In *Race, Law, and Culture: Reflections on* Brown v. Board of Education, ed. Austin Sarat. New York: Oxford University Press, 1997. 74–88.

Gates, Henry Louis, Jr. Afterword: "Zora Neale Hurston:'A Negro Way of Saying.'" In Hurston, *Mules and Men*. New York: Harper Perennial, 1990. 194–205.

———. "The Master's Pieces: On Canon Formation and the African-American Tradition." *South Atlantic Quarterly* 89.1 (1990): 89–111.

———. *The Signifying Monkey: A Theory of African-American Literary Criticism*. New York: Oxford University Press, 1988.

Gatewood, John B. "Reflections on the Nature of Cultural Distributions and the Units of Culture Problem." *Cross-Cultural Research* 35.2 (May 2001): 227–41.

Gayle, Addison, Jr. "The Function of Black Literature at the Present Time." In *The Black Aesthetic*. 407–19.

Gayle, Addison, Jr., ed. *The Black Aesthetic*. Garden City, NY: Doubleday, 1971.

Geary, Joyce. "A Chinese Girl's World." Rev. of *Fifth Chinese Daughter,* by Jade Snow Wong. *New York Times Book Review,* October 29, 1950, 27.

Gershenhorn, Jerry. *Melville J. Herskovits and the Racial Politics of Knowledge*. Lincoln: University of Nebraska Press, 2004.

Gilroy, Paul. *Against Race: Imagining Political Culture beyond the Color Line*. Cambridge: Belknap Press of Harvard University Press, 2000.

Girdner, Audrie, and Anne Loftis. *The Great Betrayal: The Evacuation of the Japanese-Americans during World War II*. London: Macmillan, 1969.

Goldschmidt, Walter, ed. *Uses of Anthropology.* Washington, DC: American Anthropological Association, 1979.

Gonzales, Rodolfo. *I Am Joaquín.* 1967. Toronto: Bantam Pathfinder Editions, 1972.

Gordon, Avery, and Christopher Newfield. "White Philosophy." *Critical Inquiry* 20.4 (Summer 1994): 737–57.

Gould, Stephen Jay. *The Mismeasure of Man.* New York: W. W. Norton, 1981.

Graham, Don, James W. Lee, and William T. Pilkington, eds. *The Texas Literary Tradition: Fiction, Folklore, History.* Austin: University of Texas Press, 1983.

Griffin, Larry J., and Katherine McFarland. "In My Heart, I'm an American: Regional Attitudes and American Identity." *Southern Cultures* 13.4 (2007): 119–37.

Guillemin, Jean. "The Micmac Indians in Boston: The Ethnography of an Urban Community." Diss. Brandeis University, 1973.

Gutierrez, Ramon A. "Ethnic Studies: Its Evolution in American Colleges and Universities." In *Multiculturalism: A Critical Reader,* ed. David Theo Goldberg. Oxford: Blackwell, 1994. 157–67.

Handelman, Jonathan. "*With His Pistol in His Hand:* Touchstone for Border Study." *Interdisciplinary Literary Studies* 3.2 (Spring 2002): 23–38.

Hansberry, Lorraine. *A Raisin in the Sun.* New York: S. French, 1984.

Harlan, Louis R. *Booker T. Washington: The Wizard of Tuskegee, 1901–1915.* New York: Oxford University Press, 1983.

Harrington, John P. *Vocabulary of the Kiowa Language.* Bureau of American Ethnology Bulletin 84. Washington, DC: Smithsonian Institution, 1928.

Harris, Trudier. "Reconnecting Fragments: Afro-American Folk Tradition in *The Bluest Eye.*" In *Critical Essays on Toni Morrison,* ed. Nellie McKay. Boston: G. K. Hall, 1988. 68–76.

Hawthorne, Nathaniel. "The Custom House." *The Scarlet Letter.* 1850. Boston: Houghton Mifflin, 1960. 5–47.

——. "Young Goodman Brown." 1835. *The Scarlet Letter and Other Writings.* New York: Norton, 2005. 178–88.

Hegeman, Susan. *Patterns for America: Modernism and the Concept of Culture.* Princeton: Princeton University Press, 1999.

Hemenway, Robert E. *Zora Neale Hurston: A Literary Biography.* Urbana: University of Illinois Press, 1977.

Herskovits, Melville J. *The American Negro: A Study in Racial Crossing.* Bloomington: Indiana University Press, 1928.

——. *The Anthropometry of the American Negro.* 1930. New York: AMS Press, 1969.

——. "The Cattle Complex in East Africa." *American Anthropologist,* New Series, 28.1–4 (January–December 1926): 230–72; 361–88; 494–528; 633–64.

——. *Franz Boas: The Science of Man in the Making.* New York: Charles Scribner's Sons, 1953.

——. *The Myth of the Negro Past.* 1941. Boston: Beacon Press, 1990.

——. "The Negro's Americanism." In Locke, ed., *The New Negro.* 353–60.

Highsmith, Patricia. 1957. *Deep Water.* New York: W. W. Norton, 1985.

——. *The Talented Mr. Ripley.* 1955. New York: Vintage Books, 1992.

Hinojosa-Smith, Rolando. *Estampas del Valle y Otras Ombras / Sketches of the Valley and Other Works.* Berkeley: Quinto Sol, 1973.

Hinojosa-Smith, "This Writer's Sense of Place." In Graham, Lee, and Pilkington, eds., *The Texas Literary Tradition*. 120–24.

Hirabayashi, Gordon. Rev. of *No-No Boy*, by John Okada. *Pacific Affairs* 53 (Spring 1980): 176–77.

"Hirabayashi v. United States." *U.S. Supreme Court, Kiyoshi Hirabayashi v. United States, 320 U.S. 81 (1943) Kiyoshi Hirabayashi v. United States. No. 870*. Argued May 10, 11, 1943. Decided June 21, 1943. https://www.tourolaw.edu/patch/Hirabayashi/

Hoefel, Roseanne. "'Different by Degree': Ella Cara Deloria, Zora Neale Hurston, and Franz Boas Contend with Race and Ethnicity." *American Indian Quarterly* 25.2 (Spring 2001): 181–202.

Howe, Irving. "Black Boys and Native Sons." *Dissent* (Autumn 1963): 353–68.

Huntington, Samuel. *The Clash of Civilizations and the Remaking of World Order*. New York: Simon and Schuster, 1996.

Hurston, Zora Neale. *Dust Tracks on a Road*. 1942. New York: Harper Perennial, 1995.

———. "The Florida Expedition." B B61. Boas Papers. Zora Hurston correspondence. 497.3 B63c 46. Philadelphia.

———. "How It Feels to Be Colored Me." 1928. In *Folklore, Memoirs, & Other Writings*. New York: Library of America, 1995. 826–29.

———. *Jonah's Gourd Vine*. 1934. In *Zora Neale Hurston: Novels and Stories*. New York: Library of America, 1995. 1–171.

———. *Moses, Man of the Mountain*. 1939. In *Zora Neale Hurston: Novels and Stories*. New York: Library of America, 1995. 335–595.

———. *Mules and Men*. 1935. New York: Harper Perennial, 1990.

———. *Seraph on the Suwanee*. New York: Charles Scribner's Sons, 1948.

———. "Stories of Conflict." Rev. of *Uncle Tom's Children* by Richard Wright. *Saturday Review*, April 2, 1938. Reprinted in *Folklore, Memoirs, & Other Writings*. New York: Library of America, 1995. 912–13.

———. *Tell My Horse: Voodoo and Life in Haiti and Jamaica*. 1938. New York: Harper & Row, 1990.

———. *Their Eyes Were Watching God*. 1937. New York: Harper Perennial, 1998.

Hutchinson, George: *The Harlem Renaissance in Black and White*. Cambridge: The Belknap Press of Harvard University Press, 1995.

Hyatt, Marshall, *Franz Boas Social Activist/The Dynamics of Ethnicity*. Westport, CT: Greenwood Press 1990.

Inada, Lawson Fusao. "Ainu Blues." In Chan et al., eds., *The Big Aiiieeeee!* 609–18.

Irons, Peter. *Justice at War*. New York: Oxford University Press, 1983.

———. *Justice Delayed: The Record of the Japanese American Internment Cases*. Middletown, CT: Wesleyan University Press, 1989.

Jackson, Lawrence. *Ralph Ellison: Emergence of Genius*. New York: John Wiley, 2002.

Jameson, Fredric. *Postmodernism: or, The Cultural Logic of Late Capitalism*. Durham: Duke University Press, 1991.

———. *A Singular Modernity: Essay on the Ontology of the Present*. London: Verso, 2002.

Johnson, Charles S. *The Economic Status of Negroes*. Nashville: Fisk University Press, 1933.

———. "The New Frontage on American Life." In Locke, ed., *The New Negro*. 278–98.

Jones, LeRoi. *Blues People*. New York: William Morrow, 1963.

Kaplan, Carla, ed. *Zora Neale Hurston: A Life in Letters.* New York: Doubleday, 2002.

Karst, Kenneth. *Belonging to America: Equal Citizenship and the Constitution.* New Haven: Yale University Press, 1989.

Kazin, Alfred. *On Native Grounds: An Interpretation of Modern American Prose Literature.* New York: Harcourt, Brace, 1942.

Kim, Daniel Y. "Invisible Desires: Homoerotic Racism and Its Homophobic Critique in Ralph Ellison's *Invisible Man.*" *Novel: A Forum on Fiction* 30.3 (Spring 1997): 309–28.

Kim, Elaine. *Asian American Literature: An Introduction to the Writings and Their Social Context.* Philadelphia: Temple University Press, 1982.

Kingsolver, Barbara. *The Poisonwood Bible.* New York: Harper Perennial, 1998.

Kingston, Maxine Hong. "Cultural Mis-readings by American Reviewers." In *Asian and Western Writers in Dialogue: New Cultural Identities,* ed. Guy Amirthanayagam. London: Macmillan, 1982. 55–65.

———. "Personal Statement." In *Approaches to Teaching Maxine Hong Kingston's* The Woman Warrior, ed. Shirley Geok-lin Lim. New York: MLA, 1991. 23–25.

———. *The Woman Warrior: Memoirs of a Girlhood among Ghosts.* New York: Vintage International, 1975.

Kinnamon, Kenneth. "*Native Son:* The Personal, Social, and Political Background." *Phylon* 30.1 (1969): 66–72.

Klein, Christina. *Cold War Orientalism: Asia in the Middlebrow Imagination, 1945–1961.* Berkeley: University of California Press, 2003.

———. "Family Ties and Political Obligation: The Discourse of Adoption and the Cold War Commitment to Asia." In *Cold War Constructions: The Political Culture of United States Imperialism, 1945–1966,* ed. Christian Appy. Amherst: University of Massachusetts Press, 2000. 35–66.

Kluger, Richard. *Simple Justice: The History of* Brown v. Board of Education *and Black America's Struggle for Equality.* 1975. New York: Vintage, 2004.

Korematsu v. United States. December 18, 1944. https://www.tourolaw.edu/patch/Korematsu/.

Larsen, Nella. *Passing.* 1929. New York: Modern Library, 2002.

Lee, A. Robert. *Multicultural American Literature: Comparative Black, Native, Latino/a and Asian American Fictions.* Jackson: University Press of Mississippi, 2003.

Lee, Robert G. *Orientals: Asian Americans in Popular Culture.* Philadelphia: Temple University Press, 1999.

Li, David Leiwei. *Imagining the Nation: Asian American Literature and Cultural Consent.* Stanford: Stanford University Press, 1998.

Limón, José Eduardo. "Américo Paredes: A Man from the Border." *Revista Chicano-Riqueña* 8.3 (1980): 1–5.

———. *Dancing with the Devil: Society and Cultural Poetics in Mexican-American South Texas.* Madison: University of Wisconsin Press, 1994.

———. "Dancing with the Devil: Society, Gender, and the Political Unconscious in Mexican-American South Texas." In Calderón and Saldívar, eds., *Criticism in the Borderlands.* 221–35.

———. *The Return of the Mexican Ballad: Américo Paredes and His Anthropological Text as Persuasive Political Performance.* Stanford: Stanford Center for Chicano Research. 1986.

Lindroth, James R. "Generating the Vocabulary of Hoodoo: Zora Neale Hurston and Ishmael Reed." *Zora Neale Hurston Forum.* 2.1 (Fall 1987): 27–34.

Ling, Amy. *Between Worlds: Women Writers of Chinese Ancestry.* New York: Pergamon, 1990.

Ling, Jinqi. *Narrating Nationalisms: Ideology and Form in Asian American Literature.* New York: Oxford University Press, 1998.

———. "*No-No Boy* by John Okada." In *A Resource Guide to Asian American Literature,* ed. Sau-Ling Wong and Stephen Sumida. New York: MLA, 2000. 140–50.

Locke, Alain, ed. *The New Negro: An Interpretation.* 1925. New York: Johnson Reprint Corporation, 1968.

Lovecraft, H. P. "The Call of Cthulhu." 1930. In *The Call of Cthulhu and Other Weird Stories,* ed. S. T. Joshi. New York: Penguin Books, 1999. 139–69.

Lowe, Pardee. *Father and Glorious Descendant.* Boston: Little, Brown, 1943.

Mailer, Norman. *An American Dream.* 1965. New York: Owl Books, 1987.

Manganaro, Marc. *Culture, 1922: The Emergence of a Concept.* Princeton: Princeton University Press, 2002.

Manganaro, Marc, ed. *Modernist Anthropology: From Fieldwork to Text.* Princeton: Princeton University Press, 1990.

Marriott, Alice. *Sanday's People: The Kiowa Indians and the Stories They Told.* 1947. Lincoln: University of Nebraska Press, 1963.

———. *The Ten Grandmothers.* Norman: University of Oklahoma Press, 1945.

Matthews, Fred H. *Quest for an American Sociology: Robert E. Park and the Chicago School.* Montreal: McGill-Queen's University Press, 1977.

Matus, Jill. *Toni Morrison.* Manchester: Manchester University Press, 1998.

Mayhall, Mildred P. *The Kiowas.* 1962. 2nd ed. Norman: University of Oklahoma Press, 1971.

McBride, Dwight A. "Speaking the Unspeakable: On Toni Morrison, African American Intellectuals, and the Uses of Essentialist Rhetoric." *Modern Fiction Studies* 39.3–4 (1993): 755–76.

McCarthy, Cormac. *Blood Meridian, or, The Evening Redness in the West.* New York: Random House, 1985.

McDonald, Dorothy Ritsuko. Introduction. In Chin, *The Chickencoop Chinaman* and *The Year of the Dragon.* ix–xxix.

McNickle, D'Arcy. D'Arcy McNickle Collection. Letter from Charles Pearce. April 6, 1929. Folder 157. The Newberry Library. Roger and Julie Baskes Department of Special Collections. Chicago.

———. *The Surrounded.* 1936. Albuquerque: University of New Mexico Press, 1978.

Michaels, Walter Benn. "The No-Drop Rule." *Critical Inquiry* 20.4 (Summer 1994): 758–69.

———. *Our America: Nativism, Modernism, and Pluralism.* Durham: Duke University Press, 1995.

———. "Race into Culture: A Critical Genealogy of Cultural Identity." *Critical Inquiry* 18.4 (Summer 1992): 655–85.

———. "Response." *Modernism/modernity* 3.3 (September 1996): 121–26.

———. *The Shape of the Signifier: 1967 to the End of History.* Princeton: Princeton University Press, 2004.

Michaelson, Scott. *The Limits of Multiculturalism: Interrogating the Origins of American Anthropology.* Minneapolis: University of Minnesota Press, 1999.

Mizruchi, Susan L. *The Science of Sacrifice: American Literature and Modern Social Theory.* Princeton: Princeton University Press, 1998.

Mody, Sanjay. "*Brown* Footnote Eleven in Historical Context: Social Science and the Supreme Court's Quest for Legitimacy." *Stanford Law Review* 54 (April 2002): 793–829.

Momaday, N. Scott. *House Made of Dawn.* 1968. New York: Perennial Classics, 1999.

——. "The Morality of Indian Hating." *Ramparts* (Summer 1964): 30–40.

——. *The Names: A Memoir.* New York: Harper & Row, 1976.

——. "The Way to Rainy Mountain." *Reporter* (January 26, 1967): 41–43.

——. *The Way to Rainy Mountain.* Albuquerque: University of New Mexico Press, 1969.

Momaday, N. Scott, ed. *The Complete Poems of Frederick Goddard Tuckerman.* Foreword by Yvor Winters. New York: Oxford University Press, 1965.

Monahan, John, and Laurens Walker. *Social Science in Law.* 4th ed. Westbury, NY: The Foundation Press, 1998.

Mooney, James. *Calendar History of the Kiowa Indians.* 1898. Introduction by John C. Ewers. Washington, DC: Smithsonian Institution Press, 1979.

——. *The Ghost Dance Religion and the Sioux Outbreak of 1890.* Ed. and abridged Anthony F. C. Wallace. Chicago: University of Chicago Press, 1965.

Mooney, James, and Franz Boas correspondence. American Philosophical Society B: B61 Boas Papers. James Mooney correspondence. Philadelphia.

Mori, Toshio. *Yokohama, California.* 1949. Seattle: University of Washington Press, 1985.

Morrison, Toni. *Beloved.* New York: Plume, 1987.

——. *The Bluest Eye.* 1970. New York: Plume, 1993.

——. Interview with Rosemarie K. Lester. "An Interview with Toni Morrison." Hessian Radio Network. Frankfurt, West Germany, 1983. In *Critical Essays on Toni Morrison,* ed. Nellie McKay. Boston: G. K. Hall, 1998. 47–54.

——. *Playing in the Dark: Whiteness and the Literary Imagination.* Cambridge: Harvard University Press, 1992.

——. *Sula.* London: Picador, 1973.

Moses, L. G. *The Indian Man: A Biography of James Mooney.* Urbana: University of Illinois Press, 1984.

Murray, Albert. *The Omni-Americans: New Perspectives on Black Experience and American Culture.* New York: Outerbridge & Dienstfrey, 1970.

Myer, Dillon S. Letter from Robert Redfield, April 12, 1943. Dillon S. Myer's Papers. Personal Correspondence File 1943–44. Box 3. Harry S. Truman Library. Independence, MO.

Myrdal, Gunnar. *An American Dilemma: The Negro Problem and Modern Democracy.* New York: Harper & Brothers, 1944.

Nash, June. "The Aztecs and the Ideology of Male Dominance." *Signs: Journal of Women in Culture and Society* 4.2 (1978): 349–62.

Neal, Larry. "The Black Arts Movement." In Gayle, ed., *The Black Aesthetic.* 272–90.

——. Introduction. In Hurston, *Jonah's Gourd Vine,* 1971. 5–7.

Neihardt, John. 1932. *Black Elk Speaks: Being the Life Story of a Holy Man of the Oglala Sioux.* Lincoln: University of Nebraska Press, 1979.

Nelson, Emmanuel S., ed. *Asian American Novelists: A Bio-Biographical Critical Source-book*. Westport, CT: Greenwood Press, 2000.

Nelson, Robert M. *Place and Vision: The Function of Landscape in Native American Fiction*. New York: Lang, 1993.

Nowlin, Michael. "Toni Morrison's *Jazz* and the Racial Dreams of the American Writer." *American Literature* 71.1 (1999): 151–74.

Nye, Wilbur Sturtevant. *Bad Medicine and Good: Tales of the Kiowas*. Norman: University of Oklahoma Press, 1962.

O'Brien, John. "Ishmael Reed." 1971. In *Conversations with Ishmael Reed*, ed. Bruce Dick and Amritjit Singh. Jackson: University Press of Mississippi, 1995. 14–24.

O'Brien, Robert W. "The Changing Role of the College Nisei during the Crisis Period: 1931–1943." Diss. University of Washington, 1945.

———. "Selective Dispersion as a Factor in the Solution of the Nisei Problem." *Social Forces* 23.3 (December 1944): 140–47.

Ogletree, Charles. *All Deliberate Speed: Reflections on the First Half Century of Brown v. Board of Education*. New York: W. W. Norton, 2004.

Okada, John. *No-No Boy*. Seattle: University of Washington Press, 1976.

Okimoto, Daniel. *American in Disguise*. New York: Walker/Weatherhill, 1971.

Omi, Michael, and Howard Winant. *Racial Formation in the United States from the 1960s to the 1980s*. New York: Routledge, 1986.

Palumbo-Liu, David. *Asian/American: Historical Crossings of a Racial Frontier*. Stanford: Stanford University Press, 1999.

Palumbo-Liu, David, ed. *The Ethnic Canon: Histories, Institutions, and Interventions*. Minneapolis: University of Minnesota Press, 1995.

Paredes, Américo. "The Folk Base of Chicano Literature." 1964. In *Modern Chicano Writers: A Collection of Critical Essays*, ed. Joseph Sommers and Tomás Ybarra-Frausto. Englewood Cliffs, NJ: Prentice-Hall, 1979. 4–17.

———. *George Washington Gómez: A Mexicotexan Novel*. Houston: Arte Publico Press, 1990.

———. "The Problem of Identity in a Changing Culture." 1978. In *Folklore and Culture on the Texas-Mexican Border*. Austin: CMAS Books/University of Texas, 1993. 19–47.

———. *"With His Pistol in His Hand": A Border Ballad and Its Hero*. Austin: University of Texas Press, 1958.

Park, Robert E. "Behind Our Masks." *Survey Graphic* 56 (May, 1926): 135–39. Reprinted in his *Race and Culture*. 244–55.

———. "Education and Its Relation to the Conflict and Fusion of Cultures." *Publication of the American Sociological Society* 13 (1918): 58–63, 261–83.

———. "Education and the Cultural Crisis." In his *Race and Culture*.316–30.

———. "Human Migration and the Marginal Man." In his *Race and Culture*. 345–56.

———. Introduction. *Shadow of the Plantation* by Charles Johnson. Chicago: University of Chicago Press, 1934. xi–xxiv.

———. "Negro Race Consciousness as Reflected in Race Literature." In his *Race and Culture*. 284–300.

———. "Our Racial Frontier on the Pacific." *Survey Graphic* 9 (May 1926): 192–96. Reprinted in his *Race and Culture*. 138–51.

———. "Personality and Cultural Conflict." In his *Race and Culture*. 357–71.

———. *Race and Culture*. Glencoe, IL: Free Press, 1950.

Park, Robert E. "Racial Assimilation in Secondary Groups with Particular Reference to the Negro." *Publication of the American Sociological Society* 8 (1913): 66–83. Reprinted in his *Race and Culture.* 204–20.

Park, Robert E., and Ernest W. Burgess. *The City.* Chicago: University of Chicago Press, 1925.

——. *Introduction to the Science of Sociology,* 3rd ed., revised. 1921. Chicago: University of Chicago Press, 1969.

Parker, Dorothy R. *Singing an Indian Song: A Biography of D'Arcy McNickle.* Lincoln: University of Nebraska Press, 1992.

Parks, Suzan-Lori. From "Elements of Style." In *The America Play and Other Works.* New York: Theatre Communications Group, 1995. 6–22.

——. *Imperceptible Mutabilities in the Third Kingdom.* In *The America Play and Other Works.* New York: Theatre Communications Group, 1995. 23–71.

Parrinder, Geoffrey, ed. *World Religions: From Ancient History to the Present.* New York: Facts on File Publications, 1971.

Peach, Linden. *Toni Morrison.* 2nd ed. New York: St. Martin's Press, 2000.

Perloff, Marjorie. "Modernism without the Modernists: A Response to Walter Benn Michaels." *Modernism/modernity* 3.3 (September 1996): 99–105.

Poltergeist. Dir. Tobe Hooper. MGM, 1982.

Posnock, Ross. *Color and Culture: Black Writers and the Making of the Modern Intellectual.* Cambridge: Harvard University Press, 1998.

Ransom, James. "Perpetuating Remembrance: N. Scott Momaday and Kiowa Storytelling." *p.o.v.: A Danish Journal of Film Studies* 18 (December 2004): 79–90. http://pov.imv.au.dk/pdf/pov18.pdf.

Raushenbush, Winifred. *Robert E. Park: Biography of a Sociologist.* Durham: Duke University Press, 1979.

Reed, Ishmael. *Conversations with Ishmael Reed.* Ed. Bruce Dick and Amritjit Singh. Jackson: University Press of Mississippi, 1995.

——. Foreword. In Hurston, *Tell My Horse,* 1990. xi–xv.

——. *The Free-Lance Pallbearers.* 1967. Normal, IL: Dalkey Archive Press, 1999.

——. *Mumbo Jumbo.* New York: Simon and Schuster, 1972.

——. "Neo-HooDoo Manifesto." *Conjure: Selected Poems, 1963–1970.* Boston: University of Massachusetts Press, 1972.

——. *Yellow Back Radio Broke-Down.* 1969. Normal, IL: Dalkey Archive Press, 2000.

Reed, Ishmael, Kathryn Trueblood, and Shawn Wong, eds. *The Before Columbus Foundation Poetry Anthology: Selections from the American Book Awards.* New York: W. W. Norton, 1992.

Review of *Fifth Chinese Daughter,* by Jade Snow Wong. *New Yorker* 26.32 (October 7, 1950): 134.

Rivera, Tomás. Interview with Juan Bruce-Novoa. In *Chicano Authors: Inquiry by Interview.* Austin: University of Texas Press, 1980. 137–61.

——. "Mexican-American Literature: The Establishment of Community." In Graham, Lee, and Pilkington, eds., *The Texas Literary Tradition.* 124–30.

——. *Y no se lo tragó la tierra/...And the Earth Did Not Devour Him.* 1987. Trans. Evangelina Vigil-Piñón. Houston: Arte Público Press, 1995.

Rodriguez, Richard. *The Hunger of Memory: The Education of Richard Rodriguez: An Autobiography.* Boston: D. R. Godine, 1982.

Rody, Caroline. "Toni Morrison's *Beloved*: History, 'Rememory,' and a 'Clamor for a Kiss.'" *American Literary History* 7.1 (1995): 92–119.

Roediger, David. *The Wages of Whiteness: Race and the Making of the American Working Class.* London: Verso, 1991.

Rosaldo, Renato. "Chicano Studies, 1970–1984." *Annual Reviews Anthropology* 14 (1985): 405–27.

———. *Culture and Truth.* Boston: Beacon Press, 1989.

———. "Fables of the Fallen Guy." In Calderón *and* Saldívar, eds., *Criticism in the Borderlands.* 84–93.

Rosen, Paul L. *The Supreme Court and Social Science.* Urbana: University of Illinois Press, 1972.

Ross, Dorothy. *The Origins of American Social Science.* Cambridge: Cambridge University Press, 1991.

Roth, Philip. *The Human Stain.* New York: Vintage, 2000.

Rowlandson, Mary. "Narrative of the Captivity of Mrs. Mary Rowlandson, 1682." In *Narratives of the Indian Wars, 1675–1699,* ed. Charles H. Lincoln. New York: Scribner, 1913. 112–67.

Rowley, Hazel. *Richard Wright: The Life and Times.* New York: Henry Holt, 2001.

Rushdy, Ashraf H. A. "Daughters Signifyin(g) History: The Example of Toni Morrison's *Beloved.*" *American Literature* 64.3 (1992): 567–97.

Saldívar, José David. "Américo Paredes and Decolonization." In *Cultures of United States Imperialism,* ed. Amy Kaplan and Donald E. Pease. Durham: Duke University Press, 1993. 292–311.

———. "Chicano Border Narratives as Cultural Critique." In Calderón and Saldívar, eds., *Criticism in the Borderlands.* 167–80.

Saldívar, Ramón. "Américo Paredes, The Border Corrido and Socially Symbolic Chicano Narrative." *Critical Exchange* 22 (Spring 1987): 11–22.

———. "The Borderlands of Culture: Américo Paredes's *George Washington Gomez* and Chicano Literature at the End of the Twentieth Century." *American Literary History* 5.2 (Summer 1993): 272–93.

———. *Chicano Narrative: The Dialectics of Difference.* Madison: University of Wisconsin Press, 1990.

———. "Narrative, Ideology, and the Reconstruction of American Literary History." In Calderón and Saldívar, eds., *Criticism in the Borderlands.* 11–20.

Saldívar-Hull, Sonia. "Feminism on the Border: From Gender Politics to Geopolitics." In Calderón and Saldívar, eds., *Criticism in the Borderlands.* 203–20.

———. Introduction to the Second Edition. In Anzaldúa, *Borderlands/La Frontera,* 1999. 1–15.

Saroyan, William. Introduction to the Original Edition. In Mori, *Yokohama, California.* 1949; 1985.

Scarberry-García, Susan. *Landmarks of Healing: A Study of "House Made of Dawn."* Albuquerque: University of New Mexico Press, 1990.

Schubnell, Matthias. *N. Scott Momaday: The Cultural and Literary Background.* Norman: University of Oklahoma Press, 1985.

Schuyler, George S. *Black No More.* 1931. New York: The Modern Library, 1999.

Shell, Marc. *Children of the Earth: Literature, Politics, and Nationhood.* New York: Oxford University Press, 1993.

Silko, Leslie Marmon. *Almanac of the Dead*. New York: Penguin Books, 1991.

———. *Ceremony*. New York: Penguin Books, 1977.

Singal, Daniel J. *William Faulkner: The Making of a Modernist*. Chapel Hill: University of North Carolina Press, 1997.

Skeeter, Sharyn. Rev. of *The Bluest Eye* by Toni Morrison. *Essence* (January 1971): 59.

Smedley, Audrey. *Race in North America: Origin and Evolution of a Worldview*. 2nd ed. Boulder, CO: Westview Press, 1999.

Sollors, Werner. *Beyond Ethnicity: Consent and Descent in American Culture*. New York: Oxford University Press, 1986.

Sone, Monica. *Nisei Daughter*. 1953. Seattle: University of Washington Press, 1979.

Staub, Michael. "(Re)Collecting the Past: Writing Native American Speech." *American Quarterly* 43 (September 1991): 425–56.

Stocking, George W., Jr. "Anthropology as Kulturkampf: Science and Politics in the Career of Franz Boas." In *The Uses of Anthropology*, ed. Walter Goldschmidt. Washington, DC: American Anthropological Association, 1979. 33–50.

———. "Franz Boas and the Culture Concept in Historical Perspective." In his *Race, Culture, and Evolution*. 195–233.

———. *Race, Culture, and Evolution: Essays in the History of Anthropology*. New York: Free Press, 1968.

Stocking, George W., Jr., ed. *The Shaping of American Anthropology 1883–1911: A Franz Boas Reader*. New York: Basic Books, 1974.

Stonequist, Everett V. *The Marginal Man: A Study in Personality and Culture Conflict*. 1937. New York: Russell & Russell, 1961.

———. "The Restricted Citizen." *Annals of the American Academy of Political and Social Science* 223 (September 1942): 149–56.

Styron, William. *The Confessions of Nat Turner*. New York: Random House, 1967.

Sue, Stanley, and Derald W. Sue. "Chinese-American Personality and Mental Health." *Amerasia Journal* 1.2 (1971): 36–49.

Suzuki, Peter. "The University of California Japanese Evacuation and Resettlement Study: A Prolegomenon." In Chan et al., eds., *The Big Aiiieeeee!* 370–411.

Swope, Richard. "Crossing Western Space, or the HooDoo Detective on the Boundary in Ishmael Reed's *Mumbo Jumbo*." *African American Review* 36.4 (Winter 2002): 611–28.

Szacki, Jerzy. *History of Sociological Thought*. Westport, CT: Greenwood Press, 1979.

Szwed, John F. "An American Anthropological Dilemma: The Politics of Afro-American Culture." In *Reinventing Anthropology*, ed. Dell Hymes. New York: Pantheon, 1972. 153–81.

Takaki, Ronald. *Iron Cages: Race and Culture in 19th Century America*. 1979. Rev. ed. New York: Oxford University Press, 2000.

Tan, Amy. "Required Reading and Other Dangerous Subjects." *Threepenny Review* 67 (Fall 1996): 5–9.

Terkel, Studs. *Race: How Blacks and Whites Think and Feel About the American Obsession*. New York: New Press, 1992.

Thomas, William I. "Race Psychology: Standpoint and Questionnaire, with Particular Reference to the Immigrant and the Negro." *American Journal of Sociology* 17.6 (May 1912): 725–75.

Thomas, William I., and Florian Znaniecki. *The Polish Peasant in Europe and America.* Vol. 2. 1918. New York: Alfred A. Knopf. 1927.

Timasheff, Nicolas S. *Sociological Theory: Its Nature and Growth.* 3rd ed. New York: Random House, 1967.

Tolan Committee hearings. House Select Committee Investigating National Defense Migration. Part 30: Portland and Seattle Hearings: Problems of Evacuation of Enemy Aliens and Others from Prohibited Military Zones, 77th Cong., 2nd sess., 2 March 1942. Exhibit 3—Statement by Robert W. O'Brien, Assistant to the Dean, College of Arts and Sciences, University of Washington [p. 11598–11599]. Accessed online at http://www.lib.washington.edu/exhibits/harmony/interrupted_lives/text/tolan.html.

Tolentino, Cynthia. "The Road Out of the Black Belt: Sociology's Fictions and Black Subjectivity in *Native Son.*" *Novel* (Summer 2000): 377–405.

Tong, Benjamin. "The Ghetto of the Mind." *Amerasia Journal* 1.3 (1971): 1–31.

Villarreal, José Antonio. Interview with Juan Bruce Novoa. *Chicano Authors: Inquiry by Interview.* Austin: University of Texas Press, 1980. 37–48.

———. *Pocho.* New York: Anchor Books, 1959.

Von Eschen, Penny M. "Who's the Real Ambassador? Exploding Cold War Racial Ideology." In *Cold War Constructions: The Political Culture of United States Imperialism, 1945–1966,* ed. Christian G. Appy. Amherst: University of Massachusetts Press, 2000. 110–31.

Walcott, Derek. *Omeros.* New York: Noonday Press; Farrar, Straus and Giroux, 1990.

Waldman, Carl. *Atlas of the North American Indian.* New York: Facts on File, 1985.

Walker, Alice. *The Color Purple.* New York: Pocket Books, 1982.

———. Foreword: "Zora Neale Hurston—A Cautionary Tale and a Partisan View." 1976. In Hemenway, *Zora Neale Hurston: A Literary Biography.* xi–xviii.

———. "In Search of Zora Neale Hurston." *Ms.* 3.9 (March 1975): 74–89.

———. *The Same River Twice: Honoring the Difficult.* New York: Washington Square Press, 1996.

———. *The Third Life of Grange Copeland.* New York: Harcourt Brace Jovanovich. 1970.

Wall, Cheryl A. "On Freedom and the Will to Adorn: Debating Aesthetics and/as Ideology in African American Literature." In *Aesthestics and Ideology,* ed. George Levine. New Brunswick, NJ: Rutgers University Press, 1994. 283–303.

Walling, William. "'Art' and 'Protest': Ralph Ellison's *Invisible Man* Twenty Years After." *Phylon* 34 (June 1973): 120–34.

Warren, Kenneth W. *So Black and Blue: Ralph Ellison and the Occasion of Criticism.* Chicago: University of Chicago Press, 2003.

Waters, Lindsay. "Literary Aesthetics: The Very Idea." *The Chronicle Review,* December 16, 2005. http://chronicle.com/free/v52/i17/17b00601.htm.

Watkins, Floyd C. *In Time and Place: Some Origins of American Fiction.* Athens: University of Georgia Press, 1977.

Webb, Walter Prescott. *The Great Plains.* Boston, 1931.

———. *The Texas Rangers.* Cambridge, 1935.

Wildermuth, John. "Jade Snow Wong: Noted Author, Ceramicist." Obituary. *San Francisco Chronicle,* March 19, 2006: B7. http://www.sfgate.com/cgi-bin/article.cgi?f=/c/a/2006/03/19/BAGNDHQOO31.DTL.

Williams, Juan. *Thurgood Marshall: American Revolutionary*. New York: Random House, 1998.

Williams, Vernon J., Jr. *From Caste to a Minority: Changing Attitudes of American Sociologists toward Afro-Americans, 1896–1945*. New York: Greenwood Press, 1989.

———. *Rethinking Race: Franz Boas and His Contemporaries*. Lexington: University Press of Kentucky, 1996.

Wilson, Midge, and Kathy Russell. *Divided Sisters: Bridging the Gap between Black Women and White Women*. New York: Anchor Books, 1996.

Winthrop, John. *The Journal of John Winthrop*. Cambridge: Belknap Press of Harvard University Press, 1996.

Wirth, Louis. *The Ghetto*. Chicago: University of Chicago Press, 1928.

Witmer, Helen Leland, and Ruth Kotinsky, eds. *Personality in the Making: The Fact-Finding Report of the Midcentury White House Conference on Children and Youth*. New York: Harper & Brothers, 1952.

Wong, Jade Snow. *Fifth Chinese Daughter*. 1950. Seattle: University of Washington Press, 1989.

———. *No Chinese Stranger*. New York: Harper & Row, 1975.

Wong, Sau-ling Cynthia. "Autobiography as Guided Chinatown Tour? Maxine Hong Kingston's *The Woman Warrior* and the Chinese-American Autobiographical Controversy." In *Maxine Hong Kingston's* The Woman Warrior: *A Casebook,* ed. Sau-ling Cynthia Wong. New York: Oxford University Press, 1999. 29–53.

———. *Reading Asian American Literature: From Necessity to Extravagance*. Princeton: Princeton University Press, 1993.

———. "'Sugar Sisterhood': Situating the Amy Tan Phenomenon." In Palumbo-Liu, ed., *The Ethnic Canon*. 174–210.

Wright, Richard. "Between Laughter and Tears." *New Masses,* October 5, 1937, 24–25.

———. "Bibliography on [the] Negro in Chicago." 1936. Box 53. Illinois Writers Project/"Negro in Illinois" Papers. Vivian G. Harsh Research Collection of Afro-American History and Literature. Chicago Public Library.

———. *Black Boy (American Hunger): A Record of Childhood and Youth*. 1944. New York: Harper Perennial, 1993.

———. "Blueprint for Negro Writing." 1937. In *Within the Circle: An Anthology of African American Literary Criticism from the Harlem Renaissance to the Present,* ed. Angelyn Mitchell. Durham: Duke University Press, 1994. 97–106.

———. "How Bigger Was Born." In *Native Son*. 431–62.

———. "I Bite the Hand That Feeds Me." *Atlantic Monthly,* 165 (June 1940): 826–28.

———. Introduction. In *Black Metropolis,* by Horace R. Cayton and St. Clair Drake. London: Jonathan Cape, 1946. xvii–xxxiv.

———. *Native Son*. 1940. New York: Perennial Classics, 1998.

———. *The Outsider*. 1953. In *Later Works: Black Boy (American Hunger) and The Outsider*. New York: The Library of America. 1991.

———. *12 Million Black Voices: A Folk History of the Negro in the United States*. New York: Viking Press, 1941.

———. *Uncle Tom's Children*. 1938. New York: Harper Perennial, 1991, 2004.

Wyatt, E. V. R. Rev. of *Fifth Chinese Daughter,* by Jade Snow Wong. *Commonweal* 53.6 (November 24, 1950): 182.

Yarborough, Richard. Introduction. In Wright, *Uncle Tom's Children,* 1991. ix–xxix.

Yonemura, Ayanna Sumiko. "Dillon S. Myer and the War Relocation Authority's Resettlement of Japanese Americans: A Racialized Planning Project." Diss. University of California at Los Angeles, 2001.

Yu, Henry. *Thinking Orientals: Migration, Contact, and Exoticism in Modern America.* New York: Oxford University Press, 2001.

INDEX

Tuskegee, 69, 119, 121, 220
typology, 81, 138, 187–90, 199–201, 332n9, 339n10

Uncle Tom's Children, 61, 64–67, 87, 118, 202, 314, 330n9
United States v. Bhagat Thind, 333n10
universalism, 10, 28, 49, 65, 107, 181, 222, 279, 294, 297, 324–25, 330n12, 330–31n13
University of California Regents v. Bakke, 342n6

Vancouver Island, 15–16
Van Vechten, Carl, 273, 316
vernacular, 26, 31, 34, 50, 64, 77, 185–86, 202–3, 205, 216–18, 270–71, 313–14, 317, 331n14
Vietnam War, 104–5, 154
Villarreal, José Antonio, 124, 162, 224
Vizenor, Gerald, 248
voodoo, 31, 33, 35–37, 204–6, 263, 265–69, 273, 283, 329n4, 330n12
Voting Rights Act, 98, 127

Walcott, Derek, 286–87, 289, 294–95
Walker, Alice, 23, 39, 51, 205–6, 208, 279, 292–93, 313, 317, 319, 325, 339n13
War Relocation Authority, 58, 142–44, 234–37
Warren, Earl, 74, 192, 335n5
Warren, Kenneth, 123, 323–24
Washington, Booker T., 52, 69, 72–73, 83–84, 87, 113, 116, 121, 125, 331n3, 333n12
Waters, Lindsay, 342–43n4
Watts riot, 98
Way to Rainy Mountain, 240–42, 244–49
Webb, Walter Prescott, 172, 300
Welch, James, 248
West, Cornell, 324
West Coast, 16, 111, 142, 234, 285, 333n4
White House Arts Festival, 127, 196, 202
Williams, Raymond, 338n8
Williams, Roger, 233–34
Williams, Vernon Jr., 328n7, 331n2

Wirth, Louis, 67, 77
Wirth, Mary, 67, 226
Wissler, Clark, 244
"With His Pistol in His Hand," 160–61, 163–76, 179–81, 224, 290–91, 297
Woman Warrior, 178, 304, 309–13, 318–19, 342n2
Wong, Jade Snow, 98–100, 102, 186, 211–12, 305, 309
  sociology in, 106–9, 111–14, 118, 311–12, 333n6, 336n8
  See also Fifth Chinese Daughter
Wong, Sau-ling, 102, 342n2
Wong, Shawn, 218, 284
  See also Aiiieeeee!; Big Aiiieeeee!
World War I, 16
World War II, 58, 99, 106, 128, 220–21, 236, 253, 336n1
  nationalizing effects of, 162, 169–70, 182, 224
  See also internment, Japanese American
Wovoka, 287, 291
Wright, Richard, 226, 260, 313–14, 331–32n8
  African American culture in, 61, 64, 159, 268, 328–29n3
  politics of, 38, 87–90, 92–93, 203, 271
  reception of, 52, 62–66, 82, 86, 118, 184, 196–97, 206
  sociology in, 63, 67, 76–87, 90–91, 115, 118, 137–38, 198, 289, 331n6, 332n9
  See also Black Boy; "Blueprint for Negro Writing"; *Native Son; Outsider; Uncle Tom's Children*

Yarborough, Richard, 64–66, 87
Year of the Dragon, 185, 210–11
Yellow Back Radio Broke-Down, 266, 271
yellow peril, 231–32
Yonemura, Ayanna, 143–44
Yu, Henry, 143–44

Zangwill, Israel, 71
Znaniecki, Florian, 69, 197
zombies, 36–37

I think dad's girlfriend is meching
anyone you too